FIFTY YEARS OF
THE HERBALIST ALMANAC

RSMyeks

OTHER BOOKS BY CLARENCE MEYER
Available from the Publisher

THE HERBALIST
AMERICAN FOLK MEDICINE
VEGETARIAN MEDICINES
HERBAL RECIPES
SACHETS, POTPOURRI & INCENSE RECIPES
ONIONS: Condiment, Nutrient, Medicine
HERBAL APHRODISIACS

THE HERBALIST ALMANAC

A 50-Year Anthology

Compiled, Written, and Illustrated by
CLARENCE MEYER

Selected and Edited by
DAVID C. MEYER

Meyerbooks, *Publisher*
Glenwood, Illinois

Published by
Meyerbooks
Box 427
Glenwood, Illinois 60425

Sixth printing, 1999

Third printing, with additions and modifications,
copyright © 1988 by David C. Meyer

Original copyright © 1977 by David C. Meyer

All rights reserved. No part of this publication may be
reproduced or utilized in any form or by any means,
either mechanical or electronic, including xerography,
photocopying, recording, or any information storage or
retrieval system now known or to be invented, without
written permission from the publisher, except by a
reviewer wishing to quote brief passages in connection
with a review written for inclusion in a newspaper,
magazine, or broadcast.
ISBN 0-916638-02-2

In memory of two herbalists
JOSEPH E. MEYER
CLARENCE MEYER
Father & Son

TABLE OF CONTENTS

Preface To The Third Printing /	9
Preface /	11
A Note To The Reader /	12
Americana And Almanacs /	13
The Botanic Age /	17
Nature's Laboratories /	79
The Race That Lived With Nature /	107
On The Farm /	127
In The Garden /	149
Around The House /	175
Beauty And Scents /	193
Kitchen Concerns /	213
Index /	251

PREFACE TO THE THIRD PRINTING

Although ten years have passed since this anthology was compiled and it is nearly fifteen years since my father completed the final issue of "The Herbalist Almanac," letters from readers and inquirers continue to arrive. If the almanac is still available, they want it. When they learn that it is no longer published annually, they want to know why. The answer is easy: No one I know could do the job as well as my father did. For over forty of the seventy-five years "The Herbalist Almanac" was published, my father single-handedly researched, compiled, wrote, edited, illustrated, designed, and pasted up each issue.

I can still see him working at these tasks. In the mornings he was at the drawing board, either writing by longhand the articles which can be found in this anthology, or he was bent over with pen and ink preparing illustrations. In the afternoons he was in the garden, cultivating favorite herbs and the many rare and unusual plants sent to him by readers from around the world. His evenings were spent reading and gleaning information from books acquired during weekly visits to the old book shops of Chicago or from English book dealers' catalogs of rarities. Remarkably, he did not require eyeglasses until he was over forty years old, after deciphering the quill-written recipes and marginal notes of a 1585 edition of Dodoens' *A Nievve Herball, or Historie of Plantes*. The resulting article, entitled "Notes From An Old Herbal," appeared in the 1946 issue of "The Herbalist Almanac" and is reprinted in this book.

I would hate to think that the time has passed for such one-person endeavors as my father undertook, for they provided him with a peaceful and meaningful life. The fruits of his labors have kept old ways within sight of new generations. His drawings are expressions of his love for life. These days he works in his garden.

David C. Meyer
Autumn 1987

PREFACE

If there is one thing that has characterized "The Herbalist Almanac" since its inception in 1925, it is the wealth of valuable and enduring material it has published year after year. Almanacs in this century have been little more than collections of weather predictions, planting guides, astrological signs and notes of historic interest—material to be consulted once and at the year's end the entire almanac is tossed away. "The Herbalist Almanac" has always contained these basic almanac contents and our readers have faithfully followed the planting guides and weather predictions and just as faithfully saved our almanacs for the essays, articles and recipes which just couldn't be thrown away. It is this material—the essays on botanical history, the descriptions and uses of plants around the world, the accounts of American Indian botany; the information for use in hunting, farming, gardening and in the home; the recipes for health, beauty, household and cooking uses—which makes up this anthology.

This is not a book of nostalgia. It contains information and recipes used a generation ago to centuries ago: time tested information still interesting, valuable and useful.

A characteristic feature of all almanacs is that on each page you might discover widely different subjects placed side by side. "The Herbalist Almanac" is no exception. Although in this anthology we have gathered material on similiar subjects under specific chapter headings, don't be too surprised if you find a recipe for removing household stains in the midst of the more serious articles or a proverb popping up among the cooking recipes. That's the nature and, incidentally, the delight of an almanac. If you happen to find two recipes for preserving flowers in two different places in the book or other examples of apparent repetition, what in fact you are finding are two different methods for accomplishing the same result. You have your choice. If you are in a hurry to locate a specific item—whether it be an article on ginseng or various references to, say, the uses of slippery elm—simply go to the index at the back of the book. Otherwise, you can either read the book from the beginning to the end or pick it up at any page and begin reading. It's that kind of book.

We believe, in this age of countless books with thousands of words and hundreds of illustrations and very little content or worth, FIFTY YEARS OF THE HERBALIST ALMANAC is a rare book. This is a book for reading at your leisure; for looking into when you *need* to know; a book for enjoyment *and* instruction. A rare book indeed!

A NOTE TO THE READER

The medicinal or therapeutic uses of the plants described in this book are not to be considered in any way a recommendation for their use as curative agents. Naturally one should not attempt to self-medicate any serious or difficult condition as there may be various causes that may require a doctor's diagnosis and treatment. The descriptions and recipes given herein are more in the nature of former recognitions and in the light of herbal lore.

AMERICANA & ALMANACS

Early American homes were like busy little factories capable of making a variety of products for comfort and survival in the virgin woodlands of the New World. Everyone, children included, had to work from sunrise to sunset for the multiple chores required to produce meager essentials.

The making of clothing was one of the most important of all products of civilization. Long before sheep could be brought to the New World for wool, wilderness lands had to be cleared and made safe for these animals. Linen was the main source of fiber for cloth in colonial times. Small plots of flax were grown in the fresh soils of newly cleared lands. Making linen fiber from flax required a multitude of processes. After the plant was grown the stalks had to be retted, hackled, dressed, spun and finally woven into material. Dyeing the spun fiber or finished cloth was also a chore of early families. Colors and mordants were obtained from plants found in their environs.

The forests provided pioneers with an assortment of game. The furs of some animals substituted for non-existent money to barter for essentials at trading settlements.

Indian corn was a godsend staple as it not only provided a substantial food, but could be easily grown in small areas as well as being easily stored until another crop was available. Dried corn was ground by hand in mortars for meal or flour to be used in a variety of dishes. It was made into bread, cakes, biscuits, muffins, grits, puddings, fritters, hominy and mixed with vegetables or meats. The ears or kernels could be roasted, boiled or fried. Corn was also an important food for poultry and farm stock. Like furs, corn was used as a medium of exchange.

Butchering was another vital chore of rural homes. This was generally done in late fall after the weather turned cold. Fresh meats were a rare treat — much of the meat was preserved by drying, smoking, pickling or packing in lard, brine, wood ashes or charcoal. Nothing was wasted: meat scraps and blood made sausages; excess fats were saved for soaps; hides for shoes, straps, harnesses, etc.

Sweets were generally a rare luxury in Early American life. An occasional bee hive provided honey and the saps drained from butternut or maple trees in spring were boiled to make an excellent sugar. Wild fruits, berries and grapes were plentiful and relished in season.

Native plants provided early settlers with a number of tasteful and health-giving teas.

Every well established old-time farm had a huge iron kettle and lye barrel in the yard. The kettle was used for boiling water and clothes, making vegetable dyes, hominy or soap. The lye barrel was placed over rocks or logs to allow a container to be placed beneath it. The top was open and the bottom of the barrel had drain holes. Several inches of small stones were kept in the bottom to allow for drainage. Over the layer of stones were dumped all the wood ashes saved from the fireplace, stove and kettle fires. Rain water leached through the ashes making a lye which drained from the bottom of the barrel into the lye container. Generally, the first drainage resulted in a weak lye so it had to be poured repeatedly over fresh ashes until the lye was strong enough to float an egg or potato. Lye was used for cleaning purposes but mainly to make soap by adding it to melted discarded fats.

Sabbath was a day of rest. After religious duties folks often visited neighbors to exchange news and pleasantries or strolled in woods or waysides to appreciate the wonders of nature. Sunday was also a day of thanks and special dinners when food supplies were bountiful. The Bible often consoled in times of scarcity and sorrow. Almanacs, in former times, were also a usual and essential item in every household. Proverbs, maxims and phrases were interspersed throughout their pages. Many homes framed their favorite sayings and hung them on the wall as reminders from straying off the righteous path.

In the old days, folks simply looked outside to observe cloud formations to determine what the weather would be for the day. Almanacs were referred to for long range prognostications. For hourly weather signs more astute forecasters studied the sky as well as actions of birds, animals, insects and plants. Our most sophisticated instruments are not more sensitive to barometric pressures than that of a spider knowing whether or not it should spin or reinforce its web. Although not as sensitive as insects, the action of animals and their intuitions afford some indication of weather to come. It is said that swine generally grunt loudly and retire to their pens upon the approach of rain. Dogs become drowsy and dull and show a loss of appetite. Cats lose their vivacity and remain indoors. Clover, wood sorrel and wild licorice close their leaves before a storm. The closing flowers of dandelion, pimpernel, goat's beard and several other flowers indicate coming of rain.

An important chore of early American life was to keep the home well stocked with medicinal plants for ailments that usually occur through the long winter months. Herbs, barks, roots, flowers and berries were gathered in season and stored in wood or tin containers or simply hung in bunches from the rafters. The fats of wild animals were saved to make salves or ungents simmered with herbs for muscle aches, strains and pains. Medicines were usually readily assimilated infusions or decoctions. People did not expect miracle cures, but their simple remedies must often have eased or cured conditions common in their mode of living. Many educated families were fortunate to own a copy of Dr. Gunn's *Domestic Medicine* or Dr. Chase's *Recipe Book* or other medical guide where professional care was scarce or unavailable. Indian remedies made of native botanicals probably saved the lives of many colonists. Emigrant families often brought seeds of medicinals from their native lands in order to maintain a tiny apothecary garden. In those trying times people also helped each other, exchanged favors, products, skills and medical knowledge.

Almanacs were first printed in the New World in the mid-1600's. They were important to keep dates and records of days, weeks, months and years for those settlements remote from all chronological order of civilizations. Adventurers, explorers and early settlers resorted to Indian methods. Weather and the habits of animals, birds, insects and plants served as general indicators of months and seasons. Phases of the sun, moon and stars also served as time indicators.

Earliest almanacs recorded events in the settlements; doings of the Indians; dates of ship arrivals; new settlers; belated news of the Old World and lists of cargo urgently needed for settlement of colonies.

Almanacs of the 1700's added Old World and Indian remedies to help colonists combat plagues and infectious diseases. Thomas Godfrey's "Pennsylvania Almanack" (1736) advised using an herb each month of the year. Motherwort was recommended for January; black alder for February; mustard seed for March [probably spring awakening]; dandelion for April [European spring tonic]; vitamin-rich parsley for May; asparagus for June [more vitamins]; whey for July; fumitory for August; horehound for September; St. Johnswort for October; tobacco for November; sage for December. "Poor Richard's Almanack," printed by Benjamin Franklin, also provided considerable medical advice from the Old World as well as medicines used by the Indians. Later almanacs added an assortment of information, recipes as well as advertisements of imports, patent medicines and products manufactured by New World industries.

"The Herbalist Almanac" began publication in 1925 when many almanacs were going out of existence. In spite of changes of modern life, "The Herbalist Almanac" has consistently retained its original format. The editor believes natural remedies, homely recipes and ideas are as durable today as they were in the past. The many nationalities which settled in the New World brought their methods and talents from their homelands and the combined mixture has left us with a treasure chest of ideas, recipes, lore and nostalgia still appreciated by descendants and Americana lovers.

For over forty years the editor of "The Herbalist Almanac" scoured through countless American books, records and news items published for more than 200 years. He has searched modern as well as the ancient herbals of the Old World for information on every conceivable use of plants. Government ethnobotany publications of the early 1900's reveal valuable information of American plants used by the aboriginals. Interesting information and recipes also were gleaned from a variety of unique sources. An elderly lady sent the writer a handwritten family recipe book she inherited from her mother. She wrote that the book has passed from one generation to another in her family and she was fearful the new generation would no longer value it. The writer has a collection of books of the 1800's, printed in limited editions by church parishioners who contributed their favorite recipes for the good of their community. A very rare home-made book is made up of Civil War era clippings pasted over pages of another old book. Subjects include medical recipes for humans and farm stock; recipes for cooking and preserving; ways to use various plants for dye; advice on farm, gardening, insect killers and repellents, and a variety of household information. Much of this valuable information has, over the years, found its way into "The Herbalist Almanac" and is as useful to present generations as it was to those of the past.

The Writer especially prizes a tiny herb doctor book entitled, *The Poor Man's Physician, The Sick Man's Friend; or Nature's Botanic Garden,* by Josiah Burlingame, printed in Norwich, New York in 1826. The book was received from Mr. E. C. Barney, who wrote: "I've handled and treasured this book and read it over the years . . . because of its beneficial herbal remedies that I have used for many years, I believe it has helped me to reach my 90th year without having what is called a family doctor. This is my personal opinion."

Mr. Barney found the book in the early 1900's when he was a boy hunting rabbits in the Wisconsin backwoods. He discovered it in the "musty cobwebby attic" of the ruins of an early settler's forest home.

CM

THE BOTANIC AGE

The BOTANIC AGE
as revealed in Parkinson's Theatrum Botanicum

At the age of 73, when most men considered themselves very old, John Parkinson published the largest herbal ever printed in the English language. This botanical encyclopedia contains descriptions and uses of some 3,800 plants. Little is known of Parkinson except that he was born about 1567 in Nottinghamshire, England, early in the 17th century—he was practicing apothecary and maintained a botanical garden filled with many rare plants. In 1629 he published his gardening book entitled Paradisus. Soon after that, he was appointed apothecary to James I and later given the grand title of Botanicus Regius Primarius by Charles I.

The Indiana Botanic Gardens copy of Theatrum Botanicum was printed in 1640. Time has almost obliterated the title and the old animal skin cover is worn smooth where hands of many generations held the massive book. The printing upon the yellowed pages appears strange—after careful study we recognize words spelled in the manner of olden times. This old style English is easily understood, but very wordy compared to the abbreviated style of today. Delving into the ponderous and quaint descriptions of plants reveals fascinating lore and interesting bits of everyday life. Plants were indeed a very vital part of economic life. From plants came foods, medicines and material for industry and arts. Plants had an important place in literature, festivities, rites and religious beliefs. In no period in the history of the world were plants employed in so many different ways.

Thought of centuries past differ little from thought of modern times—the materials used however differed radically. The materials for ideas of other days came from nature's laboratories. The materials of modern times are produced by man's chemical laboratories.

Centuries ago people did not know about vitamins and minerals, but instinctively knew that certain greens contained more health building and strength giving properties than others. People were instinctively aware of the healing properties of chlorophyl as most of their remedies for cuts and wounds consisted of fresh green herbs. Before the days of aspirin, sleeping pills and powerful stimulants, every family had its own store of botanical recipes. Such harmless herbs as cool Mints, soothing Lavender, Feverfew and Aloes were used for simple headache. For sedative folks made a pillow of Hops, hung Anise seed in a bag over the bed, or placed the fragrant Rosemary beneath their pillows. For stimulant or to "make the heart merrie," folks brewed herbal teas or smelled frequently of sweet herbs.

Hot or spicy flavored herbs added zest to foods when oriental condiments were little known or too costly. Savory seeds and sweet herbs added variety to simple menus of

THE BOTANIC AGE—*Continued*

olden times. Healthful teas were part of meals before the days of tea and coffee.

Lovely women of earlier times concocted their own beauty recipes to fit their personal type and tastes. Clothes, bath and boudoir were scented with fragrant herb mixtures.

Strong scented herbs were used as insect repellents for food, clothes and homes. Mints, Woodruff, Meadow Sweet and Lavender were used to freshen and air condition the home, Church and assembly places.

Magnificent fabrics, fine leathers, masterpieces of Tapestries were dyed with marvelous shades of plant colors. The beautiful crystal glass and colored glasses of the great Gothic Cathedrals were made from plant sources.

On the farm, herbs were used to fatten and doctor stock and poultry. Strong herb decoctions were used to protect the garden from an insect ridden world. The deadly insecticide of modern times (pyrethrum) is a plant product.

In the home, fragrant and oily Mints were rubbed on furniture for polish. Wooden, pewter and brass vessels, greasy pans and kitchen were scoured or brightened with Scouring Rush. Plants were used in innumerable and surprising ways around the home.

Weather signs, protection from elements, plagues and evils were sought in the plant kingdom. Parkinson tells how a Great King protected himself from poisoning by using Rue. He gives recipes to prevent drunkenness from too much wine, as well as a recipe for hangover. A few herbs mentioned by Parkinson still are being used in this Synthetic and Atomic Age. In Florida one still finds Aloe leaves hanging in open-air markets and homes, as Parkinson described more than 300 years ago.

Theatrum Botanicum is divided into seventeen classes or "tribes". Plants are grouped under such headings as Sweete Smelling Plants; Purging Plants; Venemous Sleepy and Hurtfull Plants and their Counter Poysons; Hot and sharpe biting Plants. Exotic plants are listed under heading Strange and Outlandish Plants. One large section is devoted to Vulnerary or Wound Herbs. This was important information of the day because people were armed with daggers, knives or swords and skirmishes and brawls were frequent. There are many antidotes for poisoning. Foods were often spoiled because of poor means of transportation preservation. Many delightful chapters take the reader through Parkinson's own garden, giving personal and quaint methods of the day.

The excerpts represented here consist of scant cross sections of a few chapters. The reader who is fortunate enough to be able to study a copy of Theatrum Botanicum no doubt would find many restful and interesting hours reading this wonderful record of the Botanical Age.

(Medical opinion has since changed as regards many old time herb beliefs. These excerpts are given for their historical interest only, and are not meant to imply in some cases, modern recognized herb actions. See Special Notice on page 1.)

SUMMER SAVORY
medicine, culinary herb

Summer Savory is both sharpe and quicke in taste, expelling winde in the stomacke and bowels, and is a present helpe for the rising of the mother procured by winde, provoketh urine and womens courses, and is much commended for women with child to take inwardly, and to smell often thereunto:—it is in familiar use with many to procure a good appetite unto meate.

MOTHER of THYME
headache

—taken inwardly, or applyed outwardly with Rosemary and vinegar to the head, it ceaseth the paines thereof.

WILD MARJORAM
liniment

—it is profitably put into those oyntments and salves, that are made to warme and comfort the outward parts or members, the joynts also and sinewes, (muscles) for swellings also and places out of joynt—The oyle made thereof is very warming and comfortable to the joynts that are stiffe, and the sinewes that are hard to molifie, supple, and stretch them forth.

SWEET MARJORAM
flavor, scented water

—used in meates and brothes to give rellish unto them, and to helpe to warme a cold stomack, and to expell winde—Our daintiest women doe put it to still among their other sweet herbs, to make sweet washing water.

SWEET BASIL
perfume, lore

—used as a sweet smelling hearbe to sweeten or perfume anything—the fragrant smell of this hearbe so comfortable to the sences, reviving them as it were, when they are dull

THE BOTANIC AGE—Continued

or distempered, may evidently declare a singular efficacy to be therein, and therefore not to be smally regarded—(Seed) provoketh Venery, and therefore was given to horses to make them apt to bred.

PENNY-ROYAL
fainting, gums, skin, water purifier
—applyed to the nostrils with vinegar, it reviveth those that are fainting or sounding: being dryed and burnt, it strengthneth the gums;—the decoction helpeth those that have itches, if the places affected bee washed therewith—put into unwholesome and stinking waters, that men must drinke (as at Sea in long voyages) it maketh them the lesse hurtful;—it lesneth the fatnesse of the body being given with wine.

MINTS
flavoring, headache, colic, bad breath, lore, etc.
—it is very profitable to the stomack, and in meates (foods) is much accepted. Applyed to the forehead or the temples of the head it easeth the paines thereof. It is also good to wash the heads of young children therewith against all manner of breaking out therein, whether sores or scabs; and healeth the chaps of the fundament—Aristotle and others in the ancient times forbade Mints to be used of Souldiers in time of warre, because they thought it did so much incite to Venery, that it took away, or at least abated their animosity or courage to fight. Divers have held for true, that cheeses will not corrupt, if they be either rubbed over with the juyce or the decoction of Mints, or laid among them. The vertues of the wild Mints are more especially to dissolve winde in the stomack, to help the chollick and those that are short-winded, and are an especiall remedy for those that have venerous dreames and pollutions in the night, used both inwardly, and the juyce being applyed outwardly to the testicals or cods—the distilled water helpeth a stinking breath, which proceedeth from the corruption of the teeth. Pliny saith, that in the time of Great Pompey, it was found out by experience of one, to cure the Lepry by eating the leaves, and applying some of them to his face, and to help the scurfe or dandroffe of the head used with vinegar.

CATNIP
cats, stomach, piles
Cats delight both to smell and eate thereof, and gladly rub themselves against it— It is also of special use for the windinesse of the stomach or belly. It is effectual for any cramps or cold aches to dissolve the cold and wind that affecteth the place, and bring warmth and comfort thereunto afterwards: The greene hearbe bruised and applyed to the fundament, there abiding for two or three hours easeth the sharpe paines of the piles, the juyce also is effectuall for the same purpose, being made up into an oyntment and applyed.

BALM
melancholy, bath, wounds, bees
Avicen confirmeth in his booke of medicines proper for the heart, where he saith that it is hot and dry in the second degree, that it maketh the heart merry, and strengthneth the vitall spirits, both by the sweetness of smell, austerity of taste, and tenuity of parts, with which qualities it is helpfull also to the rest of the inward parts and bowels. It hath a purging quality therein also saith Avicen, and that not so weake, but that it is of force to expell those melancholy vapours from the spirits, and from the blood, which are in the heart and arteries, although it cannot doe so in the other parts of the body. Dioscorides commendeth the decoction thereof, for women to bathe or sit in to procure their courses. It is used in bathing among other warme and comfortable hearbes for men's bodies or legges in the Summer time, to comfort the joynts and sinewes (muscles). The Hearbe is often put into oyles or salves to heale greene wounds—Bees doe much delight, both to have their hives rubbed therewith to keep them together, and draw others, and for them to suck and feed upon; and is a remedy against the stinging of them.

HOREHOUND
cough
Dioscorides saith a decoction of the dryed hearbe with seed, or the juyce of the greene hearbe taken with honey, is a remedy for those that are pursie, and short-winded; for those that have a cough—there is a sirope made of Horehound to be had at the Apothecaries much used, and that to very good purpose for old coughes to rid the tough flegme; as also for old men and others, whose lungs are oppressed with tinne and cold rheme to helpe to avoid it, and for those that are asthmatick, or short winded.

SAGE
lore, wash, gargle, etc.
—in Cyprus and Aegypt, after a great plague, women were forced to drinke the juyce of Sage, to cause them to be the more fruitfull. Sage is of excellent good use to helpe the memory, by warming and quickning the sences—they are perswaded in Italy that

THE BOTANIC AGE—Continued

if they eate Sage fasting with a little salt, they shall be safe that day from the danger of the byting of any venemous beast;—The use of Sage in the Moneth of May, with butter, Parsley, and some salt, is very frequent in our Country to continue health to the body; as also Sage Ale made with it, Rosemary and other good hearbes for the same purpose, and for teeming women, or such as are subject to miscary. Gargles likewise are made with Sage, Rosemary, Honisuckles, and Plantaine boyled in water or wine, with some Honey and Allome put thereto, to wash cankers, sore mouthes, and throats, or secret parts of man or woman as need requireth. And with other hot and comfortable hearbes to be boyled, to serve for bathings of the body or legges, in the Summer time, especially to warme the cold joynts or sinewes of young or old, troubled with the Palsie or crampe, and to comfort and strengthen the parts.

CLARY SAGE
eyes, poultice, tansie, beer, lore

—the seed is used to be put into the eyes to clear them from moates, or other such like things are gotten within the liddes to offend them, as also to cleare them from white or red spots in them. The Muccilage of the seed of either sort with water and applyed to tumors or swellings, disperseth and taketh them away, and also draweth forth splinters, thornes, or other things gotten into the flesh—It provoketh to venery, either the seed or the leaves taken in wine. It is in much use with men or women that have weake backes, to help to strengthen the reines, either used by itself, or with other hearbes that conduce to the same effect, and in tansies often, or the fresh leaves fried in butter, being first dipped in a batter of flower, egges, and a little milke, served as a dish to the Table, is not unpleasant to any,—some Brewers of Ale and Beere doe put it into their drink to make it the more heady, fit to please drunkards—It is used in Italy to bee given to women that are barren through a cold and moist disposition, to heate and dry up that moisture, and to help them to be fruitfull.

MULLEIN
bath, gout, colic, cattle, poultice

—a decoction of the leaves hereof, and of Sage, Marjoram, and Camomill flowers, and the places bathed therewith, that have their veins and sinewes (muscles) starke with cold, or with crampes, doth bring them much ease and comfort. It is said that there is not a better remedy found out for the hot gout then to drink three ounces of the distilled water of the flowers every morning and evening for some days together.
—the powder of the dryed flowers is an especial remedy for those are troubled with bellyaches, or paines and torments of the collick. Country men doe often give their Cattel that are troubled with coughs—The leaves also a little bruised, and laid or bound to a Horse foote that is grievously prickt with shooing, doth wonderfully heale it in a short space.

ROSEMARY
lore, eyes, fumigant, tobacco, bath, oil

Rosemary is an hearbe of as great use with us in these dayes, as any other whatsoever, not onely for Physicall, but civill purposes: the civill uses as all know, are at Weddings, Funerals, etc to bestow upon friends: the Physicall remedies, both for inward and outward diseases are many and worthy, for by the warming and comforting heate thereof it helpeth all cold diseases, both of the head, stomack, liver and belly: the decoction thereof in wine helpeth the cold distillations of the braine into the eyes, and all other cold diseases of the head and braines, as the giddinesse or swimming therein, drowsinesse or dullnesse of the minde and sences like a stupidnesse, the dumbe palsie, or losse of speech, the lethargie and falling sicknesse, to be both drunke, and the temples bathed therewith—it helpeth dimme eyes, and to procure a cleare sight, if all the while it is in flower, one take of the flowers fasting with bread and salt—the flowers and the conserve made of them, is singular good to comfort the heart, and to expell the contagion of the pestilence, to burne the hearbe in Houses and Chambers in the time of the infection to correct the aire in them—the dried leaves shred small and taken in a Pipe like as Tobacco is taken, helpeth those much that have any cough—the leaves are much used in bathings, and made into oyntments or oyles, is singular good to helpe cold benummed joynts, sinewes or members. The chymicall oyle drawne from the leaves and flowers, is a soveraigne helpe for all the diseases aforesaid, to touch the temples and nostrils with a drop two or three for all those diseases of the head and braines, as also to take a drop two or three, as the cause requireth for the inward griefes yet must be taken with discretion, lest it doe more harme than good, for it is very quick and piercing, and therefore but a little must be taken at once.

COSTMARY
medicine

—in briefe it is an especiall friend and helpe to evill, weake, and cold livers.

THE BOTANIC AGE—Continued

TRIBE 2.   *The Theater of Plantes.*   CHAP. 12.   177

Lupulus saliltarius. Hoppes.

The Place.
These plants are more frequent in these colder, than in the hotter countries, which sheweth the goodnesse of God unto us, to provide for every Country, such things as are fit for the sustentation of life; for where Vines grow not, and the water too cold and raw, to drinke simply of it selfe, there are these Hoppes chiefely bred to make drinke to serve instead of wine or water: They delight chiefly, or rather onely to grow well, in low moist grounds, where they may have moysture enough, and yet not too much; for therefore where they are planted on hillockes, as it were, there are trenches made to receive any great quantity of water, and bee conveyed away, that the plants stand not drowned therein.

The Time.
These spring not up untill *Aprill*, and flower not untill the latter end of *Iune*, the heads are not gathered, untill the middle or end of *September*.

The Names.
It is observed and much marveiled at, by our ordinary writers, that this plant should not be remembred by *Dioscorides*, *Galen*, or any other of the ancient Greeke or Latine writers except *Pliny*, who doth but onely name it and, number it among those herbes that grow of themselves, and that are used for meate with diverse nations, calling it *Lupulus salictarius*. The *Arabians* have not onely remembred it, but commended the use of it highly for many diseases, as you shall heare by and by. *Mesues* maketh it his third kind of *Volubilis* with rough leaves, among his purging plants: the Greekes at this day call it βρύον & βρυωνία. *Bryon* and *Bryonia* it is likely for the forme of the leaves and running of the branches. It is called *Lupulus & Lupus salictarius, & reptitius (quia salit & reptat per arbores, vel quia scandit salices)* of all our moderne writers, onely *Lobel* calleth it *Vitis septentrionalium*, the Vine of the Northerne regions, and *Tragus* as I sayd before thinking it to be *Smilax aspera* & the *Italians* call it *Lupolo*; the *Spaniards Hombrazillos*, the *French Houblon*, the *Germaines Hopffen*, the *Dutch Hoppe*, and we in *English Hoppes*.

The Vertues.
The first buds of the Hoppes, being layd a while in sand, maketh them the tenderer, and being boyled are used to be eaten, after the same manner that the buds of *Asparagus* are, and with as great delight for the taste, yet they have little nourishment in them: their Physicall operation therefore is to open, the obstructions of the Liver and spleene, to clense the blood, to loosen the belly, and to clense the Raines from gravell, and to cause them to make water in whom it is stayed: the decoction of the toppes of the Hoppes, of the tame as well as of the wilde, and so also the rootes doe worke the same effects, but that they are somewhat hotter than the young buds, which have more moysture in them: in clensing the blood, they helpe to cure the French disease, and all manner of scabbes, itch, and other breakings out in the body, as also all tetters, ringwormes and spreading sores, the morphew likewise and all discolourings of the skin, and are used in Agues: the decoction of the flowers and tops, are used to be drunk, to helpe and expell poyson that any one hath drunk: halfe a dram of the seede in powder taken in drink, killeth the worms in the body, it likewise bringeth down womens courses, & expelleth Vrine. The flowers and heads, being put into bathes for women to sit in, take away the swellings and hardnesse of the Mother, and is good for the strangurie, or those that very hardly make their water; the juyce of the leaves dropped into the eares, clenseth the corrupt sores, and stench arising from the corruption in them; *Mesues* saith they purge choler, but worke more effectually, being steeped in whey of goates milke: A Syrupe made of the juyce and sugar, cureth those that have the yellow jaundise, easeth the headach that cometh of heate, and tempereth the heate both of the liver and stomack, and is very profitably given in long & hot agues, that rise of choler and blood: Those bakers that will use the decoction of Hoppes, to mould up their bread, shal make thereby their bread to rise better, and be baked the sooner: *Clusius* reciteth the manner of a medecine used in *Spaine*, by women leeches, to cure the falling of the haire, caused by the french disease, in this sort. A pound of the roots of Hopps, wel washed & boyled in 8 pints of faire water, to the consumption of the third part, or a halfe if they see cause; whereof they give half a pint to drink in a morning, causing them to sweate well after: into the decoction they put sometimes, two or three roots of parsly, and as many of couch grasse, with a few Raysins of the sunne. The Ale which our forefathers were accustomed onely to drinke, being a kinde of thicker drinke than beere (caused a stranger to say of it, *Nil spissius dum bibitur, nil clarius dum mingitur, unde constat multas faeces in ventre relinquit*, that is, there is no drinke thicker that is drunke, there is no Vrine cleerer that is made from it, it must needes be therefore that it leaveth much behinde it in the belly) is now almost quite left off to be made, the use of Hoppes to be put therein, altering the quality thereof, to be much more healthfull, or rather physicall, to preserve the body from the repletion of grosse humors, which the Ale engendred. The Wilde Hoppes are generally used Physically more than the manured, either because the Wilde is thought to be the more opening, and effectuall, or more easily to come by, or that the owners of the manured, will not spare, or lose so much profit, as that which would be taken away might yeeld; yet assuredly they are both of one property, take which you will, or can get.

                                                                                                              CHAP.

Reproduction of page from Theatrum Botanicum describing Hops.

THE BOTANIC AGE—Continued

FEVERFEW
headache, beauty
—it is very effectuall for all paines in the head, comming of a cold cause, as Camerarius saith, the hearbe being bruised and applied to the crowne of the head—Some doe use the distilled water of the hearbe and flowers, to take away freckles, and other spots and deformities in the face.

CHAMOMILE
bath, stomach, colic, etc.
The bathing of a decoction of Camomill taketh away wearinesse, and easseth paines to what part of the body it be applyed. Besides, it comforteth the sinewes that are overstrayned, mollifieth all swellings, and those that are not overhard and rarifyeth those that are found together. It moderately comforteth all parts that have need of warmth, and digesteth and dissolveth whatsoever hath need thereof, by a wonderfull speedy property. It easeth all the paines of the collick and stone, as also all paines and torments of the belly, and provoketh urine gently. The flowers boyled in posset drinke, provoketh sweat, and helpeth to expell colds, aches, and paines wheresoever. The oyl of the flowers of Camomill is much used, against all hard swellings, and paines, or aches, shrinking of the sinewes, or crampes, or paines in the joynts or any other part of the body; and helpeth to dissolve wind, paines in the belly, used in glisters for that purpose.

MUGWORT
lore
It is said of Pliny, that if a Traveller binde some of the hearbe about him, he shall feele no wearinesse at all in his journey; as also that no evill medicine or evill beast shall hurt him that hath this hearbe about him.

SOUTHERNWOOD
baldness, oil, vermine
The ashes mingled with old Sallet-oyle helpeth those that have their haire fallen, or their heads bald, to cause the haires to grow againe either upon the head or beard. Durantes saith that the oyle made of Southernwood, and put among other oyntments, that are used against the French disease, is very effectual, and likewise killeth vermine in the head.

WORMWOOD
stomach, eyes, repellent, drunkenness, etc.
—the decoction or the infusion thereof taken, doth take away the loathing to meate (food)—it taketh away the blacke and blue marks in the skinne, that come after bruising or beating, if it be mingled with honey and annoynted; as also it helpeth the dimness of the eyesight being used in the same manner. Being put into Chests, or Presses, or Wardrobes, it preserveth them from wormes and mothes, etc., and driveth away Gnats, or Waspes, and such like, from any part of the body, if the skin be annoynted with the oyl thereof—the decoction with Cumminseeds taken warme, easeth the paines of the belly and chollicke by winde — It is said that if a few leaves of Wormwood be eaten, it defendeth one from surfeiting and drunkenesse. The vinegar wherein Wormwood is boyled, is especiall good for a stinking breath, that commeth either from the gums or teeth, or from corruption in the stomacke.

RUE, or HEARBE of GRACE
skin, lotion, warts, eyes, etc.
—a decoction made thereof with some dryed Dill leaves and flowers, easeth all paines and torments, inwardly to be drunke, and outwardly to bee applyed warme to the place affected. — if it be drunke after it is boyled in the wine to the halfe, with a little honey; it helpeth the gowt; or paines in the joynts of hands, feete, or knees, applyed thereunto; —It cureth the Morphew, and taketh away all sorts of warts, on the hands, face, nose, or any other parts, if it be boyled in wine, with some Pepper and Niter, and the places rubbed therewith: and with Allome (alum) and Honey, helpeth the dry scab, or any tetter or ringworme:—The eating of the leaves of Rue taketh away the smell both of Garlike and Leekes. The leaves of Rue first boyled, and then laid in pickle, are kept my many to eate, as sawce to meate, like as Sampire, for the dimnesse of sight, and to warme a cold stomacke.

AVENS
plague
Some use it in the Spring time to put the roote to steepe for a time in wine, which giveth unto it a delicate savour and taste, which they drinke fasting every morning, to comfort the heart, and to preserve it from noysome and infectious vapours of the plague.

CALAMUS
bath, bees, perfume, charm
—it is put into bathes for women to sit in, as also into Glisters to ease paines. It is

THE BOTANIC AGE—*Continued*

used in mollifying oyles and plaisters, that serve to ripen hard impostums, as also for the sweet scent thereof. It is verily beleeved of many that the leaves or rootes of Acorns (Calamus) tyed to a hive of Bees, stayeth them from wandring or flying away, and draweth a greater resort of others thereunto. It is also affirmed, that none shall be troubled with any fluxe of blood, or paines of the crampe, that weareth the hearbe and rootes about them. The rootes of Acorns or Calamus, as it is usually called, are used among other things to make sweet powders, to lay among linnen and garments, and to make sweet waters to wash hand, gloves, or other things to perfume them.

ALOE
wounds, burns, purge, piles, headache, sleep, hair, etc.
Aloe is usually hung up in houses to bee ready at hand upon all occasions, to apply a little of the juyce of a leafe presently cut off, or the piece of a leafe it selfe, upon any cut or fresh wound which is found to bee singular good to soder and heale them—the leaves also are found to bee exceedingly cold in the hot countres, and of very great use and effects for all manner of scalding with water, or burning with fire, gun powder, or the like, healing them quickly: the nature of the juyce, or Aloes it selfe, is fit to thicken, to dry, to procure sleepe, and moderately heate; it openeth the belly, purgeth the stomacke, and the yellow jaundice, and stayeth the spitting of vomiting of blood, if a dramme thereof be taken in faire water: it is not only a good purger of it selfe, but added also with other purgers to cause the lesse trouble in the stomack: it healeth greene wounds, and bringeth old sores to cicatrizing, as also those of the genitors, it healeth the chappes of the fundament, the piles and breaking forth of blood from them, being used outwardly; but assuredly it is found not convenient for those that are troubled with piles, to take thereof inwardly, because it heateth, and maketh the blood of them to be more sharpe and fretting. Being mixed with a little vinegar and oyle of Roses, and the temples and forehead anoynted therewith, about the time of rest, doth much helpe the headache, and is a meanes to procure sleepe to those that want: if it be dissolved in wine, and the head washed therewith, it stayeth the falling of, or shedding of the haire: used with honey and wine, it cleanseth all foule ulcers that happen in the mouth or throat, as also fistulaes, that happen in the yard of a man or in the fudament.

ELDER
beauty, headache, stomach, ointment
—the distilled water of the flowers, is of much use to cleare the skinne from sunne burning, freckles, morphew, or the like: Matthiolus saith both the forepart and hinderpart of the head, being bathed therewith, it taketh away all manner of the headach that commeth of a cold cause. The Vinegar made of the flowers of Elder by maceration and insolation, is much more used in France, than anywhere else, and is gratefull to the stomacke, and a great power and effect to quicken the appetite.—An oyntment made of the greene leaves, and May butter made in the month of May, is accounted with many a soveraigne remedy, for all outward paines, aches, and crampes in the joynts, nerves, or sinewes, for starknesse and lamenesse by cold and other casualties, and generally to warme, comfort and strengthen all the outward parts ill affected.

SENNA
purge, obstruction of bowels, etc.
The leaves of Sene (Senna), howsoever used are a very safe and gentle purger, as well made into pouder, and the weight of a French Crowne or dramme thereof taken in Wine or Ale, or broth fasting; as the infusion of halfe an ounce in Wine or Ale for a night, or the decoction of halfe an ounce, or if need be of six drammes, with some other herbes or rootes (but because they are a little windie, a few Aniseed or Fennell seede, and a little Ginger is to be added unto them to helpe to correct that evill quality)—it strengtheneth the senses both of sight and bearing, and procureth mirth by taking away that inward humour, which was the inward cause of sadnesse in the mind, opening the obstructions of the bowells, and causing a fresh and lively habit in the body, prolonging youth, and keeping backe old age—Senna likewise is an especiall ingredient among other things put into a bag, to make purging Beere or Ale, fit to be taken in the spring of the yeare, not only for all those diseases before mentioned, but also to clense the blood from all sharpe humours, mixed or running therewith: Purging Prunes also and purging Currants are made therewith, by boyling Sene and some other opening herbes and rootes, or if yee will without them, with some Anniseede, Fennellseede, Cinamon, Ginger and Cloves, some of these or all of them a little quantity, and according to the proportion of your Prunes or Currants, being set to stew with the decoction of your Sene, and other things above specified, these may be given to the dantiest stomack, that is without offence, and without danger, to open the body and purge such humours above specified, as troble the body.

THE BOTANIC AGE—Continued

TAMARIND
thirst, beverage, medicine

—it does exceedingly helpe to asswage the thirst, if an ounce thereof be dissolved in faire water and a little Sugar mixed therewith, or taken of it selfe; for the people of the hot countries, doe usually eate thereof in their long travells to quench their thirst, which they were never able to indure without it, to refresh themselves in the great heate, both of the Summer, and of those drie places, where no water is to be had—if a small quantity of the pulpe of Tamarinds and Cassia (Cassia fistula) and the pouder of Rubarbe be mixed together, it maketh a delicate medicine to purge the stomacke and liver, and is very effectual to helpe to expell all hot burning agues, and procure an appetite.

BLACK ALDER
lice, teeth

—the inner barke hereof boiled in vinegar, is an approved remedy to kill lice, to cure the itch, and take away scabbes, and drie them up in a very short space: the same also is singular good to wash the teeth, both to take away the paines, to fasten those that are loose, to cleanse them from corruption and to keepe them firm.

BUCKTHORN
dye

Of these berries are made three severall sorts of colours, as they shall be gathered; that is being gathered while they are greene and kept dry, are called Sappe berries, which being steeped in some Allome water they give a reasonable faire yellow colour, which painters use for their workes, and Bookebinders to colour the edges of bookes, and leather dressers to colour leather, as they use also to make a greene colour called Sappe greene, taken from the berries when they are blacke, being bruised and put into a brasse or copper kettle, or pan; and there suffered to abide three or foure dayes, or a little heated upon the fire, and some beaten Allome put into them, and after pressed forth, the juyce or liquor is usually put up into great bladders, tyed with strong thred at the head, and hung up until it be dryed, which is dissolved in water or wine, but sacke is the best to preserve the colour from starving as they call it, that is from decaying and to make it hold fresh the longer: the third colour is a purplish colour which is made of the berries suffered to grow upon the bushes, until the middle or end of November, that they are ready to droppe from the trees.

SESAME SEED
beauty, ointment, baking

The oyle is of great use and effect to anoint the face or hands; or any other part of the body, to clense the skinne, and to take away sunburning, morphew, feckles, spots and scarres or any other deformities of the skinne, proceding of melancholy: it is good also to anoint any part scalded or burnt with fire: it helpeth those sinewes that are hard or schrunke, or those veines that are too great. The seede was in ancient times much used in bread for to relish and make it sweeter, as also in cakes with honey as Poppie seed was.

ORRIS
perfume

—being beaten either alone of themselves into pouder, or with other sweete things, are used to be layed in presses, chests and wardrops, to sweeten and perfume garments of linnen, and silke especially, and all things that you will put it to.

FALSE SAFFRON
food, parrots

—are much used in Spaine and other places, to bee put into their brothes and meates, to give them a yellow colour, which doth much please them: as for any relish of spice, or hot quick taste they have none—Parrots doe most willingly feede upon the seede, yet doth it not move their bodies a white.

CABBAGE
intoxication, medicine, lore

—they are much commended being eaten before meate, to keepe one from surfetting, as also from being drunke with much wine, by restraining the vapours that else would intoxicate the braine, or being drunke, will disperse the vapours and make them quickly rise sober again; and even Galen himselfe applied the juyce thereof, to the temples of them that had paines in their heads caused by drunkenesse; for as they say there is such antipathy or enmity betweene the Vine and the Colewort (Cabbage), that the one will die where the other groweth:—the ashes of Colewort stakles, are of such drying quality that they become almost causticke, or burning, and being mixed with old grease, are very effectuall to anoint the sides of those that have had long paines therein, or any other place pained by the access of melancholike and windie humours, helping mightily to digest them. It is thought to be effectuall for all dis-

THE BOTANIC AGE—Continued

eases of the body, either inward or outward, and therefore Hrysippus wrote a vol. of the vertues, applying it to every part of the body: and the old Romans having expelled Physicians out of their territories, did for six hundred yeares maintaine their health, and helped their infirmities, by using and applying it, for their onely medicine in every disease.

KALI or GLASSEWORT
glass, castile soap

—the ashes of the hearb, beaten to powder and mixed with a certaine kind of sand, the glassemen by the heate of fire, in their fornace being molten, doe make those fine christall glasses serviceable to drinke in—Of the ashes of the Kali likewise relented into a lye, and boyled with oyle of Olives they of Spaine, etc., use to make a kind of hard sope (soap) to wash with, the one sort comming from Spaine, we call Castile sope. another from Venice, white or Venice sope.

FUMITORY
depilatory

Dioscorides saith that it hindereth any fresh springing of the haires on the eye liddes, if after they be pulled away the eye browes be anointed with the juyce that hath Gum Arabeck (Arabic) dissolved in it.

FRENCH MERCURY
lore

—the ancient writers, Dioscorides, Theophrastus and others doe relate, that if women use these herbes inwardly or outwardly, for three dayes together after conception, and that their courses past, they shall bring forth male or female children, according to that kinde of herbe they use.

MALLOW
hair, medicine, poultice, etc.

—if the head be washed therewith (leaves) it stayeth the falling and shedding of the haire thereof: the roots and seedes of the Marsh Mallow, boyled in wine or water, is with good effect used by them that have any excorations in the guts or the bloudy flixe, not so much by any binding qualitie in them, as by qualifying the violence of the sharpe cholericke fretting humors, that are the cause thereof, and by the sliminesse easing the paines and healing the sorenesse, and in some sort staying the further eruption of the bloud therefrom, at that time, or any other after—Hippocrates used to give the decoction of the rootes, or the jouyce thereof to drinke, to those that were wounded, and were ready to faint, through the expense and losse of bloud, and applied the same mixed with hony and rosen unto the wounds: The Muccilage of the rootes, and of linseede and fenegrecke (fenugreek seed) put together, is much used in pultises, ointments, and plaisters, that serve to mollifie and digest all hard tumors and the inflammations of them, and give ease of the paines in any part of the body:

CAPSICUM
teeth

—the ashes of them being rubbed on the teeth, will clense them and make them grow white that were blacke.

GENTIAN
stomach, weariness

—the rootes taken in wine helpeth those that have obstructions in their livers, or are liver growne as they call it, or have paines in their stomackes; those also that cannot keepe or relish their meate, or have dejected appetites to their meate, for hereby they shall finde present ease and remedy: being steeped in wine and drunke, it refresheth those that are overwearied with travell, and are by cold and ill lodging abroad growen starke or lame in their joyntes—Matthiolus saith that it (root) was to be gathered wheresoever it was found and fit to be kept in ones purse, as ready to be used upon all occasions.

JOB'S TEARS
prayer beads

—beyond the sea, the greatest use they make of it, is of the seede, to perforate and string them, as other things for beades, to stint God with their prayers, and tell him how many they mumble upon them, and are sure that they have done him so good service therein, that he must needs give them heaven for it.

STINGING NETTLE
laying hens, nettle rash

—if you give hennes (hens) some dry Nettles broken small, with their meate (food) in winter, it will make them lay egges all the winter more plentifully—the juice of the leaves themselves, is a present remedy to take away the stinging of the Nettles.

THE BOTANIC AGE—Continued

PLANTAIN, RIBWORT, Etc.
wounds, sores, etc.
—Briefely, all the Plantanes are singular good wound herbes, to heale fresh or old wounds and sores, either inward or outward.

HOUND'S TONGUE
hair, fresh wounds
—the leaves bruised, or the juice of them boyled in Hogges (hog) larde and applied, cureth the falling away of the hair, which commeth of hot and sharpe humours—the leaves of themselves bruised and laid to any greene wound, doth heale it up quickly.

SPURRY
cattle, chickens
—It fatteneth cattle, and so it doth also Pullaine (chickens), and as it causeth the Kine to give more store of milke then ordinary otherwise, so it causeth Pullaine likewise to lay more store of egges, which is no idle conceit, for those of Brabant, and other the parts thereabouts have found it sufficient true, by their daily use and tryall thereof.

WOODRUFF or MASTER-OF-THE-WOODS
wine, medicine, plague
The Germanes doe account very highly of this woodroofe, using it very familiarly in wine, like as we doe Burnet to take away melancholy passions, to make the heart merry; and to helpe the stomacke dejected, unto a good appetite, and the Liver being oppressed and obstructed: it is held also to be good against the Plague, both to defend the heart, and vitall spirits from infection.

LADIES BEDSTRAW
lore, ointment, foot bath
Dioscorides writeth that the roote is good to provoke bodily lust, and some say the flowers doe so also: the flowers and the hearbe likewise made into an oyntment or oyle, in oyle to be insolated or set into the Sunne, and changed after it hath stood some tenne or twelve dayes, but if it be made into an oyntment, it must be boyled in Axungia (hog's grease) or sallet oyle, with some waxe melted therein after it is strayned; which will helpe burnings with fire, and scaldings with water: the same also or decoction of the herbe and flowers, is good to bath the feete of travelers, who are surbated with travaile, and for Lackies or such like, whose running long, causeth not onely wearinesse, but stiffnesse in their sinews and joynts; for which both the decoction warme is very availeable, and so is the oyntment to use afterwards.

CLEAVERS
reducing
Galen saith it cleanseth meanely and dryeth, and is of subtill parts: it is familiarly taken in broth to keepe them leane and lanke, that are apt to grow fat.

ST JOHNSWORT
wounds, muscular aches
S. Johns wort is a singular wound herbe as any other whatsoever, eyther for inward wounds, hurts or bruises, to be boyled in wine and drunke, or prepared into oyle or oyntment, bathe or lotion outwardly, for being of an hot and drying quality, with subtill parts, it hath power to open obstructions, to dissolve tumours, to consolidate or soder the lips of wounds, and to strengthen the parts that are weake and feeble:—The oyle of S. Johns wort, eyther simple or compound, but the compound is more effectuall, is singular good both for all greene wounds, and old sores, ulcers, in the legs or else where, that are hard to be cured, and is effectuall also for cramps and aches in the joynts, and paines in the veines and sinewes, and is also good for all burnings by fire, to be presently used, or the juice of the greene leaves applyed; the hearbe dryed and made into pouder, is effectuall for wounds and sores to be strowed thereon, as the oyle or juice. The simple oyle is made of 4 ounces of the flowers infused in a pint of oyle Ollive, called Sallet oyle, and 3 ounces of white wine, for 10 or 12 dayes to bee set in the Sunne, and afterwards boyled in a Kettle of seething water, strayned forth, and refreshed with new flowers, so set in the Sunne, and in the same manner boyled, strained forth and renewed the third time with fresh flowers, which after they have lastly stood in the Sunne a fortnight or more, are to be boyled in the sayd Kettle of seething water, strayned forth, and the oyle, having some fine turpentine dissolved in it whiles it is hot, and so kept, is singular good for the purposes aforesayd.

GARDEN BURNET
wine flavor
—a friend to the Hart, Liver, and other the principall parts of a mans body; 2 or 3 of the stalks with leaves put into a cup of wine, especially Claret, as all know give a wonderfull fine rellish to it, and besides is a great meanes to quicken the spirits, refresh the heart, and make it merry, driving away melancholly.

THE BOTANIC AGE—Continued

420-Year-Old Illustration of Herb Market

MEADOW SWEET
strewing herb

—because both flowers and herbes are of so pleasing a sweete sent, many doe much delight therein, to have it layed in their Chambers, Parlars, etc. and Queene Elizabeth of famous memory, did more desire it then any other sweet herbe to strew her Chambers withall: a leafe or two hereof layed in a cup of wine, will give as quick and as fine a rellish thereto, as Burnet will.

WOOD BETONY
lore, stomach, drunkenness, weariness

—Antonius Musa, the Emporour Augustus his Physition, who wrote a peculiar booke hereof, saith of it, that it preserveth the lives and bodies of men, free from the danger of diseases, and from witchcrafts also; but it is found by dayly experience, as Dioscorides formerly wrote thereof, to be good for innumerable diseases, as Matthiolus termeth it, for it helpeth those that either loath or cannot digest their meate (food), those that have weake stomackes, or have sower belchings, or continual risings in their stomacke, if they use it familiarly, either greene or dry, either the herbe, the roote, or the flowers, in broth drunke, or meate, made into conserve, syrupe, electuary, water, or powder, as every one may best frame themselves unto, or as the time or season requireth taken any of the aforesayd wayes:—it is sayd also to hinder drunkennesse, being taken before hand, and quickely to expell it afterwards: a dramme of the powder of Betonie taken with a little hony; in some vinegar, doth wonderfully refresh those that are overwearied by travaile.

CELANDINE
warts, piles, hemorrhoides

—the juice rubbed often upon warts will take them away; it is certaine by good experience, that the decoction of the leaves and rootes doth wonderfully helpe the piles or hemorrhoides.

BOUNCING BET or SOAPWORT
soap

This Herbe is usually called Saponaria because it serveth in stead of Sope to wash any thing withall.

RAMPIONS or BELL-FLOWERS
salads, motherhood, beauty

The rootes of all sorts of Rampions, and so likewise some of the Bell-flowers, especially if they have any greater rootes than the ordinary stringie ones, are used for sallets either cold with vinegar oyle and pepper, or boyled and stewed with butter or oyle, and some blacke or long pepper cast on them; either way or any way else they are familiar to the stomacke, stirring up the appetite, and by reason of their temperate quality, causeth a good digestion, and engendreth store of milk in nurses breasts; the rootes beaten small and mixed with some meale of Lupines, clenseth the skinne from spots, markes, or other discolourings. The distilled water of the whole plants, rootes and all, performeth the same, and maketh the face very splendent and cleare.

HAZEL NUT
as food, stick for snakes and mad dogs

—while they are fresh are sweete, and much pleasing to the palate, but the much eating of them breed headache and windinesse in the stomacke, especially when they grow older, but if they be a little heated or parched by the fire, the oylinesse doth become lesse offensive:—if a snake be stroke with an Hasell wand, it doth sooner stunne it, then with any other sticke, because it is so pliant, that it will winde closer

THE BOTANIC AGE—*Continued*

about it, so that being deprived of their motion, they must needs dye with paine and want: and it is no hard matter in like manner, saith Tragus to kill a mad dog that shall be strooke with an Hasell sticke, such as men use to walke or ride withall.

ASH
snake lore
—Pliny writeth that those serpents will not abide the shadow that the Ash maketh in the morning and the evening which they are longest, nor will come neere it, and further saith of his own experience, that if a fire and a serpent be encompassed within a circle of the boughes of the Ash tree, it (snake) will sooner flye into the fire then into them:

MEDLAR FRUIT
pregnancy
—the mellowed fruite is often served among other sorts of fruite to the table, and eaten with pleasure by those who have no need of physicke, but worketh in women with childe, both to please the taste as in others, and to stay their longings after unusuall meates (foods) as also very effectuall for them that are apt to miscarry, and before their time to be delivered, to help that malady, and make them joyfull mothers.

TREFOIL (Cytisus)
fodder for cattle, increase mother's milk
—in former ages, there was much profit made by the feeding of sheepe herewith to give store of milke, and not onely to fatten them, but Bullockes and Goates also, and Hens, and all other sorts of cattell: but was planted also for Bees to feede on, as from whence they did gather more honey, then from any other plant whatsoever, and beside it abideth greene eight moneths of the yeare for their pasture, and may be kept dry the rest of the yeare following, as the dry fodder: if women that be Nurses have not any store of milke in their brests, let them steepe some of the leaves and young branches hereof in faire water all night, and being strained forth in the morning, let them take three parts thereof, with a fourth of wine, which will breede good store of milke in them, and make their children strong and able: the dryed leaves steeped all night in water, and boyled afterwards, strained and drunke is as effectuall as the juyce.

CYPRESS
hair dye, repellent
—the nuts boyled in Wine, and the hair washed therewith, causeth them to grow black
—the leaves being laid among seedes of any sort, will keep them from being eaten with wormes, and the wood in Wardrobes will preserve garment from Mothes: the wood it selfe is in no age subject to the worme, neither will the sent (scent) decay in many yeares, and therefore much desired in chests and boxes.

HOLLY
protect meats, Christmas decoration, superstition
—some use to tie the branches with leaves upon their Bacon, and Martinmas Beefe, to keepe Rats and Mice from them by their prickles: the Branches with berries, are used at Christ tide to decke up our houses withall, but that they should defend the house from lightening, and keepe themselves from witchcraft.

BAY
flavor, medicinal uses of oil
—the leaves boyled in fish broth, give a fine rellish, both to meate and broth, and helpeth to warme the stomacke and to cause digestion, without fear of casting—the oyle which is made of the berries, is very comfortable in all cold griefes of the joynts, nerves, arteries, stomacke, belly or wombe, and helpeth palsies, convulsions, crampes, aches, tremblings, and numnesse in any part, wearinesse also, and paines that come by sore travelling in wet weather, or foule wayes:

MULBERRY
lore
—a branch of the tree taken when the Moone is at the full, and bound to the wrist of a womans arme whose courses come down too abundantly, doth stay them in a short space.

BANANAS
pregnancy
—are good for woman with childe to nourish the birth.

QUINCE FRUIT
stomach, sore nipples, hoarseness
—if a little vinegar be added, it stirreth up the languishing appetite, and the stomacke

THE BOTANIC AGE—*Continued*

given to casting (vomiting), and if some spices it comforteth and strengtheneth the decaying and fainting spirits, and helpeth the liver opprest, that it cannot perfect the digestion, and correcteth chollour and flegme:—the muccilage taken from the seedes of Quinces boyled a little in water, is very goode to coole the beate, heale the sore breasts of women, who have them sore by their childrens default or otherwise: the same also with a little Sugar is good to lenesie the harshnesse and hoarsenesse of the throate, and roughnesse of the tongue.

PEARS
Perry, beverage of Middle Ages

The wilde Peares by reason of their harshnesse, are not eaten as the milder sorts are, except some good kinde stewed or baked, to serve the poore peoples dyet, the other scarse fit for the hogs to eate, and therefore are for the most part where store of them grow, beaten and pressed into a liquor which is called Perry, of especiall good use at Sea in long voyages, to mingle with their fresh water, to make it the more helpfull, or lesse offensive to those that must continually drinke water: and will after some time become so milde almost as Wine, and fit and wholesome to be drunke:—Perry is a drinke that whosoever useth at home being not accustomed to it, will wring them a little by the belly, and will a little force it downeward, but being more used to it worketh not so at all, but rather cooleth an hot or fainting stomacke, helping the digestion being temperately taken: but at Sea by the working thereof it is made more comfortable, taking away the crudity and rawnesse of the water.

GOLDILOCKS
lore

—the herbe with the flowers boiled in wine and drunke expelleth loves enchantments and all other poisons.

MOUSE-EAR
harden steel, shoeing horse

It is sayed to be so powerfull to harden iron or steele, that if any edge or pointed tool be often quenched in the juice thereof, it will cut all other iron, steele or stone very easily without turning edge or point. Alchimists did much commend the juice of this herbe, that it would congeale or fix Mercury, but all these fancies are in these times quite dispersed and driven away I thinke. It is said that if it be given any way to an horse it will cause that he shall not be hurt by the Smith that shooeth him.

YARROW
hair, stomach medicine

—the oyle made thereof stayeth the shedding of the hair; the decoction thereof made in wine and drunke is good for them that cannot reteine their meate (food) in their stomacke.

SOLOMONS SEAL
beauty aid

—the whole plant used to the face or other part of the skinne, cleanseth it from morphew, freckles, spots or markes whatsoever, leaving the place fresh, faire and lovely.

TOBACCO
abstinence

Thevet saith that women in America forbeare the taking of Tobacco, because that they have beene taught that it will hinder conception and bodily lust.

SWEET CLOVER or MELLILOT
liniment

The flowers and herbe of the white flowred Mellilot, steeped in oyle Olive, and set into the Sunne to digest for some time, and after being boyled in a Balneo (double boiler?) of hot water, and strained forth, and other fresh flowers and herbes being put thereto, and Sunned, as before and strained, and so used at the second or third time, is accounted a most soveraine Balme, both for green (fresh) wounds and old sores, for swellings, inflammations, crampes, convulsions, paines, or aches whatsoever in any part of the body, whether it be any fleshy or musculous part, or among the sinewes and veines.

HOUSELEEK
warts, corns, bites, stings

—the juice taketh away warts and cornes in the hands or feete being often bathed therewith, and the skinne of the leaves being layed on them afterwards; the leaves being gently rubbed on any place stung with Nettles or Bees, or bitten with any venemous creature doth presently take away the paine.

THE BOTANIC AGE—Continued

CHICKWEED
liniment
—when a Sinew is strayned here is a faire medicine for it; Boyle a handfull of Chickweede, and a handfull of red Rose leaves dryed in a quart of Muscadine untill a fourth part be consumed, then put to them a pint of the Oyle of Trotters or Sheepes feete, let them boyle a good while still stirring them well, which being strayned annoint the greeved place herewith warme against a fire, rubbing it well in with ones hand, and binde also some of the herbe if ye will to the place, doe so againe the next morning and evening, by which time you shall finde helpe if God will.

BORAGE
increase milk, melancholy
—the seed helpeth Nurses to have more store of milke, for which purpose the leaves are much conducing: the leaves, flowers and seede, all of them or any of them are very cordiall and helpe to expell pensiveness and melancholie, that ariseth without manifest cause, whereof came the saying, Ego Borrago gaudia semper ago, and as I sayed before called Corrago.

DANDELION
medicine for children and aged
—(root) is very effectual for the obstructions of the liver, gall and spleene, and the diseases that arise from them, as the jaundise and the hypochondriacall passion, it wonderfully openeth the uritorie parts, causing abundance of urine, not onely in children whose mesericall veines are not sufficiently strong to contain the quantitie of urine drowne in the night, but that then without restraint or keeping it backe they water their beds, but in those of old age also upon the stopping or yeelding small quantitie of urine.

SOW THISTLE
beauty aid
—the distilled water is wonderfully good for women to wash their faces to clear the skinne and to give a lustre thereunto.

WILD ROCKET
body odors and skin discolorations
—the seede taken in drinke taketh away the evill smell of the arme-holes or pits, and of the rest of the body—the seede mixed with hony and used on the face clenseth the skinne from spots, morphew, and other discolourings therein, and used with Vinegar taketh away freckles and other rednesse hapnings in the face or other parts, and used with the gall of an Oxe it amendeth foule scarres, blacke and blew spots, and the markes of the small poxe, restoring the skinne to its owne colour againe.

MUSTARD
sauce recipe
—two ounces of Mustarde seede, halfe an ounce of good Cinamon well beaten to be made up into balles or cakes, with hony and vinegar, which being dried in the Sunne are to be kept untill use to be made thereof, which then relented with a little vinegar is made into a sawce presently, very delicate and pleasing to the palate and stomacke.

ARSMART or WATER PEPPER
repellent, lore
—if the herbe be strowed in a chamber, it will soone kill all the Fleas therein; and if the herbe or juice thereof be put to horses or other catteles fores, it will drive away the Flyes that will sticke thereto, even in the hottest Summer: a good handfull of the herbe put under a horses saddle, will make him travell better, although hee were halfe tired before.

FENNEL
increase milk, hiccough, medicine, overweight
—the leaves or seede boyled in Barley water and drunk is good for Nurses to encrease their milke, and to make it the more wholesome for their Nurse children to take: the seede boyled in water stayeth the hickocke, and taketh away that loathing which often happeneth to the stomackes of sicke or feaerish persons; the rootes are of most use in Physicke drinkes and broths that are taken to clense the blood, to open obstructions of the Liver, and to provoke Urine and to amend the evill colour or complexion in the face after long sicknesse and to cause a good colour and a good habit through the whole body: Fennell—both leaves and seedes or rootes are much and often used in drinkes or brothes, for those that are grown fat to abate their unweldinesse and make them more gaunt and lanke.

CARAWAY
medicine, sharpen sight
—the seede is conducing to all the cold greefes both of the head and stomacke, the bowels or mother, as also the winde in them, and helpeth to sharpen the eye sight.

THE BOTANIC AGE—Continued

ANISE
bad breath, increase milk, colic, headache
The seede being often taken helpeth a stinking breath and to breake winde in any part of the body, bee it the head, stomacke, spleene, bowells or mother, and to provoke Urine and sleepe to them that want it: they help Nurses to store of milke for their children, to eate the seedes comfited fasting and last at night, and is very good also for teeming women or with child; the bruised seede and storax mixed together, and the fumes thereof taken being cast on quicke coales, so the head be covered over, that the fumes may penetrate the better, will soon ease the continuall headach.

PARSLEY
offensive breath, sick fish, inflamed eyes, breasts, discolorations
The leaves of Parsley eaten after Onions, Leekes, or Garlicke taketh away offensive smell of them, suppresseth the vapours that may offend eyther the head or the eyes; they use also to cast the herbe into their Fish ponds if there be any sicke among them to clense them—The leaves laid to the eyes that are inflamed with heate or are swollen doth much helpe them, if it be used with bread or meale: and being laid to womens hard breasts that come by the curding of their milk doth abate the hardnesse quickly if it be fryed with butter and applyed, and doth also take away the blacke and blew spots or markes by bruises, falls, etc.

LOVAGE
stomach medicine
—the dried roote in powder taken to the weight of halfe a dramme in wine, doth wonderfully warme a cold stomacke, helping digestion—easeth all inward gripings and paines, dissolveth winde, and resisteth poyson and infection effectually.

MALE FERN
colored glass, magic
Of the ashes of Ferne is made a kind of thicke or dark coloured greene glasse in sundry places in France—the seede gathered onely on Midsommer eve at night, with I know not what conjuring words is superstitiously held by divers, not onely Mountebankes and Quacksalvers, but by other learned men to be of some secret hidden vertue, but I cannot finde it exprest what it should be.

FEMALE FERN
repellent, laundry soap
—the fume of Ferne being burned driveth away Serpents, Gnats, and other noisome Creatures that in the Fenny Countries much molest both strangers and inhabitants that lye in bed in the night time. They use in Warwickeshire, above any other Country in this Land in steed of Sope (Soap), to wash their clothes, to gather the female Fern about midsomer and to make it up into good big balls, which when they will use them they burne them in the fire, untill it become blewish, which being then layed by, will dissolve into powder of it selfe, like unto Lime: foure of these balls being dissolved in warme water is sufficient to wash a whole bucke full of cloathes.

OAK FERN
depilatory
—it is a remedy to take away haires as Dioscorides saith, if the rootes and leaves bee bruised together and applyed after sweating.

MAIDENHAIR FERN
—the Lye made thereof is singular good to clense the head from scurfe, and eyther dry or running sores, stayeth the falling or shedding of the haire, and causeth them to grow thicke, faire, and well coloured, for which purpose some boyle it in wine, putting some smalledge seede thereto, and afterwards some oyle.

KIDNEY BEANS
horse bites
—if the greene pods be chewed in ones mouth, and applied to any place that is bitten by an horse it will helpe.

PEAS
as food
Peases are lesse windy than Beanes, but passe not forth of the body as soone as they.

FENUGREEK
fattener, headwash, poultice
Galen and divers authors said the seede was used in their times (being buried a little in earth to make them sproute, whereof many Sacke fulls are sold in the markets daily) to make them grow fat.—the decoction thereof clenseth the head and haire from

THE BOTANIC AGE—Continued

scurfe, dandraffe and running sores—a Pultis made with the meale thereof and Linseede, and the decoction of Mallowes, and a little oyle or Axungia (lard) put thereto asswageth the swelling and paines of the cods or privy parts of women, and generally all other swellings and tumors

MEDIC (varieties of Alfalfa)
cattle feed

The use of this herbe was in former times more to feede Cattell then in medicine, for it was held to be so powerfull to fatten their Horses and other beasts that they would stint them to a quantitie for feare of suffocating them, by growing thereby too fat.

DOG GRASS
medicine

—is the most medicinable grasse of all others, serving to open obstructions of the liver and gall, and stoppings of the urine, being boyled and drunke, and to ease the griping paines of the belly, and inflammations.

HORSE TAIL GRASS
staunch blood, household uses

It is very powerfull to stanch bleedings, wheresoever, eyther inward or outward, the juice or decoction thereof being drunke, or the juice, decoction or distilled water applyed outwardly—Countrey housewives doe use any of these rough sorts (varieties) that are next at hand to scoure both their woodden, peuter and brasse vessels.

COLUMBINE
sore throat

The leaves of Columbines are commonly used in lotions, for sore mouthes and throates.

BIRCH TREE
interesting uses

Many civill uses the Birch is put unto, as first to decke up houses and arbours, both for the fresh greennesse and good sent (scent) it casteth; it serveth to make hoopes to binde caskes withall; the young branches being fresh are writhed, and serve for bands unto faggots; of the young twigges are made broomes to sweepe our houses, as also rods to correct children at schools, or at home, and was an ensigne born in bundles by the Lictors or Sergeants before the Consuls in the old Roman times, with which, and with axes borne in the like manner, they declared the punishment for lesser, and greater offences, to their people.

ALDER
tired feet, fleas, dye

—the leaves put under the bare feete of travellers, that are surbated with travelling, are a great refreshing unto them: the said leaves while they have the morning dew on them, laid in a chamber troubled with fleas will gather them thereinto, which being quickely cast out, will ridde the chamber of them: of the barke is made a black dye.

BLACK POPLAR
beautify hair, ointment, mothers breasts

—the young blacke Poplar buds saith Matthiolus, are much used by women to beautifie their haire, bruising them with fresh butter, and strayning them after they have beene for some time kept in the Sunne: the oyntment called Populeon which is made of this Poplar is singular good for any heate or inflammation in any part of the body, and doth also temper the heate of wounds: it is much used to dry up the milke in womens breasts after their delivery, or when they have weyned their children.

YEW
poisonous, berries turn birds black, ancient bow

The opinion of harme that this tree worketh or preadventure some accidental harme by distemperature, either by the climate wherein it is bred, or of the persons that take it hath caused, that there is nothing of any good property recorded, by any ancient or moderne writer hereof, but still said by most to be deadly to beasts, and dangerous to men—the berries are sweete with some bitternesse—birds that feede thereon become blacke—formerly long bowes were wont to be made (of the wood) which were of great account, as well with us as with other nations long agoe.

WALNUT
dog or man bites, lore, ointment, flavoring, painters oil

(the nut) taken with Onions, salt and honey helpe the biting of a mad dogge, as also the biting of any man—Cneus Pompeus found in the treasury of Mithridates King of Pontus, when he was overthrowne a scroule of his own handwriting, of a medicine against any poyson or infection which is this, two dry Wallnuts, and as many good Figges (figs), and twenty leaves of Rue or Herbegrace, bruised and beaten together

THE BOTANIC AGE—Continued

with two or three cornes of salt, which taken every morning fasting preserveth from danger of poyson or infection that day it is taken—the kernels when they grow old are more oyly, and therefore are not so fit to be eaten, but then are used to heale the wounds of the sinewes, gangrens, and carbuncles:—(the nuts) eaten after Onions take away the strong smell and sharpnesse of them, a peece of the greene huske put unto an hollow tooth, easeth the paines—some doe use the greene huskes, dryed and made into pouther (powder) instead of Pepper to season their meates, but if some dryed Sage in pouther be put unto it, it will give it the better rellish: in the same manner doe some use the young red leaves before they grow greater, and find it a seasoning not to be dispised of poore folkes; the oyle pressed out of the kernells is farre better for the painters use, to illustrate a white colour then Linseede oyle which deadeth it, and is of singular good use to be laid on guilded workes, or on those workes of wood that are made by burning, such as are those walking staves that have workes on them or the like, to preserve the colour of the gold, or of the other worke for a long time without decay.

PEACH
rest and sleep, bald heads

The milke or creame of these kernells, with some Verven water being applyed to the forehead and temples, doth much helpe to procure rest and sleepe to sicke persons wanting it—If the kernels be bruised and boyled in vinegar untill they become thicke, and applyed to the head, or other places that have shed the haire, and are bald it doth marvellously procure the haire to grow againe.

ALMONDS
dry cough, keeping sober

—the oyle of sweete Allmonds, mixed with fine pouther (powder) of Sugar Candy is good for the dry cough, and for hoarsenesse, to take a little at once:—if one doe eate five or sixe bitter Almonds before he fall into drinking company, it will keepe him from being overtaken more than the rest.

CHERRIES
as food

Cherryes as they are of divers tastes, so they are of divers qualities, the sweete are more lubricke, and passe through the stomacke and belly more speedily, but are of little nourishment, the tart or sowre are more pleasing to an hot stomacke, and procure an appetite to meate (food).

MASTIC
teeth

—the ponther of the barke doth helpe to fasten loose teeth, and loose gummes, and of the wood is made fine and good toothpickes.

DRAGON'S BLOOD
crafts, glass

The Goldsmiths and Glasiers use it much in their workes, the one for an enamell, and to set a foile under their precious stones, for greater luster; and the other by fire to strike a crimson colour into glasse for windowes or the like.

PINE
wrinkles

There is a water destilled from the greene cones or apples that is very effectual to take away the wrinkles in the face.

GRAPES
properties of wine

I will touch onely the particular properties of wine it selfe, both as it is medicinable and nourishing, for taken moderately, and by them that are of a middle age, or well stept in yeares, or are of a cold and dry disposition and (not very young, and so their blood too hot for to abide wine) it encreaseth blood and nourisheth much: it procureth an appetite, and helpeth to digest being taken at meate (meals)—it expelleth feares, cares, and heavinesse, and breedeth alacrity, mirth and bodily pleasure—causeth quiet rest and sleepe, both to the sound and sicke that lacke it—on the contrary side, the excess thereof breedeth a distraction in the sense, the Appoplexie, and Lethargy or drowsie evill, the trembling of the joynts, the palsie, and the dropsie.

ASSAFOETIDA
tale of middle ages

Garcias saith the Indians use it to take away the loathing of the stomacke to meate (food), and to strengthen the weaknesse of it also, and is much used by them to provoke unto Venery, and causeth one to expell winde mightily, which thing was tryed by a

THE BOTANIC AGE—*Continued*

Portugall (Portuguese) as Garcias relateth it upon an Horse, whom the King of Bisnager would have bought, but that he was over subject to breake winde, but after that the Portugall had cured him thereof the King bought him, and asking how he cured him, he answered him with Assafetida given in his provender, no mervaile said the King, if he were cured with the Gods meate, yea rather with the devils said the Portugall, but softly, and in his owne language for feare of being overheard.
NOTE: Assafoetida is also known as Devil's Dung or Food of the Gods.

COCCULUS INDICUS
fish bait, lice

(the berries) are wholly spent either to make baites to catch fish, with other things for that purpose, or the pouther (powder) used to kill lice and vermine in childrens heads.

MYRRH
wrinkles in face

Matthiolus commendeth it as a singular fucus for the face to take away wrinkles that come by age, and to make it smooth and youthfull to be made into an oyle as it is called, or rather the liquor of Myrrhe, which is made with eggs boyled hard, cut in the middle, the yolkes taken forth and filled up with pouther (powder) of Myrrhe, then put into a glasse and set in a Wine cellar or moist place, and with this liquour to be bedewed: As also another way, that is, by sprinckling with white wine, a new iron dish or pan made hot in the fire, and taking first the fumes thereof unto the face, being covered over with a cloth, and then the fumes of Myrrhe in pouther, afterwards cast on it being heated againe, and the head covered as before, and this still to be used before bed time, for eight dayes together.

SPIKENARD
Caravans versus Ships

Garcais ab Orta, intreating of this Spikenard testifieth that there is but one sort knowne, and used as well by the Indian and Turkish, as the Persian and Arabian Physitions, and although some would intimate that this is not that used by the Ancients, in that Pliny setteth it down lib 12. C. 12. that it was not to be had but at an excessive price, yet that hindereth not, in regard both all the Countryes of the Indies are better husbanded then heretofore, and especially that since the Portugalls (Portuguese) had opened the way by Sea, all sortes of Drugges were provided better and better cheape by much, the charge of Caravans being excessive chargeable by their long journey and travaile, but I thinke both the Drugges and the Indies, by being more sought by Venetians and other Christians was the beginning of the reformations, for when Arabians and the like were the chiefe Merchants, much bad Merchandize was dearely sold, howsoever cheaply bought, I thinke much more adulterated by them, and the Indians also were not behind to sophisticate whatsoever they could, which the Christians I verily suppose did somewhat alter, when they became Great Merchants of Europe, and since is rectified more and more, when onely the sincere and pure is bought, and the other left on their hand to mend if they can, but yet it falleth out that the blinde eateth many a flye, I meane the ignorant is often deluded who through covetousnesse oftentimes letteth passe the better to take the worser at cheaper rates.

SASSAFRAS
New World botanical

—the first knowledge of this Sassafras or Ague tree came by the French to our Christian world, and to the Spaniards by driving out the French, who had seated themselves somewhat neere the Florida, which they claimed for themselves for they having gotten Agues, and swellings in their legges, and other diseases by lying on the ground in the open aire by bad victualls and raw drinke of water, as the French before them had, by a French man that remained among them, were taught the use of this tree, which he and his Country men had learned before of the Natives.

And now unto God Almighty Triuno, and Uno in Trinitate, who I hope hath beene at the beginning of this Worke, and holpen me through all the passages thereof, notwithstanding the multa discrimina rerum mortalium, whereof I have felt my part, to bring it to the end, for the benefit of others (who that they may make good use thereof, and not pervert it to any sinister course, is my earnest desire) be given all the praise, honour, and glory, for I am but (like the Bee, that workes out waxe and hony for others, not his owne good:) his instrument to accomplish it, receiving off from Him. Amen.

Finis

SPRING TIME

"Spryngynge tyme is the time of gladnesse and of love; for in Sprynging time all thynge semeth gladde; for the erthe wexeth grene, trees burgynne (burgeon) and sprede, medowes bring forth flowers, heven shyneth, the see resteth and is quyete, foules synge and make theyr nestes, and al thynge that semed deed in wynter and widdered, ben renewed in Spryngyng time."—from Bartholomaeus Anglicus' 688 year old manuscript.

NOTES FROM GERARD'S 1597 HERBAL

(*HERBAL BELIEFS OF THE MIDDLE AGES,* See Special Notice on Page 9)

Shepherd's Purse staieth bleeding in any part of the body whether the juice or the decoction thereof be drunke, or whether it be used pultesse wise, or in bath or any other way else.

Eyebright: It is very much commended for the eies. Being taken itselfe alone, or anyway else, it preserves the sight, and being feeble and lost it restores the same; it is given most fitly being beaten into powder; ofentimes a like quantitie of Fennell seed is added thereto, and a little mace, to the which is put so much sugar as the weight of them all commeth to.

Eyebright, stamped and laid upon the eyes, or the juyce thereof mixed with white wine and dropped into the eyes, or the distilled water, taketh away the darknesse and dimnesse of the eyes and cleareth the sight.

The parts of the powder of Eyebright, and one part of maces mixed therewith, taketh away all hurts from the eyes, comforteth the memorie, and cleareth the sight, if halfe a spoonefull be taken every morning, fasting, with a cup of white wine.

Water-mint: It is commended to have the like vertues that the garden Min hath, and also to be good against the stinging of bees and wasps, if the place be rubbed therewith. The savor or smell of the Water Mint rejoyceth the heart of man, for which cause they use to strew it in chambers and places of recreation, pleasure and repose, and where feasts and banquets are made.

Borage: The leaves and floures of Borrage put into wine make men and women glad and merry, driving away all sadnesse, dulnesse, and melancholy, as Dioscorides and Pliny affirme.

Syrrup made of the floures of Borrage comforteth the heart, purgeth melancholy, and quiteth the phrenticke or lunaticke person.

The floures of Borrage made up with sugar, do all the aforesaid with greater force and effect.

Alkanet: The gentlewomen of France do paint their faces with these roots.

Coltsfoot: A decoction made of the greene leaves and roots or else a syrrup thereof, is good for cough that proceedeth of a thin rheume.

The green leaves of Coltsfoot pound with honey, do cure and heale inflammations.

The fume of the dried leaves taken through a funnell or tunnell burned upon coles, effectually helpeth those that are troubled with the shortness of breath and fetch their winde thick and often.

Being taken in manner as they take Tobaco, it mightily prevaileth against the diseases aforesaid.

Solomon's Seal: The root stamped while it is fresh and greene, and applied, taketh away in one night, or two at the most, any bruise, blacke or blew spots gotten by fals or women's wifulnesse, in stumbling upon their hasty husbands fists, or such like.

The leaves boyled and applied in manner of a pultis taketh away the burning heate in wounds; the decoction thereof strengthneth the gummes, and fastneth the teeth.

Golden Rod hath long, broad leaves, somewhat hoary and sharpe-pointed, among which rise up browne stalkes two foot high, dividing themselves toward the top into sundry branches, charged or loden with small yellow floures; which when they be ripe turn into downe which is carried away with the winde.

It is extolled above all other herbes for the stopping of bloud in bleeding wounds; and hath in times past beene had in great estimation and regard than in these daiese: for in my remembrance I have known the dry herbe which came from beyond the sea sold in Bucklersbury in London for halfe a crowne an ounce. But since it was found in Hampstead wood even as it were at our townes end, no man will give halfe a crowne for an hundred weight of it; which plainely wetteth forth our inconstancie and sudden mutabilitie, esteeming no longer of anything, how pretious soever it be, than whilest it is strange and rare. This verifieth our English proverbe. Far fetcht and deare bought is best for Ladies. Yet it may be more truely said of phantastical Physitions, who when they have found an approved medicine and perfect remedy neere home against any disease; yet not content therewith, they will seeke for a new farther off, and by that meanes many times hurt more than they helpe. Thus much I have spoken to bring these new fangled fellowes backe againe to esteeme better of this admirable plant than they have done, which no doubt have the same virtue now then it had, although it growes so neere our owne homes in never so great quantity.

There are several modes of effecting cures by equivalent remedies; but vegetable substances afford the mildest, most efficacious, and most congenial to the human frame.—Rafinesque

Botanicals, Spices, and Gums from the World Over

Our ancestors lived in a very small, yet a very big world. The world was small because these prehistoric people did not venture far from the hiding place they called home. The world was big because vast, unknown seas, mountains and wilderness lay about them.

There was no trading in those days. Life was very simple. Foods and medicines consisted of only what man could find in the tiny area in which he lived. Nevertheless, from this area a few simple raw foods provided sufficient vital minerals and vitamines to sustain these people living under very hazardous conditions.

As man found better means of protecting himself, he became bolder and ventured farther from the place of his birth. Covering more territory meant a larger assortment of foods, botanicals and new flavors. With the development of communities we find man beginning to explore more and more the mysterious world in which he lived. It was mainly the people of the sea coasts that dared venture far from their native lands. The open seas were less to fear than the dark forests inhabited by beasts, wild races and imaginary monsters. These early sea-faring people met different people and eventually began exchanging products of their native lands. Early trade centered around the coast of the Mediterranean Sea—it was here that civilization spread from Egypt to east and northern shores. Each civilization contributed new foods, botanicals and flavors. The greatest contribution being made by the Romans, when Caesar penetrated the much feared mountain and forest barriers in the north. This conquest opened the trade routes to all Europe and the Isles.

About a century after Caesar's death, Dioscorides, a Greek Physician, traveling with the Roman armies wrote his De Materia Medica. This great work described all the medical substances then known, together with their properties and uses. For more than sixteen hundred years it served as the authority in materia medica. It was translated into Latin and other languages and preserved through the Dark Ages by the monasteries. Monks used this valuable knowledge to administer medical aid to their ailing parishioners.

Some 1300 years after Dioscorides, we hear of many new botanicals from unknown lands of the Far East. Marco Polo with his father and uncle traveled more than three years by boat, foot and horseback, to reach the distant empire of the Great Kublai Khan, Tartar ruler of all the Orient. After living twenty years in the East, the Polos returned to their native Venice with a story that was incredible to a people still suffering under the stupor of the Dark Ages. In the Polo narrative, we hear of Camphor, Sago, Brazilwood, Cassia, Silk, Cloves, Musk, Ginger, Coconuts, Cubebs, Spikenard, Galangal, Nutmeg, Sandalwood, Pepper, etc. Pepper, Cinnamon and Ginger were not new to Europe—they had been brought centuries before by traders over long, dangerous caravan routes. Because of the prohibitive prices of these spices, they were beyond the reach of common people—in fact, unknown to most of them. It was not until the 16th and 17th centuries when spices appeared in quantities and prices where the average man could indulge in a bit of these smacking new flavors.

Nations and great trading houses, seeing the possibilities of Oriental products, sent their ships out to find shorter routes to the great Oriental trade. The English and Dutch tried to reach the East via northern routes. The Portuguese found a long route around Africa and Cape of Good Hope. Columbus believed he would find a shorter route by sailing westward.

The discovery of the New World opened the doors to tremendous possibilities, the significance of which were not realized until centuries later. From the New World came potatoes and corn which helped overcome periodic famine caused by failure of seed crops. From America came only two spices, but a score of new flavors, the most important of which were cocoa, vanilla, pineapple, green and red peppers, maple sugar, etc. The Americas contributed such important new botanicals as Cinchona (Quinine), Coca (Cocaine), Golden Seal, Cascara, Serpentaria, Senega, Podophylum, Lobelia, etc. The uses of these new foods, flavors and botanicals were learned through the Indians. The great wilderness and wild tribes of South America still hold secrets that may some day serve mankind.

Today man has penetrated the botanical fields in *all* parts of the globe but the possibilities of plants are still far from being exhausted. Improved scientific methods will find new possibilities in old or little known botanicals. The mechanical equipment of science permits a greater field of research in microscopic plants and offer unlimited possibilities in studying the countless botanicals growing in the great gardens beneath the waters of the seven seas.

AGAR-AGAR is a delicate white seaweed found growing upon submerged rocks in the Indian and Malayan Seas. When boiled with sugar it forms a jelly much resembling that made from Calve's feet and is highly esteemed by Europeans and natives for the delicacy of its flavor. The following is a very old recipe for the sick: Cut a small chicken into small pieces and put over the fire with three pints of cold water, four ounces of Agar-Agar and half a teaspoon of salt. Boil an hour and strain into cups or jelly mold. Another method is to use one ounce of Agar-Agar to a pint of boiling water and flavor to taste with lemon or orange. Because of its ability to absorb and retain moisture, Agar-Agar is used for bulk action in constipation. In this way, small shreds are mixed with fruit, milk, or any other convenient vehicle. Agar-Agar has a variety of other uses, most important of which are as media for bacteria culture and the growing of tiny seeds such as orchids. Considerable quantities of the seaweed is used for making dental creams.

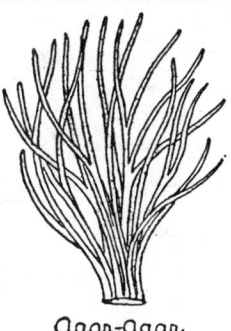
Agar-Agar

ALKANET is a pretty blue-flowered plant, native of Southern Europe. The deep red roots have long been used as a dye for coloring wine, salves, cosmetics, staining wood, etc. A beautiful rich red color is obtained by soaking dried Alkanet roots in oil or alcohol. When soaked in water, it makes a brownish hue. Alkalies render the color blue.

ALLSPICE is the dried unripe fruit of a beautiful evergreen tree, native of the West Indies. Allspice was given its name because of its resemblance in taste and odor to a mixture of cloves, cinnamon and nutmeg. In the whole form it is used for flavoring pickles, meats and gravies. In the ground form it is used in baking, puddings, relish, fruit preserves, curry powder, mince meat, meat sauces, catsup, poultry dressing, frankfurters, bologna, hamburger, pork sausage, wine, etc. In the West Indies a cordial is made from Allspice. This fruit was also an ingredient in old-fashiond sweet scent bags and potpourris. Powdered Allspice mixed with a little sugar is an old-fashioned recipe, for nausea, weak digestion and flatulency. Smith's "Dictionary of Economic Plants" states: "In Jamaica the berries are highly spoken of as a substitute for tobacco, being odoriferous, but they require a long pipe to smoke them, when they afford a treat unknown in smoking tobacco."

Alkanet

ANGOSTURA is native of Brazil and Venezuela. The bark is reputed to be febrifugal and similar to Quinine. The extract of this bark forms the basis of the bitters so highly esteemed in the United States as an aromatic bitter. It stimulates the appetite and is used also for bilious diarrhoea, dysentery and diseases which require a tonic. South American Indians use the bark to stupefy fish.

Allspice

ANISE SEED.—A flavorsome little seed used in considerable quantities from ancient times until the 17th century when many new flavors were brought to Western civilization. A very old epithet says of Anise:—"Solamen intestinorum"—the comforter of the bowels. A warm tea is useful for flatulent stomach-ache for children and adults. Gerard wrote: "The Aniseseed helpeth the ycoxing, or hicket (hiccough) and should be given to young children to eat which are like to have the falling sickness, or to such as have it by patrimony or succession." Anise seed tea is often helpful for infantile catarrh. The tea is made by pouring a half pint of boiling water on two teaspoonfuls of bruised Anise seed. The cold tea (sweetened) may be given in doses of one to three teaspoonfuls frequently. A pinch of Anise Powder with a glass of warm milk is useful as an aid in producing sleep. Anisette administered in hot water is an excellent palliative for bronchitis and spasmodic asthma. The ground seeds are used for smoking to promote expectoration. As a flavor Anise seed is used in curry powder, cheese, cookies, bread, cakes, sweet pickles and liqueurs. Anise oil is used to disguise unpleasant medicines and to perfume toilet articles. The oil mixed with lard or spermaceti makes a useful

Angostura

anise

annatto

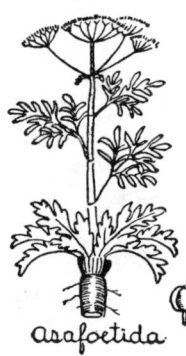

asafoetida

Balsam of Peru

ointment to destroy lice. The oil is also much used as lure on fish bait and bait for trapping small fur-bearing animals.

ANNATTO is a bush, native of tropical America. The seeds are much used to color cheese, butter, soups, rice, cosmetics, pomades, soaps, silks, varnishes, etc. The seeds are said also to be a source of Vitamines A and D.

ASAFOETIDA is native of Persia and Afghanistan. The plant has a strong, thick, fleshy root which when cut yields a milky juice and upon hardening becomes the smelly drug, asafoetida. Although strongly disagreeable in taste as well as smell, it was held in high repute in ancient and modern times by people of Western Asia, for seasoning curries and other foods. Asafoetida contains volatile oil, resin, gum, bassorin, sulphate of lime, carbonate of lime, oxide of iron and alumina, malate of lime, etc. The volatile oil and bitter resin are the active principles. The American Eclectic Dispensatory states its properties and uses are, "stimulant, antispasmodic, expectorant, emmenagogue and feebly laxative. Improper in inflammatory conditions of the system. Was used in hysteria, convulsions, spasmodic nervous diseases of females, spasm of the stomach and bowels, various irregular nervous disorders which accompany debility of the nervous system—also was used in pertussis, asthma, infantile coughs and catarrhs, croup, measles, etc., whenever there was a want of nervous energy or disposition to sink." Owing to its vile taste it is usually taken in pill form, but is often given to infants per rectum in the form of an emulsion.

The magic of science changes the smelly Asafoetida into delightful perfumes.

BALSAM OF PERU is obtained from certain tall trees native of Central America. It is a thick tenacious resin which exudes from incisions made in the bark. The resin hardens and becomes brittle with age. It is used in medicines, incense and perfumery for its balsamic and aromatic odor and taste. Soap made from Balsam of Peru makes a soft creamy lather. An ointment may be made by melting Balsam of Peru with equal weight of tallow. It is useful for chapped hands, sore nipples and minor skin diseases.

BALSAM OF TOLU is an exudation from a certain tree found on high plains and mountains near Tolu and the Magdalena province of Colombia, South America. The delicate, hyacinth-like scented resin is used as a fixative in fine perfumes. Medicinally Balsam of Tolu is reputed to be stimulant and expectorant, being used as basis for cough mixtures.

BETEL NUT.—A slender-stemmed lofty palm, native of Cochin China, the Malayan peninsula and islands. The fruit of this palm is about the size of a hen's egg, covered with a thick fibrous rind, which envelopes a hard nut about the size of a nutmeg. The nut is cut up into pieces and rolled up in a leaf of Betel pepper, to which a little lime is added and then chewed—a custom common to the whole Malayan races. It is said that many would forego their food rather than the use of Betel nut. All carry a box containing the nut, leaf and lime, which may be compared to the snuff-box of other countries. Powdered Betel nut is used in dentifrices because of its astringent properties. Mixed with honey, syrup or butter, the powdered seeds are used in veterinary medicine as a vermifuge.

BUCHU is a plant native of South Africa. The strong, fragrant leaves are used as perfume by the Hottentots to rub upon their greasy bodies. They also prepare a Buchu brandy by distilling the leaves with wine, and which they employ in all affections of the stomach, bowels and bladder. A strong decoction of the leaves is used as a wash for wounds. Buchu leaves contain diosphenol, a substance with mild antiseptic properties.

CALAMUS is a reed-like plant found growing in ditches and swamps in many parts of the northern hemisphere. This ordinary looking plant is remarkable because the leaf blades as well as the roots have a peculiar agreeable fragrance. In olden times the tops were strewn on floors in churches and public buildings on occasion of festivities. The pleasant scent was released when the herb was trampled upon. Calamus root has been used as medicine for more than two thousand years. Dioscorides mentioned that it helps the cough, "being suffited either of itself or with gum Terebinthina, the smoke thereof being taken in at the mouth through a funnell." In another part of the world—not discovered until some 1400 years later—red skinned people were also using Calamus for colds.

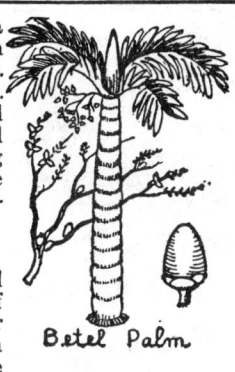
Betel Palm

Medicinally, Calamus root is an aromatic stimulant, mild tonic and stomachic, useful in flatulent colic, dyspepsia and atonic conditions of the stomach. The dried root may be chewed to relieve dyspepsia or an infusion of one ounce of root to one pint of boiling water taken in doses of a teacupful. The dried root is also chewed to clear the voice. Calamus root has been found useful as a mild stimulant in typhoid cases. In the Old World the candied root is chewed as cough lozenge.

Calamus root is used to flavor beer, cordials and in powdered form is used as a spice for certain foods. The pleasant scent of Calamus is also used for aromatic baths, perfumery and hair powders.

Indians of the Great Lakes area soaked their nets in a decoction of Calamus root in the belief that it attracted more fish.

CANELLA or White Cinnamon is a tree native of the West Indies. Its highly aromatic bark resembles cinnamon mixed with cloves. Because of its aroma it is often mixed with tobacco. Canella was formerly used by the natives as a tonic but its main use today is as a condiment, being used like oriental cinnamon. Canella oil is used to make Oriental type perfumes.

Buchu

CARAWAY SEED.—Judging by old writings, this wholesome little seed must have been very popular from Egyptian times and throughout the Middle Ages. Besides being used for flavoring many foods, Caraway had many medicinal uses. Dioscorides advised the oil for pale-faced girls. The oil or seeds was also believed to sharpen vision and promote the secretion of milk. The powdered seeds put into a poultice "taketh away blacke and blew spots of blows and bruises." Caraway was most popular with people of these old civilizations because of its comforting properties to stomach in colic and in flatulent indigestion. Considering the slow mode of travel and poor means of keeping foods, stomach-aches must have been very frequent occurrences. People often made Caraway seed tea because it "consumeth wynde and is delightful to the stomack." Caraway seed tea is still popular today for infants. It is made with one ounce of bruised seeds infused for 6 hours in a pint of cold water. Dose, one to three teaspoonfuls as often as necessary. In modern times Caraway seed is used for flavoring rye bread, biscuits, cakes, cheese, sauerkraut, pork sausage, meats (especially veal roast with sour cream), mixed pickling spice, etc. The cordial known as "Kümmel" is also made of Caraway seed.

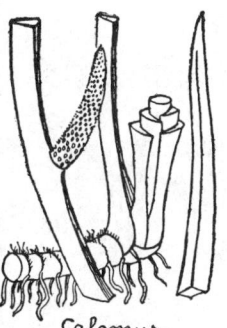
Calamus

CARDAMON is a relative of the ginger family and also native to the Orient. The delightfully fragrant seeds are used in curry powders, flavoring holiday cookies, coffee cakes, grape jelly, pickling spice, gin, rum, liqueurs, wines, etc. In Turkey one or two Cardamon seeds are chewed to sweeten the breath and to conceal liquor breath. Old-fashioned sweet bags, perfume powders and incense contained Cardamon seeds. Oil of Cardamon is used to make Lily-of-the-Valley perfume.

CASCARILLA is a small tree or shrub native of the Bahama Islands. The bark is an aromatic, bitter tonic with possibly slight narcotic properties. The bark is mixed with tobacco and smoked for alleviating nervous headaches. An infusion aids digestion and helps prevent nausea.

Canella

Caraway

CASSIA FISTULA is a tree native of India, bearing very long pods. The black licorice-like pulp of the pod has mild laxative properties. A physician and professor of medicine wrote almost 400 years ago: "The inner pulpe of Cassia is a very sweete and pleasant medicine, the which may be given without any danger to al weak people, as to women with child." The pulp may be eaten raw or pods may be crushed and placed in boiling water and decoction strained after cooling. Cassia Fistula is often employed as an ingredient in the laxative preparation known as confection of Senna (see paragraph under Senna).

CHIRATA is a slender branching annual of the Gentian family native of India. The stems are held in repute as a tonic and febrifuge by native and European practitioners.

CINNAMON is probably the first spice used by man. Ancient records reveal that it was used for more than 5,000 years. The countless flavoring uses of this valuable spice need not be enumerated.

Medicinally, Cinnamon has stimulating, astringent and carminative properties. Cinnamon powder is taken in milk for dysentery. Cinnamon brandy is taken for colds and influenza. Cinnamon brandy is made by soaking crushed Cinnamon bark a fortnight in brandy.

CLOVES are so well known in kitchen that its uses as a spice require no further explanation. Oil of Clove is used in considerable quantities to flavor cigarettes, medicines and cosmetics. A vanilla substitute is also obtained from this oil.

Medicinally, Clove is considered one of the most stimulating and carminative of all aromatics. It is given in powder form or infusion for nausea emesis, flatulence, languid indigestion and dyspepsia. A half tumblerful of hot water, poured over a half dozen bruised Cloves will secure a good night to a restless dyspeptic patient if taken just before retiring. Oil of Clove is an old-fashioned recipe to relieve toothache. A small wad of cotton saturated with oil is put into the hollow of the decayed tooth.

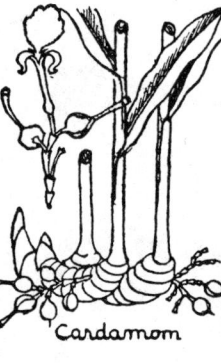
Cardamom

COCCULUS INDICUS is a climbing shrub, native of Ceylon, India and Eastern Islands. Its use in medicine is simply in the preparation of an ointment to destroy lice. It is also used as a fly poison and whole berries are thrown in water to stupefy fish.

CORIANDER SEEDS are like tiny balls, the green seeds have a disagreeable scent, but upon drying they become very fragrant. Coriander was known to ancient Egyptians and further cultivated by succeeding civilizations. Caesar's Roman legions brought the seed to northern Europe and England. As a flavor, ground Coriander seeds are used in curry powder, sausage making, "hot dogs," fresh pork, poultry stuffing, baking, to flavor gin and wherever this particular flavor is desired. In the Orient the seeds are much used in flavoring soups. The Chinese believe that the seeds possess a power of immortality.

Cascarilla

Medicinally, Coriander seeds are aromatic, stimulant and carminative. They are used mainly in veterinary practice for cattle and horses, to flavor and to disguise the taste of active purgatives and to lessen their griping tendency.

CUBEBS are the dried, unripe fruit of a vine native of Java, grown extensively in plantations under the shade of coffee trees.

Cubebs were first introduced into Europe by Arabians as pepper with tails—so called because of the short stem attached to the fruit. The King of Portugal forbade imports of this new kind of pepper for fear it should spoil the sale of other pepper.

Medicinally, Cubebs are stimulant and carminative. The crushed fruit mixed with Chamomile flowers are used as herbal smoke for nasal congestion. The whole berries are chewed for offensive breath.

Cassia Fistula

CUDBEAR is a lichen found growing on rocks in Alpine countries. This lichen yields a rich purple color which is used in dyeing woolen yarns.

It is also the source of litmus, used as a test for acids, when it becomes red, and for alkalies, by which the blue color is restored.

cinnamon

CUMIN SEED is mentioned in ancient Biblical writings and in the works of Hippocrates and Dioscorides. Like Anise, Caraway, Coriander and Fennel, Cumin was a very popular household medicine and spice of the Middle Ages. As a condiment, the seed is still used mainly in Europe to flavor bread, soups, rice, pickles, cheese, curry powder, meat dishes, etc.

As a medicine, Cumin seed was used to correct the flatulence of languid digestion, serving also to relieve dyspeptic headache and to allay colic of the bowels. In modern times, Cumin is used mainly as a carminative in veterinary practice.

DEER'S TONGUE is an herb found growing in the low pinelands of Louisiana and Florida. Bunches of this herb are often seen hung in the cabins of the Negroes of this section of country. The fresh plant has no scent, but when dried it emits a delightful, vanilla-like fragrance. The Negroes use the herb to make bitters to take when prostrated by fever. Its main use, however, is for mixing with tobacco, which it gives a pleasant aroma.

Cloves

DRAGON'S BLOOD is a substance derived from a palm tree, native of Sumatra and other Malayan islands. The fruits, which grow in bunches, are about the size of a cherry and are covered with imbricating scales of a red color, coated with a resinous substance. This is collected by placing the fruits in a bag and shaking them, the friction loosens the resin which is then formed into sticks or cakes and constitutes the Dragon's Blood of commerce. Its main uses are for varnishing and staining wood. Because of its fanciful name and its resemblance to dried blood, Dragon's Blood is used in voodoo rites, magic powders, gris-gris, etc.

DULSE is a seaweed found growing abundantly on the rocky shores of England and Ireland. It is collected at the lowest ebb of tide. The plant is eaten raw as a salad and considered useful in scrofulous complaints, its efficacy being no doubt due to the rich iodine content. Iodine is essential to proper functioning of the thyroid gland. A reputed medical authority has said premature aging may often be retarded if the system is supplied with the necessary amount of iodine.

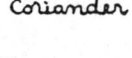
Coriander

FENNEL.—The ancients believed eating Fennel herb and using the seeds for flavoring gave strength, courage and conveyed longevity. In Imperial Roman times physicians considered this herb thus: "Ye herb itself if eaten is of force to draw down milk, as doth the seed being drank, or sodden together with Ptissana. But ye decoction of the hair (fine, hair-like leaves) being drank is good for ye nephriticall, and for ye griefs about ye bladder being diureticall. It is fitting also for ye serpent-bitten when drank with wine, and it expells ye menstrua, and in fevers doth assuage ye burning heat and nauseousness of ye stomach, being drank with cold water. Ye roots being beaten small and applied with honey do heal dog-bitings, but the juice of the bruised stalks, and ye leaves being dried in ye sun, is prepared commodiously for eye medicines such as are for ye sight-quickening and ye seed also being green together with the leaves and the branches is juiced for the same purposes, and the root at ye first putting out." (From 17th century translation of Greek manuscript.) Nineteen centuries later writers and poets still extolled the virtues of this herb.

Cubebs

Longfellow wrote:
"Above the lower plants it towers,
The Fennel with its yellow flowers;
And in an earlier age than ours
Was gifted with wondrous powers
Lost vision to restore."

Cumin

Deer's Tongue

Dragon's Blood

Dulse

William Coles wrote in Nature's Paradise:
"both the seeds, leaves and root of our garden Fennel are much used in drinks and broths for those that are grown fat, to abate their unwieldiness and cause them to grow more gaunt and lank."

Milton alludes to the aroma of the plant in Paradise Lost:
"A savoury odour bloom,
Grateful to appetite, more pleased my sense than smell of sweetest fennel."

Shakespeare's characters mention Fennel in Hamlet and Henry the Fourth.

In modern times Fennel is used medicinally mainly in purgatives to allay their tendency to griping. As a rustic medicine the bruised fresh plant is applied externally to relieve toothache, earache, and as a poultice for swellings. A hot infusion made by pouring half a pint of boiling water over a teaspoonful of bruised seeds will often comfort stomach-ache in the infant, if given in teaspoonful doses, sweetened with sugar. As a flavor dried Fennel seed are used in rye bread, sauerkraut, pickling spices, fish sauces, roast pork, etc. The whole fresh leaves are used for garnishes. When chopped up, they add delicate flavor to salads, soups, fish, potatoes, etc.

FENUGREEK SEED was most popular with old civilizations bordering the Mediterranean, and to this day this seed is still used mainly by peoples treading the dust of these ancient civilizations. As in the past the seeds are employed as medicine and for culinary purposes. Recently a famous horticulturist noted many fat Jewesses in Tunis—some of these women weighed over 300 pounds! It was discovered that the women were deliberately fattened for the marriage market on Fenugreek seed with milk and honey. The chemical composition of Fenugreek resembles cod liver oil as it is rich in phosphates, lecithin, nucleo-albumin and considerable quantities of iron. It may be employed as a substitute for cod liver oil in scrofula, rickets, anemia, debility following infectious diseases. For children one or two teaspoonfuls of the powder may be taken daily with fruit juice or jam to disguise flavor. Fenugreek seeds are very mucilaginous. A decoction made with one ounce of seeds to one pint of water forms a useful emollient when taken internally for irritated conditions of the stomach and intestines. Externally Fenugreek seed is used as a poultice for abscesses, boils, carbuncles, etc. Fenugreek seed is also used in the manufacture of condition powders, foods for horses and cattle and mixed with damaged hay to make it palatable.

FLAX is one of man's most important plants since the day he shed his animal skin clothes. Linen cloth is woven from the stalks of the Flax plant. Linen cloth has been found in prehistoric lake-cities of Switzerland and the ancient Egyptian mummies were wrapped in fine flax fibre cloth.

Flax is also important because of its seeds (linseed) having numerous medicinal and economic uses.

Medicinally, Flaxseed is used as a demulcent and emollient. Half an ounce of the seed (not bruised), infused in half a pint of boiling water forms a mucilage which is useful for cough, catarrh, dysentery and inflammatory affections of lungs, intestines and urinary passages. When not contra-indicated, the addition of lemon juice improves the flavor. It may be sweetened with loaf sugar or honey. A decoction of Flaxseed or of Flaxseed meal forms useful laxative enema, and the meal mixed with hot water forms an excellent emollient poultice. Dose of the infusion is one or two pints daily. Dioscorides compares Flaxseed to Fenugreek seed; a translation states: "The seed hath ye same power to Foenigraec (Fenugreek) discussing and mollifying all inflammation inwardly and outwardly, being sod with honey and oil, and a little water, or being taken in sodden hony (honey)."

GALANGAL is a peppery and gingery flavored root spice that was popular many centuries ago, but apparently does not suit most modern tastes. In Europe Galangal is used to flavor vinegar, beer and liqueurs.

Medicinally, Galangal is stimulant and carminative. A 1525 herbal states: "The vertue of Galangal is thus; It comforteth the stomake and maketh hym well to digest his meet (food) and unbyndeth and letteth wycked wyndes out of a mannes body." In modern times Galangal is used for sea-sickness, catarrh snuff (powdered form) and cattle medicines. It is said that Arabs use this botanical to make their horses fiery.

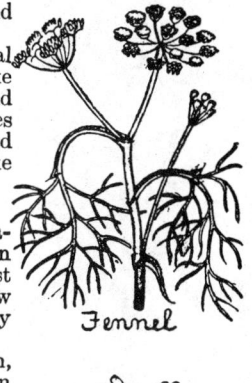
Fennel

GINGER.—Marco Polo mentions this spice in his unbelievable narrative of the 13th century. Ginger is the root of a plant cultivated in the Orient when most of the so-called Old World was still a vast wilderness. The Spaniards brought the first Ginger plants to the New World in the early part of the 16th century. The finest roots today come from Jamaica.

Ginger is one of the most valuable of all flavoring agents known, being used in many medicines, foods and beverages. It is used in making Gingerbread, cakes, puddings, pumpkin pie, cookies, curry powder, liver sausage, other sausages, minced meats, sauces, pickling spice, ginger beer, to disguise drugs, etc.

Medicinally, Ginger is stimulant and carminative being used in dyspepsia and flatulent colic. It is often added to bitter infusions. Parkinson, author of the world's most complete herbal (Theatre of Plants) wrote in 1640: "The properties of Ginger is to warme a cold stomacke and to helpe digestion, to dissolve winde both there and in the bowels, while it is fresh it is eaten in sallets; with the Indians, the roote being sliced and put among the herbs, and helpeth to mollefie and loosen the belly by the moisture therein, which then abateth much of the heate which being dry it hath, and helpeth to bind the belly. The preserved Ginger is most acceptable and comfortable to the stomacke and is availeable to all purposes aforesaid."

Fenugreek

Ginger combined with Black Willow Bark forms an excellent poultice for minor open wounds. A piece of root is often chewed for toothache. A paste made with powdered ginger and water, spread on paper may be applied to the forehead to relieve a headache from passive fulness. In India, Europeans who suffer from languid indigestion, drink an infusion of Ginger as a substitute for tea.

An American variety of Ginger (not related to the true) was used by the Indians to flavor foods—especially disagreeable or strong flavored foods. It was also used for stomach disorders. This variety is used in France by drunkards as an emetic. The American Ginger has a mild gingery flavor.

GRAINS OF PARADISE are aromatic, pepper-like seeds from a bush found growing in Africa. The seeds are used as a substitute or adulterant for black pepper and to give added strength to wines, beer, spirits and vinegar. Negroes in Africa and parts of America use Grains of Paradise seeds in voodoo rites, incense, etc.

Flax

GUARANA is a substance brought to market in recent times by traders from the Amazon jungles. Guarana is prepared from seeds of a vine. Indians pound the seeds to a meal and make a paste which is formed into rolls, becoming hard when dried and of a dark color, resembling large sausages. A beverage is prepared by grating about a tablespoonful of the substance from a roll and placing it in about half a pint of water with sugar. The beverage is much used by those employed in laborious work, especially miners. Its virtue consists in its stimulating principle similar to theine in tea. It has been reported that Japanese soldiers were supplied with Guarana to chew in order to keep up their stamina and aid in keeping courage.

GUM ARABIC is obtained from several species of Acacia native to Africa. The gum exudes from the trees naturally or is accelerated by making incisions in branches. It soon hardens and is then collected. It begins to flow at the commencement of the dry season which is

Galangal

ginger

Grains of Paradise

Gum Arabic

Henna

generally about November. About the middle of December, the Moors encamp on the border of the Acacia forest, and the harvest lasts six weeks during which time they live almost entirely upon the gum.

Gum Arabic is nutritious and demulcent. It is soluble in cold or hot water. It is used as a soothing agent in common irritated conditions of the respiratory, digestive and urinary tract and is useful in diarrhoea and dysentery. It may be given in the form of solution or lozenge; as an article of diet in cases requiring a rigid regimen, as in fevers, it is superior to other substances; it may be used for this purpose by dissolving the powdered gum, half an ounce, in five ounces of water, and sweetening with loaf-sugar, of which a tablespoonful may be given every two or three hours.

Equal parts of pulverized alum and Gum Arabic for a good preparation to check hemorrhages from small cuts, wounds, etc. Powdered Gum Arabic mixed with water is useful as a poultice for burns and scalds. Gum Arabic is much used for compounding pills, lozenges, mixtures and emulsions; also for administering insoluble substances in water, as oils, resins, balsams, camphor, musk, etc.

Mucilage of Gum Arabic: to four ounces of powdered Gum Arabic, add, very gradually, a pint of boiling water, and rub the whole until perfectly blended. May be taken as desired.

HENNA.—Few women sitting in "Beauty Shoppes" today, having their hair hennaed realize that they are using an herb used by women in Cleopatra's time and for thousands of years before in Egypt. The lovelies of these remote times also used Henna for dyeing their finger and toe nails. Even the men used the herb for dyeing their beards and coloring the manes and tails of their horses. These methods were not approved by other peoples according to this ancient writing which states in regards to captured ladies of the ancient civilization: "Then thou shalt bring her home, to thine house; and she shall shave her head and pare her nails." So strong was the prejudice against dyeing hair that women of Europe did not use Henna until the very late 19th century. From the fashion centers of Vienna and Paris, the use of Henna spread rapidly over the world.

Henna is simple to prepare. The fine cut leaves or powdered leaves are made into a paste with hot water and applied to the hair and allowed to remain until desired shade is obtained. On finger or toe nails the paste is allowed to remain over-night or paste is renewed often until the desired shade is obtained. Plain Henna adds an auburn shade to nails. Various shades may be obtained by mixing Henna with Indigo, Sage, or other dye plants

HOPS have become important in modern times, being used in great quantities in the production of beer and ale. In early times only the young sprouts of Hops were used as a pot herb. The fruit of the Hop Vine was used in the making of beer during the Middle Ages and several centuries later it entered the production of ale. Ale was made originally of malt and honey, flavored with bitter herbs such as Ground Ivy, Marjoram, and Wormwood. Early prejudice held that Hop was a wicked weed that would spoil the taste of drink and endanger the people. Later writers considered beer and ale very healthful because of the addition of Hop.

The properties of Hop are contained in the strobiles found only on female or cultivated plants. Medicinally, Hop is reputed to have tonic, nervine, diuretic and anodyne properties. The volatile oil contained in the Hop strobiles produces gentle sedative and soporific effects, the bitter principle is stomachic and tonic. An infusion of Hops is often taken to allay pain or induce sleep in cases of nervousness and disturbed mind. The strobiles are also stuffed in pillows for the purpose of producing sleep. Such pillows were first prescribed in 1787 to King George III and later for the Prince of Wales. An infusion of Hops is often taken at meals to promote digestion. It was a custom in England to drink Hop tea in Spring "to obviate the lassitude and debility felt by persons of relaxed habits on approach of warm weather." Externally an infusion of Hops with Chamomile flowers is used as warm application for muscular pains, bruises, boils, etc. Hops placed in a bag and steeped in very hot water, may be applied directly as a poultice.

In Sweden a coarse yarn and paper are made of Hop stalks. The leaves and flowers make a fine brown dye. Recipe for Hop Bitters: 2 ounces Buchu leaves, ½ pound Hops, boil in 5 quarts of water in an *iron* (NOT aluminum) vessel for an hour; when lukewarm add two ounces essence of Wintergreen and one pint of alcohol. Take one tablespoonful before each meal.

Hops

ICELAND MOSS.—Bountiful Nature proves here how well she supplies man and animals living even on the far ends of the earth. In the far north, where land is composed almost entirely of rocks and the season is too short for most plant life, Nature has planted this tough lichen upon the cold stones, and feeds it from the damp air. Iceland Moss offers a valuable food for Icelanders and Greenlanders because of its rich starch content. Natives boil the lichen in broth or dry it in cakes and use it as bread. A gruel is made by mixing the lichen with milk. An ounce of Iceland Moss boiled for a quarter of an hour in a pint of milk or water will yield seven ounces of thick mucilage. Before using Iceland Moss, it is generally soaked in cold water for several hours, after which the water is strained off and thrown away. The lichen may be again dried or used at once as desired.

Iceland Moss contains cetrarin, uncrystallizable sugar, gum, green wax with potash and phosphate of lime and about 70 per cent lichen starch.

Medicinally, Iceland Moss is demulcent and mild tonic. It is used as a demulcent in chronic catarrh, chronic dysentery and diarrhoea and as a tonic in dyspepsia convalescence and exhausting diseases. The tonic properties of Iceland Moss depend upon its cetrarin content, which, if removed by weak alkaline solutions, renders the lichen merely nutritious.

Iceland Moss

Iceland Moss may be taken in powder, syrup or mixed with chocolate. An excellent jelly is made as follows: Boil four ounces of the lichen in one quart of water; then add the juice of two lemons and a bit of the rind, with four ounces of sugar. Boil up and remove the scum from the surface. Strain the jelly through a muslin bag into a basin and set it aside to become cold. It may be eaten thus, but it is more efficacious when taken warm.

IRISH MOSS is a seaweed found in great abundance on the submerged rocks along the shores of Ireland. At low tide it is raked up, washed and dried in the sun which bleaches it to a tan color. The dried moss has little odor or taste. Boiled in water, it forms a stiff mucilage containing considerable sulphur and small amounts of iodine and minerals. Upon cooling it becomes jellied. Cold water does not dissolve Irish Moss, but swells it up. For this reason it is useful in powdered form alone or with foods as bulk for promotion of bowel elimination. As Irish Moss contains no sugar or starch, it is valuable as a nutritive for gouty persons and persons suffering from pulmonary consumption, with an excessive bodily waste. A decoction is generally prepared by boiling half an ounce of the Moss in a pint and a half of water, down to half a pint. Lemon juice may be added for flavor. Irish Moss is more nutritious boiled in milk. Before boiling in milk or water, allow moss to soak in cold water for an hour or more, then strain off the water.

Irish Moss

Irish Moss is useful in soups, custards, puddings, cold sweets, jellies and where the thickening is desired. It is also used for clarifying beer and as a base for skin creams.

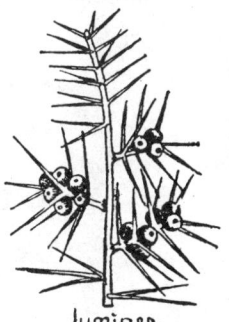
Juniper

JUNIPER.—According to tradition, when the Virgin and the infant Christ were fleeing from Herod into Egypt, they took refuge behind a Juniper bush.

Juniper is an evergreen bush or small tree found over a large part of the northern hemisphere. The berries, which require two years to mature, are parts used in medicine and flavoring gin, liqueur and bitters. In Sweden the berries are made into a conserve which is served

Liquorice

Logwood

Manna ash

Marshmallow

with cold meats. In Germany a few berries are used to flavor sauerkraut. Laplanders make a tea of the berries.

LICORICE.—No school neighborhood is complete unless it has its little candy store stocked with the black confection so popular with school boys. Liquorice is derived from a number of varieties of the sweet-rooted Glycyrrhiza growing mainly in southern Europe and southwest Asia.

Medicinally, Liquorice is demulcent, moderately pectoral and emollient. It is much used in cough medicines because of its soothing properties. Culpeper wrote: "Liquorice boiled in fair water, with some Maidenhair fern and figs, makes a good drink for those that have a dry cough, or hoarseness, wheezing or shortness of breath."

The following is an old-fashioned cough syrup: Take a large teaspoonful of Flaxseed, one ounce of Liquorice root, and one-fourth pound of raisins. Put them into two quarts of soft water and simmer down to one quart. Then add to it one-fourth pound of brown sugar candy and a tablespoonful of white wine vinegar or lemon juice. Drink one-half pint when going to bed and take a little whenever the cough is troublesome.

LOGWOOD is a small tropical tree with blood-red colored heart-wood. Its main use is for making dye of violet, blue and blackish colors. As dye the wood is chipped and fermented. Medicinally, the chipped wood (not fermented) is a mild astringent. It has been used in chronic diarrhoea and dysentery. It imparts a red color to urine and stools. Logwood should not be combined with chalk or limewater as they are incompatibles.

MANNA.—The Manna generally known today is a substance exuded from a variety of Ash tree found in Sicily and other Mediterranean regions. This Manna appears to be unknown before the fifteenth century. The Manna of the Scriptures is of doubtful source. Some authorities believe it is an exudation from the Tamarisk tree while others hold different opinions. The Manna we are concerned with is a hardened sap with a peculiar odor and sweetish taste. It is used mainly as a children's laxative or used to disguise other medicines. The codex of the British Pharmacopoeia contains a syrup of Manna to be prescribed as a mild laxative for children in the proportion of 1 part of Manna to 10 parts of water. A stronger syrup is made with the addition of Senna leaves or pods and Fennel seed.

MARSHMALLOW.—Varieties of Mallow grow over a very large part of the northern hemisphere. Where they are found, aboriginal peoples found similar uses for these mucilaginous plants. In the Middle Ages, Marshmallow was called Vismalva or Bismalva because it was considered twice as effectual as any other variety.

Marshmallow contains starch, mucilage, pectin, oil, sugar, asparagin, Phosphate of lime, glutinous matter and cellulose. An infusion with cold water takes up the mucilage, sugar and asparagin, hot water dissolves the starch content. The fresh or dried root has a pleasant flavor similar to soft white confection sold under the name "Marshmallows."

The entire plant is used medicinally, but the root containing more mucilage is considered more effectual. Marshmallow is demulcent and emollient, being useful in inflammation and irritation of the alimentary canal and the urinary and respiratory organs. Parkinson's "Theatre of Plants" states the leaves of Marshmallow are used to "loosen the belly gently—the roots are used for coughes, hoarsenesse of the throate and voyce, wheesings and shortnesse of breath, being boyled in wine, or honied water and druncke—the dried rootes boyled in milke and drunke are specially good for the chin cough."

The powdered dry roots or crushed fresh roots made into a poultice will remove obstinate inflammation when applied as hot as can be borne and renewed when dry. Slippery Elm may be added with good advantage. An infusion of Marshmallow leaves is useful for bathing inflamed eyes.

MASTER-OF-THE-WOODS is a beautiful, low growing plant native of the pine forests of Germany. The green or fresh plant has no odor; when dried it has a delightful sweet clover or vanilla-like scent. Because of its lasting fragrance it is used in pot-pourri, sachets and kept among linens for scent and woolens to drive off moths. Master of the Woods is used to flavor tobacco, snuff and liqueurs. A handful of dried herb allowed to stand overnight in a quart of light dry wine, makes the famous German May Drink. The following is taken from a 400-year old herbal, "Some say if it be put into the wine which men do drinke, that it rejoiceth the hart and comforteth the liver."

An infusion of dried Master-of-the-Woods makes a pleasant tea. Old Teutons carried this herb as a good luck charm when they went to battle.

Master-of-the-woods

MYRRH is a gum exuded from the bark of a bush native of Arabia and Somaliland. It is the same Myrrh that was so important in commerce in the early civilizations centered on the southeast shores of the Mediterranean Sea. Incense made with Myrrh and Frankincense is mentioned in very ancient Egyptian and Semitic literature. The two substances formed the bases of incense Moses fixed for Jewish ceremonial rites. Myrrh was also the main ingredient for the very ancient Egyptian Kyphi incense.

In Egyptian times, Myrrh had a large variety of medicinal uses. Modern uses have dwindled down considerably. It is used as an ingredient of dentifrices, mouth washes and for treatment of spongy gums and aphthous irritations.

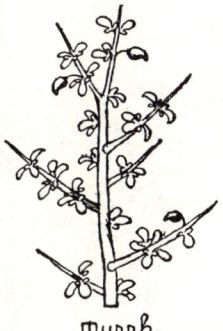
Myrrh

NUTMEG is a beautiful tree, native of the Molucca Islands, bearing luscious fruits resembling the peach. The fruit makes delicious jam, jellies and conserves with a spicy flavor. When the Nutmeg fruit ripens, it splits into halves revealing a crimson or scarlet seed which soon turns brown. The outer shell of this seed is the spice known as Mace; Nutmeg is the kernel of this seed.

The Malays believe that Nutmeg trees will not bear unless they can hear the sea and the trees must be fed with animal food. The beliefs are corroborated by the fact that trees grown near the sea and fed with animal food actually do produce the finest fruits.

In the kitchen grated Nutmeg or Mace is used as spice in apple pie, doughnuts, sweet potato souffle, topping for eggnogs, custards, bananas and berries with cream, etc.

Medicinally, Nutmeg or Mace is used for flatulence and to correct the nausea arising from other drugs, also to allay nausea and vomiting. Nutmeg is an agreeable addition to drinks for convalescents. In grandmother's day a Nutmeg tea was concocted by pouring a pint of boiling water over a crushed Nutmeg and allowing to stand until cool, then straining. One or two cupfuls were taken just before retiring to aid in restful sleep.

Nutmeg

ORRIS is obtained from three beautiful varieties of garden Iris known botanically as Iris Germanica, Iris pallida and Iris Florentina. The finest Orris is grown in the vicinity of Florence, Italy. The fresh roots of Orris have little or no scent. The characteristic violet odor is gradually developed during the drying process and does not attain its maximum fragrance for at least two years. Orris has been used for ages for its lasting natural aroma. It was the main ingredient in almost all old-fashioned perfume powders, sweet bags and pot-pourri. It is used in considerable quantities today in violet scented face powders, dental creams, violet scented soaps and cosmetics.

Whole roots of Orris, resembling the human form, are highly valued in voodoo performance and the powdered root is an ingredient in "love potions."

Orris

PSYLLIUM is a common weed in Southern Europe, the seeds of which have been used since time immemorial. Psyllium seeds yield a large amount of mucilage when soaked in water. Because of this characteristic they are used as a mechanical or lubricating laxative. The seeds are inodorous and nearly tasteless. Externally they are used like flaxseed as a poultice.

Psyllium

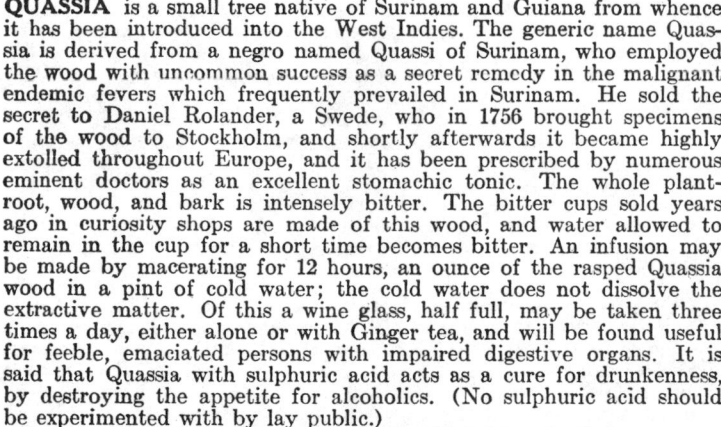

QUASSIA is a small tree native of Surinam and Guiana from whence it has been introduced into the West Indies. The generic name Quassia is derived from a negro named Quassi of Surinam, who employed the wood with uncommon success as a secret remedy in the malignant endemic fevers which frequently prevailed in Surinam. He sold the secret to Daniel Rolander, a Swede, who in 1756 brought specimens of the wood to Stockholm, and shortly afterwards it became highly extolled throughout Europe, and it has been prescribed by numerous eminent doctors as an excellent stomachic tonic. The whole plant-root, wood, and bark is intensely bitter. The bitter cups sold years ago in curiosity shops are made of this wood, and water allowed to remain in the cup for a short time becomes bitter. An infusion may be made by macerating for 12 hours, an ounce of the rasped Quassia wood in a pint of cold water; the cold water does not dissolve the extractive matter. Of this a wine glass, half full, may be taken three times a day, either alone or with Ginger tea, and will be found useful for feeble, emaciated persons with impaired digestive organs. It is said that Quassia with sulphuric acid acts as a cure for drunkenness, by destroying the appetite for alcoholics. (No sulphuric acid should be experimented with by lay public.)

Quassia is used in hair lotions. An old-fashioned plant spray to drive off plant lice was made with a strong decoction of Quassia mixed with liquid soap. A strong infusion sweetened and placed in a saucer is used to kill flies. This is harmless to house pets.

Quassia

SANDALWOOD is mentioned often in Marco Polo's 13th century narrative. The tree is native of various parts of India, particularly Malabar, as well as in the Pacific and Malayan Islands. According to the size and age of the tree, the interior is of a dark or light yellow color, and it is the heart-wood that is the valuable part; it is highly fragrant. The burning of incense has from the earliest ages been intimately connected with the religious sentiments of man—being practiced by Pagan, Jew and Christian. In the Catholic churches, various kinds of aromatic gum-resins are used, while in pagan temples Sandalwood holds the highest rank, pieces of the wood being burned before the images of their deities, and the millions of Brahmins and Buddhists, on beholding the smoke of the incense curling heavenward, presume they have performed their religious duties, and that the perfume smelt by their deity will obtain forgiveness of sins.

Sandalwood is still used in great quantities in incense and in sachets. Being an excellent fixative, Oil of Sandalwood is used in many perfumes and soaps.

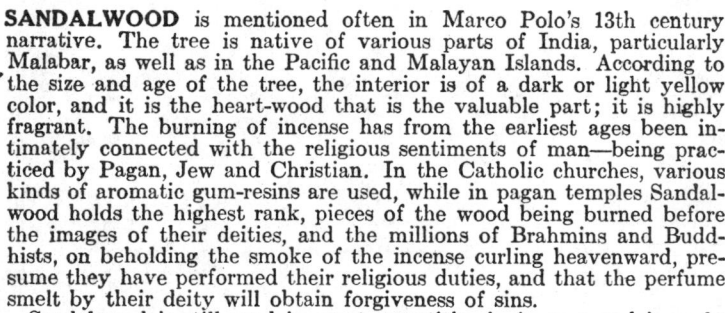

SANDARAC GUM is obtained from a small tree native of North Africa. The hard mahogany colored fragrant wood was very highly prized by the ancient Egyptians, Greeks and Romans. It is believed to be the Thyine wood mentioned in the book of the Revelation, and if it be so "the merchants of the earth" must have carried it as far as Babylon. Sandarac gum is used mainly in making of nail polishes and in pharmacy for coating pills.

Sandalwood

SASSAFRAS.—There is an old story that the scent of Sassafras carried out to sea by wind helped Columbus convince his mutinous crew that land was near. The white man found the Indians using this bark of root for beverage, medicine and flavoring. This powerful new flavor —different from cinnamon or any other highly prized spice yet found, had a particular appeal to the white man. For more than 200 years, Sassafras was exploited in disease-ridden Europe as a panacea for many ills. At one time Sir Walter Raleigh controlled a monopoly of all imports on this new botanical.

Sassafras is a shrub or tree commonly found in large areas from Texas to Florida and northward to the Great Lakes region. In leaves, color and general form, Sassafras is quite different from all other native plants. (It is especially beautiful in its Fall coloring.) The Indians were first to use the delicately fragrant leaves for flavoring; later the Creoles adopted this flavoring for soups and sauces. The strong flavored and agreeably scented bark of root was most important to the

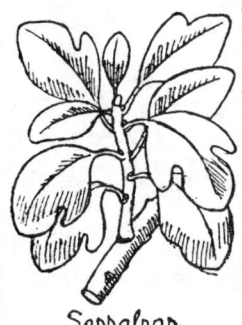
Sassafras

Indians as well as the white man. Like the Indians, the early pioneers drank a pleasant tea in the spring made of the bark of the roots. Many folks to this day follow this old custom. Bundles of sassafras bark may still be seen in fruit stores of large cities in Spring.

Medicinally, Sassafras bark of root is used as an aromatic, mild stimulant, diaphoretic and alterative. The white, spongy pith of Sassafras is used as a demulcent for inflammation of the eyes and as a soothing drink in catarrhal affections.

From Sassafras Oil are obtained derivatives used in the cosmetic and perfume industries.

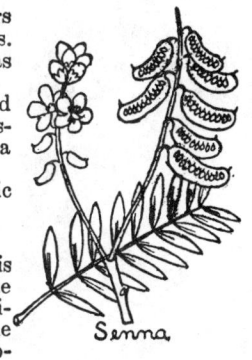
Senna

SENNA is a small shrub, native of Egypt, Nubia and Arabia. It is believed the early Arabian and Greek physicians were first to use the leaves and pods of this plant as medicine. The use spread with civilizations along the Mediterranean, through Europe and the rest of the world. In modern times the market has grown to stupendous proportions.

Medicinally, Senna is used as a purgative. The properties are described interestingly in this excerpt from Dodoens' 400-year-old herbal: "The cods (pods) and leaves of Senna taken in the quantitie of a dram do loose and purge the belly.... For the same purpose men give it to drink with the broth of a chicken or with Perrie made of Pease, or some other like liquor. The leaves of Senna taken in this sort are good for people that are given to be sad and pensive, heavy, dull and fearful, and that are sodainly afrayed for little or nothing."

An infusion taken of Senna leaves acts mainly on the lower bowel. It increases the peristaltic movements of the colon by its local action upon intestinal walls. Apparently the active principle passes out of the system in secretions unaltered because when taken by nurses, the suckling infant becomes purged. Senna taken alone is apt to cause griping. For this reason it is generally blended with other botanicals to modify its action.

American Senna

Confection of Senna: Boil equal parts of figs, tamarinds and prunes in water for about three hours. Rub soft pulp through a sieve to remove seeds. Make an infusion of equal parts of Senna leaves and Licorice roots with small parts of Fennel and Coriander seeds. After infusion is sufficiently cool and strained, combine with the first mixture of figs, tamarinds and prunes. Stir thoroughly and sweeten to taste. The laxative is taken in doses of about one teaspoonful.

Because of its mild action and being almost tasteless, Senna Pods are used as children's laxative. It is prepared by placing three or four pods into a cup of boiling water and allowed to set until cool. It is most effective taken before bedtime. The infusion may be sweetened if desired.

In America is found a variety of Senna with properties similar to the Egyptian botanical. American Senna is milder in action and pods are of no value. Early American authorities strongly advocated using our own native drug plants. Prof. Rafinesque wrote in 1828: "It has been ascertained that this plant is more efficacious than the Senna of Egypt; it ought, therefore, to supersede it altogether with us and even to be exported to Europe." A favorite recipe of an old pioneer doctor stated: "Take of Senna and Manna, each half an ounce—pour on these medicines a pint of boiling water; cover over the vessel in which you make this tea, so as to prevent the steam from escaping. This tea is to stand until it becomes cool. You are to give it to grown persons, one gill every hour or two, until it operates freely. According to the age of the person you are to give this tea in smaller doses, and as it is quite innocent, it may be given to children occasionally in very small doses until the desired effect is produced. If you wish it to act as a very mild and gentle purge, you may leave out the salts."

Sesame

SESAME SEED is used to give a nut-like flavor on bread, rolls, biscuits and cookies. The oil is used in the manufacture of margarine.

Medicinally, Sesame seeds are emollient and demulcent. Ground seeds are used for poultices like Flaxseed.

Simaruba

SIMARUBA is a tree native to French Guiana, the Islands of Dominica, Martinique, St. Lucia and Barbados. The bark of this tree was first brought to Europe in 1713 as a remedy for dysentery. It was used in France several years later to check an epidemic of flux.

Medicinally, Simaruba is a bitter tonic. It is used to restore lost tone of the intestines and to promote secretions. It is only successful in the latter stage of dysentery when the stomach is not affected. Large doses produce sickness and vomiting. An infusion is made by allowing the bark to stand in cold water rather than using boiling water. The infusion is sometimes made with equal quantity of Cinnamon bark.

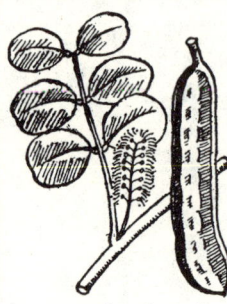
St John's Bread

ST. JOHN'S BREAD is a sweetish pod of a tree long used along the northern shores of the Mediterranean as food for humans and animals. Pods were found in kitchens and shops in the excavations of the ancient city of Pompeii (city in south Italy buried by lava from Mt. Vesuvius, A.D. 79). It is supposedly the husks of these pods that were eaten by the prodigal son and the "locusts" that St. John lived upon in the wilderness, hence the name, St. John's Bread.

Medicinally, St. John's Bread is mild laxative and demulcent. Years ago the pods were much eaten by singers in the belief that they cleared their voices. The seeds contained in the pod, being very hard, stone-like and very uniform in size, were used by jewelers as the original carat weight.

Star Anise

STAR ANISE is a star-shaped fruit of a tree native to southern Asia. The carpels of this fruit have a decided sweet anise flavor. In the Orient they are chewed after meals as an aid to digestion, to sweeten breath, for colic, incense and for flavoring foods, candies, medicines, spirits, etc. The Chinese use one or two carpels when roasting chicken; it is said to give it a delicious flavor.

Star Anise is carried by the superstitious folks as a good luck charm.

TONQUIN or Tonka Beans are seeds of a tree found in the forests of Brazil and British Guiana. When the beans are gathered they are placed in rum and soaked for 24 hours, then dried. This process brings out the coumarin and gives the beans the delicate vanilla-like scent. Tonka beans are used to give fragrance to snuff, cigars, cigarettes, pot-pourri, sachets, old fashioned perfumes, powders, etc.

Tragacanth

TRAGACANTH GUM is an exudation from a low spiny shrub native of the desert and mountain regions of Western Asia. In other days Tragacanth gum was considered "good against the cough, the roughnesse of the throte, hoarseness and roughnesse of the voyce, being licked in with honie." In modern use the gum is used mainly as a base in greaseless hair preparations, creams and cosmetics.

TURMERIC is a root of a plant related to Ginger and also native to southern Asia. The bitterish, ginger-like flavored roots are used mainly in curries, mustards, pickling spice and egg dishes. The root is also used to dye a paper yellow for testing alkaloids and boric acid. Curry Powder: 4 ounces Turmeric root, 4 ounces Coriander seed, 2½ ounces Black Pepper, 14 drams Ginger, ½ ounce Cinnamon, ½ ounce Mace, ½ ounce Cloves, 1 ounce Cardamon, 2 drams Cumin seed, 1 ounce Cayenne Pepper, 1 ounce Fenugreek seed. All ingredients should be powdered. Mix thoroughly and keep in a labeled bottle. The proportions may be varied to suit taste. Good materials are very essential for good curry.

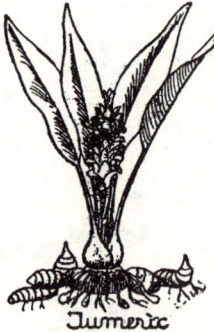
Turmeric

HEALTH TEACHING OF THE ANCIENT SCHOOL OF SALERNUM

The School of Salernum, earliest school of medicine in Christian Europe, was founded about 800 A.D. The school became world famous and survived 1000 years, when its common sense health teachings were finally smothered by political intrigue.

For the sake of clarity, simplicity and brevity, the principals of the School of Salernum were reduced to poems. They became the favorite among the educated of every class, and were looked upon like Solomon's Proverbs—useful to all who could appreciate the common sense health suggestions. The verses were considered to be the pillars of successful medical practice, without which no treatment could have any foundation in the *laws of nature*. A physician who could not quote the poems was looked upon with suspicion. So universally were the merits of the poems recognized and endorsed, that an edition was printed soon after printing was invented. Some 240 editions have since been published in practically every language.

To Live a Long Life

If thou to health and vigor wouldst attain
Shun weighty cares—all anger deem profane,
From heavy suppers and much wine abstain.
Nor trivial count it, after pompous fare,
To rise from table and to take the air.
Shun idle, noonday slumber, nor delay
The urgent calls of Nature to obey.
These rules if thou wilt follow to the end,
Thy life to greater length thou mayst extend.

Appropriate Diet for Each Season

Slender in Spring thy diet be, and spare;
Disease, in Summer, springs from surplus fare.
From Autmun fruits be careful to abstain,
Lest by mischance they should occasion pain.
But when rapacious Winter has come on,
Then freely eat till appetite is gone.

Over-drinking (of Wines)

Art sick from vinous surfeiting at night?
Repeat the dose at morn, 'twill set thee right.

Drinking Water

If very thirsty, drink just what you need,
Lest thirst should some consuming fever breed;
Nor stint yourself, but take enough, no more:
So speaks in every age majestic lore.
Yet too much water drunk the food disturbs,
The stomach frets, and thus digestion curbs.
'Mid summer heats, should you desire to drink
From fountain cool, you need not trembling shrink.
Rain water is by far the best potation,
And gives our jaded spirits exaltation.

Correcting an Improper Drink

Of all the cunning draughts that you can brew,
The best is Sage, combined with graceful Rue.
Let rose leaves be into this mixture brought.
And love's desires will quickly come to naught.

Antidotes to Poisons

The radish, pear, theriac, garlic, rue,
All potent poisons will at once undo.

Healthy Air

Let air you breathe be sunny, clear and light
Free from disease, or cesspool's fetid blight.

Things Hurtful to the Sight

Much bathing, Venus, blust'ring winds and wine,
And meats of every sort preserved in brine,
With lentils, pepper, mustard, also beans,
Garlic and onions—by such hurtful means,
With too much labor amid dust and smoke,
Weeping, or watching fires, we thus invoke,
With long exposure to the noonday sun,
The direst wrongs that can to sight be done.
But vigils are, by far, more noxious still
Than any form of single-minded ill.

Things Strengthening to Sight

Fennel, vervain, rose, celandine and rue,
Cure filmy eyes and give them sight anew.
From each a potent eyewash may be made,
To strengthen them when sight begins to fade.

Remedies for Catarrh

Fast well and watch. Eat hot your daily fare,
Work some, and breathe a warm and humid air;
Or drink be spare; your breath at times suspend,
These things observe if you your cold would end.
A cold whose ill effects extend as far
As in the chest, is known as catarrh.
Bronchitis, if into the throat it flows—
Coryza, if it reach alone the nose.

HEALTH TEACHING—continued

Remedy for Sea-sickness
Sea-sickness its fell gripe on none will fix,
Who wisely with their wine salt water mix,
And to each threatened qualm this draught prefix.

Condiments
Pepper, parsely, sage, garlic, salt and wine.
Use these, as sauce, lest meats should ill combine.

Peppers
All peppers black make food digest with haste,
Cure phlegm, and help us to repair our waste.
White pepper is the stomach's dearest friend.
And coughs and pains brings to an early end.
'Twill interrupt the chill of any fever,
Or prove, if raging high, supreme reliever.

Saffron
Saffron, 'tis said, brings comfort to mankind,
By giving rise to cheerfulness of mind.
Restores weak limbs, the liver also mends,
And normal vigor through its substance sends.

Leeks
The Leek will all young women fruitful make,
Who of its substance constantly partake.
Should ever bleeding from the nose begin,
'Twill yield at once to this drug, smeared within.
When cooked they're best; when raw they're doubly vile,
And fruitful in producing wind and bile.

Onions
Doctors in Onions different virtues see:
Quoth Galen, they should never given be
To bilious men, with whom they disagree.
Yet for lymphatics deems them wholesome food.
Asclepias praises them in highest mood.
They aid the stomach, also causes to start
A handsome color in a hairless part;
Which, with them rubbed, you thus can soon repair
Your tonsure, and bring back all fallen hair.

Cabbage
In cabbage we strange contradictions find;
Its broth will loose, its leaves in contrast bind.
But broth and leaves, when used together, prove
A laxative, and thus the bowels move.

Pears
Pears bind, preceding food; purge when they follow;
Then, after pears, of good wine take a swallow.

Prunes
Prunes cool the body and the bowels move—
To all, in many ways, a blessing prove.

Figs
Figs sooth the chest, and figs the bowels scour,
When raw or cooked with corresponding power
Both feed and fatten and relieve us too,
From every kind of swelling, old or new.

Fennel Seed
Many the virtues fennel seed displays,
First, fever in its presence never stays;
Next, it kills poison and the stomach frees,
And last, to human sight gives increased ease.

Anise Seed
The savory aniseed the stomach cheers,
And human sight improves as well as clears.
The sweeter kind all others overpeers.

Sage
Why should he die, whose garden groweth sage?
No other plant with death such strife can wage.
Sage soothes the nerves, and stills a trembling hand,
And sharpest fevers fly at its command.
The beaver, sage, and lavender will bring,
With tansy, and the cress, first gifts of spring.

Rue
Of use to sight, a noble plant is Rue;
O blear-eyed man, 'twill sharpen sight for you!
In men, it curbs love's strongest appetite,
In women, tends to amplify its might.
Let rue to chastity inclines mankind,
Gives power to see and sharpens, too, the mind;
And instantly, when in decoction, frees
Your house for-ever from tormenting fleas.

Violet
Headache, catarrh, the violet dispels.
And falling fits and drunkenness expels.

Nettle
The nettle to the sick man slumber brings;
Checks qualms, and need of all emetic things.
From painful colics patients may be freed
By eating honey which contains its seed.
When in decoction used, it will drive off
Catarrh, or any long-protracted cough;
From ventral tumors give relief as well,
And joint diseases cure with magic spell.

Hyssop
Hyssop among all purging herbs is best,
And frees from phlegm the overburdened chest.
When cooked with honey 'tis esteemed the chief
Of balms to give the lungs complete relief.
Its use, by some, is said to give the face
The highest character of human grace.

Elecampane
Elecampane brings joyous health to all
Thoracic organs, whether great or small.
To drink its juice, combined with that of rue,
Is the best thing that ruptured men can do.

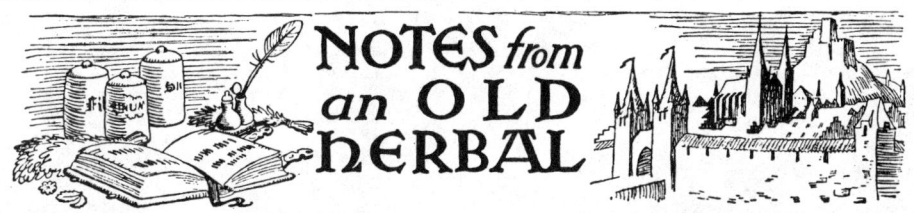

Notes from an Old Herbal

Nearly 400 years ago Rembert Dodoens, physician to two emperors and professor of medicine at Leyden, wrote his Dutch herbal, "Kruydeboeck." This wonderful herbal was written in an Age which produced many of the world's greatest discoveries and achievements. Such men as Copernicus, Galileo, Brahe and Michaelangelo helped raise civilization from the pall of the Dark Ages.

With the magnificent reign of Queen Elizabeth came the Golden Age of English Literature. Books of the native tongue became available to common people. Shakespeare was still a lad when Henrie Lyte carefully and faithfully translated Dodoens' famous herbal from French into English. The Indiana Botanic Garden's Library copy of Lyte's translation was printed in London in 1586. Our book contains many quill written recipes and notes on the margins of the pages.

Dodoens' Herbal is systematically arranged and one of the earliest attempts at classifying plants. He gives the English, German, Dutch, French, Greek and Latin names of many of the plants. A few of the strange plants of the New World, which was discovered only 62 years earlier, are mentioned in the herbal. Many of Dodoens' recipes are of ancient Egyptian, Greek and Roman origin. Many recipes are still used in the Old World today. Although quaint old superstitions still involve a few of the herbs, Dodoens' recipes do not contain the vile substances used so much by the alchemists of those days. The virtues of many of Dodoens' recipes are now known to be more or less exaggerated. Regardless of their actual value they are interesting because they represent herbal medicines in one of the most brilliant periods of world history. Many of the great people who lived in this Age (the Renaissance) employed these very recipes. Shakespeare's knowledge of herbs was very keen as his writings affirm.

Dodoens' herbal contains more than a thousand uses of "sundrie sorts of herbs, plants, pleasant and sweet smelling floures, medicinal rootes, corne or graine, fruits, trees, shrubs, rosins and gummes."

The following recipes not only show how herbs were used but also give a fascinating bit of human element to centuries past.

The ashes of Southernwood mingled with the oiles of Palma Christi, rapes, or old Olive, restoreth the hair fallen from the head, if the head be rubbed therewithal, twise a day in the sunne, or against a fire.

Southernwood steeped or soked in oile, is profitable to rub or annoint the bodie, against the benumming of members taken with cold and the brusing or shivering colds that come by fits, like as in agues.

If Wormwood be taken fasting in the morning, it preserveth from dronkennes that day.

Wormwood is good against the windines and blastings of the belly, against the paines and appetite to vomite, and the boiling up or wamblings of the stomacke, if it be dronken with Annis (Anise) seede or Sesely.

The same (Wormwood) dronken with vinegar, is good for such as are sicke with eating venemous Champions or Todestooles. (Poisonous mushrooms and toadstools).

The same (Wormwood) laid in chests, presses and wardrobes, keepeth cloth and garments from mothes and vermine. And with the oil of Wormwood, a man may annoint and rub any place to drive away fleas, flies, knats and wormes.

If Mugwort be hanged or cast into barrels or hogsheads of beere, it will preserve the same from sowring.

If the leaves or floures of Borage be put in wine, and that wine dronken it will cause men to be glad and merry and driveth away all heavy saddnes and dull melancholie.

Borage boiled with honied water is very good against the roughnesse or hoarsenesse of the throte.

The leaves (St. Johnswort) pound, are good to be laid as plaister upon burnings: The same dried and made into pouder and strowen upon wounds and naughtie, old rotten and festered ulcers, cureth the same.

The same (Yarrow) brused and laid upon wounds, stoppeth the bloud and keepeth the same from inflammation and swelling and cureth the same.

The same roote (White Water Lily) pound with water, taketh away all the spots of the skinne when it is rubbed therewithall, and being mingled with tarre, it cureth the naughty scurfe of the head.

The floures and herb of Cammomil boyled in wine and dronken, driveth forth windiness

NOTES from an OLD HERBAL—continued

and cureth the cholike, that is to say the paine in the bowels and belly.

The root (Hound's Tongue) rosted in hote imbers, and laied to the fundament, healeth the inward Hemerrhoids.

The decoction or broth of agrimonie, dronken, doth cleanse and open the stoppings of the liver, and doth strenthen the same, and is especially good against the weakness of the same.

The apothecaries of this country doe use to preserve and comfit the roote of Eryngium, to be given to the aged and old people and others that are consumed or withered, to nourish and restore them agayne.

Pepper is put into sauces to give a good smack, and taste unto meats.

Garden Parsley taken with meates is very wholesome and agreeable to the stomacke, it causeth a good appetite and digestion, and provoketh urine.

Certaine deceitfull and naughtie rogues that would be taken for cunning physitions, with their treacles, scammony, and plaisters, do gather of the fine strings and hairy rootes of Sengreene, and put them into phiols or glasses full of water, and set them openly in their shop windoes or standings, to be seene of people, whereby they make the people to beleeve, that they be wormes, which they have caused men to avoide with their powders, sugar and oyntments.

The Indian Sunne, or the golden floure of Perrowe is a plant of such stature and tallnesse, that in one sommer it groweth to the length of thirteene or fourteene foote, and in some places to the heigth of four and twentie or five and twentie foote—This plant groweth in the West India, the which is called America—Of ye vertue of this herb and floure, we are able to say nothing, because the same hath not been yet found out, or proved of any man.

(The Indian Sunne is better known today as common Sunflower. Seeds given by the Indians were brought to the Old World by early Spanish explorers.)

Hyssope sod in vinegar and holden in the mouth, swageth toothache.

The same (Hyssop) decoction cureth the itch, scurfe, and foule mangines if it be washed therewithall.

This Savorie (Summer Savory), as Dioscorides saith, is in operation like unto Time (Thyme) and is very good and necessary to be used in meates.

This herbe (Mother of Thyme) taken in meates and drinks (or broths) is a soveraigne medicine against all poison, and against the bitings and stingings of venemous beasts and serpents.

If at any time men be constrained to drinke corupt, naughty, stinking or salt water, throw Penny Royall into it, or throw the powder thereof into it, and it shall not hurt anybody.

Garden Mint taken in meate or drinke, is very good and profitable for the stomacke, for it warmeth and strengtheneth the same, and drieth up all superfluous humors gathered in the same. It appeaseth and cureth all the paynes of the stomacke and causeth good digestion.

They lay it (mint) with good successe unto the stingings of Bees and Wasps.

This herbe (Costmary) is also used in meates, as Sage and other herbes, especially in salades and sauces, for which purpose it is excellent, for it yeeldeth a proper sent and taste.

Rue eaten rawe or condited with salt, or otherwise used in meates, cleareth the sight, and quickneth the same very much: so doth also the juice thereof laid to the eies with hony, the iuice (juice) of fenell, or by itselfe. The leaves of Rue mingled with Parley meale asswageth the paine of the eies being laid thereupon.

The Arabians and their successours Physitions, do say that Rosemary comforteth the braine, the memorie and the inward sences, and that it restoreth speach, especially the conserve made of the floures thereof with Sugar, to be received daylie fasting.

The ashes or aren of Rosemarie burnt, doth fasten loose teeth and beautifieth the same if they be rubbed therewith.

The seed (Anise) chewed in the mouth, maketh a sweet mouth and easie breath and amendeth the stench of the mouth.

It (Anise) swageth the Squinance, that is to say, the swelling of the throte, to be gargled with hony, vineger and hyssope.

The seed (Anise) thereof found in a little bag or handkerchief, and kept at the nose to smel unto, keepeth men from dreaming and starting in their sleep and causeth them to rest quietly.

The perfume of it (Anise), taken up into the nose, cureth headache.

The Caruway (Caraway) seed is very good and convenient for the stomach and for the mouth, it helpeth digestion, and provoketh urine, and it swageth and dissolveth all kind of windinesse, blastings of the inward parts, and to conclude, it is answerable to Annis (Anise) seed in operation and vertue. The roots of Caruway boiled, and good to be eten like carrots.

The same (Cumin) eaten or dronken is very profitable for such as have the cough, and have taken cold, and for those whose breasts are charged or stopped; and if it be dronken

NOTES from an OLD HERBAL—continued

with wine, it is good for them that are hurt with any venemous beasts. The danger: Comyn (Cumin) being too much used, decaieth the natural complexion and lively colour, causing one to looke wan and pale.

It (Betony) comforteth the stomacke, helpeth digestion swageth belching, and the desire to vomite, if it be taken with clarified honie, in the evening after supper. The same vertue hath the Conserve thereof made with sugar and taken in the quantitie of a beane.

The seed of Ligusticum (Lovage) warmeth the stomacke, helpeth digestion and is pleasant to the mouth and taste, wherfore in times past the people of genues did use it in their meates instead of pepper, as some do yet, as witnesseth Antonius Musa.

The late writers say, that the rootes of Angelica are contrary to all poison, the pestilence and all naughtie coruption of evill or infected aire.

If one do often rub his head with aloes mingled with wine, it will keepe the haire from falling.

The same (Aloes) laid to with wine, cureth the sores and pustules of the gums, the mouth, the throte, and kernels under the toong.

The seedes (Elder), especially the little flat seede dried, is profitable for such as have the dropsie, and for such as are too fat, and would faine be leaner, if it be taken in the morning and quantitie of a dramme with wine, so that diet be used for a certaine space.

The greene leaves (Elder), pound, are very good to be laid upon hot swellings and tumors, and being laid to plaister-wise, with Deare suet, or Buls tallow, they asswageth the paine of the gout.

Ground Ivie (Ivy) brused and put into the eares, taketh away the humming noise or ringing sound of the same, and is good for such as are hard of hearing.

Amorous Apples, or Golden Apples—All the herbe is of a strange stinking savour, and it must be sowen every yeere as the cowcumbers be—The complexion, nature and working of this plant is not yet knowne, but by that I can gather of the taste, it should be colde of nature, especially the leaves, somwhat like unto Mandrake, and therefore also it is dangerous to be used.

NOTE: This Amorous Apple or Love Apple is no other than our common garden TOMATO. Dodoens lists this with "herbs that purge the bodie, noisome weedes and dangerous plants."

It (Oleander) hath scarse one good propertie. It may be compared to a Pharisee, who maketh a glorious and beautifull shewe, but inwardly is of a corrupt and poisoned nature. God grant all true Christians and Christian Realmes, whereas this tree or anie branch thereof, beginneth to spread and florith, to put to their helping hands to destroy it, and all the branches thereof; as dissimulation, covetousnes, briberie, sir symonie, and master usurie. It is high time, if it be the will of God, to supplant it. For it hath alreadie flowred, so that I feare it will shortly seede, and fil this holsome soile full of wicked Nerium. The danger: Oleander or Nerium is very hurtfull to man, but most of all to sheepe, goats, kine, dogs, asses, mules, horses and all fower-footed beasts, for it is deadly and killeth them. Yea, if they doe but drinke the water, wherein Oleander hath bin steeped or soked, it causeth them to die sodainly, as Dioscorides, Plinie, and Galen do write.

Buckwheat hath none other vertue that I know, saving that they give the greene herbe as fodder and fourage for cattell, and they feede hens and chickens with the seede, which doth make them fat in short space.

The decoction or broth of the seed (Fenugreek) dronken with a little Vineger, expelleth all evil humors, that sticke fast to the bowels.

It (Fenugreek) is good also to wash the hed with the decoction of Fenugreek, for it healeth the scurffe, and taketh away both nits and scales, or brand of the head.

The same laid to with sulphur (that is, brimstone) and honie driveth away pusthes or little pimples, wheales, and spots of the face; and healeth all mangines and scurvie itch, and mendeth the stinking smell of the armepites.

The down of this herbe (fuzzy heads of Cat-tail) mingled with swines grease well washed, healeth burnings and scaldings with fire or water.

Wooddrow is counted a verie good herbe to consolidate and glew togither woundes.

Some say, if Wooddrow be put into the wine which men do drinke, that it rejoiceth the hart and comforteth the diseased liver.

(Wooddrow is better known today as Woodruff or Master-of-the-Woods).

Malloews (Hollyhock) are good to be laid against the stingings of wasps, bees and draw forth thorns, splinters, if they be laid therupon.

The same (Marshmallow root) boiled in sweete new milke, healeth the cough, as Plinie writeth.

It (Marshmallow root) is good also against the toothach; for it swageth the paine, being boiled in vineger and holden in the mouth.

The leaves of Marshmallow being laid to with oile, do heale the burnings and scaldings with fire and water, and are good against the bitings of men and dogs, and against the stingings of bees and wasps.

NOTES from an OLD HERBAL—continued

The seede (Marshmallow) either greene or dry laid to with vineger, taketh away freckles or fowle spots of the face both white and black, but yee must annoint your selfe either in the hot sun or else in a hothouse or stewe (?).

It (Chervil) is good for people that be dull, old and without courage, for it rejoiceth and comforteth them, and increaseth their strength.

Peonie (our Garden Peony) took his name first of that good old man, Paeon, a verie ancient physition, who first taught the knowledge of this herbe.

The roote of Peonie, dried, and the quantitie of a Beane of the same dronken with Meade, called Hydromell, bringeth downe womens flowers, scoureth the mother of women brought a bed, and appeaseth the griping paines, and torments of the bellie.

Fifteene or Sixteene of the blacke cornes or seedes (Peony) dronken in wine or Meade, helpeth the strangling and paines of the matrix or mother, and is a speciall good remedie for them that are troubled with the night mare (which is a disease wherein men seeme to be oppressed in the night, as with some great burthen, and sometimes to be overcome with their enemies) and it is good against melancholicke dreames.

It (Garlic) is good against all venome and poison, taken in meates or boiled in wine and dronken, for of his owne nature it withstandeth all poison; insomuch that it driveth away all venemous beast from the place where it is. Therfore, Galen, prince of physitions, called it poore men's Treacle.

The same (Garlic) eaten rawe or boiled cleareth the voice, cureth the old cough.

It (Garlic) is very good against the toothache, for it staketh the same, pounde with vineger, and laid to the teeth; or boiled in water with a little incence, and the mouth washed therewith, or put into the hollownes of the corrupt teeth. It is of the same vertue mixt with goose grease and powed into the eares.

The same (Garlic) brused betwixt the handes and laide to the temples, staketh the olde headache.

The same (Garlic) burned into ashes, and mingled with hony, healeth the wild scab, and scurffe of the head, and the falling of the heare, being laide thereupon.

Laid to in the same manner, it healeth black and blew scarres, that remaine after bruses and stripes.

They cure the pipe or roupe of Pultrie and chickens with Garlike (garlic).

The danger: Garlike is hurtfull and nought for cholerique people, and such as be of a hot complexion, it hurteth the eies and sight, the head and kidneies. It is also nought for women with child and such as give sucke to children.

The same iuice (Onion juice) dropped into the eares, is good against deafnesse, and the humming noise or ringing of the same, and is good to clense the eares from all filthinesse and corrupt matter of the same.

It (Onion) cureth the naughty scab and itch, and the white spots of all the body, and also the scurffe and scales of the head; and filleth againe with haire the pild places of the head, being laid thereto in the sunne.

The same (Onion) laid to with capon's grease, is good against the blisters of the feete, and against the chafing and galling of the shooe.

Pythagoras saith that if Squilla (Sea Onion) be hanged over the doore or chiefe entrie into the house, it keepeth the same from all mishap, witchcraft or sorcerie.

Acatia maketh the haire black, if it be washed and often wet in the water wherin it hath bin soked.

The leaves and tender crops of Acatia do settle and strengthen members out of joynte, if they be bathed or soked in the hot bath or stue made with the broth thereof.

The decoction of Myrtel berries maketh the heare blacke, and keepeth it from falling, it cureth the evill sores of the head, and clenseth the same from roome, or scurvie scales, if the head be often washed therewithall.

It (Myrtle berries) keepeth from dronkennes, if it be taken before hand.

The dry leaves of mirtell (Myrtle) laide to with convenient ointements or salves, do heale the exulceration of the nailes, as well of the hands as of the feete, and do take away the sweat of all the bodie.

Bayberries are put into medicines that are made to refresh them that be tired, or wearied, against cramps and drawings togither of sinewes, moist and drie scurvinesse, being applied with oiles or ointments serving to the same purpose.

The oile of Bayberries is of the same vertue; also it is good against bruises, and blacke and blew marks, that chance after stripes or beatings.

NOTES from an OLD HERBAL—continued

The decoction thereof (Bayberry) in wine, or the juice thereof dropped into the eares, cureth the stinging or humming noise of the same, and is good against hardnes of hearing and deafnes.

Some hold, that the branches or bowes of Rhamnus stickt at men's doores and windowes, do drive away sorcerie and enchantments that witches and sorcerers do use against men.

The oile of ripe olives doth mollify, it swageth paine, dissolveth tumors or swellings, it is good against the stiffenes of members and cramps, especially when it is mixt or compounde with good herbes. Oile Olive is very apt and profitable to make all sorts of oiles, whether they be of herbs or flowers; for it doth easily and readily draw unto it the qualities and vertue of those herbes or flowers, with the which it is set to be sunned, or otherwise sod and prepared.

The ashes of the barke of Willow mingled with vineger, causeth warts to fall off, taketh away the hard skin or brawne that is in the hands or feet which is gotten by labour, and the cornes in a man's toes or fingers, if it be laid thereupon.

The leaves (Black Alder) be good fodder, or feeding for kine, (cows) and cause them to yeeld store of milke.

The fruit or berries of Juniper is good for the stomack, lungs, liver and kidneies; it cureth the old cough, the gripings and windinesse of the bellie, and provoketh urine to be boiled in wine or honied water and dronken.

Also it (Juniper) is good for people that be bruised or squat by falling, to be taken in the aforesaid manner.

Juniper or berries thereof burned, driveth away all venomous beasts, and all infection and corruptions of the aire; wherefore it is good to be burned in a plague time, in such places whereas the aire is infected.

The Egyptians in times past, kept their dead bodies with Cedria (Cedar); for it keepeth the same whole, and preserveth from corruption; but it consumeth and corrupteth living flesh.

WRITTEN NOTES AND RECIPES
From the Margins of the Pages of Dodoen's Herbal

Judging by this very old style script the following recipe regarding SAVIN was probably written soon after the book was published.

The above script reads.
The leaves Boyled in oyle olive and kept therein killeth the wormes in Children, yf their Bellyes Bee annoynted therewith:/. The leaves poudered and given in milke, or muskadine is of the same effect ./.

It (Concoction of Cedar) killeth Lyce and all such vermine, wherefore, whatsoever is annointed with the same, Mothes, Wormes, and such other vermine, shall not hurt it at all.

The leaves (Savin) pounde and laide to with hony, cureth ulcers, and staieth spreading and eating sores; they do scoure and take away all spots and speckles from the face or body of man.

The leaves (needles) of Pine tree healeth greene (flesh) woundes, and boyled in vineger, they swage the toothache.

Mastick (Mastic) is very good for the stomacke, for it strengtheneth the same, and stayeth vomiting, swaging all the paine and greefe of the same, and reviveth the appetite which was dulled.

The same holden in the mouth and chewed upon, doth dry and comfort the braine, stayeth the falling downe of humours, and maketh a sweete breath.

They use to rub the teeth with Masticke, to whiten the same, and to fasten them that be loose and to comfort the jawes or gums which be loose and weake.

A philosophical note:
"By ever learning, Solon waxed old
For tyme hee knew, was better farr than gold;
Fortune would give him gold, which would decay
But fortune cannot give him yesterday."

A botanist wrote:
"there is much of it (Snap Dragon) in Broughton woodes", Dated 1631. Elsewhere the same writer states: "This kinde (Maidenhair Fern) groweth on the northsyde of the Church of Haxey".

NOTES from an OLD HERBAL—continued

Horehound or an unknown mixture with this herb, was held in very high esteem centuries ago according to this partially mutilated note: "against the rough and wheasing of the lunge. Doth above creditt ease such as have been long sick of any consumption of the lunge, as hath bene often proved by the learned phisitions of the College in London."

The following note is very interesting because it reveals that Summer Savory (Bohnenkraut or Bean Herb) is more than a flavoring herb for beans, peas, etc.,—"and therefore more fitt for medicine. It makes thinn and marvelously prevailes against wynde (wind), therefore it is with much good successe Boyled (boiled) and eaten with Beanes, pease and other wyndie pulses (leguminose plants). If it bee applyed to the Belly in a fomentation, it forthwith helpeth the mother preceeding of wynde."

Here are some very old uses for our Old Fashioned English Daisies (Bellis perennis):

"The juice (concoction) of the leaves and roote snift up into the nostrelle purgeth the head mightely of foule and filthy slimy humoure and helpeth the megrim."

"The juice putt into the eyes, cleares them and taketh away their watering."

"The juice of the leaves and roote given to little doge with milke keepeth them from growing."

Space does not allow printing all these old recipes and notes. The following, however, represent a general cross section. Many of the recipes were ruined when this herbal was "restored" some 60 or 70 years ago. It was given a new cover and the pages were trimmed down in order to even them up. By this thoughtlessness many lines were partially or entirely cut off.

. . . not only that, but (Wormwood) also quickly refresheth the stomach and belly after large eating and drinking.

The roots (Burdock) stamped, streyned with a drought of ale, is a most approved medicine for synde and cold stomach.

It (St. Jameswort) is much comended, not without cause to helpe the old aches, paynes in the armes, hippes, legge, boyled with hoge grease to the forme of an oyntment.

The juice of houseleeks takes away cornes from the foot and feete yf they bee washed and bathed therewith every day, night as it were emplastered with the skin of the sayd houseleeks, which certainlye takes them away without incision or such like cutting as it hath bene sufficiently expimented and tryed.

A little fine treacle spread upon a leaf of mulleyn (Mullein) layed to the pyles or hemeroides curethe the same.

The husbandmen in Kent doe give their catle the leaves of mulleyn (Mullein) to drinke against the cough of the lunge, being an excellent approved medicine for the same whereupon they call it Bullocke lungwort.

It (Motherwort) is judged to bee soe forceable yt is thought it tooke his name cardiaca of the effect: It is also reported to cure convulsions, crampes, to kill all kindes of wormes in the Belly. It is a remedy for the cough nurren in cattell for that cause is much desired of husbandmen.

The powder of fenell (Fennel) seed drunke for certaine dayes together preserveth the sight.

Angelica leaves steeped in ale a night and taken in the morning, a good Draught, purges the belly from ill humours; clenseth ye bloud.

Steeped in viniger (Galbanum) scattereth, dissolveth and putteth clean away all hard, old, cold swellinge, tumoure, Botches (?) and hard lump growing about the joynte.

The roote (Elecampane) Boyled soft and mixt in a morter with fresh Butter and the powder of ginger maketh an excellent oyntment against the itch, scabs, mangynesse.

Ground Ivy stampt; mixed with a little ale and hony and strayned taketh away the pin, web or any greife out of the eyes of horse eye or cow or any other Beast, Being squirted into the same with a squirt.

The flower of hoppes (Hops) make bread light; the lump to bee sooner and easy leavened, yf the meale bee tempered with liquor wherein they have been boyled.

Burneings: apply juice of ye rootes (Malefern) with rose water or cold water, to heale it when all other things faile.

The iuice of it (Sorrel) in summer is a profitable sause (sauce) in many meate (food) and pleasant to the taste. It cooleth a hot stomack, moveth appetite to meate, tempereth the heate of the liver and openeth the stopping thereof.

Water-cresses Being Boyled in wine or milke and drunke for certaine dayes together is very good and effectuall against the scurvye.

The oyle of Wallnutte, made in such manner as oyle of almonde, maketh smooth the hande and face and taketh away scales, skurfe, black and blew marke that come of strypes and bruyses.

Willows brought into chambers, sett about the bede of those that bee sick of agues for they doe mightily coole the heate of the aire; which thing is a wonderfull refreshing to the sick patiente.

The gum mastick hath the same vertue yf it be released in wine and given to drink, and the falling sicknesse.

MEDIEVAL ELDER FOLKLORE

Some fourteen or fifteen hundred years ago hordes of barbarians poured out of the forests fringing the edge of a civilization that had grown soft.

The work and accumulations of many centuries were destroyed. Upon the ruins these barbarians built their wretched hovels and established their own mode of life.

It was during these Dark Ages of history in which fear, superstition and magic clouded and haunted the remains of civilization.

European Elder, being a comparatively common plant, was known to the barbarians as well as the civilized world. The myths and legends of the past mixed with the superstition of the barbarians made it one of the most notorious plants of all the plant world.

One of the oldest legends held that it was Elder wood that was used for making the Cross of Calvary. Judas, the betrayer, was believed to have hanged himself from an Elder tree. Sorrow and death was believed to hover over this plant.

Folk avoided burning or disturbing the growth of Elder for fear of evil or ill luck.

Household articles made of Elder were believed to haunt the owners.

When the plant grew around dwellings, it was said to ward off witches, evil influences and evil spirits. The leaves gathered on the last day of April and fastened over windows, doors or other openings, were considered certain protection against witches that try to enter.

A cross made of Elder and fastened over stables kept evil from animals.

A twig tied into three or four knots and carried in the pocket was a charm against rheumatism.

It was long believed that refuge may be safely taken under Elder in a thunderstorm because the Cross was made therefrom and so lightning never strikes it.

If an Elder bush flowers after being trimmed in the shape of a cross and planted over a new grave, it was believed the soul of the person lying beneath was happy. Green branches were buried with the corpse to protect it from witches and evil spirits. The drivers of hearses even carried whips made of Elder wood.

It was believed that a child would stop growing if whipped with an Elder stick.

A popular belief held that summer began when Elder was in flower and ends when the berries are ripe.

The unpleasant soporific odor of Elder is said to be harmful to those that sleep under its shade. Few plants will live long under the bush because of peculiar Elder exhalation.

A very old legend held that "he who stood under an Elder tree on Midsummer Eve would see the King of Fairyland ride by attended by all his retinue."

Sticks of Elder were believed to kill serpents and drive off robbers.

The hollowed sticks were used to make smoking pipes and musical flutes. The shrillest and most sonorous instruments were made of wood "which grew beyond the voice of the cock-crow."

Despite all the superstition which enveloped Elder the plant has long been valued medicinally. The berries are still used to make excellent wine, syrups and rob. The flowers mixed with Peppermint leaves make a pleasant beverage. An old fashioned cream for whitening and softening the skin was made by simmering Elder flowers in fresh lard. The flowers were strained off and the lard again simmered with fresh flowers. Concoctions made of Elder leaves or flowers have been used for centuries as beauty aides.

Elder flowers placed in wine vinegar and allowed to stand near heat made the old fashioned Elder vinegar.

ROMAN WORMWOOD

For three or four years it was a problem what to grow successfully on the north side of our house, in the narrow 10-inch space between the sidewalk and the house. We tried the ever-faithful Petunias but they became lanky and straggly, as did other annuals. We wanted something that would look prim and fresh the entire season.

When Roman Wormwood began to crowd neighboring perennials in a border, we moved it to our narrow north side space and this problem was solved.

This variety of Artemisia grows only about 18 inches high, with fragrant, lacy, gray-green leaves. Flower heads are one-eighth inch wide and whitish-yellow. For us, even in the perennial border, the flowers often failed to develop. They are insignificant, however, and as the shrubby plant trims well, making a neat and compact hedge, it serves its purpose well in a narrow ribbon planting. As it is quick growing, our space was filled in one season's time.

Weather conditions do not affect it. It stands up under drought and hot southwest winds. As we have no trees north of the house, it does get some direct rays of the late afternoon sun.

In late summer we cut branches of A. pontica and dry them to put into bags as moth preventive. The Pennsylvania Dutch laid branches of it in their pantries to keep out ants, so 'tis said.—By P. G.

Roman Wormwood is an old-fashioned garden plant.

FERTILIZING IVY, WANDERING JEW, AND PARTRIDGE BERRY

Dissolve in one gallon of water the following: 1 tsp. saltpeter, 1 tsp. epsom salts, 2 tsp. baking powder (no alum), 2 tsp. washing ammonia.

Put one tablespoon in a pint of water and use only this water for watering plants; no plain water being used.—"Garden Club."

LORE AND QUAINT RECIPES OF A 200-YEAR-OLD ENGLISH HEALTH BOOK

Properties of Meats

BEEF: Is a nourishing, but gross food, breeds thick strong blood, and is to be avoided either roasted, boiled or baked, by sedentary persons, and those of weak nerves, or sickly habits; but to such as work hard, or take much exercise, and have strong health, it is a grateful, a necessary, a strengthening, and a wholesome food.

VEAL: Is a nourishing and wholesome food, and light of digestion to the stomach; and the more so, when plain dressed, as are all other foods.

LAMB: Is a tender and light food, and may be indulged to tender constitutions, according to the case.

PORK: Is a very nourishing, but a very gross food. This as well as beef, may do well with constitutions inured to labor and exercise; as indeed any food may; but the learned Dr. Cheyne tells us that it ought to be forbidden to the valetudinary and weak and studious.

BACON: Is a light and easy food, moderately eaten; but salt or hard meats are unkindly to scorbutick constitutions.

FOWLS: Of all sorts are generally an innocent, easily digested, and wholesome food; especially when plain dressed, and not seasoned with high and unnatural sauces.

FISH: Some sorts of fish, in small quantities, and plain dressed, such as Whitings, Flounders, etc., are not improper for sickly or weakly persons.

Properties of Vegetables, Greens and Fruits

PEAS: Are all of them of a gross and windy nature, and the dishes and soups made of them should be well seasoned with hot spice for that reason, to avoid colicky disorders. When green they are good for sharp and salt bloods, because they are sweet and smooth.

BEANS: Of whatever sort, are hard of digestion, and windy. They should be eaten with a good deal of spice, and drank plentifully after, that their mealy parts may not turn to a paste in the bowels or blood.

KIDNEY BEANS: Are mealy, but not so glewy and windy as the other sorts; but are apt to turn sour, and gripe. The flower of the common bean is used much in poultices for different maladies. People of sedentary lives should not be too free with them, because of their viscosity.

BEET-ROOTS: Boiled, are loosening, cool and smooth, provoke urine, temper hot and cholerick blood; and being assisted in their cooling property by vinegar, are good after a debauch, to refresh and cool.

GARLIC: Is good in splenetick constitutions, worms, inveterate coughs, and against the bite of a mad dog, taken inwardly. 'Tis pity its offensive smell should make it so obnoxious to Englishmen, who want it more than foreigners, and yet use it less. It has been found experimentally to be good in jaundices and dropsies, and in asthmas from cold phlegm.

ONIONS: In an inferior degree, partake of the qualities of garlic.

PARSNIPS: Are sweet, nourishing, and balsamick to the blood. They are diuretic, promote venery, provoke the menses, and are good in phlegmatic cases.

TURNIPS: When boiled, are sweet and smooth nourishment, for asthmatic and coughing people. They are, however, windy and cold, and not fit for weak stomachs. The more they are boiled, the less windy they are, and easier digested.

SPINACH: Is cooling and loosening, and tempers sharp, hot blood.

LETTUCE: Of all kinds, is cooling and opening, and good after a debauch. It is good also for wet nurses, promoting milk, especially in warm constitutions. If too plentifully eaten by those in years, they hinder the appetite. Physicians hold that the distilled water of lettuce is a promoter of sleep.

CLARY: Is good in colicky cases, strengthening the stomach, and promoting digestion.

SAGE: Thins the blood, is good in most nervous cases, in palsies, lethargies, etc., and much used, will cure the trembling of the hands.

APPLES: Cool and loosen, and help the appetite; but are not good for cold stomachs, says a good physician.

PEACHES: Used before a meal, will serve to create an appetite; after a meal, to keep the body open; and are pectoral. Cold constitutions, however, should not touch them at all; and hot ones with moderation, especially of those that are produced in the latter season of the year.

STRAWBERRIES: Are cooling and di-

LORE AND QUAINT RECIPES—continued

uretic, and therefore an infusion of them may be of service in the gravel. But women eating of them too greedily at a certain time, may endanger the stopping of the course of nature. They agree with most palates, and as they gratify thirst, and cool the tongue, a moderate use of their juice may be allowed in burning or bilious fevers, mixed with the juice of a lemon and spring water. The seeds obtained by shaking the ripe fruit in water, are excellent in the stone.

RASPBERRIES: Also raise an appetite, and, like mulberries, cool and refresh warm and hot blood.

CUCUMBERS: The juice of cucumbers is too cold for some stomachs, and ought not to be taken by such as have thin and poor blood. The juice of an unripe cucumber is purgative. Cucumbers are useful, but are as bad as poison to be eaten when hot by exercise, etc.

Properties of Spices

CINNAMON, MACE, NUTMEG, CLOVES, GINGER, PEPPER: Are all heating; and all Spices are bad for melancholy persons, but generally very useful and agreeable to cold constitutions, if moderately used.

PEPPER: Is a wholesome ingredient in pea soup, fish, oysters, eggs, milk, or any diet of a glewy nature; but care must be used not to take too much, which will inflame, and perhaps corrode, the stomach. It is properly used in colicky cases, and in soreness in the stomach; but not too freely at once. It has put off a fit of an ague, swallowing six or eight corn an hour or two before—but as it inflames all those humours it can't carry off, care must be taken, that by too much freedom with it, an ague is not blown into a continual fever. It is also good against the poisonous effects which sometimes follow the eating of mushrooms—also in cases where opium has produced ill effects, and has relieved children who have been busy with the poisonous berries of night-shade, being administered in all they take after the berries are vomited up. (In such cases consult a physician at once.)

CLOVES: Are good against wind in the stomach. They corroborate the nerves, and all nervous parts, such as the stomach, the bowels, and womb—and by a discreet and frequent use are good as a dietary addition in the whites, and other simple feminine disorders, taking a little of the powder in a glass of red wine now and then, occasionally, as they are affected.

GINGER: Is good in colicky and sour humours, in windy and asthmatic cases, if not inflammatory. It opens the obstructions of the nerves and womb. Is good in cold palsies —but in hectical dispositions, or in case of bleeding, must be avoided. Yet, it is one of the wholesomest of the Spices.

Refreshing the Spirits

The following of the plough hath been approved for refreshing the spirit, and procuring appetite: But to do it in the ploughing for wheat or rye, is not so good, because the earth hath spent her sweet breath in vegetables put forth in summer. It is better, therefore, to do it when barley is sowed. But, because ploughing is tied to seasons, it is best to take the benefit of the air of the earth new-turned up by digging with a spade—or, if that be too tiresome and laborious, to stand by him that digs.

Ladies may receive great benefit by kneeling on a cushion and weeding; and these things may be practiced in the best seasons, which is ever the early spring, before the earth weakens her virtues by putting forth her vegetables; and in the sweetest earth that can be chosen, and when the dew is a little off the ground, for fear of too moist a vapour. This excellent author says he knew a great man that lived long, who had a fresh clod of earth brought to him every morning as he sat in his bed, and he would hold his head over it a pretty while, and if, says he, in digging of new earth a little malmsey or greek wine were poured in, that joining with the vapour of the earth, would still more comfort the spirits.

Tonic-stimulant for the Appetite and Stomach

Take roots of Calamus aromaticus, Spanish Angelica root, of each one drachm; Gentian root, two drachms; tops of Centaury, Roman Wormwood, of each a quarter of a handful; Coriander seeds, half a drachm. Just simmer them together in a pint of spring water; then strain, and add of compound Gentian water, four ounces. Make four doses of it. Drink in the morning fasting, and at five of the clock in the afternoon, and eat nothing till an hour after.

The cure of all relaxations of the nerves (the source of chronical diseases) must necessarily often begin at the stomach and guts.

The great rule of eating and drinking for health is to adjust the quality and quantity of our food to our digestive powers.

All crammed poultry, and stall-fed cattle, and even vegetables forced by hot beds, tend more to putrefaction, and consequently are more unfit for human food than those brought up in the natural manner.

Plain dressed food is easier of digestion than what is pickled, salted, baked, smoked, or any-way high seasoned.

Where exercise is wanting (as in studious persons), there is the greater need of abstinence; for these eight ounces of animal, and twelve of vegetable food, in twenty-four hours, is sufficient.

LORE AND QUAINT RECIPES—continued

Strong and spirituous liquors freely indulged become a certain, though a slow, poison.

Chocolate is so heavy and hard of digestion that it can never be fit for the stomachs of weak and tender people.

Smoking tobacco without drinking after it, chewing, or snuffing the gross-cut leaf in a morning, are useful to phlegmatic constitutions—but to dry and lean habits, they are pernicious. Snuff is just good for nothing at all.

Old age should carefully guard against all the injuries of weather; should lessen the quantity, and lower the quality of their food gradually, as they grow older, even before a manifest decay of appetite force them to it; and in short descend out of life by as gradual steps of ailment as they ascended into it.

Gout Recipe of Mr. Miller of Chelsea

Speedwell herb is found an excellent general systemic tea remedy. The method is to make a tea of the dried herb—the quantity to be used is about a quarter of an ounce, from which four common dishes of tea may be drawn. These are to be drank every morning, as felt needed. To this, some add the dried herbs of Bog-bean and Ground-pine, which they mix in equal quantities, and make a tea of them, from which many persons have received great benefit.

Pile Recipes

For an excellent easer simple of pains, take of the herb Toad-flax with the flowers, as much as you will; boil it with hog's lard till it grows green and makes an ointment. For use, add a proper quantity of the white of an egg.

Rosemary eaten every morning with a little honey will quite take away the piles.

Onion or leek, roasted under the ashes, with Oil of Roses, and a little Safron, is highly recommended. A leek, fried with butter in a pan, is an admirable remedy.

Oil of Amber used by itself cures the most violent pain.

Hiccough Recipes

If the distemper is obstinate, and the patient strong, vomits are proper.

Some apply a fomentation, hot, to the stomach, with a sponge; or hot bread moistened with vinegar boiled with castor, pepper and mustard.

An ounce of Skirret roots, boiled in a pint of good red port, and a large coffee cup full taken blood warm, when the hiccough is troublesome, has been of service in this case.

Cough Recipes

Boil good turnips in water, and having expressed the juice, mix with it as much finely powdered sugar candy as will bring it into a kind of syrup—of which let the patient swallow a little as slowly as he can from time to time.

Take dried Coltsfoot leaves, a good handful, cut them small and boil them in a pint of spring water, till half a pint is boiled away; then take it off the fire, and when it is almost cold, strain it through a cloth, squeezing the herb as dry as you can, and then throw it away, and dissolve in the liquor an ounce of brown sugar candy finely powdered, and give the child (if it be about three or four years old, and so in proportion) one spoonful of it cold or warm, as the season proves, three or four times a day (or oftener, if the fits of coughing come frequently) till well, which will be in two or three days—but it will presently almost abate the fits of coughing.

Common Colic

Take about half a drachm of expressed Oil of Nutmegs. Dissolve this in some spoonfuls of good wine, which the patient is to take as hot as conveniently he can.

A medicine prescribed to King Charles I to fasten teeth

Take a pint of spring water, and put to it four ounces of brandy. Let the patient wash his mouth with the mixture of these every morning, and twice or thrice a day besides, and let him in the morning roll for a little while, a bit of rock alum to and fro in his mouth.

To Prevent the Nail Growing Into the Toe

If the nail be hard, and apt to grow into the corners, scrape it very thin, whenever you pare your nails, with a bit of glass, which will by degree make the corners fly up, and grow flat.

To Make Dr. Stephen's Water

From a Recipe He Himself Gave to the Archbishop of Canterbury

Take Cinnamon, Ginger, Nutmeg, grains of Paradise, Cloves, Anise seeds, Fennel seeds, Caraway seeds, of each two drams; Sage, Chamomile, Marjoram, Lavender, of each a small handful; Mints, Red roses, Pellitory of the Wall, Rosemary and Thyme, and wild Thyme, of each a small handful. Break the spices fine, bruise the herbs small, and put them into a gallon of Bourdeaux red wine, and let them stand 24 hours, stirring them; then put them into a limbeck, and keep the first water by itself, for it is best. The second water is good, but not equal with the first. It comforts the spirits, and helps conditions that arise from cold, and comforts the stomach. With this water the old doctor preserved his life till he was not able to go nor ride, having kept his bed five years, when others thought it impossible for him to live one year. He owned before his death that he never used any other physic than this.

HERBAL CHARMS

The following botanicals have no value for conditions mentioned. We sometimes hear of ailments being prevented or "cured" by these herbal charms, but actually the ailment was a temporary or non-existent condition—the charm merely incurred a faith cure.

Herbal charms were very popular in the Old World many centuries ago, when superstition and imagination were wide-spread. Among rustics there still exists remnants of these old time beliefs. In England, one hears of folks wearing Tansy herb in their shoes, in the belief that it will cure ague, or a hank of Flax worn round the loins as a cure for lumbago.

In Holland and Germany, it was believed that if Mugwort herb was gathered on St. John's Eve, it gave protection against disease, as well as misfortunes.

Italian peasants believe if a fresh peach leaf is placed on a wart, then buried, the wart will fall off when the leaf is decayed.

A necklace of Job's Tears was a very popular preventative for goiter, until recent times, when the discovery of iodine and its importance was realized.

An old gypsy belief held that a piece of asafoetida hung around a child's neck, was protection from all disease.

A 2000 year-old belief held "If any have ye herb Artemisia with him in ye way, it dissolves weariness, and he that bears it on his feet, drives away venemous beasts and devils." The same writer says in regard to Vervain—"When any shivers with an ague, let one taking ye branches from this stand only before him that hath ye shivering, and forthwith he is cured."

Gerard wrote that an infusion of Feverfew drunk and fresh plant bound to wrists was of "singular virtue against ague".

About a century ago in England, a certain Mr. Morley published a pamphlet, advising the root of Vervain tied with white ribbon to be worn around neck of scrofulous people.

"Dioscorides saith that the herbe Antirrhinum being hanged about one preserveth from being bewitched, and maketh a man gracious in the sight of people." Turner later wrote "all these are but the dreames of sorcerers."

In America we may still find people believing that a Buckeye carried in the pocket, would prevent, as well as cure rheumatism.

Even the American Indian had an herbal charm for rheumatism. The placing of Goat's Rue leaves in moccasins was supposed to be a cure and preventative.

Lord Bacon states that in his time, it was common for people to wear bands of green Periwinkle tied around the calves of their legs to keep away the cramp.

Parkinson wrote that a wreath of Periwinkle "worn about the ankle, defendeth them that wear it from the crampe." Fleabane "bound to the forehead is a great helpe to cure one of frensie."

One of the most popular remedies for ague was made with Bucks-horn Plantain. The old recipe required "hanging the roots with the rest of the herb about the neck—nine whole plants for men—seven plants for women and children."

A 300 year old Herbal states—"that if the whole plant (Meadow Rue) both herbe and roote, be hung up in a chamber, or tied to the necke of any person doth free them from any danger or harme."

The countrie shepherds of Germany, as Tragus reporteth, doth use to hang it (Night Shade) about cattells neckes, when they are troubled with the disease they call Die Hynsch, which is a swimming in the head, causing them to turne round.—from an old herbal.

"Dioscorides saith Madwort is an Amulet to expell charmes, that shall be used upon man or beast, and that tyed with a scarlet cloth to cattell that are diseased, it helpeth them."

Matthiolus saith that the greene herbe of Celandine, worn in their shooes that have the yellow jandies, so as their bare feete may tread thereon, it will helpe them of it.

HOUSEHOLD HINTS FROM AN OLD RECIPE BOOK

Tar may be removed from either hands or clothing by rubbing well with lard and then washing well with soap and water.

To Keep Lard Fresh: To every eight gallons of lard add one quart of strained honey.

Ants: To keep ants from any dish or pail, draw a circle of chalk around it.

To Take Out Scorch: If a shirt bosom or any other article has been scorched in ironing, lay it where the bright sunshine will fall directly on it. It will take it entirely out.

How To Make Furniture Look New: Take three parts of sweet oil, one part spirits of turpentine and mix them. Rub off all the dust, and apply the mixture with a flannel cloth.

To Make Washing Easy: Mix one tablespoonful of kerosene oil with a pint of soft soap, and soap all the boiled clothes; put them in soak over night and very little rubbing will be necessary.

To Make Sour Fruit Sweet Without Sugar: To two pounds of fruit when cooking, add one teaspoonful of soda.

To Keep Off Mosquitoes: Dip a piece of sponge or flannel in camphorated spirits and make it fast to the top of the bedstead. A decoction of pennyroyal or some of the bruised leaves rubbed on the exposed parts will keep these insects away.

INTERESTING FACTS AND LORE GLEANED FROM OLD HERBALS
How Dreadful Disease Was Carried to Europe

In the yere of our Lorde God 1493, in the wars that the Catholic king had in Naples, with King Charles of Fraunce, that was called greate heade: in this tyme sir Christofer Colon (Columbus), came from the discoverie that he had made in the Indias. He brought a greate number of Indians, bothe men and women, which he carried with him to Naples, where the Catholic King was at that tyme, who had then concluded the wars, for that there was peace between the two Kings, and the hostes did communicate together, the one with the other. And Colon (Columbus) being come thether with his Indians, the most part of them went with the fruite of their countrie which was the Poxe (syphilis) the Spaniards began to have conversation with the Indian women, in such sorte, that the men and women of the Indias, did infecte the Campe of the Spaniards, Italians and Almaines (Germans), the Catholic king had then of all these Nations, and there were many that was infected of the evill. And after the hostes did common together, the fire did kindle in the camp of the king of Fraunce: of the which did follow that in short tyme, the one and the other were infected to this evill seed: and from thence it hath spred abroad into all the worlde.

At the beginning it had diverse names: The Spaniards did think that it had been given them by the Frenche men, and they called it the Frenche evill. The Frenche men thought that in Naples, and of them of the Countrie, the evill had been given them, and they called it the evill of Naples. And they of Almaine (Germany) seyng that of the conversation of the Spaniards, they came to it, they called it the Spanishe Skabbe, and other called it the Measelles of the Indias, and with much truth, seyng that from thence came the evill.—From Monardes "Joyfull Newes out of the Newe Founde Worlde," Year 1577.

Washington, Victim of Contemporary Practice

In reading the official report of the death of General Washington, says Dr. Reid, I should imagine there were few medical persons who did not feel astonishment at the extraordinary manner in which that great man was treated by his physicians, during his last and fatal indisposition.

Some time in the night of the 13th of December, it is said, the General was seized by a disease called the cynanche trachealis or croup. During the same night he sent for a bleeder, who took from him 12 or 14 ounces of blood. Next morning a physician was sent for, who arrived at Mount Vernon at 11 o'clock; when, imagining danger in the case, he advised the calling of two consulting physicians.

In the interval, however, he thought proper to employ, in spite of the 12 ounces that had already been expended, two copious bleedings. Now, when we consider that these are called copious, and the other is not noticed as such, and all the indifference with which a future most copious bleeding, is afterwards mentioned, we may presume that each of these was at least 20 or 25 ounces. After this two moderate doses of calomel were administered. I know not exactly, what an American moderate dose of calomel may be; but if it is fair to presume it be in proportion to the bleedings, we may conclude that it was at least very considerable.

Upon the arrival of the first consulting physician, it was agreed, that, as there were no signs of accumulation in the bronchial vessels of the lungs, they should try another bleeding. Now this appears to be perfectly inexplicable. As there were, at present, no signs of accumulation in the bronchial vessels of the lungs, they were driven to another bleeding. Hence it will be seen, that this last bleeding was to produce an accumulation in the bronchial vessels of the lungs! There was great difficulty of breathing, great inflammation; but as there was as yet no accumulation in the lungs, they were determined to induce that also, and as a likely means of inducing it, had recourse to the most extravagant effusion of blood. This is not an unfair interpretation of their words; but it could not have been their real meaning; their real meaning it is impossible to discover. In addition to all their previous venesections, thirty-two ounces are now drawn! The medical reader will not be surprised to find that this was unattended by any apparent alleviation of the disease.

In the next place, vapors of vinegar and water are frequently inhaled. Two doses of calomel were already given, but this is not deemed sufficient; ten grains of calomel are added; nor is even this sufficient. Repeated doses of emetic tartar, amounting in all to five or six grains, are now administered. It is said, the powers of life now seemed to yield to the force of the disorder. To many, it may appear that the yielding of the vital principle, in these circumstances, was not altogether owing to the force of the disorder. The pa-

Washington—Continued

tient, lying in this feeble, nearly exhausted state, is to be still further tormented. Blisters were next applied to his extremities, together with a cataplasm of bran and vinegar to his throat. It is observed that speaking, which was painful from the beginning, now became scarcely practicable. When we reflect upon the extreme weakness to which the patient must, by this time, have been reduced, and that he had both a blister and a cataplasm of bran and vinegar to his throat, can we wonder that speaking would be scarcely practicable! Respiration grew more and more contracted and imperfect, until after 11 o'clock on Saturday night, when he expired without a struggle. — From Mattson's *American Vegetable Practice*.

"WONDER DRUG" OF THE 16th CENTURY

While the Spanish sought gold in the New World, the English were busy scouring the Eastern shores for Sassafras, the "wonder drug" of the 16th Century. The demand for this botanical was so tremendous that it became a virtual "gold mine" for Sir Raleigh, who held monopolist control of its importation.

Early French and Spanish explorers brought first attention of this New World botanical to Europe. The following account, written almost 400 years ago, did much to start the fires of publicity in plague-ridden Europe. Soldiers returning to Europe, explorers, etc., fanned the flames until nobody felt safe from diseases unless they had some Sassafras:

"The Frenchemen, which had been in Florida at that tyme, when thei (Spanish) came into those parts, thei had been sick the moste of them, of greevous and variable diseases, and that the Indians did show them this Tree, and the manner how thei should use it, and so thei did, and thei healed of many evilles, which surely it doeth bryng admiration, that one onely remedy should do so variable, and so marveilous effectes.

"After that the Frenche men were destroyed, our Spaniards did begin to waxe sicke, as the Frenche men had done, and some which did remain of them, did show it to our Spaniards, and how thei had cured themselves with the water of this merveilous Tree, and the manner which thei had in the using of it, showed to them by the Indians, who used to cure themselves therewith, when thei were sick of any grief.

"Our Spaniards did begin to cure themselves with the water of this Tree, and it did in them greate effectes, that it is almost incredible: for with the naughtie meates and drinking of the raw waters, and sleeping in the dews, the most part of them came to fall into continual Agues, of the which many of them came to opilations, and of the opilations thei came to swell, and when the evil began, immediately it began to take away the luste that thei had to their meate (food)—and then came to them, other accidents and diseases, as such like Fevers are accustomed to bring, and having there no remedie to be healed, thei did what the Frenche men had counsailed them, doing that which thei had done, which was in this forme.

"Thei took up the root of this Tree, and tooke a piece thereof, suche as it seemed to them best, thei cut it small into very thin and little pieces, and cast them into water, at discretion, that which thei saw was needful, little more or less, and thei sodde (soaked) it the time that seemed needful, for to remaine of a good coulour, and so they drank it, in the morning fasting, and in the daie tyme, and at dinner and supper, without keeping any more weight, or measure, than I have said, nor more keepyng, nor order then this, and of this thei were healed of so many griefes, and evill diseases. That to hear of them what thei suffered, and how thei were healed, it doeth bring admiration, and thei which were whole drank it in place of wine, for it doeth preserve them in healthe: as it did appeare verie well by theim, that hath come from thence this yere, for thei came all whole and strong, and with good coulours, the which doeth not happen to them that dooeth come from those partes, and from other conquestes, for thei come sicke and swollen, without coulour, and in shorte space the most of them dieth, and these soldiers doeth trust so much in this wood, that I beyng one day amongst many of them, informing myself of the thynges of this Tree, the moste parte of them tooke out of their pockets, a good peece of this wood, and said: Maister, doe you see here the wood, that everyone of us doth bryng for to heale us with all, if we do fall sicke, as we have been there: and thei began to praise so muche, to confirme the marvelous workes of it, with so many examples of them that were there, that surely I gave greate credite unto it, and thei caused me to believe all that thereof I had heard."

Today Sassafras is simply thought of as a rustic "Spring Tea" used to "thin" the blood that has been sluggish through long, cold winters, and semi-hibernating habits. The "Spring Tea" custom is of Indian origin.

Sassafras is used in modern medicine as an aromatic, stimulant, diaphoretic and alterative.

Annise seede chewed in the mouth, maketh a sweete mouth and easie breath, and amendeth the stench of the mouth—Recipe of Middle Ages.

"All flesh is grass."—Isaiah.

67

LIVED TO BE 103 YEARS OLD THROUGH TEMPERANCE

Almost 500 years ago there lived in Italy a youth named Louis Cornaro. Louis was of delicate constitution with a high-strung temper and many dissipating habits. By the time he was 35 years old, his health was so completely impaired that doctors no longer could help him with their medicines. He was warned to change his life or expect death very soon.

We will use parts of Louis Cornaro's own treatise on how he cured himself and gained such control over his health that he outlived his doctors, relatives and friends by many, many years.

I Resolved to Live a Temperate Life

"The food I was to use was such as belonged to sickly constitutions, and that in small quantity. This they had told me before: But I, then not liking that kind of Diet, followed my Appetite, and did eat meats, pleasing to my taste, and when I felt inward heats, drank delightful wines, and that in great quantity; telling my physicians nothing thereof, as is the custom of sick people. But after I had resolved to follow Temperance and Reason, and saw that it was no hard thing to do so, but the proper duty of man; I so addicted myself to this course of life, that I never went a foot out of the way. Upon this, I found within a few days that I was exceedingly helped, and by continuance thereof, within less than one year (although it may seem some incredible) I was perfectly cured of all my infirmities.

"Being now sound and well, I began to consider the force of Temperance, and to think thus with myself: If Temperance had so much power as to bring me health; how much more to preserve it! Wherefore I began to search out most diligently what meats were agreeable unto me and what disagreeable: and I purposed to try, whether those that pleased my taste brought me commodity or discommodity; and whether that Proverb, wherewith Gluttons used to defend themselves, to wit, *That which favours, is good and nourisheth,* be consonant to truth. This upon trial, I found most false; for strong and very cool wines pleased my taste best, as also melons, and other fruit; in like manner, raw lettuce, fish, pork, sausages, pulse, and cake and piecrust, and the like; and yet all these I found hurtful.

"Therefore trusting on experience, I forsook all these kind of meats and drinks, and chose that wine that fitted my stomach, and in such measure, as easily might be digested; above all, taking care never to rise with a full stomach, but so as I might well both eat and drink more. By this means, within less than a year I was not only freed from all those evils which had so long beset me, and were almost become incurable; but also afterwards I fell not into that yearly disease, whereinto I was wont, when I pleased my Sense and Appetite. Which benefits also still continue, because from the time that I was made whole, I never since departed from my settled course of *Sobriety,* whose admirable power causeth that the meat and drink that is taken in fit measure, gives true strength to the body, all superfluities passing away without difficulty, and no ill humours being engendered in the body.

"Yet with this diet I avoided other hurtful things also, as too much heat and cold, weariness, watching, ill air, overmuch use of the benefit of marriage. For although the power of health consists most in the proportion of meat and drink, yet these forenamed things have also their force. I preserved me also, as much as I could, from hatred and melancholy, and other perturbations of the mind, which have a great power over our constitutions. Yet could I not so avoid all these, but that now and then I fell into them, which gained me this experience, that I perceived that they had no great power to hurt those bodies which were kept in good order by a moderate Diet: So that I can truly say, That they who in these two things that enter in at the mouth keep a fit proportion, shall receive little hurt from other excesses.

"This *Galen* confirms, when he says, that immoderate heats and colds, and winds and labours, did little hurt him, because in his meats and drinks he kept a due moderation, and therefore never was sick by any of these inconveniences, except it were for one day only. But mine own experience confirmeth this more, as all that know me can testify: For having endured many heats and colds, and other like discommodities of the body and troubles of the mind, all these did hurt me little, whereas they hurt them very much who live intemperately. For when my brother and others of my kindred saw some great powerful men pick quarrels against me, fearing lest I should be overthrown, they were possessed with a deep Melancholy (a thing usual to disorderly lives), which increased so much in them, that it brought them to a sudden end; but I, whom that matter ought to have affected most, received no inconvenience thereby, because that humour abounded not in me.

"Nay, I began to persuade myself, that this suit and contention was raised by the Divine Providence, that I might know what great power a sober and temperate life hath over our bodies and minds, and that at length I should be a conqueror, as also a little after it came to pass: For in the end I got the victory, to my great honour and no less profit, whereupon also I joyed exceedingly, which excess of joy neither could do me any hurt: By which it is manifest, That neither melancholy nor any other passion can hurt a temperate life.

Recuperating Powers Strengthened Through Temperance

"Moreover, I say, that even bruises, and squats, and falls, which often kill others, can bring little grief or hurt to those that are temperate. This I found by experience, when I was seventy years old; for riding in a coach in great haste, it happened that the coach was overturned, and then was dragged for a good space by the fury of the horses, whereby my head and whole body was sore hurt, and also one of my arms and legs put out of joint. Being carried home, when the Physicians saw in what case I was, they concluded that I would die within three days: nevertheless, at a venture, two remedies might be used, letting of blood and purging, that the store of humours and inflammation and fever (which was certainly expected) might be hindered.

"But I, considering what a orderly life I had led for many years together, which must needs so temper the humours of the body, that they could not be much troubled, or make a great concourse, refused both remedies, and only commanded that my arm and leg should be set, and my whole body anointed with oil; and so without any remedy or inconvenience I recovered, which seemed as a miracle to the Physicians; whence I conclude, that they that live a temperate life can receive little hurt from other inconveniences."

"But my experience taught me another thing, also, to wit, that an orderly and regular life can hardly be altered without exceeding great danger."

Danger of Changing Temperature Life

"About four years since, I was led, by the advice of physicians, and the daily importunity of my friends, to add something to my usual stint and measure. Divers reasons they brought, as, that old age could not be sustained with so little meat and drink; which to gather strength, which could not be but by meat and drink. On the other side, I argued that Nature was contented with a little, and that I had for many years continued in good health with that little measure; that Cusom was turned into Nature, and therefore it was agreeable to reason, that my years increasing and strength decreasing, my stint of meat and drink should be diminished rather than increased, that the patient might be proportionable to the agent, and especially since the power of my stomach every day decreased. To this agreed two Italian Proverbs, the one whereof was, *'He that will eat much, let him eat little'*; because by eating little he prolongs his life. The other Proverb was, *'The meat which remaineth, profits more than that which is eaten;* by which is intimated that the hurt of too much meat is greater than the commodity of meat taken in moderate proportion.

"But all these things could not defend me against their importunities. Therefore, to avoid obstinacy and gratify my friends, at length I yielded, and permitted the quantity of meat to be increased, yet but two ounces only; for whereas before, the measure of my whole day's meat, viz. of my bread, and eggs, and flesh, and broth, was twelve ounces exactly weighed, I increased it to the quantity of two ounces more; and the measure of my drink, which before was fourteen ounces, I made now sixteen.

"This addition, after ten days, wrought so much upon me, that of a cheerful and merry man I became melancholy and choleric, so that all things were troublesome to me; neither did I know well what I did or said. On the twelfth day, a pain in the side took me, which held me two and twenty hours. Upon the neck of it came a terrible fever, which continued thirty-five days and nights, although after the fifteenth day it grew less and less; besides all this I could not sleep, so, not a quarter of an hour, whereupon all gave me for dead.

"Nevertheless, I, by the grace of God, cured myself only with returning to my former course of Diet, although I was now seventy-eight years old, and my body spent with extreme leanness, and the season of the year was winter, and most cold air; and I am confident that, under God, nothing help me, but that exact rule which I had so long continued; in all which time I felt no grief, save now and then a little indisposition for a day or two.

"For the Temperance of so many years spent all ill humours, and suffered not any new of that kind to arise, neither the good humours to be corrupted or contract any ill quality, as usually happens in old men's bodies, which live without rule; for there is no malignity of old age in the humours of the body, which commonly kills men, and that new one which I contracted by breaking my diet, although it was a fore evil, yet had no power to kill me.

"By this it may clearly be perceived how great is the power of order and disorder; whereof the one kept me well for many years, the other, though it was but a little excess, in a few days had so soon overthrown me. If the world consist of order, if our corporal life depend on the harmony of humours and elements, it is no wonder that order should preserve, and disorder destroy. Order makes arts easy, and armies victorious, and retains and confirms kingdoms, cities, and families in peace. Whence I conclude, That an orderly life is the most sure way and ground of health and long days, and the true and only medicine of many diseases."

LIVED TO BE 103 YEARS OLD, THROUGH TEMPERANCE—continued

Becoming Your Own Doctor

"Neither can any man deny this who will narrowly consider it. Hence it comes that a Physician, when he cometh to visit his patient, prescribes his physic first, that he use a moderate diet; and when he hath cured him commends this also to him, if he will live in health. Neither is it to be doubted, but that he shall ever after live free from diseases, if he will keep such a course of life, because this will cut off all causes of diseases, so that he shall need neither Physic nor Physician: yea, if he will give his mind to those things which he should, he will prove himself a Physician, and that a very complete one; for indeed no man can be a perfect Physician to another, but to himself only. The reason whereof is this: Every one by long experience may know the qualities of his own nature, and what hidden properties it hath, what meat and drink agrees best with it; which things in others cannot be known without such observation as is not easily to be made upon others, especially since there is a greater diversity of tempers than faces. Who would believe that old wine should hurt my stomach, and new should help it, or that cinnamon should heat me more than pepper? What Physician could have discovered these hidden qualities to me, if I had not found them out by long experience? Wherefore one to another cannot be a perfect Physician. Whereupon I conclude, since none can have a better Physician than himself, nor better Physic than a Temperate life, Temperance by all means is to be embraced.

"Nevertheless, I deny not but that Physicians are necessary, and greatly to be esteemed for the knowing and curing of diseases, into which they often fall who live disorderly: For if a friend who visits thee in thy sickness, and only comforts and condoles, doth perform an acceptable thing to thee, how much more dearly should a Physician be esteemed, who only as a friend doth visit thee, but help thee!

"But that a man may preserve himself in health, I advise, that instead of a Physician a regular life is to be embraced, which, as is manifest by experience, is a natural Physic most agreeable to us, and also doth preserve even ill tempers in good health, and procure that they prolong their life even to a hundred years and more, and that at length they shut up their days like a Lamp, only by a pure consumption of the radical moisture, without grief or perturbation of humours. Many have thought that this could be done by *Aurum potabile,* or the *Philosopher's stone,* sought of many, and found of few; but surely there is no such matter, if Temperance be wanting."

Sensual Men and Belly-gods

"But sensual men (as most be) desiring to satisfy their Appetite and pamper their belly, although they see themselves ill handled by their intemperance, yet shun a sober life; because, they say, It is better to please the appetite (though they live ten years less than otherwise they should do) than always to live under bit and bridle. But they consider not of how great moment ten years are in mature age, wherein wisdom and all kind of virtues is most vigorous; which, but in that age, can hardly be perfected. And that I may say nothing of other things, are not almost all the learned books that we have, written by their Authors in that age, and those ten years which they set at nought in regard of their belly?

"Besides, these Belly-gods say, that an orderly life is so hard a thing that it cannot be kept. To this I answer, that *Galen* kept it, and held it for the best *Physic;* so did *Plato* also, and *Isocrates,* and *Tully,* and many others of the Ancients; and in our age, *Paul the Third,* and *Cardinal Bembo,* who therefore lived so long; and among our Dukes, *Laudus,* and *Donatus,* and many others of inferior condition, not only in the city, but also in villages and hamlets.

"Wherefore, since many have observed a regular life, both of old times and later years, it is no such thing which may not be performed; especially since in observing it there needs not many and curious things; but only that a man should begin, and by little and little accustom himself unto it."

Temperance Regardless of Employment

"Neither doth it hinder, that *Plato* says, That they who are employed in the commonwealth, cannot live regularly, because they must often endure heats, and colds, and winds, and showers, and divers labours, which suit not with an orderly life: For I answer, That those inconveniences are of no great moment (as I showed before) if a man be temperate in meat and drink, which is both easy for commonweal's men, and very convenient, both that they may preserve themselves from diseases, which hinder public employment, as also that their mind, in all things wherein they deal, may be more lively and vigorous.

"But some may say, He which lives a regular life, eating always light meals and in a little quantity, what diet shall he use in diseases, which being in health he hath anticipated? I answer first, Nature, which endeavours to preserve a man as much as she can, teacheth us how to govern ourselves in sickness: for suddenly it takes away our appetite, so that we can eat but a very little, wherewith she is very well contented: So that a sick man, whether he hath lived heretofore orderly or disorderly, when he is sick, ought

LIVED TO BE 103 YEARS OLD, THROUGH TEMPERANCE—Continued

not to eat but such meats as are agreeable to his disease, and that in much smaller quantity than when he was well. For if he should keep his former proportion, Nature, which is already burdened with a disease, would be wholly oppressed. Secondly, I answer better, that he which lives a temperate life cannot fall into diseases, and but very seldom into indispositions, because Temperance takes away the causes of diseases; and the cause being taken away, there is no place for the effect.

"Wherefore, since an orderly life is so profitable, so virtuous, so decent, and so holy, it is worthy by all means to be embraced; especially since it is easy and most agreeable to the nature of Man. No man that follows it, is bound to eat and drink so little as I: No man is forbidden to eat fruit or fish, which I eat not: For I eat little, because a little sufficeth my weak stomach; and I abstain from fruit, and fish, and the like, because they hurt me. But they who find benefit in these meats may, yea ought to use them; yet all must needs take heed lest they take a greater quantity of any meat or drink (though most agreeable to them) than their stomach can easily digest: So that he which is offended with no kind of meat and drink, hath the *quantity*, and not the *quality* for his rule, which is very easy to be observed.

"Let no man here object unto me, That there are many, who though they live disorderly, yet continued in health to their lives' end: Because, since this is at the best but uncertain, dangerous, and very rare, the presuming upon it ought not to lead us to a disorderly life.

"It is not the part of a wise man to expose himself to so many dangers of diseases and death, only upon a hope of a happy issue, which yet befalls very few. An old man of an ill constitution, but living orderly, is more sure of life than the most strong young man who lives disorderly.

"But some, too much given to Appetite, object, That a long life is no such desirable thing, because that after one is once sixty-five years old, all the time we live after is rather death than life: But these err greatly, as I will show by myself, recounting the delights and pleasures in this age of eighty-three, which now I take, and which are such as that men generally account me happy."

Enjoying Health and Life at 83

"I am continually in health, and I am so nimble, that I can easily get on horseback without the advantage of the ground, and sometimes I go up high stairs and hills on foot. Then I am ever cheerful, merry, and well-contented, free from all troubles and troublesome thoughts; in whose place joy and peace have taken up their standing in my heart. I am not weary of life, which I pass with great delight. I confer often with worthy men, excelling in wit, learning, behaviour, and other virtues. When I cannot have their company, I give myself to the reading of some learned book, and afterwards to writing; making it my aim in all things, how I may help others to the furthest of my power."

(The above 300 year old translation of Cornaro's "Treatise of Temperance and Sobriety" was made by George Herbert, noted English author of religious subjects.)

LONGER LIFE THROUGH MENTAL ATTITUDE

The following excerpt was taken from a treatise by John Worlidge, printed in 1676:

"Gardens and orchards themselves, have been esteemed the purest of human pleasures, and the greatest refreshments of the spirits of man: for the exercises of planting, grafting, pruning, and walking in them, very much tendeth to salubrity, as also doth the wholesome airs found in them, which have been experienced not only to cure several distempers incident to our nature, but to tend toward the prolongation of life.

For nothing can be more available to health and longer life, than a sedate quiet mind, attended with these rural delights, a healthful air, and moderate exercise, which may here be found in all seasons of the year."

The maddening pace of modern times, the alarming increase in the number of insane, and the staggering death toll from heart attacks, impresses upon us more and more how important good mental attitiude is in maintaining health.

Most of us have experienced reactions in our stomach, when in grief, temper or other mental disturbances. A mind in which morbid thoughts, jealously, hate and anger are continually stirred and brewed, will agitate and sap body strength to a point where it becomes an easy victim to disease.

Practice good mental habits as you would practice good physical habits. Creating pleasant home surroundings, attending Church, reading good literature, healthy sports and games, gardening, and a general return to nature will do wonders in keeping a healthy mental state.

Early writers believed that the smelling of fragrant herbs and listening to music did much to influence mental and physical conditions.

WONDERS(?)
Predicted in the Year 1704 A.D.

'Twas pronounc'd in all the Chambers and in the Courts of Princes, that the Chymical medicines would make Life Immortal, by Preventing and Curing every Distemper; and that therefore Hippocrates and Galen and Celsus, (who had no Chymical Medicines) and all the Voluminuous Writers since the Restoration of Learning, were to be despis'd and neglected—and that no Physician ought to confess, having read and considered 'em, without the mark of Publick Infamy.—(*From Pitts Antidote, by R. Pitt, M.D. Fellow and Censor of the College of Physicians, and fellow of the Royal Society, and Physician of St. Bartholomew's Hospital.*)

1956 A.D. People Alarmed by Ever Increasing Use of Chemicals

The marvels of chemistry can not be denied, but they have no place in the human body, simply because the body assimilates only the organic products of Nature. Today we find chemicals in our drinking water and many beverages, and most all of our foods and medicines. We eat chemicals by the tons, daily. Chemists say we eat this in such minute quantities it cannot possibly harm us. The minute quantities, of course, refers to a single meal—they do not tell you that the average adult EATS HIS WEIGHT IN FOOD every 6 to 8 weeks! As for the power of minute quantities, let us refer to a lecture by a noted doctor:

"Minute amounts of chemicals can have the most fantastic effects on our bodies. For instance, the mineral cobalt is essential in our diet if we are not all to die of pernicious anaemia. Yet all that each one of us needs daily is only one fifty-millionth of a piece the size of an aspirin tablet. So it seems silly to say minute amounts of chemicals cannot affect the body, when a microscopic fragment of cobalt is all that stands between our life and death.

The harmlessness of a chemical cannot be proved when it is to be taken daily for many years. Animal experiments are valueless partly because we are not rats nor even apes, chiefly because if we are going to eat a chemical every day for sixty or eighty years we want experiments carried out on animals for that length of time. This is obviously impossible. Man is the only laboratory animal of value as a guide to man's needs. Take as an example aniline dyes, which are one of the few chemicals whose long-term effects we do know. By unhappy chance workers in aniline dye factories have acted as human guinea pigs. Aniline dyes cause cancer of the bladder. But a man may have to be exposed for twenty or more years to the minute amounts he breathes while at work before he develops cancer. And, even more frightening, he may not develop the cancer until fifteen years after he has left the factory. No Animal experiments could have given us this information. But, having got it, one might suppose no aniline dye could ever be added to our food. Yet what dyes do you suppose give such weird colours to some cakes, ices, soft drinks, jams, bottled fruits, chocolates, dyed fish? Are you surprised to hear that cancer of the bladder has increased by fifty per cent, in the last ten years? Are you quite happy when you remember you have been eating agenized flour for just over twenty years and so, by analogy with the dyes, its effects might now start to appear?"

An excerpt from another lecture states: "Fresh fish is the only food left to us, which is never contaminated or even made poisonous with chemicals. Nearly all prepared foods may and do have chemicals added: even vegetables, fruit, meat and milk may have chemicals in them, because these chemicals have been used on the farm lands, or used as preservatives."

"Man's first disobedience, and the fruit of that forbidden tree, whose mortal taste brought, death into the world and all our woe with loss of Eden."—Milton

The Lord hath created medicines out of the earth; and he that is wise will not abhor them.—Ecclesiastes XXXVIII, 4.

"There is nothing like herbs—they have made me feel wonderful at 73 years of age. They are a God-send."—C.K.R., Wilmington, Del.

FOLK MEDICINES

Folk medicine, like other folk lore, gives a keen insight into the lives, hopes, fears, and misfortunes of "less" sophisticated people. Also it indicates the more prevalent diseases of a group. Even today there are thousands of communities where the major part of the population is more or less illiterate, so that its news, knowledge and entertainment are generally perpetuated through word of mouth, even from generation to generation. Invariably in such a society there is allusion to medicinal and charm cures.

In the Arkansas hills corn starch and brown "floar" (flour) are used for heat. Sweetened water in which cherry bark has been soaked is considered fine for coughs. Peach-leaf tea is recommended for hair tonic and worms. Egg membrane or prickly pear is used for draining boils. Red oak bark is used for "die," poke-root for "each" (itch), and gum turpentine is chewed for sores in the mouth, toothache or a sore throat. Water allowed to stand in a hollow red oak (or most any hollow) stump until it is black will sure smooth the "rinkills" out of one's face. Dogwood bark is the old stand-by for chills, but a cotton yarn dipped in turpentine and tied around the waist with a knot over the navel is regarded as a sure cure for the malaria. "Black hall" (Viburnum) root is used for "wimin's ailins," black draught (Ilex) for physic tea, and sassafras tea for a "blood thinner."

In the southern states "home remedies" are varied and numerous. The bark of red oak is made into a tea or poultice for bringing "a rising to a head," and for ground itch and other skin diseases. A tea made from the root of the "red shank" (Rumex) is used as a wash for sore mouth. The bruised green leaves of huckleberry in the form of a cold-water tea are supposed to cure pyorrhea. A boiled tea decocted from the bark of the wild plum just before blossoming time is used in asthma. Onion bulbs are good for swelling and pneumonia. For an emetic, the bark of elderberry bush should be skinned upward, but to settle the stomach it must be peeled downward. Cottonseed tea with a little sulphur is used for colic. Snuff and tobacco are remedies for cuts and wasp stings. Cedar balls are used in the form of a poultice for rheumatism and bruises. Green moss from the bark of oak trees in the form of a tea is used for salivation. A decoction from the limbs of "tag" alder is supposed to purify the blood. Bark of the limbs of the persimmon tree is chewed as a cure for diarrhea. The fruit of the persimmon just before ripening is used to prevent swelling and soreness from cuts or bruises. Tea made from corn fodder will make measles break out. The seed of Jerusalem Oak cooked in molasses candy is used for worms in children. The root of swamp root makes poultices for sores. Poplar bark, dried and ground, is said to give results in dropsy. Fig leaves are smoked for asthma. Two drops of blood from a "bessie bug" (bed-bug) dropped into a child's ear is the accepted cure for ear-ache. Blackberry root tea is used for diarrhoea. A tea from wild cherry bark is good for coughs, as is dogwood-bark. Water in which Indian turnip rhizome has been placed is given for colic and pains, and tea from the root of green meadow for kidney trouble. An Irish potato should be carried in the pants pocket for chills, and asafoetida tied on a string around the neck, is a charm against certain diseases. A pocket knife held on the back of the neck is said to stop nose bleeding. Willow bud tea is used for chills and horse-radish root tea for colds. In Arkansas, peach-tree bark is employed as a poultice for risings. A tea from sheep-sorrel leaf is used for lung colds, and one from the inner bark of the hickory tree as an expectorant. Black root (Aletris) tea is used as a purgative. Ground-ivy vine is a remedy for hives for babies.

STRANGE OLD BELIEFS

It was believed in England that Rosemary will not grow well in the garden unless the mistress is master in the house.

From a 1525 Herbal: "Make thee a box of the wood of Rosemary and smell to it and it shall preserve thy growth."

Another old European belief held that if one chewed a clove of Garlic before running a race, it would keep the garlic chewer well ahead of his competitors. Garlic was also hung on race horses for the same results.

"He who sees Fennel and gathers it not, is not a man but a devil."

Gerarde wrote in regard to Hound's Tongue herb: "It will tye the tongues of Houndes so that they shall not bark at you if it be laid under the bottom of your feet."

William Coles wrote in 1656, "If a footman take Mugwort and put it into his shoes in the morning, he may goe forty miles before noon and not be weary."

A very old legend: When the herb Water Pepper was placed under the saddle, it would enable the horse to travel long distances without becoming hungry or thirsty. The ancient Scythians used the herb for this purpose.

Culpeper wrote, "The leaves of the Lesser Perriwinkle, if eaten by man and wife together, will cause love between them."

Pliny said of Common Evening Primrose: "Of such virtue is this herbe that if it be given to drink to the wildest beast that is it will tame the same and make it gentle."

In the Middle Ages when people were haunted by magic and superstition, it was believed that if Agrimony was laid under a man's head it would cause heavy sleep until it was removed.

Another old belief: Any article which held a few Caraway seeds was believed to be theft-proof. (Too bad this is not true!)

In Italy stables are popularly thought to be protected by a sprig of Juniper from demons and thunderbolts, just as we suppose the magic horseshoe to be protective to our houses and barns.

The Chinese believed Coriander seeds possessed a power of immortality.

Superstitious folk used to hang branches of Fennel with St. Johnswort over doors to keep out evil spirits.

From a 1539 Herbal regarding Mugwort: "Yf this herbe be within a house there shall no wycked spyryte abyde."

In Holland and Germany it was believed that if Mugwort herb was gathered on St. John's Eve it gave protection against disease and misfortunes.

The Ancient Greeks believed that Basil would grow better if they cursed while sowing the seeds.

An old legend held that if sprigs of Rosemary were placed under the head it would deliver the sleeper from all evil dreams.

Certain tribes of American Indians believed that if leaves of Goat's Rue were placed in the moccasin it would cure rheumatism.

An ancient Greek and Roman belief held that if Rue was stolen from the neighbor's garden it would grow better in his own. The plant does well in anybody's garden if given well drained soil and a sunny location.

A belief that still exists in Italy: If a fresh peach leaf is placed on a wart then buried, the wart will fall off when the leaf is decayed.

Elder was commonly planted around English cottages as a protection against witches.

An old proverb regarding Flaxseed: "If put in the shoes it preserves from poverty."

Peasants of Sussex put Tansy herb in their shoes in the belief that it will cure ague.

A cross made from wood of Elder and fixed to the barn was believed to protect cattle from all harm.

HERBS FOR THE EYES

Bancke's Herbal says of an infusion made of Wormwood: "It doth away the black mist in a man's eyes, and cleareth the sight."

A quaint old rhyme:
"Noble is Rue! It makes the sight of eyes
 both sharp and clear;
With help of Rue, Oh! blear-eyed man! thou
 shalt see far and near."

For this reason the painters of old ate Rue with most of their meals. The Italians and peoples of Balkan States still use it (sparingly) in salads, meats, cheese, etc.

Culpeper made this very extravagant claim: "Eyebright made into a powder and then into an electuary with sugar, hath powerful effect to help and to restore the sight decayed through years.

OLD FASHIONED MEDICINAL PREPARATIONS

Syrup Manna: Manna flakes, 10 ounces; hot water, 12 ounces. Make a solution, strain, and add 1 pound sugar. Dissolve by gentle heat. This is a useful laxative. Dose: 1 tablespoonful or more.

Infusion of Flaxseed: Linseed, 1 ounce; Licorice root, ½ ounce; boiling water 2 pints. Macerate for two or three hours near the fire, in a covered vessel, strain and add lemon juice sufficient to make it agreeable. It may be given as a common drink in catarrh.

Mucilage of Gum Arabic: As an article of diet, the proper proportions are an ounce of gum arabic to a pint of boiling water. The solution is allowed to cool before it is used. Gum Arabic is very nutritive, and life can be sustained on it alone for some time.

Sage Tea: Dried Sage leaves, ½ ounce; boiling water, 1 quart. Infuse for half an hour and then strain. Sugar and lemon juice may be added in the proportion required by the patient. In the same manner may be made balm and other teas.

Jelly of Carragreen or Irish Moss: Irish Moss (Carrageen), ½ ounce; fresh milk, 1½ pints. Boil them down to a pint. Remove any sediment by filtering or straining and then add the requisite quantity of sugar, with lemon juice or peach water to give it an agreeable flavor. To be used freely. The moss, before being used, should be well washed in cold water, to remove its saline taste.

Coughs of Colds: Boil two ounces of Flaxseed in one quart of water; strain and add two ounces of rock candy; ½ pint of honey, juice of three lemons; mix and let all boil well; let cool and bottle. Dose: One cupful on going to bed, ½ cupful before meals. The hotter you drink it the better.

Vienna Purgative: Take of Manna, 1 ounce; Senna, 1 drachm; Cream of Tartar, 30 grains; Powdered Coriander and raisins, of each, ½ drachm; water, 5 ounces. Reduce by boiling to 2 ounces, and take before breakfast.

Confection of Senna: Take of Powdered Senna, 4 ounces; Powdered Coriander, 2 ounces; Purging Cassia, 8 ounces; Tamarinds, 5 ounces; sliced prunes, 3 ounces; bruised figs, 6 ounces; sugar, 15 ounces; water, enough. Mix well together into a conserve. Dose, ½ drachm to 4 drachms at night.

Aromatic Drops: Take of bruised **Angelica**, 1 ounce; Sweet flag, 1 drachm; Fennel seed, 2 drachms; Anise seed, 4 drachms; Catnip, 4 drachms; Motherwort, 4 drachms; infuse in 8 ounces of alcohol for four days, often shaking and keeping warm; then add 8 ounces water, and Cayenne Pepper, 1 drachm. Dose, ½ to 1 teaspoonful. Useful to relieve wind colic and to promote perspiration and refreshing sleep.

Good Samaritan Liniment: Take of alcohol, 1 quart; Oil of Sassafras, Oil of Turpentine, Balsam of Fir, Chloroform, Tincture of Catechu and Tincture of Guaiacum of each 4 drachms; Oil of Origanum, 1 ounce; Oil of Wintergreen and Gum Camphor, of each 2 drachms. Mix. This is one of the noblest liniments yet formulated for the relief of muscular aches, bruises, sprains, headaches, burns, etc.

Magic Liniment: Take of alcohol, 1 quart; Camphor, 4 ounces; Oil of Turpentine and Oil of Origanum, of each, 2 ounces; Olive oil, 1 ounce. Mix.

OLD FASHIONED POULTICES

How to make a good Linseed Poultice: Rinse a bowl with boiling water to heat it then pour in sufficient boiling water; with one hand sprinkle into the bowl the meal while with the other stir the mixture constantly with a spoon or spatula till sufficient meal has been added to make a thin and smooth dough. This should be done rapidly, otherwise the poultice will be almost cold when made. The meal should always be added to the water with constant stirring as here directed, for if the water be poured over the meal, the two ingredients are not well blended, and a lumpy knotty mass is the result. The dough thus made should be spread quickly and evenly over a folded piece of warm linen, cut ready to receive it. Linseed Meal, 4 ounces; Olive Oil, ½ ounce; Boiling Water, 10 ounces. Mix and apply.

Slippery Elm Poultice: Powdered Elm bark and boiling water formed into a thin paste. Sometimes a small portion of laudanum is added which makes a grateful application to abscesses, felons, painful bruises, etc.

Charcoal Poultice: Make a bread and milk poultice in the usual way, then sprinkle finely powdered charcoal over it and apply. Valuable for cleansing old sores and for arresting mortification.

Flax Seed Lemonade

Four tablespoons whole Flax Seed, 1 quart boiling water poured on Flax Seed, juice of two lemons. Sweeten to taste; steep three hours in a covered pitcher. If too thick, put in cold water with the lemon juice and sugar. Ice for drinking. It is splendid adjunct in colds.

POPULAR TEA OF OLD ENGLAND

The passing centuries have not changed the old English custom of drinking Nettle tea when one feels "out of sorts". It is believed this health habit was brought to the Isles by the early Roman conquerors who used Nettle tea to help them withstand the rigorous climate.

Stinging Nettle

This old custom would have been long forgotten if it had not proven beneficial generation after generation.

The ancients, of course, knew nothing of vitamins and minerals but we know now that Nettle herb is one of the richest botanical sources of these important elements. Most modern English herbals extol the use of this tea for toning up the system in general. The herb was often found in herbal longevity formulae. The tea is also used as a "spring tonic".

Nettle tea is generally taken 4 times a day. The first cup taken upon arising, 2d and 3rd are taken between meals and the 4th cup taken upon retiring. The tea may be taken hot or cold. It is made like Chinese teas—sweetened and flavored with lemon to taste.

Old-time Longevity Beliefs

"Make thee a box of the wood of Rosemary and smell to it, and it shall preserve thy youth."

also "If thou be feeble, boyle the leaves of Rosemary in cleane water and washe thyself and thou shalt wax shiny."—Banckes Herbal.

"It (Chervil) is good for people that be dull, old, and without courage, for it rejoiceth and comforteth them, and increaseth their strength."—Dodoens Herbal.

Regarding Balsam of Gilead: "The women of Egypt, herewith has Alpinus showeth, preserve their beauty and young forme for a long time.—Parkinson Herbal.

"How can a man die in whose garden there grows Sage?" The tea is highly regarded in parts of Europe.

Laplanders believed if they chewed and smoked Angelica root as tobacco, it would prolong their life.—Herbal Delights.

American Indians believed that roots of Indian Cup-plant would make an old man young again.—Horton's Botanic Medicine.

The ancients believed eating Fennel herb and using the seeds for flavoring foods gave one strength, courage, and conveyed longevity.

HEALTH ADVICE FROM AN OLD ENGLISH RECIPE BOOK

January: "For your own health, keep your body warm, let good diet and wholesome be your Physitian, and rather with exercise than sawce encrease your appettie."

February: "Take heed of cold, forbear meats that are flimsy and phlegmatick, and if need require, either purge, bathe as Art shall direct you."

March: "Bathe often, purge not without good counsel and let your diet be cool and temperate."

April: "Either purge or bathe as you shall have occasion, and use all wholesome recreation; for than moderate exercise in this month, there is no better physick."

May: "Use drink that will cool and urge the blood, and all other such physical precepts, as true Art shall prescribe you, but beware of Mountebanks, and old wives tales, the latter hath no ground and the other no truth, but apparent cousenage."

June: "Distill all sorts of plants and herbs whatsoever. And lastly for your health, use much exercise, thin dyet and chast thoughts."

July: "Abstain from all physick, and neither meddle with Wine, Women nor other wantonness."

August: "Let Physick alone, hate wine and onely take delight in drinks that are cool and temperate."

September: "Use Physick, but moderately, forbear fruits that are too pleasant or rotten, and as death shun ryot and surfeit."

October: "Refuse not any needful physick at the hands of the learned Phystian, use all moderate sports, for anything new is good which reviveth the spirits."

November: "For your health, eat wholesome and strong meats very well spiced and drest, free from rawness; drink sweet wines and for digestion ever before cheese, prefer good and moderate exercise."

December: "And lastly, for your health eat meats that are hot and nourishing, drink good wine that is neat sprightly and lusty, keep thy body well clad and thy house warm, forsake whatsoever is flegmatick and banish all care from thy heart for nothing is more unwholesome than a troubled spirit."

MORE VITAMINS ARE NEEDED IN WINTER

For Winter Salads: For vitamin richness, use the curd of broccoli and cauliflower raw; wonderfully rich in vitamin A: celery tips and green leaves may be 100 times richer in vitamins than the bleached heart; red cabbage contains over thirty times as much vitamin A as white.

Lore of Ancient Herbals

Phillips wrote in 1831 "that a stone taken out of the human body, on being wrapped in Chamomile, will in a short time dissolve. Hence, says Coles, it is evidently an excellent remedy for that complaint, if the syrup or decoction of the flowers be taken in a morning, fasting.

The Romans admired radishes as a winter sauce to their meat; but it was observed that they injure the teeth, and yet, says Pliny, they will polish ivory, which is the tooth of an elephant.

Spearmint, when dry, and digested in rectified spirits of wine, gives out a tincture which appears by daylight a fine dark green, but by candlelight a bright red color. A small quantity is green by daylight or candlelight; a large quantity seems impervious to daylight, but when held between the eye and the candle, or between the eye and the sun, it appears red. If put into a flat bottle, it appears green sideways; but when viewed edgeways, red.

The common Ivy (Hedera helix) at one time held in great repute as a help in the preventative of drunkenness and antidote to the effects of "heady" wines.

Anise seed, they say, being eaten an hour, when that they shall sleep, it doth make a pleasant and delectable dream.

Yarrow, or Clary herb, was formerly used to give an intoxicating quality as well as a bitterness to beers.

Parsley herb, when rubbed against a glass goblet or tumbler, will break it. The cause of this phenomenon is not known.

Many people shun onions on account of the strong, disagreeable smell they communicate to the breath. This may be remedied by eating walnuts, or a few raw parsley leaves, immediately after, which will effectually overcome the scent, and cause them to sit more easy on the stomach.

"The very smell of Mint alone, recovers and refreshes the spirits, as the taste stirs up the appetite. Mint was put into milk to keep it from turning sour or curdling. For this reason, those who generally drink milk take Mint with it, for fear it should coagulate or curdle in the stomach."

"The blossoms of Nasturtiums have been observed to emit electric sparks towards evening, which was first noticed by the daughter of the illustrious Linnaeus, who could not credit the account until he had seen the phenomenon. It is seen most distinctly with the eye partly closed.

"The flowers, being of so excellent a color for candlelight, are often used to garnish dishes."

The Romans gave Garlic to their laborers to strengthen them, and to their soldiers, with an idea that it excited their courage. They also fed their game-cocks with Garlic, previous to fighting them.

The odor of Garlic is so powerful and penetrating that, if it be applied to the feet, its scent is soon discovered in the breath, and when taken internally, its smell is communicated through the pores of the skin, even to the fingers.

If you have taken Garlic, and wish to sweeten your breath, the eating of baked beet-root will entirely take off the offensive smell.

Glasswort or Saltwort: It is from the ashes of this plant that the salt called alkali is extracted, which being mixed with a fine sort of sand, makes the glass called crystal. The Venetians manufacture it into those beautiful glasses so much esteemed.

The ashes of this seaside plant, made into lye, and boiled with oil, make the best soap.

It is called Sage in English from the French word SAGE (wise), from the property it is said to possess of strengthening the memory, and thus making people sage or wise.

"A wine of the infusion of the tops (Eyebright) for ordinary drinking; this is much commended by Arnoldus de Villa Nova, being put into new wine before it works; they that cannot get wine go to the charge of it, may tunn it up with new Ale or Beer; this wine, saith he, not only helps the dimness of the sight, but the use of it makes old Men to read small Letters without Spectacles, who could scarcely read great ones with their Spectacles before; and he affirms that it did restore their sight who had been a long time blind."

Herbs and Spices: These things are rich in minerals, vitamins, and medicinal principles, and have valuable tonic effects when used regularly. Broadly, herbs go with vegetables, spices with fruits, seeds with starchy foods. There's no food richer in vitamin C than parsley. Paprika is a vitamin C source, too. Try dill seeds with potatoes, mint with peas, cinnamon with banana, vanilla with apples, and ring the changes often.

A Spring Tonic for children is freshly grated raw carrot, sprinkled with a little powdered aniseed. Mildly laxative, and the ideal vermifuge (destroyer of internal worms) for infant systems.

A Nerve Tonic Fruit: If your nerves are shaky, make good use of apples this month. Use windfalls for apple juice—cut and mash one pound of apples, unpeeled with cores, add one pint of water, bring to boil and simmer for twenty minutes; cool and strain, sweeten with honey and drink often. For breakfast —grate sweet apples, add a pinch of nutmeg, and eat with cereals.

HERBS ARE COMING BACK

There are very few cooking recipes printed to-day that do not call for one or more flavoring herbs.

Old attics, dusty book shelves, and second-hand book stores are being scoured for forgotten herbals. Many of these neglected books are now fetching fantastic prices.

A few years ago, many folks scoffed at Grandma's homely remedies. Now, more and more, science is proving that many of these old-fashioned medicines really are good. Penicillin—prize of the 20th Century, was one of Grandma's old remedies. The possibilities of this minute plant led to many other valuable anti-biotic mold discoveries.

For ages, people over the entire world have used fresh leaves of certain plants as a poultice, to hasten healing of wounds. Science now tells us that the green substance in plants, known as chlorophyll, contains definite healing properties.

For ages, people of the Mediterranean shores ate garlic as a health measure. It is now known that the cloves have powerful penetrating and antiseptic properties.

It was common knowledge in Europe, what vegetables, and foods had strengthening properties. These same plants are now known as vitamin and mineral-rich foods.

Asclepias, helonias, aletris and licorice were favorite remedies of the "Yarb" doctors and rustics. For "female troubles" modern researchers have proven that the botanical contain significant amounts of estrogenic hormones.

Mountain folks in the Ozarks and Alleghanies used a decoction of sumach root as a "flu" remedy. Recently, researchers found that the remedy does show promise against the virus that causes "flu."

For thousands of years, Chinese herb doctors used ma huang for asthmatic conditions. Ephedrine—derivative of ma huang is now widely used by modern physicians in shock, hemorrhage, low blood pressure and asthma.

A botanical panacea of the ancient Egyptians was found by researchers to be helpful in relieving and preventing angina pectoris.

Modern researchers are delving into the medicines of aboriginal peoples, as well as the ancients.

In South America plant explorers found Amazon Indians dabbing their arrow points with an herbal decoction which paralyzed the game they hunted, without effecting the flesh. This powerful drug plant is now being used to relax muscles of patients undergoing surgery. It has been found to be a valuable aid in shock therapy in mental disease, and in the treatment of some forms of paralysis.

In Africa, another botanical used on arrows, offers a potential source of cortisone, the drug that promises new hope for arthritis and rheumatic fever.

In Mexico, steroid hormones, used in the treatment of cancer, arthritis, gout and asthma, are derived from a species of dioscorea.

In the jungles of Ecuador, head hunting Indians use a combination of botanicals to shrink heads to the size of a baseball. It has been reported that these head shrinking botanicals, injected into patients in advanced stages of cancer, prolong life, modifies or eliminates pain, stopped hemorrhages, and reduces cancerous tissue.

The possibilities of herbal remedies appear to be unlimited. Research is only in the beginning state. It will require centuries of work by the world's greatest scientists, to tap nature's vast laboratories on land and sea.

MEDICINE MAN WINS TRIBUTE

Successful treatments of functional diseases by the modern physician and surgeon cannot compare with the record of cures attained by the shaman (medicine man), says bulletin edited by Prof. James G. Leyburn.

Modern medicine will begin to approach "the arts of the shaman in effectiveness" when it becomes not only a biological science as well. The article states that when "our physicians and surgeons approach the record of the shaman, the millenium of medicine will be near."

Scientific medicine deserves its plaudits, but "they give no grounds for the common practice of depreciating primitive shamanism. The medicine man, the witch doctor, the shaman, was a creature of superstition—granted. But he got results. He actually cured patients." —News Item.

PROVE ALL THINGS, HOLD FAST THAT WHICH IS GOOD

The numerous systems scattered wide abroad,
Compare them closely by the Word of God;
Hold fast the good, have all things truly tried
By that all comprehensive guide.
What'er is false, reject without delay;
Uphold the right, and cast the rest away.

NATURE'S LABORATORIES

NATURE'S LABORATORY

Some 200,000,000 years ago the HORSETAIL GRASS was a mighty family of tree size plants growing with gigantic clubmosses and  ferns in a strange world of steaming bogs, swamps and shallow lakes. Plants of this remote age grew prodigiously but were short lived. Millions of years of accumulation of dead plants formed our valuable coal fields.

Evolution has made little change in the Horsetail Grass thru these vast ages. Today it is an insignificant dwarf amongst a flowering vegetation of an entirely different plant world. The plant still prefers low damp sandy locations. Horsetail Grass contains such a quantity of silica that it came in considerable use in Europe for polishing woodwork, pewter and metals. Medicinally the plant was used as a diuretic.

GOLDEN SEAL is a native of our own land. Its value was learnt from the Indians by early trappers, hunters and adventurers.  Golden Seal grows in small colonies in rich woods. The leaves of the different forest trees provide a leaf-mulch mixture which blend over winter to provide renewed fertilizer for this valuable drug plant each year.

MORMON VALLEY PLANT or EPHEDRA grows in the saline soil of arid lake beds of Rocky Mountain regions where practically little other  vegetation survives. It was long used medicinally by the Indians and early Spaniards and later adopted by explorers and frontiersmen as a medical drink as well as a pleasant, refreshing beverage. They called it DESERT TEA or TEAMSTER'S TEA. It is still preferred by some cowboys. A similar species of Ephedra known as MA-HUANG has been used by the Chinese herbalist for colds, coughs, headache and fever for more than 4,000 years. Only recently has modern science acknowledged its value. It is the source of drug known as Ephedrine.

BLADDERWRACK thrives in the salty waters along rocky shores of the Atlantic Ocean. It is a natural source of iodine.

BEECH DROPS is a very odd dull red little plant with neither leaves nor green coloring. It is a parasite that grows upon the roots of Beech  Trees. The plant is astringent and used locally on minor cuts, wounds and bruises.

NATURE'S LABORATORY

Brought from Europe, TANSY escaped the old Colonial garden and became a vagabond over a large part of North America. Even where the seeds settle and sprout, the plant will not remain permanently. Before the mother plant drains the soil of its essential fertilizers, shoots travel on to new and fresh soil, establishing new clumps which in turn start off more new travelers. The old plants dwindle until weeds take complete possession of the depleted soil. The powerful virtues contained in Tansy probably accounts for its quick soil depletion and the plant's traveling habit.

TANSY was mentioned in writings as early as 5000 B.C. It reached the height of its popularity during the Middle Ages when it was put to every use imaginable. Leaves were worn in shoes in belief that it would relieve ague. The mashed leaves were used as poultice for skin trouble, sprains and swellings. Rubbed on meats it was one of the early attempts of preserving. Branches of the herb were kept near foods to shoo off ants and flies. Folk of that day evidently liked very strong flavors as the fresh herb was used for flavoring puddings, cakes and omelets.

TANSY contains tanacetin, tannic acid, volatile oil, resinous substance and sugar. Its action is anthelmintic, tonic, stimulant and emmenagogue. The herb tea is taken in moderate doses.

The essential oil derived from TANSY is very powerful, drastic in action and poisonous in overdoses. It should only be used internally by practitioner's directions.

A curly-leaved variety of TANSY makes a very beautiful garden plant.

SQUILL or SEA ONION is a juicy, bulbous plant found growing in dry sandy soil along the shores of the Mediterranean. The bulb rests on top of the soil, being anchored down and fed by many, very deep growing fibrous roots.
The bulb acts as a store house to feed the young bulblets. They are protected under the heavy skin of the plant until the youngsters have built up enough supply to live until their own roots have time to reach nourishment. When the bulblets are freed, the wind rolls them to locations of their own.

SQUILLS were valued as medicine as early as 500 B.C. They were used by the ancient Greeks, Egyptians and Romans. Arabian physicians introduced the drug into European medicine after the Dark Ages. Their preparations are still in use. Although the fresh leaves of the *plant are used as a home remedy for minor cuts and burns*, the dried bulb is the part used in the drug market. Because of its powerful properties, the drug should only be administered internally by physicians. The bright green, shiny long leaves resemble hanging silk ribbons. Flowers grow in spikes on the end of a tall careening stalk.

An herbal printed about 1833 said of COMFREY, "This is so common that a description would be useless." Although grown in almost every garden for use as a home remedy, it is practically forgotten today. The plant somewhat resembles Nicotinia but is coarser.  While most plants shed their leaves to the winds in the fall, COMFREY retains the season's top growth to refertilize the plant for the following year.

COMFREY has been used to alleviate man's sufferings from remote ages. The roots contain considerable mucilage and small parts of allantoin, tannin and starch. They are demulcent, mildly astringent and expectorant. The fresh leaves or fresh roots are used as poultice on sprains, swellings, bruises, cuts and boils and abscesses.

IRISH MOSS is a seaweed found in great abundance on submerged rocks along the shores of Ireland and other parts of the world. At low tide, when the seaweed is exposed or available at shallow depths, it is raked up and dried in  the sun which bleaches it to a tan color. The dried herb has a mucilaginous, saline taste.

IRISH MOSS is being used in increasing quantities for various new purposes. As food and medicine, the plant has been used for generations in regions where it was found. Because of its power to absorb water and expand, POWDERED IRISH MOSS taken with foods is useful as bulk for promotion of bowel elimination. Boiled in water, IRISH MOSS forms a stiff mucilage containing considerable sulphur and small amounts of iodine and minerals. Iodine is essential to proper functioning of the thyroid gland. A reputed medical authority has said premature ageing can be retarded if the system is supplied with the necessary amount of iodine. As IRISH MOSS contains no sugar or starch it is a very valuable nutritive for diets. The vegetable pectin of IRISH MOSS is useful in soups, custards, puddings, cold sweets, jellies and where thickening is desired.

Botanically, ICELAND Moss is not a moss but a LICHEN. Herbs like golden seal, ginseng and blood root live off the "fat of the land"; LICHENS thrive where soil has not yet been made. Rocks offering no foothold and less plant nourishment are the "gardens" of LICHENS.  They attach themselves so firmly to rocks that to remove them completely the rock must be broken! ICELAND Moss has neither root, stem nor leaves. The light greyish or brown tinged plants form colonies resembling fragments of carpeting made of paperish tissues. The plant derives its nourishment from the moist air. They do not grow near gaseous and smoky air of cities. Years of lichen accumulations forms the first soil which is eventually taken possession of by green plants if the climate is not too cold. ICELAND Moss grows in Great Britain and north to the polar regions. In Iceland and Greenland it covers vast barren, rocky land. Here it is assured of plenty of moisture from the heavy fogs which that part of the world is noted for.

Because of the lichen starch content (about 70 per cent) ICELAND Moss forms a valuable food for Icelanders. Dried cakes are eaten like bread. An easily digested gelatinous broth is made by boiling the plant. Boiled with milk ICELAND Moss forms an excellent nutritive and tonic. Its tonic virtues depend upon its cetrarin which, if removed, renders the lichen merely nutritious. Liquid in which ICELAND Moss has been boiled becomes firm jelly on cooling.

THEY SEASON IT WITH BOTEKA

Boteka. The whole leaves are used for seasoning. The cut leaves are used as a tea for indigestion and tonic.

NATURE'S LABORATORY

CHA MATE is found growing in the depths of the great South American virgin jungles. Its roots draw their stimulating virtues from a soil, enriched by the accumulation of fallen vegetation of ages. From this Garden of Eden, Indian gatherers bring the leaves to sophisticated civilization.

DAMIANA thrives under the strong ultra violet rays of the tropical sun. It is gathered and dried with great care to assure fullest value. Damiana is a mild tonic and diuretic.

LUCERNE: Note depth and spread of its roots to absorb its valuable nourishment. It is one of the richest known plants for lime and organic salts. For full strength we eliminate all stems and worthless parts.

SWEET FLAG grows in shallow bays along rivers and streams where its aromatic roots derive a rich nourishment from old vegetation, washed into the bays. Calamus is an aromatic, carminative, tonic and vulnerary.

MANDRAKE thrives under Oak Trees, where its shallow roots feed on the soil fertilized by tannin bearing leaves fallen from Oak. Roots of Mandrake are cathartic, cholagogue, alterative, emetic, diaphoretic, emmenagogue and vermifuge.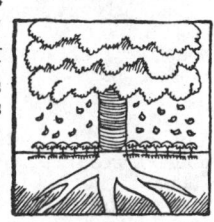

YELLOW DOCK grows most luxuriantly where there is evidence of iron in soil. Its stout roots absorb this valuable mineral to make it digestible for man. Its properties are alterative, tonic, depurative, astringent and anti-scorbutic.

GOBERNADORA, THE DESERT PLANT

Gobernadora is a dark olive-green bush found growing in great colonies in the scorching sands of the Mohave desert where drought has shriveled up practically all other plant life. To sustain life, the roots of Gobernadora penetrate 20 to 30 feet into the soil and branch off in all directions. The thick pulpy bark of the root acts as a reservoir to store water in rainy season and to feed the top plant during the drought season. In order to seal this precious moisture and to resist sharp, cutting sand storms, Nature has given Gobernadora varnish-coated tiny leaves. These leaves are further protected by moving edgewise against the blistering heat of the desert sun. Like most desert vegetation, the golden flowers of this plant burst forth during the brief winter rains.

Because of the leanness of desert land, there is a fierce struggle between plants and animals for existence. Juicy cacti are armed to the roots with vicious spines. The fresh green yuccas are actually strands of dry tough fibre. If small plants are not protected with irritating hairs, they usually are flavored with a strong taste or scent. Gobernadora grows in perfect safety among hungry browsing animals and insects in spite of being the only "green" in the barren desert.

The entire plant of Gobernadora has a strong, resinous odor. Mexicans call the plant "Hediondilla" or the little bad smeller. Col. Fremont, famous explorer and pathfinder, considered the odor of the plant "singular and very agreeable." The smoke from the plant is said to give beans baked in molasses a pleasant tang and delicious flavor.

The early Spaniards found the Indians using Gobernadora when they came to the desert country. The herb still is popular among modern Indians as well as Mexicans. It has been reported that Indians of the Vallecito region use a decoction of the leaves as a hair tonic. The United States Bulletin, "Trees and Shrubs of Mexico," (vol. 23, part 3) states: "The flower buds, pickled in vinegar, are said to be eaten like capers. The plant is much used in domestic medicine, especially for rheumatism, a decoction of the leaves being employed for baths or fomentations. The decoction is said, also, to have remarkable antiseptic properties, and is applied to bruises and sores. A reddish brown lac is often deposited upon the branches by a small scale insect. This lac is used in some parts of Mexico for dyeing leather red, and the Coahuilla Indians of California employ it as cement. The Pima Indians of Arizona drink a decoction of the leaves as emetic, and apply the boiled leaves as poultices to wounds and sores."

EVERGREEN NEEDLES USED FOR SCURVY 400 YEARS AGO

Vitamin C, the scurvy-preventer, was recently found by Russian botanists to be present in ordinary pine needles. This discovery was hailed as significant and very properly so, because although the concentration in pine needles is not great, Russia has simply unlimited quantities of evergreen trees.

However, although the discovery is new from a biochemical angle, from the viewpoint of practical medicine it is not. Without knowing anything about vitamins. American Indians 400 years ago knew how to cure scurvy with a tea made from evergreen needles.

Dr. Maurice Donnelly of the U. S. Soil Conservation Service research laboratory in Riverside, Calif., calls attention (*Science*, Aug. 6) to a passage in Parkman's classic historical work, *Pioneers of France in the New World,* which tells of the troubles of the French explorer Jacques Cartier and his party in Canada, just four centuries ago. Twenty-five of the men were dead of scurvy, and only three or four were still able to get about in anything like full vigor.

Cartier, walking one day near the river, met an Indian, who had been as sick as the rest a short time before, but now appeared to be perfectly healthy. When questioned, the Indian told his white chief of making a drink of the leaves of a certain evergreen. The Frenchman tried it on his men, and in a week they used up all the foliage of a large tree. Recovery of the party began immediately.—*Science News Letter.*

INDIAN SALVE

The Indians boiled the resinous buds of Balm of Gilead in fat to make a salve for dressing wounds and put up the nostrils for cold in the head.

JOE PYE WEED

When I was a child I used to gather great bunches of Joe Pye weed for my mother. It was used as a cure for coughs and colds. A syrup was made from it. There is also a white variety which is better than the red.

Do you know how it derived its name? Joe Pye was the name of an Indian who cured typhus fever in New England by means of this plant.

I can testify as to its healing properties for coughs. The Cough Syrup of the Joe Pye Weed, or Thoroughwort, as it is sometimes called, is made of the blossoms and leaves, steeped and boiled down, molasses added; then boiled to a syrup. It was bitter —like horehound.—Mrs. R. M. F.—From *Madison Cooper's Gardening Magazine.*

SOME MEDICINAL PLANTS OF NORTH AMERICA

Used by Indian Medicine Men, Botanic Physicians, "Regulars," "Yarb" Doctors, etc.

Much of this material is taken from early American herbals, the authors of whom were professors and doctors, highly regarded in the medical field of their time. Much of this botanic materia medica is lightly or totally ignored by modern practitioners. (See special notice, Page 1).

ALETRIS—Aletris farinosa

"Aletris was held in high repute by the aborigines as a stomachic, bitter tonic, and emmenagogue; from them it passed into the hands of the laity and herbalists. The first notice given of its action upon the female organs of reproduction, is in Eclectic practice, where it receives consideration in chlorosis, dysmenorrhoea, engorged uteri, amenorrhoea, and prolapsus."

Modern research has proven that this botanical has estrogenic properties.

BLACKBERRY—Rubus villosus

"Of the vegetable astringents, says Prof. Chapman, this I have reason to believe is among the most active and decidedly efficacious in certain cases. To the declining stages of dysentery, after the symptoms of active inflammation are removed, it is well suited, though I have given it, I think, with greater advantage under nearly similar circumstances, in cholera infantum. To check the inordinate evacuations which commonly attend the protracted cases of this disease, no remedy has ever done so much in my hands. Even 2 or 3 doses will sometimes so bind the bowels that purgatives became necessary. Being so powerfully astringent, this medicine is useful in all excessive purgings, and especially in the diarrhea of very old people, as well as when it occurs at the close of diseases."

BLACK COHOSH—Cimicifuga racemosa

"A favorite remedy among all tribes of the aborigines, being largely used by them in rheumatism, disorders of menstruation, and slow parturition."

"Dr. Williams says: "Indians and quacks recommend its use in rheumatism, etc"—and then he recommends it himself!

BLUE COHOSH—Caulophyllum thalictroides

"The aborigines found in Caulophyllum their most valuable parturient; an infusion of the root drank as tea, for a week or two preceeding confinement, rendering delivery rapid and comparatively painless. They also used the root as a remedy for rheumatism, dropsy, uterine inflammation, and colic. These uses have been proven reliable by all methods of practice since.

There is hardly an American remedy in our Materia Medica that needs, and probably merits, a more thorough proving, upon females especially, than Caulophyllum."

BONESET—Eupatorium perfoliatum

Millspaugh wrote in 1887—"There is probably no plant in American domestic practice that has more extensive or frequent use than this. The attic, or woodshed, of almost every country farmhouse, has its bunches of the dried herb hanging tops downward from the rafters, during the whole year, ready for immediate use should some member of the family, or that of a neighbor, be taken with a cold. How many children have winced when the maternal edict—"drink this Boneset; it'll do you good," has been issued; and how many old men have craned their necks to allow the draught to the quicker pass the palate!" The use of a hot infusion of the tops and leaves to produce diaphoresis, was handed down to the early settlers of this country by the Aborigines, who called it by a name that is equivalent to Ague-weed.

Fever and ague was so common, that it was considered as something to be expected on the frontier, like hard work. "He aint sick, he's only got the ager," was the attitude taken by the settlers.

Boneset is diaphoretic only when given in generous doses of the hot *infusion;* a cold *decoction* is claimed to be tonic and stimulant in moderately small, laxative in medium, and emetic in large doses.

BUGLE-WEED—Lycopus virginicus

Rafinesque thought exceedingly well of its general properties, and as a means of producing diaphoresis without debility; he judged it a tonic sedative, and found it very useful in hemoptysis, and internal inflammation; he further claims that it acts somewhat like digatalis, lowering the pulse, without producing any bad effects, *nor accumulating in the system.* Dr. Williams speaks of the plant as being one of the most valuable styptics we possess in our vegetable Materia Medica. Most writers accept the idea that the plant is narcotic—we, however, infer, both from our own experience, and that of others, that it is only a sedative, in that in removes by check-

MEDICINAL PLANTS—continued

ing hemorrhage, that nervous excitability and mental fear always accompanying such conditions.

BUTTERNUT—Juglans cinerea

Decoction made with the inner bark is a mild cathartic. Millspaugh wrote that "it acts without colic, and is said to leave none of the constipating effects so frequently following general cathartics. In diarrhoea and even dysentery it receives many encomiums from botanic physicians."

The unripe, half formed fruits of Butternut, make fine pickles. The sap, gathered in its season, forms—on boiling—a fine sugar, equal if not superior to that of the maple. The leaves, bark and unripe fruit, afford a dye of a chocolate-brown color, for woolen goods, which, with that of the Black Walnut, was used in the South to a great extent, during the Civil War, as a dye for soldiers' uniforms.

CALAMUS—Acorus Calamus

Rafinesque wrote in 1828: The warm infusion, like tea, cures the wind cholic (colic) of infants, sailors, etc."

Some years ago this writer was talking with a rustic in the hills of Tennessee. During our conversation, my friend pulled out a good sized root of Calamus from his pocket, and bit off a piece. He said "I always carry this to chaw, whenever I get belly-ache."

Wisconsin and Minnesota Indians soak their nets in an infusion made of Calamus and roots of Sarsaparilla, for catching white fish. It is said the net still smelled of the decoction after being in water for 12 hours.

Calamus is still used today for its refreshing aroma. In powdered form it is used for sachet and toilet powders. The distilled oil is used in perfumery. The candied root was a popular confection in colonial times. In medicine, it is used mainly for flavoring.

CRANESBILL—Geranium maculatum

"It is one of the most powerful astringents we possess."

Its internal use has been recommended in dysentery and cholera infantum, but astringents *are not always* admissible in these complaints, at least in their early stages, during the existence of much active inflammation, or during the presence of any substance requiring to be removed.

It is highly extolled for its styptic power in stopping hemorrhages of wounded vessels. The powdered root in doses of a teaspoonful, thrice or four times a day, or a decoction in milk, used as a common drink, is said to be excellent in checking immoderate menstrual discharges, also the whites, and gleets, and obstinate diarrhoea.

In consequence of the virtue of the geranium having been so often experienced about Woodbury, in cases of hemorrhage, the inhabitants have been induced to cultivate the plant in their gardens, and it would be well if their example were followed by everyone in the country. Providence has diffused the valuable plant over every part of our country, yet as it grows principally in the woods, and the accident it is intended to relieve may admit of no delay—and often happens in winter when the plant cannot be found, it should be transferred to every garden, that it may be at hand when wanted.

FEVER BUSH—Benzoin aestivale

"A decoction of the buds or wood is an excellent febrifuge, and from this valuable property, it receives its name. It is an ancient Indian remedy for all inflammatory complaints, and likewise much esteemed on the same account, by the inhabitants of the interior parts of the colonies."—from Carver's Travels.

FRINGE TREE—Chionanthus virginica

Indians used the bark as an astringent vulnerary, and the bark of the root as a tonic after long and exhaustive diseases. Old botanic physicians considered a decoction of the bark as trustworthy diuretic.

GOLD THREAD—Coptis trifolia

"It is also greatly esteemed both by the Indians, and the Colonists, as a remedy for any soreness in the mouth, but the taste of it is exquisitely bitter." — from Carver's Travels.

LADY'S SLIPPER—Cypripedium pubescens

A striking and strangely beautiful native plant. Used by the Indians wherever they found the plant. Lady Slipper "acts as a sedative to the nerves in general, causing a sense of mental quiet and lassitude, and subduing nervous and mental irritation, having no baneful nor narcotic effects. It seems also to quiet spasms of voluntary muscles, and hysterical attacks, especially in women."

LIFE EVERLASTING — Gnaphalium polycephalum

"The herb, as a masticatory, has always been a popular remedy, on account of its

MEDICINAL PLANTS—continued

astringent properties, in ulcerations of the mouth and fauces, and for quinsy. Hot fomentations of the herb have been used like Arnica, for sprains and bruises, and form a good vulnerary for painful tumors and unhealthy ulcers. The dried flowers are recommended as a quieting filling for the pillows of consumptives."

MAY APPLE—Podophyllum peltatum

"This plant constitutes one of the principal remedies used by the American aborigines, by whom it is especially valued on account of its cathartic action."

PENNYROYAL—Hedeoma pulegioides

A tea extensively used in domestic practice, as an aromatic, stimulant and carminative in colic of children; a diaphoretic in the beginning of colds; and in large doses of a hot infusion, together with the foot bath, in Amenorrhoea. In the latter trouble, if of recent occurrence, it will often bring in the menses nicely—and combined with a gill of brewer's yeast, it frequently acts well as an abortivant, should the intendee be not too late with her prescription. The oil is anti-emetic, anti-spasmodic, and rubefacient in rheumatism. With raw linseed oil, it makes an excellent dressing for recent burns.

PIPSISSEWA—Chimaphila umbellata

Dr. Wolf has reported a number of cases of ischuria and dysoria, arising from various causes, in which the Pipsissewa given in infusion, produced the most evident relief, and took precedence over a variety of remedies which had been tried. His method of administering it was to give a tablespoonful of strong infusion, with a little syrup, every hour. In all the cases he has detailed, small as the dose was, it gave relief in a very short time. In one case its effect was so distinctly marked, that the disease returned whenever the medicine was omitted, and was removed on resuming its use. A tonic operation attended its other effects, so that the appetite was improved and digestion promoted during the period of its employment. It is valuable as a diuretic.

BUTTERFLY WEED or PLEURISY ROOT—Asclepias tuberosa

"This fine vegetable is eminently entitled to the attention of physicians, as an expectorant and diaphoretic. It produces effects of this kind with *great gentleness,* and without the heating tendency which accompanies many vegetable sudorifics. It has long been employed by practitioners in the Southern States, in pulmonary complaints, particularly in catarrh, pneumonia, and pleurisy, and has acquired much confidence for the relief of these maladies."

Indians boiled the thick roots of food. They prepared a crude sugar from the flowers, and ate the young seed pods after boiling them with buffalo meat. Canadian tribes use the young shoots as a pot herb.

PHYSIC ROOT—Leptandra virginica

Millspaugh believed this plant to be "the most graceful and attractive of all American Veronicas." One of the many Indian remedies handed down by them to the botanics, and extensively used in domestic practice, from our earliest settlements. Rafinesque states—"The dried roots are commonly used in warm decoction as a purgative and emetic, acting somewhat like the Eupatorium and Verbena hastata. Some boil it in milk for a milder cathartic, or as a sudorific in pleurisy."

PRICKLY ASH—Xanthoxylum americanum

Its speedy relief of rheumatism is said to occur only when it causes perspiration. For this disease, a pint a day is taken, of a decoction of 1 ounce of the bark boiled in a quart of water. It is a powerful stimulant to healing wounds or indolent ulcerations.

"Many physicians place great reliance on its powers in rheumatic complaints, so that apothecaries generally give it a place in their shops. It is most frequently given in decoction—an ounce being boiled in about a quart of water. Dr. G. Hayward, of Boston, informs me that he formerly took this decoction in his own case of chronic rheumatism, with evident relief. It was prepared as above stated, and about a pint taken in the course of a day, diluted with water sufficient to render it palatable, by lessening the pungency. It was warm and grateful to the stomach, produced no nausea, nor effect upon the bowels, and excited little, if any, perspiration."

"I have given the powdered bark in doses of 10 and 20 grains, in rheumatic affections, with considerable benefit. A sense of heat was produced at the stomach by taking it, but no other obvious effect. In one case, it effectually removed the complaint in a few days. I have known it, however, to fail entirely in obstinate cases, sharing the approbrium of failure with a variety of other remedies."

MEDICINAL PLANTS—continued

POKE WEED—Phytolacca decandra

This American weed has migrated to Europe, where it is rather common in all the countries bordering upon the Mediterranean Sea.

The medical use of Poke-root were handed down to domestic and botanic practice by the aborigines, who valued it as an emetic, and the berries as a palliative of syphilitic and gonorrhoeal rheumatism.

Poke ashes of stalks yield 67 per cent alkaline carbonate, and 42 per cent caustic potash.

RAGWEED—Ambrosia artimisaefolia

Probably the rankest of all native American weeds, its pollen causing hay fever discomforts to countless thousands, during its flourishing period. It is said to be very effective as an application for poison ivy, if fresh leaves of Ragweed are rubbed upon the inflamed parts until discolored by the juice of the leaves.

RED RASPBERRY LEAVES

"The leaves, made into a strong tea is one of the best things known for canker, and may be used with good success in all bowel complaints of children. This made into a tea, sweetened, and a little milk put to it, is a very pleasant drink, and may be used freely, as it is perfectly harmless."

SASSAFRAS—Sassafras variifolium

Rustic "Spring tea" used to "thin" the blood that has been sluggish through long, cold winters, and semi-hibernating habits. The custom is of Indian origin.

An old botanic physician advised "those who wish to break themselves of chewing tobacco, will find the pith of Sassafras an agreeable substitute."

SENEGA or SENECA SNAKE ROOT—Polygala senega

More certain success attends the use of Seneca in pneumonia, and some diseases related to it. In the advanced stages of pneumonic inflammation, after venesection and the other usual remedies have been carried to their proper extent; and the cough still remains dry and painful, while the debility of the patient forbids further depletion—in these cases, I have often found a decoction of the Seneca root to afford very marked relief, by promoting expectoration, and relieving the tightness and oppression of the chest. Various medical writers have spoken favorably of its employment in these cases. It has been found injurious, from its stimulating properties, when given at too early a stage, or during the prevalence of much acute inflammation.

SNAKE-ROOT or SERPENTARIA—Aristolochia serpentaria

Related to Canada Snake-root and Black Snake-weed. Millspaugh wrote "Strange as it may seem, almost all the species are esteemed by the natives of the countries in which they grow, as remedies against the poisonous effects of snake bites—this use being fully known to each nation, without previous communication with each other."

Medicinally, Serpentaria has been classed among the diuretics, warm stimulating tonics, and diaphoretics.

Dr. Chapman states it is admirably suited to check vomitings and to tranquilize the stomach, more particularly in bilious cases. It is given for this purpose in a decoction, in the small dose of half an ounce, or less, at a time, and frequently repeated. The most common form of exhibiting Snake-root is in infusion, for which purpose half an ounce may be steeped in a pint of boiling water for 2 hours in a covered vessel.

SPIKENARD—Aralia racemosa

"These (the berries) are of such a balsamic nature, that when infused in spirits, they make a most palatable and reviving cordial."—Carver's Travels.

SQUAW VINE—Mitchella repens

"One of the many plants used by the American aborigines as a parturient, frequent doses of a decoction being taken during the few weeks just preceding confinement. It has also been found to be a valuable diuretic and astringent, and to have an especial affinity to various forms of uterine difficulties."

STONE ROOT—Collinsonia canadensis

"In the mountains of Virginia, Kentucky, Tennessee and Carolina, the root of this genus is considered as a panacea, and is being used outwardly and inwardly in many disorders. It is applied in poultice and wash, for bruises, sores, blows, falls, wounds, sprains, and contusions, and taken like tea for headaches, colics, cramps, dropsy, indigestion, etc."

Dr. Hooker judges the principle so volatile that all infusions should be made in a tight vessel.

SWEET FERN—Comptonia asplenifolia

The leaves of this small American bush have a delightful piny fragrance. Indians used the leaves in smudge fires, and lined their baskets with them when gathering highly perishable berries. An infusion of dried leaves

MEDICINAL PLANTS—continued

was used for checking diarrhoea. A strong decoction is used as a fomentation in rheumatism and bruises.

Howard wrote in 1854: Sweet Fern leaves make a very grateful, pleasant tea, with the addition of cream and sugar, which children rarely, if ever, refuse.

SWEET SCENTED GOLDEN ROD—Solidago odora

Bigelow wrote in 1818: "Sweet Scented Golden Rod is used in some parts of the United States as an agreeable substitute for tea, and it has for some time, been an article of exportation to China, where it fetches a high price."

TURTLEBLOOM—Chelone glabra

Long a favorite laxative and purgative among the Indians and Thomsonian physicians. A botanic physician wrote in 1836—"This makes an excellent bitter, and for those who are fond of physic, will answer an agreeable purpose."

WATER LILY—Nymphoea odorata

"The roots, in a decoction, were much esteemed by Indian squaws, as an internal remedy, and as an injection or wash for leucorrhoea. Its properties in this direction being due to its great astringency."

Juice of the roots, mingled with that of lemons, is used to remove freckles and pimples from the face.

WHITE ASH—Fraxinus americana

"The leaves of this tree are said to be so highly offensive to the rattle-snake, that reptile is never found on land where it grows—and it is the practice of hunters to stuff their boots with White Ash leaves as a preventative of the bite of a rattle-snake. It was asserted that the Indians used to defend themselves from this snake by carrying White Ash leaves about their persons." How much dependence might be placed in this, is hard to tell.

WILD GINGER—Asarum canadense

Several country practitioners, who have employed it, have spoken to me favorably of its effect as a warm stimulant and diaphoretic. As a substitute for Ginger in common domestic use, I know of no indigenous article which promises so fairly as this.

WITCH HAZEL—Hamamelis virginica

"When this shrub is in bloom, the Indians esteem it a further indication that the frost is entirely gone, and that they might sow their corn. It has been said that it is possessed of the power of attracting gold or silver, and that twigs of it are made use of to discover where the veins of these metals lie hid; but I am apprehensive that this is only a fallacious story."—Carvers "Travels Through the Interior Parts of North America."

Note: a good Spring herald for a race that has no calendars. Some folks still use the forked branch of Witch Hazel in searching for treasures beneath the soil.

WILD YAM—Dioscorea villosa

"Dioscorea has held a place in domestic and general practice for a long period, as almost specific in certain forms of bilious colic."

WINTERGREEN—Gaultheria procumbens

"These (the berries) are preserved during the severe (winter) season by the snow, and are at that time in the highest perfection. The Indians eat these berries, esteeming them very balsamic, and invigorating to the stomach. The people inhabiting the interior colonies steep both the sprigs and berries in beer, and use it as a diet drink for cleansing the blood from scorbutic disorders."—Carver's "Travels Through the Interior Parts of North America in the years 1766, 1767, and 1768.

Another writer states "An infusion of the leaves has been used to communicate an agreeable flavor to tea, also as a substitute for that article, by people in the country."

SLAVE AMULETS OR CHARMS

In his native Africa, the negro believed that certain roots contained wondrous powers over all life. An evil root hidden in the hut of one's enemies was sure to bring misfortune to the hut's occupant. On the other hand, if it was suspected that such an article was hidden in the hut, one could obtain another root to counteract the action of the hidden item, by carrying it on a string around the neck, or elsewhere on person. When bad luck persisted, it was a sign that the amulet did not contain sufficient power of counteraction. In this case, a still more powerful root was sought.

Generations after the negroes were hauled away to the New World as slaves, their ancient African beliefs still continued. The slaves found strange new plants with power analogous to African plants.

A very old apothecary record mentions a brisk sale of Blood root among slaves. The roots were believed to have power to avert spells wrought by other unfriendly negroes, and to exert, also, a propitiatory or fascinating influence upon the opposite sex. The color of the Blood roots was considered very important. Salmon colored roots were considered "queen's roots" or "she" roots. The dark red roots were considered "king's roots" or "he" roots.

"Old-man-in-the-ground"—"Solomon's Seal" and "Sweet Fern" were also used to chase away evil spells.

THE FOLKLORE OF GINSENG—FABULOUS CHINESE MEDICINE

The first treatise on medicinal plants in the Orient, was compiled some 5,000 years ago by Emperor Shen-nung, popularly known as the Father of agriculture and medicine. Shen-nung placed Ginseng at the head of all herbal remedies, holding that it is "a tonic to the five viscera, quieting the animal spirits, strengthening the soul, allaying fear, expelling evil effluvia, brightening the eyes, opening up the heart, benefiting the understanding, and if taken for some time, it will invigorate the body and prolong life."

To-day—50 centuries later—Ginseng is still highly regarded as a "panacea" in China. A modern Chinese writer avows that it is "most energy giving, distinguished by the slowness and gentleness of its action."

Those who could afford Ginseng, took the root 3 or 4 times a day, as a health measure. Chewing the root or taking the tea was a "must" before and after strenuous work, or indulgences. Opium smokers used the tea for "hangovers." It was indeed a very poor chinaman who could not afford a bit of the root for his "day of departure." A cup of tea, given on his deathbed, was believed to be effective in holding off the "grim reaper" long enough to enable the person to settle his earthly affairs and bid friends and loved ones farewell.

The high esteem the Chinese held for Ginseng was conveyed to Europe, then to America in the early part of the 18th century by Father Jartoux, a missionary to China. Father Jartoux witnessed the collection and the use of Ginseng. He made a drawing of the plant, accompanied by a description, and recorded its uses. An early American account gives us an excellent description of Father Jartoux's experiences, and the discovery of a Ginseng species in the New World. We quote in part —"While on a journey among the mountains of Tartary, Father Jartoux met in various instances with the plant, and with the people employed in collecting it. He states that the root is found principally in thick forests, upon the declivities of mountains, in the banks of torrents, and about the roots of trees. It never grows in the open plains or valleys—but always in dark shady situations, remote from the sun's rays."

The Chinese consider Ginseng as possessing unequalled medicinal powers, and their physicians have written many volumes upon the qualities of the plant. It is made an ingredient in almost all the remedies which they give to their nobility—its price being too high for the common people. The sick take it to recover health, and the healthy to make themselves stronger and more vigorous. They affirm that it removes all fatigue, either of body or mind, dissolves humours, cures pul-

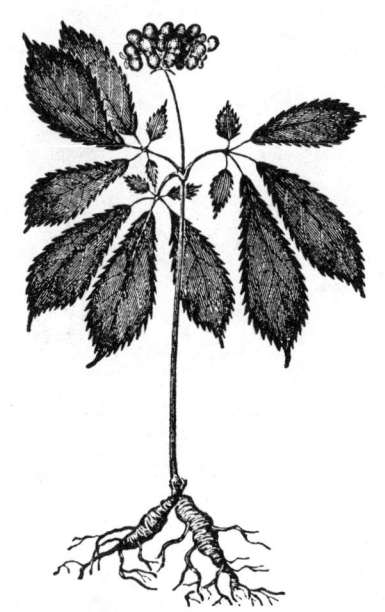

monary diseases, strengthens the stomach, increases the vital spirits, and prolongs life to old age.

Father Jartoux became so much of a convert to the virtues of the plant, that he tells us that after having taken half of a root, he found his pulse quicker and fuller, his appetite improved, and his strength increased so as to bear labour better than before. On another occasion, finding himself so fatigued and wearied as to be unable to sit on horseback, a mandarin in his company, perceiving his distress, gave him one of the roots. He took half of it, and within an hour was not sensible of any weariness.

"The Chinese use a decoction of the root, for which they employ about a fifth part of an ounce at a time. This they boil in a covered vessel with two successive portions of water, in order to extract all its virtues."

"The report of the high value of Ginseng at Pekin led to an inquiry among Europeans, as to whether the plant was not to be found in parallel latitudes, in the forests of North America. Father Lafiteau, a Jesuit missionary among the Indians, after much search, found a plant in Canada answering the description, and sent it to France. In 1718 M. Sarrasin published in the Memoirs of the Academy, an account of the American Ginseng; which, together with one published by Lafiteau the same year, seemed to put its identity with the Chinese vegetable, beyond a doubt.

Soon after this the French commenced the collection of the root in Canada, for exportation. For this purpose they employed the Indians, who brought it to the merchants for

FABULOUS CHINESE MEDICINE—continued

certain compensation. At one period, the Indians about Quebec and Montreal were so wholly taken up in the search for Ginseng, that their services could not be engaged for any other purpose. The American English engaged in the same traffic, and although the plant is a rare one in the woods, very large quantities of the root were collected. The shipments to China proved extremely profitable.

Ginseng became a big business. George Washington noted in 1784—"In passing over the mountains, I met numbers of persons and pack horses going in with Ginseng." Daniel Boone gathered the root in Kentucky, and took it up the Ohio river to ship to Philadelphia.

The export of Ginseng did much to save infant United States from economic collapse after the Revolutionary War. American shipowners took great quantities to China, and came back loaded with spices, tea and silks. Ginseng was common in the Alleghany mountain ranges and the midwest. An 1836 Herbal states—"This root abounds in great plenty throughout the woods and fields of Vermont." Gunn wrote in 1834—"It is found in great plenty among the hills and mountains of Tennessee, and brought in to Knoxville daily, for sale." Another old record mentions that "Ginseng laid the foundation of many a splendid fortune in New England."

The Chinese demand for Ginseng attracted the attention of practitioners, but the sweetish flavored roots had already earned a reputation among early pioneers, who chewed the root like licorice for appetite, and as a substitute for tobacco. Isolated mountain folk brewed the young roots as a health tonic for the young and aged.

One of the earliest native accounts is given by Samuel Henry, in his "American Medical Family Herbal." Henry advises—"Take one pound of the fresh roots, cut small, put them in a gallon of old Jamaica spirits, and let it stand in the sun for 2 weeks—every now and then shaking the vessel. In all weaknesses from excess in venery, pain in the bones from colds, and gravelly complaints, let the patient take a wineglass of this tincture 3 times a day, on an empty stomach. I knew a man in New Jersey, who was so debilitated and afflicted with pains in his bones, that he expected nothing but death every day, who by taking the Ginseng in rum, was able to follow his business on the farm, and his pains were entirely removed in a few days."

An old Kentucky recipe relates—"Ginseng gives all its strength and virtues by being steeped in whiskey."

Gunn's Family Physician, a very popular medical guide of pioneers states—"It is useful in nervous debility, weak digestion and feeble appetite, and as a stomachic and restorative. It is considered a very valuable medicine for children—and has been recommended in asthma, palsy, and nervous affections generally. Dose: Of the powdered root, from 1 to 2 teaspoonfuls in a little hot water, sweetened; of decoction—from a fourth to a half teacupful 2 or 3 times a day.

A Materia Medica book of a later period regards Ginseng as "a mild sedative and tonic to the nerve centers, improving their tone, if persisted in, and increasing the capillary circulation of the brain. It is given in cerebral anaemia, and if combined with other tonics, is capable of doing some good. It is also prescribed in the failure of digestion, incident to nervous prostration, and general nerve irritation."

American medical authorities regard Ginseng merely as a mild stomachic and demulcent.

A former United States Consul at Seoul, Korea, mentions the following in an official report: "From personal experience and observation, I am assured that Korean Ginseng is an active, strongly-heating medicine. Western people appear to regard the virtues of Ginseng claimed by Orientals rather contemptuously — as imaginary and based on superstition. The evidence are that the mystic value attached itself to Ginseng after its virtues had been practically ascertained." (U.S. Consular reports, No. 65).

Volumes have been written by the most eminent physicians of China on the virtues of Ginseng. Over 400,000,000 people have been using it for centuries. As a race these people are our equals in native intelligence, and by far our superiors in natural art.

Taking all into consideration, it may be well to suspend judgment regarding the medical qualities of their panacea.

About 20 years ago there were many reports of Russians making extensive research with Ginseng. The results of this research was never made public. In the early part of the Korean war, a report states "Russians grab entire Korean supply of Ginseng, valued at $120,000,000."

To-day, shipments of Ginseng are much smaller that they were 200 years ago, but still practically all the root, grown or gathered in the wild state is shipped to the Orient. The market has fluctuated since the days of Lafiteau, but Ginseng is still the most expensive botanical in the entire vegetable kingdom. It is strange that a botanical so highly prized by the oldest civilization on earth, should be so little regarded by the western world. Researches have been made—but it is doubtful as to whether they were made under the latest and more improved methods.

WONDERS OF THE PLANT WORLD
African Tree Mammoth

The Baobab tree (Adansonia digitata) is believed to be the giant as well as the oldest living member of the plant world These trees are found over a wide range in Africa. Records reveal specimens growing more than 30 feet in diameter and 95 feet in circumference; the horizontally outstretched branches were so large that natives could sleep upon them comfortably.

The Baobab are generally hollow. Dr. Livingstone mentioned one in which 20 to 30 men could lie down and sleep as in a hut.

From the depth of the incrustations formed on the bark which the Portuguese navigators of the 15th century used to cut in the large Baobabs which they found growing on the African coast and by comparing the relative dimensions of several trunks of known age. Adamson concluded that a Baobab of 30 feet in diameter must have lived at least 5,000 years!

In the Egyptian Sudan area, natives depend entirely upon the Baobab for their water supply, which is found in the hollow trunk of the tree. It is stored by nature during the rainy seasons. The capacity of the tree usually is about 250 gallons of water. Villages are only found where the Baobab grow. Natives have a name for each of their trees, "Mother of Honey," "Mother of Gloves," "The House of Birds,' "The Spreading" are typical titles for these tree-wells.

The Boabab belongs to the same family as the mallow or the hollyhocks, and is also emollient and mucilaginous in all its parts. The dried and powdered leaves constitute the lalo, which Africans mix with their food. The fiber contained in pounded bark is used in making baskets and strong cord. The fruit of Baobab hang on long stalks and resemble yellow cucumbers. They contain a white farinaceous substance of an agreeable acidulated taste. This is a favorite food of monkeys. For this reason the tree is sometimes referred to as Monkey-bread. The expressed juice of the fruit, when mixed with sugar, forms a cooling drink used in putrid fevers; this juice is also used as a seasoning for corn-gruel and other food.

Colossal Herb

Gunnera insignis is the Latin name for this shy giant that seems to prefer to live on inaccessible sides of mountains of Guatemala and Panama. The huge leaves measure from 4 to 5 feet across and resemble our common pot geranium. One leaf is capable of serving several people as an umbrella. Gunnera bears a large stalk covered with thousands of small brownish, wind-pollinated flowers. A similar species of Gunnera is found in the mountains of Hawaii.

Water Lily Bears Largest Leaves in World

In the year 1801, botanist Haenke was sent to investigate the flora of Bolivia. In a marsh off a tributary of the Amazon River he came upon gigantic water lilies. The size of the leaves so astounded the botanist that he fell on his knees in admiration. The plant was later named Victoria regia in honor of Queen Victoria. The circular leaves measure up to seven feet across with upturned edges. The leaves are strengthened by a marvelous framework of veins which are capable of sustaining weight up to 150 pounds!

The huge flowers of Victoria regia are nocturnal. It is a marvelous sight to watch them open in early evening. What is practically a bud with only a little white gleaming between the spaces of the calyx, is an hour later a creamy-white, wide open, strongly scented flower. About noon the next day the flower closes and then opens again 3 or 4 hours before dark, the color then being decidedly pink. By next morning the flower has faded and begins to sink below the surface of the water.

Bushes and Trees on Stilts

The Mangrove (Rhizophora) is a bush or small tree growing on stilt-like roots in the salty waters of tropical oceans. Its almost impenetrable growth forms living breakers that resist the most violent hurricanes and high seas. Many varieties of shells cling to Mangrove roots. Early writers called Mangrove the Oyster Plant; they believed the shells were part of the plant because they clasped the roots so firmly. The leaves of Mangrove are evergreen. The seeds begin to germinate and send out roots while they are yet attached to the parent branches. The fruit-bearing new root falls into water and floats in such a manner that new growth can take hold when it touches muddy bottom. Low tide reveals dense growths of short, upright "sticks" beneath the Mangroves; these root growths are said to supply the plant with oxygen.

The bark of Mangrove is a rich and limitless source of tannin.

Sargassum Weed

Sargassum weed itself is of little interest—pieces are often tossed up along our Atlantic shores. The sea weed is famed for its formation of the Sargasso Sea, a great floating mass lying in the Atlantic Ocean, several hundred miles southeast of Bermuda. This sea of weeds is estimated to be 1100 miles long and approximately 400 miles wide. Ocean currents have held the mass in the same location and general form for ages.

Sargassum also played a part in shaping the history of America. Fantastic tales were circulated throughout Europe how vessels were mired in Sargasso Sea. Early Spanish navigators avoided the treacherous sea by sailing more southward. In this way their endeavors led more to South America.

Sargassum weed has brown stems and finely divided branchlets bearing slender pointed leaves varying from olive-yellow to delicate green. The plant is kept afloat by many air-filled, pea-size berries which it bears.

The Sargasso sea is inhabited by giant squid, luminescent fish, shrimp, crabs, mollusks, sea spiders, etc. It is a favorite feeding grounds for strange monsters from the deep.

Luminous Moss

For many years botanists heard of a luminous moss growing in parts of New Hampshire but the information was generally vague and people who investigated found no evidence of such plants. Evidently the moss escaped detection because of its tiny growth and the luminosity becomes apparent only at certain times. It was finally tracked down so reliable data could be given about it. The luminous moss is known botanically as Schistostega pennata. It was described as being like dazzling green-gold carpeting, flashing one minute, then, as quickly, dim into invisibility. The writer considered it the most beautiful thing of the sort in all nature.

Luminous moss is about ½ inch high at full growth and is found in dark, damp caves or earth cellar floors in the vicinity of Lost River Gorge, Franconia and Dixville Notches, New Hampshire.

Moving Leaves

The Telegraph Plant (Desmodium gyrans) is a slender shrub native of India. It attains a height of 2 to 3 feet, having trifoliate leaves, the center one being elliptical and about 2 inches long, the 2 side ones being small, about ½ inch in length, which are in almost constant motion, rising and falling alternately, but not in regular time, sometimes resting. They are most active in early morning, and in large plants many may be seen moving at the same time; their rise and fall are compared to the railway telegraph signals. Plants are grown as a novelty.

Tree with Many Trunks

The Banyan (Ficus bengalensis) tree is native of India. An old tree covers such a wide area that it resembles a forest rather than a single tree.

The Banyan drops its aerial roots from branches like ropes when still quite young. These roots soon take firm hold in the ground, thicken and become like pillars with age. This process continues until an incredible area is covered. One old tree in India is said to be capable of sheltering 7,000 men.

The Hindus are peculiarly fond of the Banyan tree. They consider its long duration, its outstretching arms and overshadowing beneficence, as emblems of the Deity; they plant it near their temples, and in those villages where there is no structure for public worship, they place an image under a Banyan, and there perform a morning and evening sacrifice.

The Banyan is much cultivated in Miami, Florida area as a shade tree.

The Sensitive Plant
(Mimosa pudica)

A rather ordinary looking little plant with striking sensitive habits. Its neat rows of leaflets fold up instantly upon the slightest contact, and the stalks move downward as though they were trying to withdraw from contact with the object. Most plants have power to move their leaves with light, weather, etc., but no plant in the world has such instantaneous power of movement as Sensitive Plant (also called Humble Plant.) Some botanical writers also credit the plant with being able to "produce a whisper-like noise." Sensitive plant bears small round pink flowers. Grown in pots as a novelty.

The Strangler Fig

The seeds of this plant murderer are distributed by birds. The Strangler begins as an air plant lodged on a tree or palm and sends down twining roots around the trunk of the host tree as it develops. After the roots reach soil, the Strangler grows prodigiously. The twining roots become great octopus-like arms which tighten their embrace so firmly that death of the victim is inevitable. As the host decays in the arms of the Strangler more and more growth is added

WONDERS OF THE PLANT WORLD—cont.

until all is fused into a solid trunk, leaving little trace of the victim. Strangler Figs are occasionally seen in hammocks of southern Florida.

Insect Eating Plants

Most plants must stand helplessly by while they are being devoured by insects. Nature has, however, reversed this feeding arrangement by giving many plants the power to eat insects. The insect-eating or carnivorous plants grow over a wide range in the plant world and use several methods for trapping their live food.

The most ingenious of all carnivorous plants is the Venus Flytrap. It is a small plant with roundish leaves capable of opening and closing like a clam. The outer edges of this trap are lined with tentacles. Insects are induced to enter into the gaping "mouth" by a sweet substance exuded by the leaf. After the prey enters the sensitive leaf closes immediately upon its victim. The tentacles seal all escape and appear to apply pressure to squeeze the life and juice from the insect. When it is thoroughly digested, the tentacles release their grip and leaves open up again disgorging the dried shell of the victim and is ready for its next.

The Trumpets and Pitcher Plants are the more common types of carnivorous plants. Pitcher Plants have round pitcher shaped leaves and Trumpet plants have long tubular leaves. Both vegetable containers are attached to the main plant at the base of their leaves. The Leaves of these plants are lined inside with hair-like glands that serve a twofold purpose—they provide digestive fluids and their downward direction prevent victim from escaping the death vessel. Insects are attracted inside the leaves by a vile odor resembling decayed meat. The victims drown in the water contained in the bottom of the leaves and are dissolved and absorbed by the plant. The leaves of Pitchers or Trumpets torn open often reveal a startling number of wings and other indigestible insect remains.

RESURRECTION PLANT or ROSE OF JERICHO

This marvelous plant lives in the deserts of Palestine, Syria, Mexico, etc. The "plant" is actually a seed with small branches folded up into a ball. When ripened it is dropped off by the mother plant, then rolled about by desert winds until rainy season. When placed in a saucer or dish of water, the seemingly lifeless ball quickly opens out its beautiful rosette of fern-like leaves.

NATURE PULLS TEETH

The adventurer or nature lover, traveling in Cuba, never has to look up a dentist in order to have a tooth extracted, unless he is one of those thoroughly modern chaps who detest natural methods. Nature has provided a way that saves dentist bills and pain, too. The only requirement is that the tooth must have a hole in it. Into this hole there is packed some sawdust of the Guayacan, or Guaiacum tree. In the course of a day or two the tooth may be very easily extracted with no other aid than the fingers and completely without pain.

Note: Interesting if true.

HERBAL LORE

In heathen mythology Quince was devoted to the goddess Venus, as being the emblem of love, happiness, and faithfulness, and has been supposed to be the golden fruit of the fancied garden of Hesperides, defended by the dragon.

In the West Indies, negroes plant a vine known as "Overlook" (Bean family) along boundries of their plantation in belief that the plant acts as a watchman, and protects their property from plunder.

An old legend held that Archangelica (Angelica) was revealed in a dream by an angel, to cure the plague—also that it blooms on the day of Michael the Archangel (May 8th, old style) and is therefore a preservative against evil spirits and witchcraft.

An ancient Old World belief held that any article was protected from robbers if a few Caraway seeds were sprinkled on it.

Old writers claim that Hounds Tongue leaves placed in the shoe will keep dogs from barking at you. It is said the plant derived its name from its power in tying the tongues of hounds.

Culpepper wrote that if the leaves of Periwinkle are eaten by man and wife together, it causes love between them.

Fennel was used with St Johnswort and other herbs, in mediaeval times, as a preventative of witchcraft and other evil influences —being hung over doors on Midsummer's Eve.

In the Middle Ages Flax Flowers were believed to be a protection against sorcery.

The Bohemians have a belief that if seven year old children dance among Flax, they will become beautiful, and the whole plant was supposed to be under the protection of the Goddess Hulda, who, in Teuton mythology, was held to have first taught mortals the art of growing Flax, of spinning and of weaving it.

In the Middle Ages Paeony seeds were strung as a necklace, and worn as a charm against evil spirits.

GARDEN SAGE

*Longevity Herb of the Middle Ages
Flavoring Herb of Modern Times*

This herb with a strong fragrance and warm taste, derived its botanical name from an old latin word meaning "to be saved." The plant was highly regarded as medicine since very ancient times, but was particularly popular during Middle Ages as medicine for long and healthful life. The following sayings are typical of Old European regard for Sage:

He that would live for aye must eat Sage in May.

Why should a man die whilst Sage grows in his garden?

Sage the Savior.

Sage helps the nerves and by its powerful might, Palsy is cured and fever put to flight.

Sage is singularly good for the head and brain, it quickeneth the senses and memory, strengtheneth the sinews, restoreth health to those that have the palsy, and taketh away shakey trembling of the members.

Garden Sage

With the passing of centuries, the use of Sage spread throughout the world. Time however, has given the herb a different sort of popularity. People of modern times have acquired a particular liking for the flavor of Sage with foods. It is used to impart its healthy aroma and flavor to tomato dishes, poultry stuffing, soups, butter, cheese, sausage and fatty meats, such as pork, duck and goose. The pungency of Sage enables the stomach to digest fat meats more easily.

Because of the strong flavor of this herb it must be used very sparingly with foods. A pinch of herb will go a long way. Fine flavors can only be obtained from seasonal fresh herbs.

Many of the old time medicinal properties of Sage have been disproved or forgotten. Peasants along the northern shores of the Mediterranean sea still eat the herb as a preservative of healthful long life. Folks who prefer the mild action of herbal medicines use Sage as a stimulant tonic in debility of digestion generally. An early copy of American Dispensatory states that "infusions of the leaves with the addition of a little lemon juice, prove an useful diluting drink in febrile disorders."

The French drink freely of tea made from Sage, which they call "Grecian tea." The Chinese were also fond of Sage tea. They obtained it from the Dutch merchants who traded them one pound of Sage, for three pounds of Chinese tea.

A certain English doctor attributed his vigorous old age to drinking Sage tea. This doctor carried his supply of Sage along whenever he went traveling.

Sage tea is prepared in different ways to suit different tastes. The following is a simple method of preparing the tea. About ½ to 1 teaspoonful of dried Sage leaves steeped in a cup of boiling water, the saucer being placed over the cup so that none of the volatile oil escapes. Strain off leaves when the desired strength tea is obtained. Milk, sugar, lemon, or lime may be added. Sweeten with honey, or maple syrup if desired. Do not steep herb teas with metal strainer or metal container.

SAGE GARGLE FOR SORE THROAT DUE TO COUGHS

To ½ pint of very strong Sage tea add 1 level teaspoonful powdered Cayenne, and 2 tablespoonfuls each, of the following: strained honey; common salt; and pure cider vinegar. Mix and bottle for use. Gargle as often as necessary, keeping in affected parts as long as possible. Another old recipe advises a little vinegar, honey, alum, and borax with strong Sage tea. The gargle may be further improved with an addition of a small amount of Golden Seal root and Sumach berries or bark.

A warm tea of Sage, drunk freely, is an excellent remedy for colds, and coughs. It checks perspiration, and is a cooling drink in fevers.

The following old-fashioned recipe, is intended to protect and keep medicinal properties of Sage in the throat as long as possible: Simmer a handful of Sage in enough hog's lard to cover herb. When most of properties of herb are extracted, strain off, and repeat process with a fresh batch of sage. Strain off herb. When sufficiently cool, give in teaspoonful doses, three or four times a day. This old recipe advises also, that this be rubbed on the neck, with a small amount of Sassafras oil.

SLEEPLESSNESS

Use a pillow of Hops instead of feathers. It often induces sound, refreshing sleep. Herbal medicine: An ounce each of Hops and Skullcap. Pour a pint of boiling water, cover closely and let it steep until cold. Strain. Dose: Half a small teacupful about an hour before each meal. These methods are harmless.

FIRST COLD OF THE WINTER?

Don't fight it down. Have a hot bath and quick rub down, retire to a warmed bed, no food except hot Boneset tea, rest for at least twenty-four hours. Your body will get over it quickly, and will tend to be immunized against another cold for months.

LICORICE
Man's Oldest Medicinal

Ancient Chinese divided their drugs into three classes, according to their reputed properties. Licorice was listed amongst drugs of first class because "They preserve the life of man, and therefore resemble Heaven. They are not poisonous. No matter how much you take, and how often you use them, they are not harmful. If you wish to make the body supple, improve the breath, become old in years without aging in body, then make use of drugs of this class."

Licorice is one of the principal drugs of the "Susruta," a record that is said to have been revealed to Susruta by Brahma himself, who composed this book before the creation of man. Like the Chinese, the Hindus considered Licorice a general tonic, beautifying agent, and elixir of life.

When the 3000-year-old tomb of King Tut-Ankh-Amen of Egypt was opened, archeologists found quantities of Licorice stored with fabulous jewelry and magnificent art works.

Hippocrates mentioned uses of Licorice in 400 B.C. Theophrastus, "Father of Greek Botany," described Licorice in 200 B.C. as "useful against asthma or dry cough, and in general troubles of the chest, and is also administered in honey for wounds. It has the property of quenching thirst, if one holds it in the mouth; wherefore they say that the Scythians, with this and mares'-milk cheese, can go for eleven or twelve days without drinking."

Pliny wrote 1900 years ago: "The juice of Liquirice reduced to a thicke consistence, if it be put under the tongue, is singular for to cleare the voice. In like manner, it is supposed very wholesome for the breast and liver. And therewith, both thirst and hunger may be slaked and allaied. Which is the cause that some have called it Adipson; and in that regard ministered it to those persons who be fallen into a dropsie for to prevent and take away their thirstinesse."

Licorice is mentioned in practically all botanical records of mankind. Its use has survived after many a civilization grew—developed to great powers—declined and finally disappeared into the rubble and dust of the ages. Its use has spread throughout the world almost as rapidly as man explored, conquered and moved into new territories.

Today the root is used in huge quantities the world over, as a medicinal as well as a flavoring agent for beverages, foods, tobaccos, etc.

In the first World War, the French provided their troops with a beverage made of Licorice root. For generations peoples of Southern Europe and the Mediterranean regions have used Licorice beverage as a tonic and "blood purifier." The decoction is used instead of plain water in many European industries, especially in iron and steel mills, where workers must endure considerable heat.

Keith wrote in "Fads of an Old Physician," "Licorice is a useful remedy for relieving the symptoms caused by acrid matters in the stomach. I know nothing to equal it, and I have used it for this purpose for at least 40 years. It does not, like the alkalies, convert acids into more or less inert salts, but it seems to remove their irritating effects in some other way and the result in relieving the irritation of the nerves of the stomach is much the same. Many object to the use of alkalies, especially of soda if used frequently and in large quantities as it often is, as injuring the coats of the stomach and thus doing permanent mischief. But this evil does not attend the use of Licorice. It, in some way of its own—for it is neither from mere dilution nor from neutralizing the acid, removes the irritable quality of the acid or acrid mass and adds nothing deleterious to the contents of the stomach. It certainly relieves, often in a very remarkable way, the innumerable pains and discomforts, which arise from irritations of the gastric nerves. I have known relief from Licorice in a very large number of cases, both of dyspepsia and sleeplessness.

"Licorice may, of course, be abused if taken to enable one to consume with less immediate discomfort too much or improper food, but of itself it seems to have no evil qualities whatever. To most people it is pleasant to take and I have sometimes given it in considerable quantity.

"Many years ago when visiting in East Lothian, a Doctor told me he had found Licorice very useful in a way I had not known. Many farm servants, who smoked strong tobacco, could not look at breakfast until they had a smoke. This was always relieved by taking a bit of Licorice on getting up. He had got great credit from their wives for this prescription, so I concluded that the men's temper had also suffered. This is the only doctor I have met who knew the value of Licorice.

LICORICE—continued

"I have heard recently of many who have gotten much benefit from Licorice. Messrs. Hillaby, large manufacturers of Pontefract cakes, etc., wrote me that their work women, when pregnant, took it in large quantities as it kept off sickness. I have long used it in the same cases."

Licorice root is soothing in coughs, hoarseness, bronchial irritations and asthma—affording relief by lubricating the throat, and loosening tough phlegm. The demulcent properties are also found useful in stomach complaints, arising from a deficiency of the natural mucus which normally defends the stomach against acrimony of foods and fluids secreted in it.

Licorice is soothing to irritated kidneys or urinary passages. Phillips' "Kitchen Garden," written in 1831, states—"Licorice cureth the sharpnesse and smarting of the urine, and also the filthy corruption and mattering of the same, being boiled in water and drunk often." The same author advises for heartburn, "Chew Licorice and swallow down the juice and spit out the rest." For stuffy nose, "Seethe Anise seeds and Licorice in water to the one halfe and streine it and drink it at evening hot and at morning cold."

Licorice is often combined with laxatives for the young and aged. It is used to give flavor and modify actions of many medicines. It is used to cover the flavor of bitter, acrid and nauseous drugs, such as quinine, chloride of ammonia, sulphate of magnesia, senna, hyoscyamus, ipecacuanha, aloes, squills, blood root, senega, etc. Licorice is often combined with mucilaginous substances, such as marshmallow, acacia, tragacanth, sesamum, slippery elm, flaxseed, comfrey, etc., for medicines used in affections of mucous membranes, especially of the respiratory organs.

The flavor of Licorice is generally liked by all children. Probably no other flavor from the vast laboratories of the world's plant kingdom is more universally liked, than the smooth, mellow flavor of Licorice.

Remarkable Properties of Licorice

"Licorice sugar will not crystallize nor ferment, even when yeast is added."—Chemistry of Common Life.

The root of Licorice yields a substance known as glycrrhizin, which is fifty times as sweet as cane sugar.

Although sweeter than sugar, Licorice has the remarkable power to quench thirst, where practically all other sweets increase thirst. For this reason, early practitioners prescribed Licorice in dropsies.

Female Hormone Found in Licorice

Discovery of a female sex hormone in the Licorice root was reported in 1951 by two research scientists of a noted College of Pharmacy. Estrogen, the hormone discovered in Licorice root, is one of the female sex hormones used in the treatment of menopause. —News Item.

Note: In a recent trip to Dominican Republic, this writer found Licorice under the name of Pimande being offered in the native markets. My informant advised steeping pieces of the root in rum for a long period before using. This use appears common where the Spanish have settled.

Good Old Fashioned Cough Syrup with Licorice

Take 1 oz. Boneset, 1 oz. Slippery Elm, 1 oz. stick Licorice, and 1 oz. Flaxseed. Simmer together in 1 quart water until the strength is entirely extracted. Strain carefully, and add 1 pint best molasses and ½ lb. loaf sugar. Simmer them all well together, and when cold bottle tight. Try this for common croup, bronchitis and other simple affections of the lungs and throat. The mixture is soothing and contains no harmful ingredients.

Instead of tea or coffee, drink Alfalfa tea—it is a rich source for vitamins. Add Peppermint leaves to Alfalfa tea to improve taste.

SLIPPERY ELM USED BY INDIAN WOMEN

"A lady told me that an old Indian doctor said "Our women use Slippery Elm bark freely, and they have easy childbirth." That this has proved to be beneficial to expectant mothers has been attested to by others who have tried it."—From an old News Item.

TO INVITE RESTFUL SLEEP

Just before retiring drink a tea made in the following manner: To 1 cup of boiling water stir in a teaspoonful of chamomile flowers and cover the cup with a saucer. Allow to stand until cooled enough to drink. May be sweetened if desired.

The tea is also soothing in nervous conditions.

Chamomile tea with a pinch of ground ginger is beneficial for loss of appetite or distaste for food.

May be given freely to children in teaspoonful doses.

"With health, everything is a source of pleasure; without it, nothing else, whatever it may be, is enjoyable. It follows that the greatest of follies is to sacrifice health for any other kind of happiness, whatever it may be—for gain, advancement, learning or fame, let alone, then, for fleeting sensual pleasures." —Schopenhauer.

GARLIC

Early in the last century an infectious fever epidemic broke out in the poor quarter of Old London. Garlic-eating French priests went about visiting patients with impunity. The English in general did not eat garlic—when their clergy visited patients they in turn fell victims of the disease.

The odor of Garlic is so penetrating and diffusible, that even external aplication of it to the soles of the feet or any other part of the body will cause the lungs to exhale its odor, and the taste may be perceived in the mouth. It may also be detected in the flesh, and even in the eggs of fowls, geese, etc., that have eaten it.

Garlic possesses mild antiseptic and bactericidal properties. The fumes alone, of freshly crushed garlic, have the power to kill certain disease-producing germs.

Garlic was used in great quantities as an antiseptic in World War I. The raw juice was expressed, diluted with water and put on swabs of sterilized Sphagnum moss, which were applied to the wound. Where this treatment was given, it proved that there were no septic results, and the lives of thousands of men were saved by its use.

Medicinally, Garlic is used as a diaphoretic, stimulant, diuretic and expectorant. It is still used in many old-fashioned home recipes.

The bruised Garlic bulb mixed with olive oil or lard has been applied externally to scrofulous tumors, gout, burns, etc. It has proved helpful for children affected with whooping cough if rubbed on the chest and between the shoulder blades.

For children's coughs due to colds: Take 1 oz. of the expressed juice of Garlic to 1½ ounces of lump sugar. Give teaspoonful four or five times daily.

For bronchitis or croup: Bruise bulbs and apply warm as a poultice. Garlic syrup may be taken in teaspoonful doses every half hour for a few doses in croup and 5 teaspoonfuls daily in bronchitis.

Asthmatic cough: Take 2 good handfuls of Coltsfoot leaves, 1 oz. of garlic and 2 quarts of water, boil down to 3 pints, strain and add 8 ounces of sugar to the liquid, boil gently for 10 minutes. Take a half cupful occasionally. Another old recipe: Take a number af garlic cloves and boil until they are soft, then dry them well. Put an equal quantity of good vinegar to the water in which garlic cloves were boiled, add sugar and boil into a syrup. Pour syrup over dried bulbs and place in covered jar for use. Take a bulb or two in morning, fasting, with a little of the syrup.

Garlic applied to the feet at night is good to help remove feverish symptoms. It is said when it is applied to the feet of children it quiets and promotes sleep.

Old household medicine guides recommend garlic for nervous stomach, nervous vomiting, nervous cough and nervous children.

Modifying Garlic Flavor

Old Medical Herbals advise using ground Caraway seeds with Garlic to modify its strong scent and taste. Caraway blends very well with Garlic.

The late Dr. Martin discovered through extensive experiments that apple eaten with Garlic effectively deodorized Garlic without destroying its medicinal effects. The doctor also found Garlic taken internally was often very effective for chronic sores and many cases of rheumatism responsive to it.

Garlic Ointment for External Use

Place bruised garlic and clarified lard in a jar, allow to stand in pan of boiling water until cold. Do not strain. Keep jar covered.

Garlic Syrup

Place bruised Garlic in crock (NO metal container). Pour over enough heated sugar-water syrup to cover garlic. Use liquid as desired—do not strain.

HERB TONICS

Thyme tea helps breathing, and clears phlegm. Mint tea is a good stomach tonic. Parsley and celery tea do much for the kidneys. Sage is helpful to the liver. Simply pour a cupful of boiling water over a teaspoonful of the dried herb, allow to infuse a few minutes and then drink.

Try Rubbing Garlic on That Baldhead

Men who are worried about falling hair should cut down on their before dinner Martinis, rub a little garlic on their noggins and exercise regularly according to a scalp specialist.

Heavy drinking and dietary excesses of almostly any kind are apt to cause a person to lose his hair.

Baldness may also be caused by illness, eyestrain, worry, overwork, and hypertension. Hats do not affect the hair growth unless they are very tight.

In most cases, a man's hair line begins to recede because of lack of stimulation at the roots of the hair. To avoid this the scalp should be vigorously massaged every day. The use of certain stimulants will help, too. One of the best known is Garlic. It can be purchased in processed form completely deodorized.—News Item.

You can make Tasty Meals out of cheap cuts of meat by using Culinary Herbs.

A PRESCRIPTION WITH 5000 YEARS OF HISTORY

"Those Universal Remedies," writes Nicholas Culpeper, omniscient herbalist of the seventeenth century, "Aurum Potable and the Philosopher's Stone cure all Diseases . . ." The superstition of an elixir of life died hardly. This precious fluid that would renew the vital tissues was the sort of thing people have always wanted so badly to believe. The wish was father to the thought.

Yet there are other and older traditions in the history of medicine that have cropped up pretty regularly in successive chapters of history. There is truth at the bottom of every well and these persistent traditions are not to be confounded with superstition. One of the more notable of them concerns the properties of garlic.

With quite astonishing consistency the virtues of that homely herb have resounded through the annals of the ages. They were known to the Egyptians 5,500 years ago. They are mentioned in the Hindoo writings of 3,000 years ago; in a Sanscrit treatise of 2,500 years ago; in a medieval treatise of Salerno 800 years ago; in a notable medical work published in London 300 years ago; in the report of a series of scientific experiments carried out by doctors in New York 30 years ago; and in the record of investigations by medical men in France some five years later. It takes a pretty hardened skeptic to ignore testimony so faithfully documented as that. There can be no suspicion of collusion between experimentalists distributed over a period of fifty centuries!

Curiously enough, the sum total of what all these practitioners of East and West have testified about the activities of garlic is not so very much unlike the mythical attributes that the alchemists sought in the elixir of life. If garlic is not a universal remedy and a renewer of health and youth, it appears at least to come nearer to that dream than any known thing given by nature for the use of man. Nor is there anything specially magical about this—certainly nothing to strain the reasonable powers of belief. It is all quite simple and entirely natural. Consider a homely example. Most of us who have lived through the austerities of spring cleaning and interior decorations know the old recipe of half an onion left in a newly painted room. This, of course, is no mystic ritual: it originates in the common knowledge that a raw onion cleanses the air around it by attracting into itself any impurity it discovers there. There are grimly picturesque stories from the seventeenth century about the days of the great plague of London. They tell of whole households saved from the scourge by the good offices of garlic —which contains the same basic properties as the onion but in a very much stronger form. Oil of garlic, in fact, is a natural and a very potent disinfecting medium.

That brings us to Lord Lister, the celebrated British medical authority of last century. Lister worked on the principles of human antisepsis and this was his verdict: "When we have produced an antiseptic which can be taken internally without risk of injury to cell tissue, we shall have conquered infectious disease."

Most ills that we suffer come to us as the result of internal poisoning. This poisoning arises in various circumstances and shows itself in many ways—most of them more or less painful. Normally we attempt to treat each of these disturbances according to its specific symptoms. Indeed, it is possible to "cure" the symptom without ever getting to grips with the underlying cause of all the trouble.

Lister saw very clearly that if you could treat your own body with an internal disinfectant you would be well on the way to tackling many kinds of illness by one and the same means—that is by killing the germs and eliminating the poisons that always attack your system at its weakest points, and so produce the local symptoms. But there was one bad snag about this question of internal disinfection and that also Lister realized quite clearly. The snag is that, in dealing with your own body, you are dealing with human tissues. You may cope with external diseased conditions quite successfully by the use of carbolic acid, chlorides, permanganates. But you can't take these antiseptics into your internal pipes and ducts. Such disinfecting agents would poison and blister and burn up your organic tissues. They would injure if not kill the patient as well as the germs: the remedy would be worse than the disease.

What, then, is necessary for effective internal use is an antiseptic which does not destroy the vital tissues and natural secretions of the body and whose antiseptic function is not in turn destroyed by them. That is where Lister left the matter.

Now let us get back to our garlic, because garlic—that immemorial remedy of nature— does contain a natural oil that is not only powerfully antiseptic but which can be used within as well as without. It possesses, as we have already seen, the priceless property of cleansing whatever it contacts. Not only does it destroy bacteria within the system and detoxicate the poisoned areas: it exercises also a positive action in toning the lymphatic cells of the body, and purifying the blood stream and the intestines. It is the lymph surrounding every cell of the body that is the favorite lurking place for waste matter and irritants. Oil of garlic has the useful habit of penetrating the lymphatic fluid, breaking up toxic accumulation and passing it out of the body by way of the blood stream through pores, kidneys and intestines.

GREATEST LABORATORIES ON EARTH

"The operations of a simple plant humble us, and like the handwriting on the wall, though seen by many, can be explained but by One."

In the thin layer of surface soils covering the earth are stored vital elements necessary to man's very existence. These inorganic elements are poisonous in their natural form. They MUST be processed and VITALIZED by plants before they become digestible to any living creature upon earth.

The elements made soluble by rain water, are drawn by the roots of plants, and brought up into the leaves where they are combined with carbon dioxide from the air. The rays of sunlight and the power of green substance (chlorophyll) in plants, transform the water and air solution into wonderfully complex substances, which form the plant's structure.

There are ninety-two elements KNOWN to present-day science, some of them very rare, but all of them have some physiological importance and all occur in the plant world. The complexity of the marvelous chemical processes, carried out by plants, can only be vaguely imagined. Each variety of plant prepares its own particular formula, and many varieties, in different parts of its structure. The hundreds of thousands of different plants, form as many different formulae. Certainly in the vast laboratories of the Fields and Forests, must be all man's needs for health and long life.

CHLOROPHYLL—KEY TO LIFE

Chlorophyll is the green substance found in leaf tissues of all plants. IT IS A KEY LINK BETWEEN THE SOIL AND ALL LIVING CREATURES UPON IT—THE LINK THAT HAS BAFFLED MEN OF THOUGHT FOR AGES.

If chlorophyll stopped functioning, all life on earth would soon perish. Chlorophyll is chemically closely related to blood, but differs greatly from it in function. The main components of blood are globin and hemin. The molecule of hemin and the molecule of chlorophyll are essentially alike, except that the iron in hemin is replaced by magnesium in chlorophyll.

The replacement of the one element, magnesium, by another, iron, completely reverses the catalytic function of the molecule. Chlorophyll has power to transform raw earth materials into living substances, digestible to man. Haemoglobin or blood, carries oxygen with which sugar is broken down by respiration.

In recent years, science awakened to the fact that chlorophyll is important to health, and appears to have unlimited possibilities. Unlike so many of our so-called "wonder drugs," CHLOROPHYLL IS KNOWN TO BE ABSOLUTELY HARMLESS.

CHLOROPHYLL FOR WOUNDS

Since very ancient times, people in all parts of the earth, have used the green substance of plants to heal open sores, wounds, etc. Even as children, most of us remember how mashed leaves of green plantain was applied to wounds. All green plants, of course, can not be used for wounds, because many contain irritating substances, as well as chlorophyll. On the other hand, many healing herbs contain potent agents that aid the action of chlorophyll. Scientific research found that chlorophyll also minimizes foul odors, and running and cancerous sores.

A poultice of chlorophyll has proved of benefit in healing many skin troubles, bone infections, and leg ulcers.

Powdered chlorophyll, taken internally, offers wonderful possibilities in the treatment of gastric and duodenal ulcers.

CHLOROPHYLL AS A CATALYST

Researchers are now delving into the possibilities of Chlorophyll in cases of anemia due to faulty diet, and in the catalytic action of Chlorophyll as a corrective or preventative for either overactive or underactive conditions of metabolism. It is known that Chlorophyll aids in oxidation processes in living cells, and it is believed also, to make more use of oxygen in the blood stream.

According to science, the brain requires seven times as much oxygen, as any other part of the body. Brain cells die seven times as rapidly as other cells of the body, when deprived of oxygen. The increased mental alertness reported by users of Chlorophyll Tablets, may be due to Chlorophyll's ability as an oxidation catalyst.

The stimulating action of Chlorophyll in producing new cells, may also prove beneficial in retarding degenerative diseases of old age.

CHAMOMILE FLOWERS POPULAR MEDICINE

Chamomile as Tonic and Stomachic

Phillips wrote in 1831 "no simple in the Materia Medica is possessed of a quality more friendly and beneficial to the intestines than Chamomile." An old Materia Medica states —"as an aromatic tonic, stomachic and corroborant, we know of no single agent that is superior to Chamomile." The tea is valuable in enfeebled states of the digestive organs, occurring either as a primary disease, or dependent upon some acute affection when attended by common symptoms of indigestion, heartburn, flatulency, etc. In such affections, particularly if accompanied by a sluggish state of the intestinal canal, the COLD infusion, made by steeping for 24 hours, ½ ounce of Chamomile flowers to a pint of water, and combined with Ginger, Cardamons, or other alkalies, is grateful to the stomach. The cold infusion taken in moderate doses, 2 or 3 times a day is also useful for enfeebled stomach during recovery from typhoid and intermittent fevers.

Chamomile Tea for Women

Chamomile tea has been used as a tonic to anaemic girls for many generations. The tea has been found to have a special effect on the stomach, kidneys and sweat glands. Women, particularly, seem to benefit from the general toning influence of Chamomile tea, especially during the years of adolescence and menopause. It is a very old remedy for arresting excessive flooding during menses, when taken upon retiring.

Chamomile tea is efficacious for hysterical and nervous affections peculiar to women. Women prone to nervous headaches, or that form of biliousness which follows nervous strain, caused by quarreling, reprimand, etc., may also be benefitted by a cup of Chamomile tea.

Of all the plants which won in the olden times, a reputation for their sanatory properties, none have retained more credit in modern days than the Chamomile. In villages it is regarded as supply in the very best of tonics—and Chamomile tea is taken in the early morning with unhesitating faith.
—From Flowering Plants of Great Britain.

Grandmother's Chamomile Tonic

Take ¼ oz. Chamomile flowers; ¼ oz. cut Gentian root; ¼ oz. Columbo root; ¼ oz. dried orange peel; 50 whole cloves and 1¼ pints of cold spring water. Put ingredients into a bottle or jug, and pour over the water. Allow to stand 24 hours—shake occasionally —then strain off liquid. Take 3 tablespoonsful fasting every morning.

Another Recipe from an old family doctor book, used especially for women: Put ½ ounce of Chamomile flowers into 1 quart of Madeira, Malaga or Port wine. Steep for 24 hours—then strain. Dose: Half a wine-glassful 2 or 3 times a day.

Other suitable tonics may be combined, such as Spikenard, Columbo and Gentian roots, in equal parts: The whole should be covered with nearly a pint of boiling water. When cold, put all into a bottle, and add a quart of wine. An excellent restorative.

Chamomile Tea for Young and Old

Chamomile tea is valuable in cases involving convalescence or general debility. Aged persons should drink a wine-glassful of the tea, with a pinch of Ginger an hour or more before dinner, to create an appetite.

Another Recipe for the appetite is made as follows: Take 3 tablespoonsful Chamomile flowers; 2 teaspoonsful powdered rhubarb root and 1 teaspoonful Coriander seeds. Make into a tea by adding a quart of boiling water, and allow to stand over night. A wine-glassful is to be taken half an hour before dinner.

WARM Chamomile tea is soothing for infants of a restless nature, and with a tendency to colic. Infuse 4 or 8 Chamomile flowers in a cupful of boiling water—keep covered with a saucer, and allow to steep until moderately warm—then strain. Begin with a dose of ½ teaspoonful and increase to 1 teaspoonful if necessary. Give to baby just before each feeding. The tea is also good during the teething period, to soothe pain—and for diarrhea in children when stools are green. Dose—1 teaspoonful every 2 or 3 hours.

PREPARING CHAMOMILE TEA

To 1 cup of boiling water, stir in 1 teaspoonful of Chamomile flowers, and COVER CUP with saucer. Allow to steep until cool enough to drink—then strain. Tea may be flavored with a slice of lemon and sweetened with honey, if desired. NEVER boil Chamomile flowers, and ALWAYS keep infusion COVERED when steeping.

Drink Chamomile tea in small doses.

ICELAND MOSS

Iceland Moss is a tonic demulcent, and also nutritious. As a demulcent and soothing remedy, it is given in coughs, bronchial affections, and in low and exhausted conditions of the system, it is valuable also as a nutriment. It is good in dyspepsia, on account of its tonic properties. The way to use it is in mucilage, which is made by covering a handful of the Moss with from 1 pint to 1 quart of boiling water; let stand two or three hours; then strain and sweeten with honey or molasses, adding a little lemon juice, if you like, and a bit of the lemon peel —to be used freely, at pleasure. Boiled in sweet milk, it is still better as a nutriment and tonic, especially in low stages of consumption and other debilitated conditions; also for children.

Iceland Moss

ICELAND-MOSS TEA

Wash 1 ounce of Iceland-Moss in cold water. Then heat with water up to nearly the boiling point, and reject the liquid, which has extracted much of the bitter principle. Next boil with a pint of water for ten minutes in a covered vessel, and strain with gentle pressure while hot. The result is mucilaginous demulcent liquid, with mildly-bitter tonic properties. It may be flavored with sugar, lemon peel, or aromatics.

HOW TO MAKE NEW CANDLES FROM OLD ONES

Reshaping and recoloring candles is not a complicated process. First, melt the candles, then add the desired color of wax crayon (remove wrapper) to the melting candles. Since crayons are of a waxy composition, they will mix easily with the candles.

The big thick candles are popular for many occasions. Make one right at home by using a paper milk carton as a form. Use a tall slender candle for the center, if possible, then the wick will be centered more easily. If no tall candle is available, tie a weight to one end of a closely twisted, soft cotton string and a pencil at the other end. The weight will fall to the bottom of the carton. The pencil placed on the carton top will keep the wick in place while the hot wax is poured into the form. After the wax hardens, the carton can be cut away leaving a big candle which can be the center of many attractive centerpiece.

A great variety of shapes in candles can be made by using "molds".

ARROW ROOT

Arrow Root is used as a light, nutritious diet, for children after weaning, and for delicate persons during convalescence, in the form of a jelly, made by boiling a little of it, and seasoning it with sugar, lemon juice, fruit, jellies, and the like. It is generally liked by children, and next to tapioca, is, perhaps, the best article of the kind known. It is very good as a diet during recovery from bowel complaints, fevers, and the like, both for grown persons and children.

Arrow-root Broth for Invalids

Put two teaspoonfuls of Arrow-root, which mix gradually with enough water or milk, stirring it with a spoon, let it boil a few minutes, and if made with milk, add only a little butter, sugar, and salt, or serve plain; but if made with water, add the eighth part of the rind of a fresh lemon to boil with it; when done add a glass of port or sherry, sugar, a little salt, and a small piece of butter, unless prohibited.

Arrow-root Jelly

Put a good teaspoonful of Arrow-root into a basin, which mix smoothly with two spoonfuls of water, then add enough boiling water to make it about the consistency of starch, stirring all the time, pour it into a stewpan, and stir over the fire until it has boiled two minutes; add a little cream, a small glass of wine, and a little sugar, and serve.

Arrow-root Water

Put half a gallon of water to boil with two apples (quite ripe), cut each apple into eight slices, without peeling them, throw them into the water—add a stick of cinnamon; let the whole boil half an hour, then mix two large spoonfuls of Arrow-root with half a pint of cold water, very smoothly, and pour it into the boiling water, let the whole boil ten minutes, and pass it through a sieve; when cold it will be light and thickish.

Orangeade with Arrow-root

Put a quart of water in a stewpan to boil, into which put two moist dried figs, each split into two; let it boil a quarter of an hour, then have ready the whole of an orange cut in thin slices, a little of the peel included, sweetening with sugar candy, and adding a teaspoonful of Arrow-root mixed with a little cold water, which pour into the boiling liquid at the same time you put in the orange. Boil two minutes longer; then pour into a jug which cover closely with paper until cold, then pass it through a sieve; add a teaspoonful of honey, and it is ready for use. The Arrow-root makes it very delicate.

FINDS SOIL LACKS SULPHUR, ESSENTIAL PLANT ELEMENT

An acute shortage of sulphur, essential element in plants that supports human life, has been disclosed.

A noted doctor states that sulphur has proved to be "the most underrated plant nutrient."

New analytical techniques that are more accurate than those previously available have shown that plants need from two to 100 times as much sulphur as was formerly believed. Sulphur in plants is the ultimate source of all sulphur for animals.

Sulphur-deficient soils are found particularly in rural areas, distant from industrial operations, where relatively little of the element is precipitated from the air. Sulphur is a constituent of protein and has long been known to be essential to plant growth. Sulphur also effects the formation of chlorophyll.—From Science News Letter.

NOTE: In the human body, sulphur purifies and tones the system. One must have sufficient food sulphur in the diet for luxuriant hair, and a beautiful and rosy complexion. It promotes bile secretions and enables the liver to take up the 16 mineral elements.

IRISH MOSS RICH IN SULPHUR

Irish moss contains much sulphur and iodine and in consequence is a valuable addition to our diet at the present time. It is free from starch and sugar and so diabetics can eat it.

A good drink in iodine deficiency is to soak half an ounce of dried Irish moss in cold water and then to boil it in a pint of water for five minutes. Strain and drink from one to four fluid ounces three times a day.

Irish Moss

Irish moss puddings are a popular dish in Ireland and they are similar to a blanc-mange. To make one, soak a quarter of an ounce of dried Irish moss in cold water for twenty minutes. Take each piece out separately and trim off any discoloured stalks. Put half a pint of milk and half a pint of water into a saucepan and bring to the boil. As soon as it boils add the Irish moss and stir until the pudding thickens; this will take about three minutes. Strain. Sweeten and flavour with lemon or vanilla essence. Pour into a wet mould and when cold and set turn out like a blanc-mange and serve. Some people flavour them with cinnamon; in this case add the cinnamon to the milk when bringing it to the boil.

Another delicious and health-giving dish is Irish moss jelly. Soak an ounce of dried Irish moss in cold water. Put it into a saucepan with a quart of water, the juice of two lemons and the grated rind of one, and four ounces of sugar. Bring to the boil.—Skim the scum off carefully. Strain through a jelly bag and pour into a mould that has been rinsed in cold water. Stand in cold spot to set. Other fruit juices can of course be substituted for the lemons.

JELLIED DRIED FRUIT—IRISH MOSS

½ lb. dried fruit
½ teacup washed Irish Moss
1½ pints water

The method depends partly on the kind of dried fruit used. Thus, for dried bananas, figs or prunes, everything goes into the pan together; but for raisins or sultanas, these should be put in about 15 minutes before the cooking is finished.

Snip off any foreign matter from the Irish Moss, and then with scissors cut up the remainder into smallish pieces. Then put Irish Moss into a bowl and run cold water over it to remove dust.

Wash the dried fruit in warm water quickly.

Put fruit and Irish Moss in enamel pan and bring all to boil, then turn down heat low, otherwise everything boils over. Even putting lid on saucepan means trouble in this respect. In about 30 minutes the liquor in the pan is getting quite thick, so stir from time to time.

(Some people dislike the sight or presence of undissolved pieces of Irish Moss in the finished mixture, though this is really fanciful. However, if this is considered objectionable, the Irish Moss should be cooked separately from the fruit, in one pint of the water. This enables the Irish Moss liquor to be strained off and stirred into the cooked fruit.)

Pour all into a suitable dish and cover with plate. As soon as it is cold it has become a solid jelly. Just before serving, grate the outer rind of a lemon or orange (if you happen to have one) over the top. If not all used at one meal, be sure to keep it covered.

When dried bananas are used, they should be cut into half-inch pieces after being washed.

The flavour of dried fruits is definite enough to make this dish attractive. The same is true of many fresh fruits. But if the fresh fruit has a delicate flavour, some flavouring can be added, such as cloves for apples, cinnamon for pears (ground cinnamon being more suitable), remembering, of course, that ground spice is easily overdone.

DICTIONARY OF RUSTIC NAMES OF PLANTS

In early New England days an Indian, called Joe Pye, attracted considerable attention because he effected marvelous cures with herbal medicines. It was said his teas were made mainly of Eupatorium Purpureum. Although Indian Joe is long forgotten, Eupatorium Purpureum is known to this day as Joe Pye Weed.

Like Joe Pye, nobody knows who King was anymore, but the common Evening Primrose is still called King's cure-all.

Many herbs are dubbed according to their effects. Loco or Crazy-weed is known to drive stock "loco." Narcotic varieties of poppy are called Headache plants. The fruit of poisonous Jimson Weed is referred to as Madapple or Devil's Apple. Henbane Root is called Insane Root. Sheep-laurel, Lamb-kill, Calf-kill, Sheep-poison all refer to Kalmia Latifolia. Because Veratrum Viride causes irritation to sensitive skin the plant is called Itchweed or Tickle-weed. Ragweed has earned the name of Hay-fever-weed.

Wherever the Hungerweed grew it was belived there would be crop failure and folks would go hungry.

Horsetail Grass was called Pewterwort in olden times because it was used for polishing pewter ware. Houseleek is also called Homewort or Thunder-plant because when planted on the roof it was supposed to be a protection from lightning. Compass Plant or Pilot Weed was very useful to early pioneers traveling over the plains country. The closing of the flowers of Poor-man's-weather-glass is supposed to be a sign of rain. Because its juice is used for warts, Celandine is known also as Wart-weed. Whiskey or Rum Cherry is wild Black Cherry. The Castor Oil Plant hardly needs identification—the seeds are poisonous, the oil is laxative in small doses.

Go-to-bed-at-noon is an elaborate name for Meadow Salsify because of the peculiar habit of its flowers which close in early afternoon. Welcome-to-our-house is a variety of Spurge which is usually planted near door steps. Good-bye-Summer is a late flowering wild Aster. The wooly leaves of Mullein are referred to as Adam's-flannel or Old Man's-flannel. Whip-poor-will's boots refers to peculiar leaves of Sarracenia Purpurea.

Plants have been named according to their uses, appearance and peculiarities. Many of the names are of Indian origin. The rustic names of some plants have become the base of the official botanical name. An unknown number of names exist in tiny communities and out-of-way settlements. One plant may have as many as twenty-five or more entirely different names in as many different localities. The following list consists of plants that are definitely identified and recorded in flora guides:

Abscess-root or Sweat-root: *Polemonium Reptans.*
Adam's Cup: *Sarracenia Purpurea.*
Ague Bark: *Ptelea Trifoliata.*
Ague Grass or Colic Root: *Aletris Farinosa.*
Ague Weed: *Gentiana Quinquefolia.*
Ague Weed or Boneset: *Eupatorium Perfoliatum.*
All-heal, Cut Heal, St. Gorge's Herb: *Valeriana Officinalis.*
Appalachian Tea, Carolina Tea, South Sea Tea: *Ilex Vomitoria.*
Asthma Weed: *Lobelia Inflata.*

Backache-brake: *Athyrium Filix-Foemina.*
Backache-root: *Lacinaria Spicata.*
Belly-ache Weed or White Golden Rod: *Solidago Bicolor.*
Blood-staunch, Canada Fleabane: *Erigeron Canadense.*
Blue Mountain Tea: *Solidago Odora.*
Breast-weed or Lizard's-tail: *Saururus Cernuus.*
Bruise-wort: *Saponaria Officinalis.*
Bruise-wort or Bonewort: *Bellis Perennis.*

Canada Tea or Mountain Tea: *Gaultheria Procumbens.*
Cancer-weed: *Salvia Lyrata.*
Colic-root or Blazing Star: *Lacinaria Squarrosa.*
Colic-root or Wild Ginger: *Asarum Canadense.*
Colic-root or Wild Yam: *Dioscorea Villosa.*
Colic Weed, Turkey Corn, Squirrel Corn: *Bicuculla Canadense.*
Colicwort, Parsley Piert: *Aphanes Arvensis.*
Coolwort: *Tiarella Cordifolia.*
Consumption-weed or Wintergreen: *Gaultheria Procumbens.*
Convulsion Weed, Fitroot, Indian Pipe: *Monotropa Uniflora.*
Cough-root: *Trillium Cernuum.*
Coughweed: *Tussilago Farfara.*
Culver's-physic: *Leptandra Virginica.*
Cure-all: *Geum Rivale.*
Cut-heal, Set-well, All Heal: *Valeriana Officinalis.*

Dakota Potatoe, Indian Potato: *Apios Tuberosa.*
Dropsy-plant: *Melissa Officinalis.*
Dye Leaves: *Symplocos Tinctoria.*
Dyer's Weed: *Genista Tinctoria.*
Dysentery-weed: *Lappula Virginiana.*

Emetic Holly, Indian Black Drink: *Illex Vomitoria.*
Emetic-weed: *Lobelia Inflata.*

Fever-bush or Spice-bush: *Benzoin Aestivale.*
Fever-cup: *Sarracenia Purpurea.*
Fever-plant or Phthisic-weed: *Isnardia Palustris.*
Fever Root or Feverwort: *Triosteum Perfoliatum.*
Feverweed: *Dasystoma Pedicularia.*
Flux-root: *Asclepias Tuberosa.*
Flux-weed: *Isanthus Brachiatus.*

Flypoison: *Chrosperma Muscaetoicum.*
Gall-weed or Ague Weed: *Gentiana Quinquefolia.*
Gout-weed or Gout-wort: *Aegopodium Podagraria.*
Heal-all: *Clintonia Borealis.*
Heal-all: *Orchis Orbiculata.*
Heal-all: *Scrophylaria Marylandica.*
Heal-all or Self-heal: *Prunella Vulgaris.*
Heal-bite or Heal Dog: *Alyssum Alyssoides.*
Healing-blade, Houseleek: *Sempervivum Tectorum.*
Healing-blade: *Plantago Major.*
Healing Herb: *Symphytum Officinale.*
Indian Bread: *Psoralea Esculenta.*
Indian Dye Root: *Hydrastis Canadensis.*
Indian Paint: *Blitum Capitatum.*
Indian Physic: *Porteranthus Stipulatus.*
Indian Soap Berry: *Sapindus Drummondii.*
Indian Tobacco: *Nicotiana Rustica.*
King's Cure, Pipsissewa: *Chimaphila Umbellata.*
Labrador Tea: *Ledum Groenlandicum.*
Liberty Tea: *Lysimachia Quadrifolia.*
Life Root: *Senecio Aureus.*
Liver-flag: *Iris Versicolor.*
Lungwort: *Pulmonaria Officinalis.*
Mexican Tea: *Chenopodium Ambrosioides.*
Nerve Root, Lady Slipper: *Cypripedium Pubescens.*
New Jersey Tea: *Ceanthus Americanus.*
Oswego Tea: *Monarda Didyma.*
Phthisic-weed: *Ludwigia Palustris.*
Pilewort: *Scrophularia Marylandica.*
Pleurisy-root: *Asclepias Tuberosa.*
Poor-man's Soap: *Spiraea Tomentosa.*
Rheumatism Root: *Apocynum Cannabineum.*
Rheumatism Root: *Dioscorea Villosa.*
Rheumatism Root: *Chimaphila Maculata.*
Rheumatism Root: *Jeffersonia Diphylla.*
Rheumatism Wood: *Apocynum Androsaemifolium.*
Scrofula-Plant: *Cistus Canadensis.*
Scrofula-Plant: *Scrophularia Marylandica.*
Scurvy-Grass: *Barbarea Verna.*
Scurvy-Grass: *Cochlearia Officinalis.*
Shoofly or Horse-fleaweed: *Baptisia Tinctoria.*
Small-pox Plant: *Sarracenia Purpurea.*
Soap-weed: *Yucca Glauca.*
Soapwort: *Saponaria Officinalis.*
Soldiers Woundwort: *Achillea Millefolium.*
Spiritweed or Paint Root: *Gyrotheca Tinctoria.*
Styptic Weed, Coffee Weed, Nigro Coffee: *Cassia Occidentalis.*
Sweat-root: *Hydrophyllum Virginianum.*
Sweat-Weed: *Althea Officinalis.*
Sweating-weed: *Hibiscus Militaris.*
Throat-root: *Geum Virginianum.*
Throat Wort, Throat Root: *Geum Rivale.*
Toothache-grass: *Campulosus Aromaticus.*
Toothache-tree: *Aralia Spinosa.*
Toothache-tree: *Zanthoxylum Americanum.*
Touch-and-heal: *Arnica Montana.*
Vanilla Plant: *Trilisa Odoratissima.*
Walpole's Tea: *Ceanothus Americanus.*
Weather Glass: *Anagallis Arvensis.*
Weathercock: *Impatiens Biflora.*
Wormwood: *Artemisia Absinthium.*
Woundwort: *Stachys Arvensis.*
Youthwort: *Drosera Rotundifolia.*

INTERESTING—IF TRUE

An authority claims that the odor of garlic is so penetrating that if it is placed on the soles of the feet, the air exhaled from the lungs would have the odor of garlic.

(Garlic was used in considerable quantities as an antiseptic in England during the last Great War.)

It is said if the poles on which hop vines grow are shaken up by wind, there is an electrical murmur resembling distant thunder.

Pliny wrote of the healing virtues of Comfrey which is also known as Healing Herb, Knit-back or Bone-set: "and the roots be so glutinative that they will solder or glew together meat that is chopt in pieces, seething in a pot, and make it into one lump. The same bruysed and lay'd in the manner of a plaister, doth heale all fresh and green wounds."

From an English Herbal regarding Water Cress: "In the warm summer months, the flowers have been observed about the time of sunset to give out sparks, as of an electrical kind which were first noticed by a daughter of Linnaeus."

Besides the citric, tartaric and malic acids as well as gum, pectin and starch contained in the fruit of TAMARIND, the pulp possesses traces of gold in its composition.

After lying on exhibit for more than twenty years in the museum of St. Bartholomew's Hospital Medical School, a Squill bulb was found starting to grow.

From "The Boke of Secretes of Albertus Magnus of the Virtues of Herbes, Stones and Certaine Beastes": How to revive a drowning insect! If drowning flies or bees are put in warm ashes of Pennyroyal "they shall recover their lyfe after a little tyme as by ye space of one houre."

A German doctor advanced the theory that fresh lemon juice is a kind of elixir vitae, and if a sufficient number of lemons be taken daily, life may be indefinitely prolonged.

An old herbalist wrote in regard to ashes of Rosemary: "Smell it oft and it shall keep thee youngly."

Because of its nitrate of potash content, Borage herb emits sparks and faint explosive sounds when burnt. The juice of the fresh plant contains 30 per cent. nitrate of potash and the dried herb 3 per cent.

ORGANIC SUBSTANCE OF PLANTS

Inorganic substances disturb the proper functioning of the organs of assimilation and elimination. They are considered unfriendly and in most cases dangerous and injurious and very difficult to assimilate. Organic substances, however, such as are found only in plants are easily and quickly assimilated and do not disturb the system.

The following plants contain such organic salts:

Plants Containing Iron

Yellow Dock	Burdock
Strawberry Leaves	Toad Flax
Stinging Nettle	Meadow Sweet
Silver Weed	Devils Bit
Rest Harrow	Mullein Leaves
	Salep

Plants Containing Iodine

Irish Moss	Sarsaparilla
	Iceland Moss

Plants Containing Calcium

Horsetail Grass	Plantain
Toad Flax	Silver Weed
Cleavers	Shepherds Purse
Meadow Sweet	Mistletoe
Coltsfoot	Rest Harrow
Pimpernel	Chamomile
	Dandelion

Plants Containing Silicon

This is found in all plants but in Horsetail Grass in particular.

Plants Containing Sulphur

Silver Weed	Rest Harrow
Stinging Nettle	Pimpernel
Fennel Seed	Shepherds Purse
Coltsfoot	Eyebright
Calamus	Plantain Leaves
Waywort	Scouring Rush
Broom Tops	Meadow Sweet
	Mullein

Plants Containing Phosphorus

Calamus	Meadow Sweet
Caraway Seed	Marigold Flowers
Chickweed	Licorice Root

Plants Containing Potassium

Walnut Leaves	Birch Bark
Mistletoe	Nettle Leaves
Chamomile Flowers, German	Borage
	Waywort
Primrose Flowers	Dandelion
Calamus	Yarrow
Plantain Leaves	Mullein
Coltsfoot	Comfrey
American Centaury	Sanicle
Fennel	Oak Bark
Eyebright	Carrot Leaves
	Summer Savory

Plants Containing Magnesium

Meadow Sweet	Toad Flax
Rest Harrow	Silver Weed
Devils Bit	Broom Tops
Black Willow Bark	Carrot Leaves
Walnut Leaves	Mullein Leaves
Primrose	Mistletoe

Chlorine. All plants contain more or less Chlorine in the form of Sodium Chloride.

Plants Containing Sodium

Waywort	Stinging Nettle
Fennel Seed	Mistletoe
Black Willow	Meadow Sweet
Rest Harrow	Devils Bit
Cleavers	Shepherds Purse

Directions for Use

The roots and herbs listed here are absolutely harmless. They may be used in any combination. For an example, let us assume you desired a general formula containing Iron, Iodine and Calcium. You could take one or two herbs listed under Iron, one or two listed under Iodine and one or two listed under Calcium. Take equal parts of these herbs and mix them; then put a heaping teaspoonful of the mixture into a cup of boiling water—let it stand until cool and drink one to two cupfuls of the tea a day. A very good combination of this kind would be equal parts of Yellow Dock Root, Irish Moss and Horsetail Grass.

MAGIC MATÉ

Theodore Roosevelt, in his book "*Through the Brazilian Wilderness,*" says: "Maté . . . used in most of the South American states, should not be forgotten. With it, a native can do a wonderful amount of work on little food. Upon the tired traveler it has a very refreshing effect. Some experiments have been made lately with the use of Matte in the German army, and probably it would be valuable for the use of our own troops."

Shunk de Goldfein, the famous French scientist, says: "Matte is a first class stimulant for the muscles, nerves and brains; it facilitates digestion without affecting the heart or disturbing the sleep. It helps the perfect function of the intestines and kidneys."—*The Press Medicale.*

MEXICAN MATÉ

Mexicans, living in the parched desert regions under tropical sun, refresh themselves with "Mexican Maté."

THE RACE
THAT LIVED WITH NATURE

HERBS USED by the INDIANS for MINOR AILMENTS

Through the ages of actual contact with plants, the Indians learned the value of every plant about them. It was not a scientific knowledge but an instinctive knowledge through the closest possible association and experience with plants in all their stages of growth.

Contact with the white man and the disruption of their normal lives was the beginning of the decline of Indian uses of plants. Systematic recording of Indian medicines began only in the last century when the majority of tribes were already driven far from their native home and familiar plants. The uses of plants by many tribes have been lost forever.

Indian medicines were limited to plants available in their own or neighboring territories in which they lived. A varied flora grew in the different soils and climates of the prairies, woods, mountains and deserts. Despite the abundance or scarcity of medicinal plants, tribes of the different localities found different plants to treat similar conditions. The actual medicinal value of these different plants naturally varied considerably.

Canada Snakeroot is found growing mainly in the rich moist woodland soils of the north central states. The tribes living in this area used the aromatic roots for indigestion and stomach troubles. Several thousand miles to the northwest other tribes were using another variety for the same purpose. Still another variety, commonly known as Virginia Snakeroot grows mainly in the dry woodlands of the southeastern states. The roots of this plant are also used for stomach disorders by Southeastern tribes. This variety is far superior to Canada Snakeroot and Northern Snakeroot. Its use has been adopted by the white medicine men.

A few plants such as Golden-rod, Alder, Yarrow and Artemisia grow over a large part of North America and Europe. Regardless of how distant apart and unknown the Indians were to each other, they discovered similar uses for these wide-ranged plants. Although the species may differ, Alder was used for its astringent properties by tribes where the shrub or tree was found.

Since very ancient times, Yarrow was used by the white man. In another world unknown to the white man, Indians were using other varieties of Yarrow for similar ailments.

For more than five thousand years, the Chinese were using Ephedra for bronchitis and cough. Thousands of miles away in the hidden valleys of Nevada, Indians were using a similar variety of Ephedra for ailments as the Chinese were using the Oriental species.

In Europe, Rhamnus frangula was being used by the white people for its laxative properties. In remote sections of the northwest, American Indians were using Rhamnus purshiana for laxative. As the white people eventually came in contact with the Indians of the northwest they learned about the new variety of Rhamnus. They recognized it as a superior variety and eventually replaced the old world variety for the Indian variety. It is better known today as Cascara sagrada.

While the Indians did not know the chemical constituents of their medicine plants, centuries of experiment taught them the hidden virtues. The Indians knew just what season an herb contained its fullest properties. They knew that an herb found growing in certain soils and locations was superior medicinally to the same plant growing in an unfavorable location. The Indians believed that bark growing on the sunny side of trees was stronger than bark found on the shady side. They knew what part of the plants were best used and applied them in the manner most effective. The Indians understood the strength of their medicines. This is remarkably evident when they used such drastic medicine as Poison Oak, Poison Ivy, Poison Hemlock, and Stramonium. They were taken internally for certain conditions with counter-balancing botanicals in special doses.

In Colonial times and early pioneer days the white man often went to the Indian medicine man for help. Today many of these old Indian medicines are recognized and used by the white man. Modern chemistry has proved how remarkable and correct the majority of the Indian remedies were used.

HERBS USED BY THE INDIANS FOR MINOR AILMENTS—Continued

Among the better known Indian drug plants are: Witch Hazel, Prickly Ash, Culver's root, Cranesbill, Blue Cohosh, Golden Seal, Sassafras, Senega Snakeroot, Wild Cherry and Mayapple. Many other Indian medicines are not used because the white man has other sources for the same drug. Among the great variety of botanicals used by the Indians there probably are other valuable drugs which may some day come to the white man's use.

Indian therapy was not limited to herbal decoctions, applications, poultices and washes. They used herbal steam baths, performed simple surgery, amputations and understood the use of splints. *(Where Birch bark was available, splints were made of very thick bark. It was heated and bent to the desired shape, after which it became rigid as Plaster of Paris. Splints were also made of thin cedar. Tying the splint with basswood twine added greatly to its rigidity.—Densmore, Ethnobotany of the Chippewa).*

The white man learned the use of enema from the Indians. The Indians knew how to administer nourishment or medicine also by means of enema.

The Indians probably were the first people that carried a "First Aid Kit." Tribes of the Great Lakes Regions carried pieces of Senega Snakeroot for "general health" and roots of common Plantain for emergency in case of snakebite and other wounds.

The Indians would have disappeared long before the white man's arrival if he was ignorant of the plants about him.

If these plants did not aid him he could not have survived the rigorous conditions he was subjected to.

Judging by the available records, the Indians apparently were plagued with colds. They suffered many accidents causing wounds, bruises, burns, etc. Their diet of wild foods brought them disorders as refined diet did to the white man.

ACHES: Creek Indians used twigs of Spice Bush *(Benzoin aestivale)* for a c h e s. They drank the infusion and also used it in steam baths.

BLISTERS: The Cherokee made a decoction of a variety of Sumach *(Rhus copallina, Rhus typhina or Rhus glabra)* to use as a wash on blisters. These Sumachs contain considerable tannin and are useful as astringent.

BOILS: Mississippi Valley tribes made a poultice of the roots of Staghorn Sumach *(Rhus typhina)* or Devil's W a l k i n g Stick *(Aralia spinosa).* The rare Adam and Eve *(Aplectrum hyemale)* roots were used when available. The Great Lakes tribes used inner bark of Basswood *(Tilia Americana)* "to cause boils to open" and pounded roots of Wild Sarsaparilla *(Aralia nudicaulis)* "to bring a boil to a head or to cure a carbuncle." The Wailakis of California used the fresh corm of Dogtooth Violet as poultice and the grated dried root of Petasites palmata to dry up boils.

BRUISES: The Tewa Indians of New Mexico mixed dough with the ground leaves of common Dandelion for application on bruises. In the Northwest, I n d i a n s used Rocky Mountain Sage *(Artemisia tridentata)* as a poultice and farther south the Yuki Indians made a strong decoction of dried Elderberry flowers to use as a lotion for sprains and bruises. In the Great Lakes area Indians applied heated leaves of fresh plantain for bruises and swellings. Other botanicals used were: Alder bark *(as poultice)*, Yellow Water Lily root *(as poultice,)* Great Willow herb *(as wash)* and Lousewort herb *(as poultice).* Poultices were usually made with dried botanical. They were moistened with water when needed, then applied directly and held in place with bandage.

BURNS: The Zuni Indians ground the entire plant of Yarrow *(Achillea lanulosa)* mixed it with cold water and applied this to burns. They also made a poultice of the mashed roots of Winter Sage *(Eurotia lanata).* In the British Columbia section, Indians burned Horsetail Grass and used the ashes for burns. The ashes were sprinkled thickly over the burn and kept in place with a bandage. The ashes were also mixed with animal greases or oils and smeared over burns. In California, Indians made poultice of the mashed roots of Cynoglossum grande to draw out inflammation from burns and scalds. This same Cynoglossum is now used as an ornament in gardens. The Great Lakes Tribes used a number of plants for burns. The Potawatomi made poultice of Joe-Pye Weed leaves. The Meskwaki used leaves of Thimbleweed, C a n a d a Wormwood or pounded roots of Wild Sarsaparilla as poultices. An infusion made from Blood Root was used to bathe burns and to relieve the pain. The Chippewa made a poultice of pulverized leaves *(dried)* of Anise-Hyssop. The paste is said to prevent blisters and to take out the fire of burns. The same Indians also made a poultice of inner bark of Tamarack. It was made either with fresh chopped bark or moistened dried bark. Another poultice used consisted of flowers of several plants: equal parts of Anise Hyssop, Coneflower, Golden-rod, and Wild Sunflower. All flowers were dried. When needed they were moistened and applied to burns and held with bandage. When the poultice became dry it

HERBS USED BY THE INDIANS FOR MINOR AILMENTS—Continued

was not removed. It was moistened again with cold water. This flower combination was held to be very strong. It is said that if a small handful of flowers were steeped in a quart of water and a person washed their hands in this infusion, they could thrust their hands in boiling water and not be scalded. *(A test would not be worth the chance!)* The Chippewa considered poultice paste made with water and dry flowers and leaves of Wild Bergamot especially good for scalds.

Indian preparing herbal decoction in bark container. Stones are heated in campfire and placed in container with water. As stones cooled, they were returned to fire and others substituted until water was brought to boiling point.

COLDS: Like the white man, the Indian also had an assortment of medicines for colds. The Indians of the Great Lakes area seemed to be particularly bothered with head colds. In the Northwest the Thompson Indians drank a hot decoction made with water and Rocky Mountain Sage (*Artemisia tridentata*). The same tribe also drank a tea made of Wild Mint herb. It was used in steam bath for severe colds. Farther south the Pomo Indians drank a decoction made with California Sage (*Artemisia heterophylla*). In the southwest desert country the Pueblo tribes used a tea made with Wormwood (*Artemisia frigida*). In this same territory Indians used a mild tea made with Horsetail grass for babies with cold. In Mendocino County of California, Indians made a tea of the aromatic leaves of Yerba Santa for colds. It was highly valued for other ailments as well. The early Spanish missionaries adopted the Indian Medicine—later it was admitted into the U. S. Pharmacopoeia. An infusion made with Gum Plant (*Grindelia*) was also a popular Western medicine for colds. This herb was much used as a tea. In the Middle West, Indians used infusions made with one of the following botanicals: Live-Everlasting herb, Golden rod roots, Mountain Mint herb, Boneset herb, Mullein (*leaves and root*), Inner bark of Wild Cherry, White Oak or White Pine. Some of these teas were adopted by the early pioneers and are still being used by folks in homes, villages or hamlets off the beaten trail. The following recipe sounds very much like grandmother's favorite onion prescription. The Chippewa made a decoction of the roots of Wild Onions sweetened with honey for children suffering from colds. For adults they used a tea made of the sweet scented calamus. For a head cold they snuffed up the pulverized root of Calamus. For a hard dry cough, they made an infusion of common Burdock leaves. This was taken after a coughing spell. The Chippewa also drank an infusion made either with Red root (*Ceanothus ovatus*) or Spikenard root (*Aralia racemosa*). Neighboring tribes made a tea of Black Eyed Susan roots. For head colds the resinous buds of Balm Gilead were boiled in fat to make a salve which was rubbed into the nostrils.

CONSTIPATION: Probably the most widely used of all Indian medicine today is Cascara sagrada (*Rhamnus Purshiana*). The tree is native to the Pacific Northwest. The Thompson Indians used a mild decoction as a laxative, and a stronger decoction as a physic. The same Indians used a decoction of the whole plant of Sedum spathulifolium to relieve children of constipation. In the southern Central states, Indians used the leaves of American Senna as a laxative in the same way the Africans and ancient Egyptians were using the African variety of Senna leaves. Mayapple is very common in the Middlewest. The root was used by many tribes of this area as a physic. Because of its drastic action, it was generally used with other botanicals. The Chippewa Indians made a decoction with one quart of water with five dried roots of Culver's root (*Leptandra virginica*) for physic. Self Heal herb (*Prunella vulgaris*) with Catnip herb formed a combination used for physic. The Chippewa made a special decoction of Bittersweet, (*Celastrus scandens*) for infants. The following recipe is interesting because of its exacting dosage. A tea was made of Calamus root. It was prepared by scalding (*not boiling*) the root. The amount of root used was determined according to size or age of the patient. The root was measured with the length of the patient's index finger, whether an infant or an adult. Dose was about a half cupful.

CUTS: The Creek tribes used the mashed roots of Ginseng to stop the flow of blood from cuts. (*Centuries ago this plant was quite common in our woodlands. During the California Gold Rush days, Chinese were imported for menial labor. In those days Ginseng was already considered a valuable herbal so it was carried by trappers, hunters, adventurers, quacks and pioneers to*

HERBS USED BY THE INDIANS FOR MINOR AILMENTS—Continued

California. Something about this peculiar, sweet-tasting root had great attraction to Orientals. They sent some home—soon there was a great demand and exorbitant prices offered. Wood folk, pickers and even Indians gathered this precious plant until it has become practically extinct in wild form.) The Choctaw, Koasati and other neighbors of the Creeks used Fringe Tree bark (*Chionanthus virginica*). The dried bark beaten with a small quantity of water added was used as a poultice for cuts and bruises. A strong decoction was used as lotion to bathe wounds. In the Southwest desert lands, Panamint Indians rubbed the fresh bruised herb of the strong scented Thamnosma into wounds. The Tewa smeared pine resin over cuts and sores to exclude air. The Pima applied the boiled leaves of Gobernadora as poultice to wounds and sores. The Zuni pulverized the roots of Eriogonum *fasciculatum* and used it as poultices for cuts of any kind and for arrow or bullet wounds. The Zuni also used a decoction of Red Willow as a wash for wounds. Doctor Mathews observed that wounds thus treated "healed in a short time." In the North and Eastern sections poultices and lotions were made and used in the same way with botanicals native of these sections. Poultices were made with Butterfly weed roots, Yellow Dock roots, Swamp Valerian roots, Hazelnut Bark and many others. A special Chippewa formula was as follows: Boil equal parts of dried White Pine (*bark of young tree*) with inner barks of Wild Plum and Wild Cherry in water until all have become soft. Strain and keep the decoction. Pound the woody material into a mash and dry. Keep the dried mash from contact with rust or dirt. When the medicine is needed soak the dry mash thoroughly with the strained decoction and apply. Keep in place with a clean bandage.

EYES: (*Sore or Strained*) Although the Indians never developed writing (*except picture writing*) their eyes became sore or strained also. The search for food and the battle of life depended upon keen sight. Indians often named their plants according to the way they were used. "Put into Eyes" is the Indian name for a plant better known today as Prairie Zinnia (*Crassina grandiflora*). The Zuni crushed the flowers in cold water and the strained liquid was used as eyewash. "Weak Eye Tea" is an Indian name for a tree better known today by another Indian name. The more common name is Wahoo (*Euonymus atropurpureus*). A mild decoction was considered valuable for eye troubles by Lake tribes. Of the numerous "sore eye" medicine used, the following were considered most popular among many tribes: Infusions made with either St. Johnswort or St. Andrew's Cross. Mild infusions made with any one of the following: Alder Bark, Bearberry leaves, Yarrow herb, Chickweed herb, Blackberry root, Black Oak bark, Choke Cherry bark or bark of Button Bush. Ginseng root was also used for sore eyes. The pounded root was soaked in cold water, then strained. An interesting recipe of Southern Indians was made by gathering the young buds of Sassafras and placing them in cold water. The mixture was allowed to stand several hours in hot sun. The glutinous substance which formed was used for sore eyes.

FATIGUE: In the southeastern states Indians drank a decoction made by boiling dried roots of Cherokee Bean or Coral Bean root (*Erythrina herbacea*) "when legs have become sore from walking too far."

INFLAMMATION: The forest Potawatomi used the beaten fresh leaves of Common Plantain to bind upon swellings and inflammations. The Chippewa applied Plantain in another way. They smeared bear grease on the fresh leaves and applied this to the inflamed part and renewed as soon as leaves became dry or heated. For winter use the leaves were dried, greased and packed in piles and wrapped tightly. The Chippewa also made a poultice of the chopped fresh Plantain roots spread on the fresh Plantain leaves. They sometimes added chopped Wild Ginger root with this poultice. For inflammation of the joints the Chippewa made a decoction of Joe Pye Weed root. This was applied externally as a lukewarm wash. The same Indians also made a poultice of Lady Slipper root. The root was dried, then moistened for the poultice.

Indian pulverizing dried botanicals in stone mortar. Mashed or pulverized botanicals are generally mixed with water and applied as poultices.

INSECT BITES: In the northwest, Indians made a wash by mashing Yarrow to a pulp in cold water. The liquid was used for insect bites. The Great Lakes Indians applied the leaves of Yarrow as poultice for spider bites. The dried flowers of Golden-

HERBS USED BY THE INDIANS FOR MINOR AILMENTS—Continued

rod boiled in water is used as lotion for bee stings. Southern Indians made a poultice of the mashed fresh leaves of Sassafras for bites and stings.

MEASLES: The information regarding this ailment is vague. Records simply state that the Choctaw drank an infusion of Sassafras bark of root for measles. Sassafras tea is still popular in the spring among old fashioned folk.

MOUTH SORES: The Indians were either little bothered by mouth sores or possibly such medicines were not recorded and lost for all time. In the Southern states the Choctaw and neighboring tribes made a wash for mouth sores of the powdered ashes of Silver Grass (*Chrysopsis graminifolia*). In the Great Lake regions an infusion of Gold Thread roots or White Water Lily roots were used. An infusion of the root of Wild Cranesbill (*Geranium maculatum*) was used as mouth wash especially for children.

POISON IVY: This obnoxious weed seemed to be most prevalent in the Great Lakes regions, as we find the only Indians medicines used were from this area. The Menomini Indians used either Shepherd's Purse or Peppergrass for poison ivy. The dried herb was boiled in water to make a strong infusion. When lukewarm it was applied as a wash. The same Indians also used the fresh juice of Wild Lettuce (*Lactuca canadensis*) on poison ivy. Huron H. Smith, one of our best authorities on the Indians of the Great Lakes area wrote in regards to Spotted Touch-me-not (*Impatiens biflora*), "This is accounted a valuable medicine among the Forest Potawatomi who use the fresh juice of the plant to wash nettle stings or poison ivy infections. The writer knows that it instantly alleviates the sting of Stinging Nettle and has it from the Indians that it will cure and alleviate the itching of Poison Ivy." Today this Indian medicine is used by the white men living in the Wisconsin Indian Reservations Area.

SKIN: The Alabama Indians used a decoction of the inner bark of Prickly Ash to rub on itching skin. In the North other tribes used Sweet Fern leaves for the same trouble. The Forest Potawatomi made a salve of Tacamahac or Balsam Poplar. "The winter buds are melted with mutton or Bear tallow to form an ointment for persistent sores and for eczema." The Chippewa used a wash of Bittersweet for skin eruptions and itch. The same Indians used Yellow Dock root or flowers and leaves of Bergamot for children. The decoction of Bergamot was used as a wash. The pulverized dried roots of Yellow Dock was moistened and applied directly to the skin, being held with bandage. (*Yellow Dock root contains considerable iron. Bergamot contains Thymol, an antiseptic much used in modern medicine.*) The Thompson Indians of the Northwest sprinkle the pulverized leaves of Yarrow on eruptions of the skin. They also made a wash of Yarrow for chapped or cracked hands, pimples, rashes and other skin troubles. According to H. Smith, the Wisconsin Menomini rubbed the fresh juice of Wild Lettuce on skin eruptions. The Choctaw and other Southern tribes boiled the bark of Magnolia to "bathe the body to lessen or prevent itching due to prickly heat."

Squaw bundling botanicals for winter use. Barks and roots are tied up in tight bundles. Herbs are hung in shade. Before they become brittle dry they are also bound up in bundles. Berries, flowers and seeds are placed in leather bags after being thoroughly dried.

SORES: Next to cold medicines, we find that the Indians used a large and varied assortment of medicines for sores. A probable explanation for this may be that the Indians did not know how to make soap. A few tribes did, however, discover and used saponaceous plants such as Chlorogalum, various Yuccas, Sapindus, etc. These soap-making plants were used mainly to wash the scalp and hair. In the Northwest, Thompson Indians used the ashes of Bunchberry (*Cornus canadensis*) on sores. Another method they employed was toasting Bunchberry leaves until dry enough to pulverize. This powder was sprinkled on sores. Pulverized Yarrow herb was also used by this tribe. In California, the Concow Indians made a poultice of the leaves of Manzanita (*Arctostaphylos manzanita*) or used the fresh juice of Milkweed (*Asclepias eriocarpa*) for cuts and sores. The Wailaki used the grated root of Petasites palmata to dry up running sores. The Yuki dried the root of Wyethia longicaulis, moistened it again and applied it as poultice for running sores. The lichen known botanically as Everina valpina was commonly used by several tribes. In the southwest desert country, Pima Indians pulverized the roots of White Rhatany (*Krameria Grayi*) for

HERBS USED BY THE INDIANS FOR MINOR AILMENTS—Continued

dressing sores. Other varieties of Rhatany found growing in Mexico and South America were used in the same way by Indians of these areas. A Peruvian variety is much used in modern medicines. The Tewa at Santa Clara used an infusion of Pentstemon torryi for dressing sores. This beautiful plant is now being used in ornamental gardens. The Tewa used several other medicines. They made a soapy lather with the dried herb of Gilia longiflora "for sores on any part of the body." The pulverized roots of Globe Mallow (*Sphaeralcea lobata*) was "applied to wounds caused by snake bites and to sores in which considerable pus appears. The pus is said to be drawn out by the action of this remedy." Other varieties of Mallow were used in the same way in Europe since very ancient times. In the Eastern regions we find few medicines for sores. The Eastern tribes were naturally the first tribes to suffer the loss of their native homes after the whites began to push westward. The Catawba Indians made a salve either with roots of Lyre-leaved Sage or roots of Pinweed (*Lechea*) for sores. Great Lakes Indians used various poultices for old sores. They were usually made with any one of the following botanicals: leaves of Cudweed (*Artemisia ludoviciana*), bark of Wahoo (*Euonymus atropurpureus*), mashed fresh roots of Wild Sarsaparilla, Shining Willow bark, leaves of Alum-root (*Heuchera americana*), Slippery Elm bark. The last named bark is still much in use in medicine.

SORE THROAT: The minty leaves of Monarda menthaefolia was a popular remedy among the Tewa of New Mexico as a treatment for sore throat. A decoction of the herb was taken internally and at the same time a small quantity of the dried and ground herb was inclosed in a narrow strip of deerskin or calico and worn by the patient around the neck. This variety of Monarda was also used by the Indians to flavor meats. In the Mississippi valley, Indians gargled with a decoction made of Red Oak Bark. Huron Smith recorded several interesting recipes of the lake Indians. He states, "The Pillager Ojibwe, use the orange-red juice of the Blood root to cure sore throat. The juice is squeezed out on a lump of maple sugar and this is retained in the mouth until it has melted away." In the "Ethnobotany of the Menomini Indians," a bulletin of the Milwaukee Museum, he states, "The roots (*Gold Thread, Coptis trifolia*) yield an astringent mouth wash for sore throat of babies, and it is much used for teething babies. This wash also cures cankers in the mouth." The Chippewa used several sore throat remedies. A decoction made with any one of the following was used as a gargle: Tansy root, Calamus root, inner bark of Choke cherry, Prickly ash root, Slippery Elm bark. Other method was to chew any one of the following: Tansy root, Golden-rod root (*Alabama Indians chewed the flowers of golden-rod for sore throat*), Sweet Cicely root, Calamus root, Slippery Elm bark. It is interesting to note that the Chippewa Indians adopted a few of the white man's herbs such as Catnip, Tansy, etc. The plants originally came from Europe. They probably learned to use these herbs through the French with whom they were allies in the battle against British dominance.

SPLINTERS, SLIVERS: The Zuni Indians prepared a poultice by mashing the burs of common Cocklebur with squash seeds and grains of corn. A little water was added to make a paste. The mixture was applied externally to extract cactus needles or splinters, to heal wounds from nails and for similar purposes. The paste was held on with a cloth bandage. The medicine is applied morning and evening until the cactus spines or splinters are brought to the surface.

STOMACH DISORDERS: For many centuries varieties of Artemisias were household medicine in the Old World for stomach disorders. Indigestion must have been very common occurrences in olden times as foods were handled carelessly and with little means of keeping it. Across the sea, far beyond the trade routes of white man's sail ships, the Indians were also using varieties of Artemisia. The plants were different than any Old World Artemisia, but nevertheless related and containing similar bitterish qualities. The range of the New World Artemisia was mainly on the eastern and western slopes of the Rocky Mountains. Where the plant was available, Indians used it generally for stomach disorders. Records state in regards to Artemisia filifolia (*White Sage*): "This is a favorite remedy with the New Mexican Tewa. Bundles of this plant are dried for winter use. It is chewed and swallowed with water, or drunk in a hot decoction, as a remedy for indigestion, flatulence, biliousness, etc. A bundle of the plants steeped in boiling water and wrapped in a cloth is applied to the stomach as a hot compress." The same authority writes in regard to Artemisia tridentata (*Rocky Mountain Sage*), "All the New Mexican Sages are used at Santa Clara in the treatment of indigestion, and this species, the most pungent of all, is considered a very effectual remedy, though disagreeably strong. It is certainly useful in dispelling flatulence. It is also said to be a good remedy for a constant feeble cough with ineffectual expectoration. In both cases the leaves are chewed and swallowed." (*The Artemisia were also used much in colds, see chapter under that heading.*) In regards to Artemisia frigida (*Wormwood Sage*), "This plant is used in the same way

HERBS USED BY THE INDIANS FOR MINOR AILMENTS—Continued

as Artemisia filifolia." Out of the range of the Artemisias we find a fragrant and spicy family of plants being used by different Indians for stomach disorders. Indians in the south and eastern regions soaked (*not boiled*) the roots of Virginia Snakeroot (*Aristolochia serpentaria*) in water. The extract was drunk to relieve pains in the stomach. An infusion of Heart-leaf Snakeroot (*Asarum arifolium*) was used for the same trouble. In the Great Lakes regions Indians made a decoction of the gingery scented Canada Snakeroot (*Asarum canadensis*) for indigestion and colic. Some tribes used a small piece of the root with foods that "does not agree with a person" or meats that may be spoiled. The root is cooked with mud catfish to improve their flavor. Indians used Canada Snakeroot with any inedible foods, believing this to make them palatable. A northern variety of Snakeroot (*Asarum caudata*) was used in similar ways by Indians of those regions. The Chippewa used a combination formula consisting of equal parts of Blue Cohosh and Coneflower roots. The mixture was steeped in boiling water. Where neither Artemisia or Snakeroots were available, we find Yellowroot (*Zanthorrhiza apiifolia*) or Colic-root (*Aletris farinosa*) used as infusions for stomach disorders.

TOOTHACHE: When the early pioneers penetrated the Indian country, they found the natives using a bark of a prickly branched tree to relieve toothache. The bark was put in the cavity and packed around the aching tooth. The pioneers followed the Indian method; finding it effective, they referred to the tree as the Toothache tree. This name still clings to the tree which is also now known as Prickly Ash. Indians beyond the range of the Toothache Tree found numerous substitutes for their aching teeth. The Zuni chewed the root of Bull Nettle (*Solanum elaeagnifolium*) and packed the cavity of the aching tooth with this. Other desert Indians used tobacco leaves in or around aching tooth to stop pain. In California the Yuki and neighboring tribes used the fresh root of Yellow Poppy (*Escholtzia*). In the Mississippi Valley, Golden-rod seems to have been a panacea among some tribes. The roots of this common weed were also used around aching teeth. The fine rootlets of Skunk Cabbage and bark of Button Bush were also used to relieve toothaches.

VOMITING: Usually where the Indian Cup Plant is found, squaws made a tea of the dried roots of this plant to alleviate the vomiting of pregnancy. Desert Indians used a tea made of Cocklebur for diarrhea and vomiting. Record did not reveal the part of the plant used.

(See Special Notice, Page 9)

LIST OF PRINCIPAL AUTHORITIES REFERRED TO

BUSHNELL, DAVID I., JR.: The Choctaw of Bayou Lacomb, St. Tammany Parish, Louisiana.
CHAMBERLIN, RALPH V.: The Ethnobotany of the Gosiute Indians of Utah.
CHESTNUT, V. K.: Plants Used by the Indians of Mendocino County, California.
DENSMORE, FRANCES: Uses of Plants by the Chippewa Indians.
ROBBINS, WILFRED W., HARRINGTON, JOHN P., FREIRE-MARRECO, BARBARA: Ethnobotany of the Tewa Indians.
SMITH, HURON H.: Ethnobotany of the Menomini Indians.
SMITH: Ethnobotany of the Forest Potawatomi Indians.
SMITH: Ethnobotany of the Ojibwe Indians.
SMITH: Ethnobotany of the Meskwaki Indians.
STEVENSON, MATILDA C.: Ethnobotany of the Zuni Indians.
TAYLOR, LYDA A.: Plants Used as Curatives by Certain Southeastern Tribes.
TEIT, JAMES A.: Ethnobotany of the Thompson Indians of British Columbia.
Numerous articles and papers of unknown contemporary authors.

INDIAN MINT TEA

When the white man came to America he found the Indians drinking a mint tea in the same way as white folks had done in Europe for many centuries before. The native American mint is known today as Wild Mint, Mentha canadensis. The plant has a distinctive mint fragrance similar to American Pennyroyal. The tea is prepared like ordinary tea. The dried mint leaves are allowed to steep several minutes (according to tastes) in boiling water, then strained. Lemon may be added.

MANY IMPORTANT FOOD PLANTS, MEDICINES INTRODUCED BY INDIANS

During the late war some of the greatest comforts supplied to our soldiers in the trenches came from vegetable products which are a heritage from the American Indians—cigars, cigarettes, chocolate, cocoa, peanuts, preserved pineapples, maple sugar, some of the most nourishing foods, such as potatoes, maize in the form of popcorn, canned corn, corn bread, corn flakes, dried and canned beans, sweet potatoes and tapioca.

PIONEERS AND THEIR MEDICINE MEN

The pioneers followed the trails of the Indians, early adventurers, and fur traders. They came with their families, with confidence in themselves, and faith in God.

Their first homes were log cabins roofed with bark or straw. Mud sealed cracks protected them from the harsh winds, rain or snow. As there was no glass, windows were tiny openings fitted with shutters. In summer they were kept closed during the night to keep out dreaded miasmas, or lurking Indians. Flies, gnats and mosquitoes were smoked out with smudge fires. Cabins were dark, damp and dingy. A fireplace made of stones or dirt, piled around logs, afforded the only light. The luxury of candles came later. Floors were of dirt covered with straw. In the smoky rafters hung skins, furs, dried meat, corn and such native medicines as Pleurisy root, Physic root, Colic root, Emetic weed, etc. From July to October, there was always a pot of Ague tea brewing. It was considered a strengthening tea and a protection against ague—most common of all pioneer ailments.

The pioneer often had to use river or stagnant water for cooking and drinking purposes. If the water tasted badly, Indian mint, Wintergreen, Blue Mountain tea or other aromatic botanical was boiled in the water to conceal the taste. Many of these flavoring plants have become popular teas in areas where the botanicals are found.

As the pioneer severed contact with the civilized world, everything needed had to be produced at the wilderness home. Before the ground could be planted, it had to be cleared with whatever tools were brought along. Corn or wheat meal had to be ground in mortar by hand, before it could be baked into bread. Clothing was made from deer skins. Cotton was unknown to the first settlers. Until the country was safe from Indians and wild animals, settlers could not raise sheep for wool. Flax seed could easily be carried and grown in almost any soil. Linen, derived from Flax, had to be harvested, rotted, hackled, dressed, spun and woven before it was ready to be cut and sewn for clothing. Hickory, Walnut, Oak, Sumach, or other native botanicals supplied dyes for cloth materials. Soap for cleaning garments was rendered from discarded fats, with the aid of ashes.

Early pioneers found the water abounding with fish, and the forests filled with deer, turkey and other game. Wild pigeons—a favorite food—often blackened the sky, as they were so plentiful. In summer and fall, the woods hung heavy with wild plums, berries, grapes and nuts of many sorts.

As the cold weather set in, the fruits of the forest disappeared—lakes and rivers froze over, and game became scarce. Long severe winters and deep snows taxed the pioneers' larder to the point of starvation. Only the strongest and most fortunate survived famine, weather conditions, illness and attacking Indians. The road westward was strewn with the bones of fathers, mothers, and children—and often entire communities.

Settlements of early America had very few school-trained doctors. Boston, the metropolis of the New World, boasted of only one regular graduated physician, one hundred years after the city was founded. There were no medical schools—only wealthy students were able to go to Europe to study. For two hundred years doctors learned their trade by apprenticing themselves to someone who came about his trade by experience. Medicine was practiced by people in all walks of life. Parsons and preachers apparently were most numerous in practice. Their advice was sought in illness—as well as in religious and legal matters. Several presidents of Harvard College practiced and compounded their own concoctions. In Connecticut an old doctor had a negro servant, who cared for his horse and helped him in his medical practice. When the doctor died, the servant took over his practice and became a very successful physician. The old doctor's patients flocked to the servant doctor.

Many women also practiced medicine. Their success sometimes had tragic repercussions. Several were banished or hanged as witches because their wonderful cures, made of simples, were ample proof of their diabolic powers. Foreign trained physicians were at this time preaching that nature was a devil that had to be kept out of the sickroom by the doctor, who battled all symptoms with mercury, calomel and bleeding.

Indians also practiced medicine among the white people. Indian Joe Pye achieved great success in treating certain ailments common in early America. His principle medicine was a decoction made from the roots of a tall weed, which bears pale lavender flowers. To this day, this plant is known as Joe Pye Weed (Eupatorium purpureum).

Many townspeople of early America doctored themselves. Their methods and recipes were generally of old world origin—being handed down from one generation to another. Old World medicinals were grown in the kitchen garden. Peonies, Feverfew, Mari-

PIONEERS AND THEIR MEDICINE MEN—continued

golds, Larkspurs, etc., went into infusions or decoctions for the ailing. Pinks, sweet herbs and mints were the flavoring herbs and spices of the day. Everybody had their clump of tansy to make bitters that were taken religiously before and after breakfast.

Peddling squaws came into town with bundles of Sassafras, Slippery Elm, Spikenard, salves made of bear grease, deer fat, Balm Gilead Buds, Prickly Ash, etc. Indian medicines found ready market during seasons when ailments were most prevalent.

Squaws served as domestics in colonial homes. They often used their native medicines in the care of the sick, and taught their white employers ways of preparing native products for the kitchen table.

The new settlements were plagued with ailments, caused by hardships and unaccustomed climatic conditions, as well as from many ailments found in Europe. Josselyn reported "Three ships arrived at Salem bringing a great number of passengers from England; infectious diseases amongst them."

Native plants were the sole source of medicines of the pioneers, who left the Old World influences and medicaments of the new settlements.

In almost any backwoods community there was someone who showed more aptitude in treating the sick, than his fellowmen. It was natural for neighbors to call on this person in case of illness, when their own methods failed. If the service of this person was of no avail, he of course was never called upon again. Many of these backwoods "doctors" proved very successful in their simple mode of treatments. As their medicines were mainly of Indian origin, they became known as the Indian herb doctor. Often they could neither read nor write. Their schools were the fields and forests, with Indians and nature as instructors. In everyday life, the Indian herb doctor went about his tasks as preacher, farm helper, or whatever trade provided livelihood.

As the Indian herb doctor was a pioneer, his trail led ever westward with his fellowmen, until vast frontiers were settled to the Pacific shores.

After the Revolution, the American scene changed. Pseudo-European culture, silk, lace and powdered wigs, were brushed aside by the rugged dynamic culture of a new nation. The skill and crafts of the immigrants layed the foundation for the great industrial age.

The 19th Century was the Golden Age of Native American Herbals. It was the Age of Samuel Henry, Bigelow, Barton, Rafinesque, Millspaugh, and other noted medical botanists. The American herbals contain the knowledge of Indian medicine men, botanic doctors, preacher doctors and Indian herb doctors. Many of these valuable Herbals found their way into great institutional libraries, only to be buried under massive data of the new science of chemistry. Many of these native Herbals also found their way into the hills and valleys—far from the routes of a fast moving—fast changing world, where they are still used and ready to give aid, where professional care is beyond immediate reach.

"Nature was the first teacher of the medical art; instinct and chance were guiding its first steps and comparative reasoning did the rest."
—Tschirch.

IT IS ONLY AS GOOD AS YOU THINK

The following excerpt was taken from Carver's "Travels Through The Interior Parts of North America in the Years 1766, 1767 and 1768":

An elderly Indian Chief gave the account to Captain Carver: "Whilst they (the Indians) were crossing a plain, they discovered a body of men on horseback, who belonged to the Black People, for so they call the Spaniards. As soon as they perceived them, they proceeded with caution, and concealed themselves till night came on; when they drew so near as to be able to discern the number and situation of their enemies. Finding they were not able to cope with so great a superiority by day-light, they waited till they had retired to rest; when they rushed upon them, and, after having killed the greatest part of the men, took eighty horses loaded with what they termed white stone. This I suppose to have been silver, as he told me the horses were shod with it, and that their bridles were ornamented with the same. When they had satiated their revenge, they carried off their spoil, and being got so far as to be out of the reach of the Spaniards that had escaped their fury, they left the useless and ponderous burden, with which the horses were loaded, in the woods, and mounting themselves, in this manner returned to their friends."

HASTE MAKES WASTE

THE RACE THAT LIVED WITH NATURE

The following excerpts were taken from Baron Lahontan's "New Voyages to North America." His travels were made in Canada and in the vicinity of The Great Lakes more than 250 years ago. The record is most interesting because it gives a first hand report of the Indians before they became influenced by the white man. Lahontan considered the Indian "the honestest man in the world."

INDIAN INTUITION

"They have a wonderful idea of anything that depends upon the attention of the mind, and attain to an Exact Knowledge of many Things by Long Experience: To cross a Forest (for instance) of a Hundred Leagues in a straight line, without straying either to the Right or Left; to follow the Tract of a man or Beast upon the Grass or Leaves: So they know the Hour of the Day and Night exactly, even when it is so cloudy, that neither Sun nor Stars appear."

"They are as ignorant of Geography as of other Sciences, and yet they draw the most exact Maps imaginable of the Countries they're acquainted with."

INDIAN PHILOSOPHERS

" 'Tis very strange, that having no advantage of Education, but being directed only by the Pure Light of Nature, they should be able to furnish matter for a Conference which often lasts above three Hours, and which turns upon all manner of Things; and should acquit themselves of it so well, that I never repented the time I spent with these truly Natural Philosophers."

INDIAN FOODS

"Their Victuals are either Boild or roasted, and they lap great quantities of the Broth, both of Meat and of Fish: They cannot bear the taste of Salt or Spices, and wonder that we are able to live so long as 30 years, considering our Wines, our Spices, and our Immoderate Use of Women."

INDIAN PHYSICAL CHARACTERISTICS

" 'Tis a great rarity to find any among them that are Lame, Hunch-back'd, One-ey'd, Blind or Dumb. Their eyes are large and black, as well as their Hair; their Teeth are White like Ivory, and the Breath that springs from their Mouth in Expiration is as pure as the Air that they suck in, in Inspiration, notwithstanding they eat no Bread; which shows that we are mistaken in Europe in fancying that eating of meat without Bread makes one's breath stink."

HEALTH AND LONG LIFE OF THE INDIANS

"The Savages are very Healthy, and unacquainted with an infinity of Diseases that plague the Europeans, such as the Palsey, the Dropsey, the Gout, the Phthisick, the Asthma, the Gravel, and the Stone: If a Man dies at the Age of Sixty Years, they think he dies young, for they commonly live to Eighty or an Hundred; nay, I met with two that were turned of a Hundred several years."

INDIAN MOTHERS

(Squaws) "Never make use of Nurses unless it be when the mothers are out of order, and they never wean their children, but suckle them so long as they have milk, with which indeed they are plentifully provided."

EARLY INDIAN OPINION ON HEALTH, SICKNESS, AND WHITE MAN'S HABITS

"In a Conference I had one Day with a Savage, the Barbarian said with a great deal of Sense, that a good Air, good Water, and Contentment of Mind could not indeed keep a Man's Life from coming to an end, but that at least it must be owned, that these Advantages contribute in a great measure to make a Man run through the course of his Life without being sensible of any Disorder or Inconvenience. *They make a Jest of the Impatience of the Europeans, who would be cured as soon as they are sick.* They allege that our fear of Death, occasioned by the invasion of the least Fever, does so inflame and fortify the Disease, that oftentimes we fall a Sacrifice to Fear itself; whereas if we looked upon our Illness as a Trifle as well as Death, and kept our Bed with Patience and a good Heart, without offering Violence to Nature, by cramming down Drugs and Medicines, the good old Dame would not fail to Comfort and Refresh us by degrees."

"There's no Wound or Dislocation that they (the Indians) cannot cure with the Simples or Plants, whose Virtues they are well acquainted with; and, which indeed is singular, their Wounds never run to a Gangrene (infection). But after all, this is not to be imputed to these Herbs, nor to the air of the Country, but to their hail Constitution; for notwithstanding the use of these very Remedies a Gangrene invades the Wounds of the French, who questionless are harder to cure than the Savages. This People attribute our liableness to Gangrenes, and

THE RACE THAT LIVED WITH NATURE—continued

indeed all our Diseases, to the Salt that we eat; for they cannot taste any salt thing without being sick unto Death, and drinking perpetually. They cannot be persuaded to drink Ice-water, for they allege that it enfeebles the Stomach, and retards Digestion."

Note lines—"They (Indians) make a Jest of the Impatience of the Europeans, who would be cured as soon as they are sick." The white race is much more spoiled to-day. Not only must our medicines be fast acting, but pleasant to take also. As herbs are mild, their action is slow. Herbs have a natural affinity to the body, leaving no violent reactions, characteristic of some of our modern wonder drugs.

* * * * *

Nature, Time and Patience, are the Three Great Physicians.—An old Proverb.

TOO MUCH OF A GOOD THING IS WORSE THAN NOTHING

He's had his fill, when he the banquet leaves;
He's eat too much—his stomach heaves:
His rich and dainty food, how much he loathes,
The monstrous load now from his stomach flows;
Nature's relieved — she teaches thus quite plain,
To eat too much of good things, brings much pain.

* * * * *

The first physicians by debauch were made,
Excess began and doth sustain the trade.
—Dryden.

To give gloss to smooth leaved house plants, dip a bit of cotton in milk, and dab and wipe leaves carefully.

If fountain pen gets clogged, fill with vinegar to clean out.

YE OLDE APOTHECARY SHOPPE

In the early days of America, medical supplies were sold in stores that stocked groceries, dry goods, hardware, dyestuffs, farm tools, etc. As the old medicinal gardens disappeared in rapidly growing towns and cities, the drug trade developed into an individual business. The art of compounding became a profession. As there were very few ready-made preparations, everything in the Apothecary was home-made. The druggist prepared syrups, confections, medicated waters, and perfumery. He made his own soda water, seidlitz and soda powders, pills and compounds. He manufactured inks, sealing wax, putty, linseed oil, varnishes, paints, etc. Probably the most tedious and laborious work in the Apothecary shop was the reducing of botanicals, chemicals and colors into powder form. The materials were pounded by hand in stone, brass or lignum vitae pestles, and mortars.

The principal medicines in the old Apothecary shops were of botanical origin: "Jamaica pepper" (allspice); "Pepper-nails" (cloves); "Sneezing snuff" (hellebore); "King of Oils" (oil of origanum); "Stink-weed" (stramonium); "Indian tobacco" (lobelia); "Gum Dragon" (gum tragacanth); and "Devils dung" (assafoetida) were common names for popular medicinals.

Catnip was the orthodox remedy for colic in babies, as Mint and Pennyroyal were for the same complaint in adults. Sweet Fern was esteemed as a cure for pimples; Boneset for fevers; Horehound for coughs and colds; Saffron for measles; Celandine for warts; Pellitory for toothache; Sumach berries for sore throat; Blackberry bark and root for diarrhoea, and Blessed Thistle for nearly every imaginable disease.

Oatmeal was sold by the ounce. It was used as a poultice, and sometimes prescribed to be taken internally.

Opium was sold to anyone that could afford it. Wealthy addicts bought it by the pound, and the poor by the quarter pound and half-ounce quantities. A contemporary writer states: "To the rich, opium was a destructive, dreamy and benumbing intoxicant, and to the poor it afforded a temporary refuge in forgetfulness. It was easy to tell the regular opium eater, by the peculiar puffed appearance of his face, and the semi-opaqueness and dead-yellow color of his complexion."

In 1712 green and bohea teas were sold like medicine in Boston Apothecaries. The tea was boiled in water, the usual way, and strained off. The tea water was discarded, and the tea leaves were eaten—some preferred a bit of butter or salt on the soggy leaves, to make them more palatable.

HERBS USED BY THE INDIANS FOR FOWLS AND ANIMALS

Indians fed their horses Wild Lupine (Lupinus perennis) to make them "spirited and full of fire." It is also used by the white man for fodder and is said to be highly nutritious and wholesome if not fed in too large amounts and fed before the seeds mature. Lupine was also used by the Indians to control horses by rubbing the herb on the hands or person handling the animals.

When the Meskwaki Indians captured wild geese they fed them with Horsetail Grass. This was said to fatten them quickly. The Ojibwe feed this herb to domesticated ducks.

The Potawatomi Indians burned the bark of Quaking Aspen (Populus tremuloides) for ashes which they mixed with lard. This salve was applied to sores on horses.

The Meskwaki fed the inner bark (trunk) of Celtis occidentalis to ponies as a "conditioner."

The Zuni Indians of New Mexico call Wild Four O'Clock (Allioniaceae) "Great young fowls all eating food." The blossoms of the plant are fed to newly-hatched turkeys.

The Forest Potawatomi chop the root of Sweet Cicely into fine bits and add it to oats or other seeds which they give to their ponies to make them fat and sleek. Small quantities of the root is taken by the Indians themselves as a "fattener."

An infusion made of the leaves of Coral Bean (Erythrina arborea) is said to be used by the Seminole of Florida for canine diseases.

The Yuki Indians of Mendocino County, California make a decoction from the bark of Populus fremonti to use as a wash for sores on horses caused by chafing.

The Yuki use a decoction made from dried Elderberry flowers as a wash for open sores in domestic animals.

"When a horse gives out and is ready to drop" the Chippewa made a decoction with water and Psoralea root (P. argophylla). This was applied liberally to the chest and legs of the animal.

The same Indians mixed the powdered roots of Prairie-smoke (Sieversia ciliata) with horse's feed. "This was used before a race so the horse would not get winded."

From the "Ethnobotany of the Thompson Indians of British Columbia" (p. 514) regarding Yellow Pine Gum, Pinus ponderosa. "The best gum, which is white, is melted and mixed with an equal quantity of animal fat of good quality, preferably that of deer. The two are cooked together slowly in a pan and stirred until thoroughly mixed. While quite hot it is poured on sores after the latter have been cleaned with warm water and soap. This is a special means of treatment for old running sores. The application is repeated at intervals of 2 or 3 days until the sore has partly healed. After this ordinary ointments and powders are used to complete the healing. The horse is not used until the sore is well healed and if possible it is turned out on green pasture.

BOTANICALS USED BY INDIANS FOR HUNTING AND FISHING

Indians of the Great Lakes region were among the finest hunters of North America. Their keen knowledge of wild life, and skillful hunting methods were often mixed with herbal good luck charms. The Indians knew that the deer carries its scent or spoor, in between its toes, and whenever the foot is impressed into the ground, other deer or other animals can detect its presence. The peculiar scent was successfully imitated by the Indians, with roots and herbs. The roots of Blue Wood Aster was one of nineteen that was used to make smoke to attract the deer near enough to shoot it with bow and arrow. It is said that white men drive the deer away when he smokes cigarettes or cigars, but the Indians bring them closer. Other plants used to attract deer: Large leaved Wild Aster, root smoked; Canada Fleabane, disk florets smoked; Philadelphia Fleabane, disk florets smoked, and Swamp Persicaria, flowers smoked. Other roots, seeds, bark and flowers were used in mixtures for smoking to attract deer.

To sharpen their power of observation, Indian hunters drank a tea made of Heal-all root (Prunella vulgaris). For good luck the hunter drank a tea made from dried leaves of Pyrola, or carried the black stems of Maidenhair fern.

Indians of the Great Lakes also employed botanicals for trapping and fishing. The root of Alternate-leaved Dogwood was boiled in water to make a wash for muskrat traps The peculiar scent attracted this animal. The cool scented leaves of Mountain Mint were used as traps to catch minks. A wash made from roots of Kidney Liverwort was used on traps to attract other fur bearing animals. The Indian trapper boiled his traps in water with maple bark to deodorize them so that the animal would not detect the scent of the previous one which had been caught in the trap.

The sweet scented roots of Calamus, mixed with roots of Wild Sarsaparilla, were boiled in water to make a lure for fish. The nets were soaked in this decoction first before being used. It is said the scent of these botanicals still was on the net after being in water many hours

INDIAN FISH FACTS
By Chief Blackbird

Black Bass—Largemouth
The Indians call this fish the bulldog of fresh water fish. It is chubby, stout and well muscled. These will fight with dash and spirit. Typical habitat of the largemouth is weedy, rather shallow and warmer water. Their usual roost is under lily pads. Today many artificial baits are used to catch the bass, but, it is not the intention of the author to give baits other than those used by Indians. The most general method used by the Indians in catching the bass is by casting for them, using long poles amongst weeds and lily pads. On the hook is attached medium size frogs. Smaller bass are caught using minnows and worms.

Muskellunge
Here is the king of all fresh water fish, and a fighter. It grows pretty large, and a savage striker. Trolling is one method used by the Indians to catch this fish. The bucktail, that the whites copied from the early Indians, was used. A large hook was concealed in a portion of a buck's tail. Other baits used are live sucker and chub minnows, small perch, field mice, strips of fish, and frogs. Be sure you play your fish out before trying to land him as he is a fooler.

Smelts
The sweetest little eating fish in the market. In Chicago, this little fish is as popular as Minnesota's pike. For bait use small minnows, crawfish, or parts of other fish.

Yellow Perch
They can be caught almost any hour of the day. A fish good to eat, but hard to scale. The regular baits are small minnows and worms, but they will readily take grasshoppers, grubworms, crawfish, strips of perch belly, and even their eyes.

White Perch
Somewhat larger than yellow perch, but have similar habits. Use same kind of bait as yellow perch.

Your Line
An 18 lb. test silk line is generally the standard all-around line for casting. But, for still fishing, or, trolling for the big ones we would advise using a stronger line.

Sunfishes—Several Species
A family fish who dwells in lakes and ponds. Perfect pan fish. The sunfish is a sporty fish, and will fight every ounce of its weight until landed. Several belonging in the sunfish family are: The Blue Sunfish, the Bluegill, the Orangespot, the Long Ear, Pumpkinseed, the War Mouth. Fish these almost any hour of the day, with the exception of the hours between 2 and 4 p.m. The real bait is angleworm, but they will take nightcrawlers, crickets, grubworms, grasshoppers, and even small minnows.

The Bullhead
They are found in muddy bottomed lakes or rivers. Fish these on the bottom, using a small hook. Angleworms and chunks of liver are the baits. Fish these late evenings and nights.

The Catfish
Fish these same as above. The more stinkest baits you use for Catfish, the better chance you have of attracting them, because like other fish they have a keen sense of smell. They will go a long way up stream to reach a bait. Your author has also caught many Cats, yes limits, using small frogs and parts of other. Other baits used, doughballs, chicken entrails, crawfish, grasshoppers, and minnows. For a good reliable stink bait recipe send dime and stamp.

The Carp Family
The Carp: Fish these near bottom using small hook and doughballs.

The Sucker: Fish these near bottom using small hook, and angleworm for bait.

Buffalo Fish: Should be fished same as sucker.

The Sheep Head
A good eating fish, but somewhat rich. In Minnesota rivers the Indians use angleworms for bait. Fish these near bottom using heavy sinkers, no bobber, and a smaller hook. These will fight with dash and spirit. They bite very slow—a slow slight jerk should remind you to set the hook.

Walleyed Pike
A delicious dish. Belongs to the perch rather than the pike family. During early spring the walleye seeks the shallow waters, over sandbars, rocky reefs and swift waters. Shinner minnows about 2½ inches long with a spinner attached and dropped to within a foot of the bottom is one method used by the Indians, known as stillfishing. Jerk the line a little at intervals to draw the fish's attention.

They bite on the minnow very slow, so give them plenty of time before setting hook. Then, there is the trolling method, using the same bait and tackle.

Angle-Worm
An earthworm used as bait for angling. When first handled the ladies' call it "Icky."

Great Northern Pike
Northerns feed early in the mornings and late in the afternoons. At this time they will be found in weedy and shallow water feeding. During the midday heat look for them in deeper waters. The Indians use shinner, chub, or sucker minnows measuring about 4 inches long. Always hook the minnows lightly before the dorsal fin. Let him have the minnow about a minute before setting the hook. The pike usually runs with the minnow first, turns it before swallowing head first. This fish, like the "muskie," must be played out with precaution. Many a northern has fallen back into the water because of carelessness.

The Pickerel
Fish same as pike above. Same bait.

Small Mouth Bass

The small mouth bass is the cousin of the large mouth. It is fished much like the large mouth, only that the smallmouth habitat is rocky, cold and deeper water. Fish using same bait as large mouth. Other live lures for both mentioned bass are: Minnows, beetles, small perch, shawfish, grasshoppers. The Indians also used small bullheads in catching this fish.

Crappie and Calico Bass

Excellent pan fish. These two fish are similar to each other. For bait use small minnows, crickets, grubworms. They will take cutbaits, but minnow is the bait.

Rock Bass

They can be found in rocky bottoms. For bait use same as above.

Scientific Fishing

Fishing is like a trade or profession, and contrary to the belief of many that all one needs is a lake full of fish.

First of all, a person needs to know the spots on the lake. Then, you need to know their feeding habits. You need to know, according to season, just where and what time to fish them. The moon, the direction of the wind are points also observed by our expert Indian fishermen. And other points. So fishing is an art.

INDIAN FLAVORING HERBS

The Indians used very few flavoring agents simply because they were not necessary with wild foods. In different parts of the country they did, however, have an herb or two for flavoring certain foods.

The Indians of the Southwest used Western Horsemint (Monarda menthaefolia) for flavoring meats. A lemon-scented variety of Monarda (citriodora) was used especially with rabbits. The Choctaw Indians gathered the leaves of Sassafras after they have turned red in the fall. The leaves were sun-dried then pulverized. "About a teaspoonful of this powder added to a kettle of soup gives it a glutinous quality and the flavor also is relished." Wild Ginger root was a very popular flavoring agent for Indians of the Great Lake Regions. The roots were especially used for strong flavored meats and fish.

INDIAN HERBAL LORE

According to an old Panamint Indian squaw, medicine men drank a tea made from the strong scented Thamnosma in order that they may find long lost things. She added it makes the drinker "crazy like coyotes."

Old Zuni Indians of New Mexico believed when one touches a Datura blossom with moist hands, the impression will be imprinted on the hand and wherever the hand touches the body. The blossoms will appear on the hair if the hand is placed on the head.

The Meskwaki Indians chewed the root of Great Ragweed to drive away fear at night. The same tribe believed when the pulverized herb of Cardinal Lobelia is thrown to the winds it would dispel an approaching storm.

In times of gales or strong winds, the Thompson Indians chewed the root of Peucedanum macrocarpum and spat it against the wind in the belief this would calm the elements.

When the Wild Sunflower blooms prolifically, the Pueblo Indians believe it is a sign of an abundant harvest.

The Wailakis of California have a superstition to the effect that Meadow Rue (Thalictrum polycarpum) is capable of making dead Indians have bad dreams if it is allowed to grow on their graves. When, therefore, their living friends feel their conscience troubled, they go out to the grave, and, if they find the plant growing there, they dig it up, and, as a sort of propitiation for their neglect, wash their heads with the juice from the crushed stems and leaves.

The Thompson Indians believed if the whole plant of Asarum candatum with roots or sometimes only the stems are put in bedding of infants when they are restless or ill, it is said to make them quiet or well. (The dried roots have a delightful fragrance which is retained for many months).

Pueblo tribes chewed the root of Scarlet Penstemon and rubbed it over the rabbit-stick or boomerang to insure success in the hunt. "A rabbit-stick thus treated is sure to kill every rabbit at which it is aimed, provided the thrower has a good heart."

INDIAN VEGETAL DYES

Indian dyes were made very simple compared to white man's vegetal dyes. Usually the dye plant was just boiled in a minimum quantity of water with a mordant or fixer containing tannin such as oak bark or alder. Some dye plants required no fixer. The material to be dyed was generally immersed in the hot dye water after it was boiled long enough to produce the desired shade. If the proper shade was not obtained with the first immersion, the process was repeated with two or more dippings.

While the Indian methods were simple, the range of colors were very limited. Apparently the best and easiest colors obtainable were shades of red, brown and yellow.

Many fine Indian dyes were lost because their makers never divulged their secrets. Others were forgotten because they were replaced by white man's dyes.

The following formulae are boiled with a minimum quantity of water. The intensity of color is determined by the quantity of dye material used and the length of time it is boiled.

Scarlet Red—2 parts Blood root, 1 part Wild Plum bark, 1 part Red Osier Dogwood bark, 1 part Alder bark.
Light Red—1 part Red Osier Dogwood, 1 part Alder Bark.
Dark Red—Hemlock bark, rock dust added to set color.
Mahogany Red—Blossoms of Coreopsis cardaminefolia.
Brownish Red—Inner bark of White Birch.
Red Brown—Alder Bark. Immerse cloth in boiling liquid.
Orange Red—Fresh or dried Blood root.
Red Yellow—Bark of Black Oak.
Orange Shade—Equal parts of Sumach root and Blood Root.
Orange Yellow—Whole FRESH GREEN plant of Jewel Weed steeped in boiling water. Rusty nails added to deepen color.
Yellow—Yellow Dock Roots.
Yellow—Sumach Roots.
Yellow—Inner root of Oregon Grape.
Yellow—Gold Thread Roots.
Ecru—1 part Blood Root, 1 part Wild Plum, 1 part Alder.
Black—Boil charcoal made of the bark of Black Walnut.
Deep Black—Butternut bark with Blue clay.

INDIAN CORN

This colorful corn is still used by the Indians of the Southwest as food. The dried ears make attractive decorations for the table and Fall festivities. They range from shades of red, blue-black, yellows and striped. Some ears develop solid colors, others contain multi-colored kernels.

INDIAN METHODS

KEEPING BERRIES: When the Indians gathered berries, they lined the bottom and sides of their baskets with Sweet Fern leaves. After the baskets were filled with berries, more leaves were used as a cover. This is said to help keep berries from spoiling too rapidly.

FOODS: Dehydrated foods have become very important to the modern warriors because of the reduced weight, size and retention of the essential nourishing values of the foods. Dehydration of foods is by no means new. For centuries before the present war, Indians dehydrated meats, vegetables and fruits for winter use and for supplying compact supplies for their warriors and hunters. Most foods were dried in similar manner as our present day methods except corn, which the Indians parboiled. When half cooked the kernels were removed, then dried on mats in the sun.

UTENSIL CLEANERS AND POLISHERS: Like the white folk of the Old World, Indians also used scouring rush for cleaning and polishing wood utensils.

PLANTING CORN: It was the signal for the Indians to plant corn when the Flowering Dogwood started blooming. At corn planting time, the Zuni Indians sprinkled the corn with twigs of Artemisia frigida dipped in water "that it may grow in abundance and be well developed."

BUG KILLER: The liquid from the boiled herb and roots of Mandrake was used by the Indians on their potato plants. This was said to kill potato bugs as well as bug's eggs in the ground.

INSECT REPELLENTS: In the Old World the white folk used the bruised leaves of European Elder to repel flies. The common American variety of Elder served the Indians for the same purpose.

The Indians built smudge fires of green branches of either Sweet Fern or Sweet Gale to drive off pesty mosquitoes.

The Yuki of California place the culled plants of Pogogyne parviflora in or about their houses to drive away fleas.

The Choctaw Indians of Louisiana scatter the fresh leaves of Hickory about to drive away fleas.

INDIAN LOVE CHARMS AND BELIEFS

The Indian woman was very much like her white sister in employing charms to attract the male. While the white lady used perfumes, cosmetics and other articles for lure, the Indian woman sought her love charms in the fields and forests.

The tuberous root of Beth Root or Trillium was a favorite love charm. The root was rubbed on the body of one desiring a mate, or pieces of the root were cooked and secretly mixed with the food intended for the warrior the girl desired.

The root of Giant Vetch was specially used to bring back a mate that went astray. The root was rubbed on the body, then wrapped up and placed under the pillow.

The following method advertised to an entire tribe that the squaw was seeking a mate: The lonely girl or woman cut a two foot length of branch, with a forked end, from a Menziesia bush. This was waved in the air, accompanied with songs. The method was at least a fair warning for the confirmed Indian bachelor.

Apparently the most successful way of obtaining a husband was with the following recipe: Get some hairs of warrior desired, and press them with hairs of the would-be wife, and some Bedstraw herb. Just as they stick together, so would the desired warrior stick to the squaw. The squaw who revealed this secret obtained a new husband every time she lost one. She lost 7 husbands—number 8 was still sticking.

Among tribes of the northwest, Avens was employed by the male, and Columbine by the female, to gain affection of the opposite sex. The root of Dutchman's Breeches was a popular love charm among Great Lake Indians. The lovesick warrior either throws the root at the girl desired, or chews the root and blows out the scent in order to attract the girl. To be sure she catches the scent, the Indian circles around the girl until she is so completely subdued, she will follow him wherever he goes, even against her will.

The following love charm required some skill: The warrior gathered Indian Paint Brush flowers, and concealed them upon the woman he desired. If this could be done without her knowledge, it would measurably weaken her resistance. A simpler method, was to carry the root of Wood Betony, when contemplating making love advances. This root was also used to reunite quarreling lovers. The root was chopped up and put into their food without their knowledge.

Rubbing the juice of Wild Orchid upon the cheek, was believed to be a sure method of securing a good husband.

The Indian dandy smoked a mixture of tobacco and Purple Meadow Rue or Wild Columbine seeds when he called on his favorite lady friend. This was supposed to bring luck.

A mixture consisting of Cardinal Lobelia and Great Blue Lobelia, was used as an anti-divorce remedy. The ground up roots were secretly put into some common dish, which was eaten by both man and wife. The quarrel was soon over, and they live happily together.

INDIAN POISON IVY LOTION

I am sending you a sample of weed found here in Minnesota in the marshes, which an Indian gathered and put on some W. P. A. workers for ivy poisoning, as they were working in bush land. He squeezed the juice on affected parts, and it healed right up. He also claims it is a cure for other surface caused skin troubles. One man had eczema on his hands and the distress didn't bother him after using this weed.—Writes Mrs. W. W.—Hinckley, Minn.

NOTE: Sample received was Jewel Weed or Wild Touch-me-not (Impatiens biflora).

N. H. Smith also mentions this herb in his book "Ethnobotany of the Forest Potawatomi Indians" published by Public Museum of the City of Milwaukee, Wisc. Smith states "This is accounted a valuable Medicine among the Forest Potawatomi who use the fresh juice of the plant to wash nettle stings or poison ivy infections. The writer knows that it instantly alleviates the sting of Stinging Nettle, and has it from the Indians that it will alleviate the itching of Poison Ivy."

SWEET ELM BARK—FOOD AND MEDICINE OF PIONEERS AND INDIANS

When crops failed or long severe winters exhausted food supplies, Indians and pioneers alike, were often saved from starvation by the use of Sweet Elm bark. This emergency source of food had the advantage of being available when all other sources of food failed. The use of Sweet Elm bark as food spread with the early colonies until the day when the vast forests were converted into farm lands.

Sweet Elm or Slippery Elm bark, as it is better known today, is obtained from trees which were in Indian times very common over a wide range of eastern parts of the New World. A thin layer of inner bark is the part used for food and medicine. This inner bark when dried has a delicate scent and slightly sweetish taste. Infused with water, Slippery Elm becomes very mucilaginous, with wonderful strengthening, soothing and healing properties, being harmless to infants and the aged. This bark is still recognized as an "Official drug."

Slippery Elm bark was highly extolled by herbalists in early American times. Samuel Henry, botanist, and "member of College of Physicians and Surgeons, and of the Medical Society of the City and Country of New York" wrote in 1814—"I have found it effectual for ulcers, burns, scalds, scorbutic affections, whites, gleets and recent clap: and is the best poultice that I know of for fresh wounds, burns and ulcers. Its constant use (as tea) is very proper for pregnant women during the seventh month." The American Dispensatory, printed in 1818, states: "It is useful in pleurises and forms an excellent poultice for tumours, and liniment for chaps." The American Eclectic Dispensatory (1855) states: "A tablespoonful of the powder boiled in a pint of new milk affords a nourishing diet for infants weaned from the breast, preventing the bowel complaints to which they are subject, and rendering them fat and healthy."

Slippery Elm bark is recognized in modern times for its soothing properties in cases of irritations of stomach and intestines. The powder mixed with milk is wholesome and nutritious. It is easily digested, and owing to the fact that it absorbs noxious gases, it is useful for inducing restful sleep, when taken at night. It is beneficial for infants and adults who have a tendency to constipation. The slippery nature ensures an easy passage during the processes of assimilation and elimination. The soothing action of Slippery Elm bark prevents many infantile stomach and bowel troubles which often sow the seeds of serious and chronic troubles later in life.

SLIPPERY ELM TEA

Make smooth paste with one teaspoonful of powdered Slippery Elm and small quantity of cold water, then pour on slowly a pint of boiling water, stirring until thoroughly mixed. Flavor with nutmeg or lemon if desired. This tea is excellent in cases of irritation of the mucous membrane of the stomach and intestines. The unsweetened Slippery Elm taken three times a day gives excellent results in gastritis, gastric catarrh, mucous colitis and enteritis, being tolerated by the stomach when all other foods fail. The tea is very soothing for coughs in bronchitis, bleeding from the lungs and consumption.

SLIPPERY ELM TEA WITH EGG

Beat up an egg with teaspoonful of the powdered bark. Pour boiling milk over mixture and sweeten to taste.

SLIPPERY ELM COMPOUND FOR COUGHS

To 1 pint of boiling water, add pinch of Cayenne, slice of lemon, 3 tablespoonsful honey, and 1 ounce of cut Slippery Elm bark. Allow to stand ½ hour, and strain. Take frequently in small doses.

SLIPPERY ELM USED AS POULTICE

For wounds, ulcers, burns and inflamed surfaces: Mix powdered Slippery Elm bark with hot water to make a smooth paste. Spread paste on clean cloth, bandage and apply over the parts affected. In cases of abscesses and old wounds, the Slippery Elm paste should be spread between cloths. If applied to parts of body where there is hair, the face of the poultice should be smeared with olive oil before applying. This poultice is very soothing and healing

Here is an excellent remedy for an infected sore. Break an egg and put the white in a cup, add a teaspoon of fine brown sugar and 1½ teaspoons of powdered slippery elm bark. Stir and mix. Do not beat. Cover the sore with a thin coating of the mixture and change it every 15 minutes.—Mrs. J.C.

HERBS USED BY THE INDIANS FOR HAIR

The Tewa Indian squaws steep the leaves of Apache Plume (Fallugia paradoxa) in water until they become soft. The infusion was used to wash the hair to promote its growth according to ethnobotanists.

The Thompson Indians of British Columbia soaked the flowers, leaves and stems of Prairie Flax (Linum lewisii) to make a wash for the head of pubescents, especially female. It is believed to be good for the hair and when used on the skin it enhances its beauty. The same tribe also used Wild Tobacco (Nicotiana attenuata). Teit states in his Ethnobotany of the Thompson Indians: "A decoction of the plant is used as a wash for the head to remove loose dandruff. Some Indians think its use will keep the hair from turning gray until very late in life. They say they think the use of soaps procured from the whites for washing the head and hair causes the latter to become dry, scanty, and prematurely gray. When the Indians used only their own head washes and oils and method of treatment for the hair people had very fine hair and it did not usually turn gray until they were very old." More natural diets and out of door life may also have helped.

INDIAN SOAPS AND SHAMPOOS

Growing along the dry hillsides and plains of California may be seen countless clusters of strap-leaved plants. In summer these clusters are staked with very tall stalks bearing bluish green buds. In the afternoon, small white, lily-like flowers burst forth and almost as rapidly shrivel up and die. This is Chlorogalum, the Indian Soap Plant.

Soap-plant or Chlorogalum has a large bottle shaped bulb which is wrapped in coarse hair-like fiber. This fiber was used by the Indians for bedding, brushes, etc. The powerful saponin properties of Soap-plant are contained in the bulb proper. "When crushed and rubbed into any fabric with water it froths up like ordinary soap. Long before the advent of the white man this was most extensively used for soap by the Indians, and even now many old squaws use it in preference to the ordinary article. Others prefer it especially in cleansing baskets and in washing their hair; and, indeed, on account of the absence of any alkali it is really preferable for washing silk and any delicate fabrics. It is used considerably for the special purpose of removing dandruff from the scalp. The hair is left very soft and glossy." (Chesnut—*Plants Used by the Indians of Mendocino Co., Calif.* P. 320).

The roasted bulb of Soap-plant was used antiseptically as a poultice on sores.

Across the Rocky Mountains grew two other varieties of Indian Soap plants. Along the northern slopes may be found Yucca glauca, to the south through Arizona, New Mexico and Texas may be found Yucca baccata. The large roots of both plants provide an excellent lather. Before the introduction of commercial soap, these plants provided the main washing medium for the Indians of this area. The roots are still employed for shampooing the hair, for washing woolens and native cotton fabrics. The soap was prepared by placing the chopped dried roots into a cloth bag then allowed to steep in warm water. After a few minutes the water is briskly stirred with the bag of roots until a good lather is produced.

CIVILIZATION ADOPTS INDIAN LAXATIVE

When the early adventurers and traders penetrated the Pacific Northwest in their endless search for gold and furs, they paid no attention to the peculiar tree bark being used by the Indians of this region.

As time passed a new type of white people came with their families, covered wagons, a meagre assortment of tools and seeds. Until these families were well established the fields and forests had to supply all their needs. The peculiar bark found so much in Indian equipment was soon adopted by the pioneers as a substitute for medicine no longer obtainable after moving beyond the borders of civilization. Missionaries called this bark Cascara sagrada or Holy Bark, believing it to be the Chittemwood of the Bible.

Cascara is a small tree found growing on the western slopes of the Rocky Mountains from Northern California to British Columbia. Medicinally Cascara is similar in action to its related European Buckthorn. The Indian bark is, however, considered superior and has almost entirely replaced the Old World variety.

Cascara bark improves with age. A strong decoction acts as physic and a mild infusion is used as laxative. The British Pharmaceutical Codex (1934) states: "It is a useful laxative in haemorrhoidal conditions. Small repeated doses after meals are more effective in chronic constipation than a large dose taken at night." The U. S. Dispensatory states: "Cascara Sagrada belongs to the group of vegetable cathartics whose activity depends upon the presence of one or more hydroxymethylanthraguinones—in the treatment of chronic constipation it acts very favorably. It often appears to restore tone to the relaxed bowel and in this way produces a permanent beneficial effect."

Herbalists generally believe best results are obtained when Cascara is mixed with other herb simples.

ON THE FARM

EARLY AMERICAN RECIPES FOR CARE OF LIVE STOCK

Ring-Worms on Horses: Take tobacco ashes, wet with vinegar, apply it, and it will cure them.

To Make Hogs Grow Fat and Well: Never wean your pigs till six weeks or three months old; feed them only twice a day, as nigh twelve hours apart as possible; give them their regular allowance, and no more than they will eat up clean; give a hog weighing 50 lbs. two ounces sulphur in sweet milk and Indian meal fall and spring; keep them in summer in grass yard, well rung, where they can get water; keep their pen clean, and in winter give them a warm pen and a clean dry nest; never keep more than four in one pen.

To Have Your Sows Pregnant: Give them eight or ten ears of roasted corn.

To Get Horse Colts: Put your mare before the full of the moon and when the sign is below the heart.

To Make a Star on Forehead of Horse: Take pickled mackerel and bind it on any shape you wish, for three or four days, repeating, and it will produce a white spot. Rub a white spot made by the saddle (in the spring, before he sheds his coat), with bacon grease, and it will be black, or have its natural color.

To Keep Flies from Horses: Take the leaves of garden pumpkins or cucumbers, pound, strain out the juice, and wash your horses with it; or wash them with the juice of mallows; or take pulverized verdigris, boil in vinegar, and wash with it. Be careful and keep it from the eyes.

For Raising Calves: Boil for two calves, one pint of flax seed ten minutes in water, and put in skim milk, warm. Give cattle warm water to drink in cold weather.

To Stop Blood in the Nose or Elsewhere on Horse: Pound the tender tops of Hyssop and put them in the nose, or bind them on the wound.

Wind Colic in Horses: Take a quart of warm water, one pint gin, one pint molasses, two gills powdered mustard seed, pour it down, and drive the creature around briskly.

To Stop Cattle Vomiting: Boil tansy and mint, equal parts, and give one quart once an hour till it stops.

For Cough in Sheep: Take Coltsfoot, Lungwort, and Maiden Hair, each two ounces, boil them in one quart water strong, sweeten with honey, and give one gill a day to sheep.

For Fever in Sheep: Dissolve one-half ounce saltpetre in one gill water, and one gill vinegar, and give it to them.

For Staggers in Sheep: Dissolve ½ ounce Assafoetida in ½ gill warm water, and put ½ spoonful in each ear.

EARLY AMERICAN FARM AND GARDEN RECIPES

To Prevent Black Flies from Destroying Gardens: Plant buckwheat among your other seeds, and let it stand until the plants are out of their way.

To Preserve Cucumbers and Squashes from Flies and Worms: Make a strong tea of Hops and Elder leaves, and mix a little flour, and whitewash the plants.

To Destroy Cut Worms and Hessian Flies: Take the water that you boil potatoes in and sprinkle your grain and plants. It destroys insects from the egg to the fly.

To Keep Insects from Cucumbers and Squashes: Sprinkle them with weak hen dung water; or wet a quill with spirits turpentine, and put in the hill.

To Destroy Caterpillars on Fruit Trees: Smoke them well with sulphur, pitch or rosin, and it will destroy them on herbs and flowers.

To Drive Rats and Mice from Barns: Take the plant called Hounds' Tongue, pound it with a hammer, and put it in your grainery, or barn, or in your cellar, and they will leave very quick.

To Preserve Peach Trees from mildew: In March or April, take away all the turf and dirt you can and not hurt the roots, and put fresh rotten turf in its place.

To Preserve Fruit Trees: Pour hot soap suds around your trees, and wash them with thin soap in the fall and spring; scrape off the moss and rough bark, and cut off the nubs and gummy spots.

To Cut Hardwood Timber to Make It Durable: Cut it in October, November, December and January, in the old of the moon, when the sap is down. Cut all kinds of timber that sheds its leaves in the fall, in the third quarter of the moon—but, if possible, in the winter. It is more durable when cut in the month of December, which is the best month. Evergreen timber must be cut in the second quarter of the moon, and in the fall and winter. All kinds of timber cut in December, as above stated, will last as long again as it will, cut in June.

To Kill Canada Thistles: Cut them in June, July and August, when the sign is in the heart, in the old of the moon.

To Save Bees: About the first of May, raise your hive and lay salt under the edges of the hive.

Fall Plowing: Fall plowing kills weeds, worms, and grubs.

Burdock Leaf Poultice: The leaves of this plant, wilted by the fire, and applied to an external injury, will allay the inflammation, and ease pain—and they are good pounded and put on to a bruise or sprain, as it will give immediate relief.

HERBAL MIXTURES FOR ANIMALS
LAXATIVE FOR SHEEP
Epsom Salts, 1 ounce
Ginger, ⅛ teaspoonful
Gentian, 1 teaspoonful
Warm Water, 2 ounces
Linseed Oil, 1 ounce

The above may be given alone, or with gruel, to a full grown sheep; and from one-fourth to one-half to a lamb, according to its age.

GENERAL TONIC FOR SHEEP
Gentian, 2 teaspoonfuls
Columbo, 2 teaspoonfuls
Ginger, ½ teaspoonful

Give in 4 ounces of warm gruel.

STIMULATING DRINK FOR CATTLE
Epsom Salts, 1 pound
Ginger, ½ ounce
Carbonate of Ammonia, ½ ounce

Pour 1 qt. of boiling water upon the ingredients; stir them well and give when milk-warm.

STIMULATING DRINK FOR CATTLE
Ginger, powdered, ½ ounce
Caraway Seeds, 6 teaspoonfuls
Allspice, ½ ounce

Mix in a quart of warm waater.

DIARRHEA IN CALVES
Prepared chalk, 2 teaspoonfuls
Powdered Catechu, ½ teaspoonful
Ginger, ½ teaspoonful
Essence Peppermint, 5 drops

Mix, and give twice a day.

BLOOD TONIC FOR HORSES
Powdered Gentian, 2½ ounces
Powdered Sassafras Bark, 2 ounces
Powdered Elecampane, 2 ounces
Powdered Skunk Cabbage, 1 ounce
Powdered Cream Tartar, 1 ounce
Powdered Saltpetre, 1 ounce
Powdered Ginger, 1 ounce
Powdered Sulphur, 1 ounce
Powdered Blood Root, 1 ounce
Powdered Buchu Leaves, 1 ounce

If your horse is in bad health, give a tablespoonful of the above twice a day in bran mash; or in chronic cough give a tablespoonful once a day for fifteen days.

TRAINING BALKY HORSES
Whirl him rapidly round until he is giddy. In order to do this take him from the vehicle. Don't let him step out, hold him to the smallest possible circle. It will not take more than a couple of doses to effectually cure him.

MANGE ON HORSES
Tobacco, 2 ounces
Water, 1 quart
Soft Soap, 2 ounces
Sulphur, 2 ounces

Boil the tobacco in the water, strain and add the soft soap and sulphur.

STOMACH DISORDER IN HORSES
Powdered Gentian, ½ ounce
Powdered Ginger, 1½ teaspoonfuls
Carbonate of Soda, 1 drachm

Molasses to form a ball.

OINTMENT FOR HORSES HOOFS
Rosin, 4 ounces
Beeswax, 4 ounces
Lard, 8 ounces
Honey, 2 ounces

Mix slowly and gently, bring to a boil; then add less than 1 pint of spirits turpentine; then remove and stir till cool. The above is considered an excellent remedy for cracked hoofs.

TO FATTEN HORSES
Many good horses devour large quantities of hay and grain, and yet continue poor, and the more they eat the poorer they appear to grow. The fault is, that the food is not properly assimilated. If the usual feed has been unground grain and hay, nothing but a change will make any desirable change in the appearance of the animal. In case oil meal cannot be obtained readily, mingle a bushel of flaxseed with a bushel of barley, one of oats, and another bushel of Indian corn, and let it be ground into fine meal. This will be a fair proportion for all his feed. Or the meal or barley, oats and corn, in equal quantities, may at first procured and ¼ of oil cake mingled with it when the meal is sprinkled on cut feed. Feed 2 or 3 quarts of the mixture 3 times daily with a peck of cut hay and straw. If the horse will eat that amount greedily, let the quantity be gradually increased, until he will eat 4, 5 or 6 quarts at every feeding, 3 times a day. So long as the animal will eat this allowance the quantity may be increased a little every day. But always avoid the practice of allowing the horse to stand at a rack well filled with hay. In order to fatten a horse that has run down in flesh, the groom should be very particular to feed the animal no more than he will eat up clean and lick his manger for more. Follow the above suggestions and the result will be satisfactory.

PROTECTING HORSES FROM GADFLY
The bites of the gadfly are so troublesome in their effects that it is sometimes desirable to prevent them if possible. This is effected by making a strong infusion of the fresh green bark of the Elder, washing the flanks, etc., with it before going out.

HOW FOLKS KEPT FOODS WITHOUT REFRIGERATORS OR ICEBOXES

Fish were preserved in a living state for 14 days or longer without water, by stopping their mouths with crumbs of bread steeped in brandy, pouring a little brandy into them, and then placing them in straw in a moderately cool situation.—From 1846 Recipe Book.

Oysters were kept alive and fattened (if healthy) by the following method: Wash the outside of the shells with clean water and a broom, till all the slime is removed. Then put them in layers in a tub, with sprinklings of oatmeal and salt. Just cover them with clear water. Keep the tub covered, and change water and meal every day. They must also be kept free from slime. The water may be almost as salty as sea water.

To Preserve Eggs for many Weeks: As soon as possible after the eggs are taken from the nests, brush each one separately with a thin solution of gum Arabic, being careful to leave no portion of the shell uncovered by it. The half of each egg must first be done and left to become dry, before the remainder is touched, that the gum may not be rubbed off any part by its coming in contact, while wet, with the hand as it is held to be varnished, or with the table when it is laid down to harden. Eggs will remain fit for use for a very long time if carefully kept; but attention should always be given to the cleanliness of the shells before they are stored, as when these are soiled, and then excluded from the air, they will sometimes become very offensive. Those which are collected immediately after the harvest are the best, both for eating and for putting up in store: They should be collected in dry weather when they are required to be kept.

Preserving Butter in Brine: To three gallons of brine strong enough to bear an egg, add one quarter pound good loaf sugar, and one tablespoonful of saltpetre; boil the brine, and when it is cold strain carefully. Pack butter closely in small jars, and allow the brine to cover the butter to the depth of at least four inches. This completely excludes the air. If practicable make your butter into small rolls, wrap each carefully in a clean muslin cloth, tying up with a string; place a weight over the butter to keep it all submerged in the brine. This mode is most recommended by those who have tried both.

Preserving Sausage Meat: Take fresh-made sausage, make it into balls as for the table, cook it slowly, but well done; then lay it evenly in a tin can or earthen jar, pouring all the grease that fries from the meat over it, as each layer is placed in the can. When done cooking the meat should be entirely covered with lard to exclude the air.

To Salt Meat: In the summer season, especially, meat is frequently spoiled by the cook forgetting to take out the kernels: one in the udder of a round of beef,—in the fat in the middle of the round,—those about the thick end of the flank, etc., if these are not taken out, all the salt in the world will not keep the meat.

The art of salting meat is to rub in the salt thoroughly and evenly into every part, and to fill all the holes full of salt where the kernels were taken out, and where the butcher's skewers were.

A round of beef of 25 pounds will take a pound and a half of salt to be rubbed in all at first, and requires to be turned and rubbed every day with the brine: it will be ready for dressing in four or five days, if you do not wish it very salty.

In summer, the sooner meat is salted after it is killed the better, and care must be taken to defend it from the flies.

In winter, it will eat the shorter and tenderer if kept a few days (according to the temperature of the weather) before it is salted.

In frosty weather, take care the meat is not frozen, and warm the salt in a frying pan. The extremes of heat and cold are equally unfavourable for the process of salting; in the former the meat changes before the salt can effect it; in the latter it is so hardened, and the juices are so congealed that the salt cannot penetrate it.

If you wish it red, rub it first with saltpetre, in the proportion of half an ounce and the like quantity of moist sugar, to a pound of common salt.

You may impregnate meat with a very agreeable vegetable flavour, by pounding some sweet herbs and onions with the salt: You may make it still more relished by adding a little savoury spice.

To increase your reputation as a cook, try combining Sage with pork or beans; Dill seed with new potatoes; Thyme or Basil with tomatoes; Mint with peas; Anise seed with carrots—both in salads and when cooking. A pinch of herb—fresh or dried—goes a long way.

VARIOUS USES FOR PEPPERMINT

If those who are suffering from violent simple headache, bind Peppermint across their forehead, they will soon experience relief and ease.

A cupful of Peppermint tea taken every morning and evening, assists the digestion.

The powder renders the same service if one or two pinches are taken daily in the food or in water. It is a most excellent, time-honored stomachic!

Tips from Old Garden Books

Pliny wrote almost 2000 years ago that the sowing of beans is equal to manure for land, and enriches it exceedingly; and that in the vicinity of Macedonia and Thessaly, the custom was to plough them into the ground just as they began to bloom.

The foliage of Sweet Potatoes is much relished by cattle; and cows that are fed upon it yield an increased and improved quantity of milk.

A board rubbed over a stake driven into the ground, will drive earthworms to the surface.

On the Isle of Jersey, Strawberry plants are covered over during cold weather with layers of sea-weed, a plan which is said to increase the size and goodness of the fruit.

Charcoal powder applied to the roots, darkens the flowers of the dahlia, the rose, the petunia, etc. Peat application to roots, changes the red of the hydrangea to blue; while many chemical salts in minute proportions modify or enrich the colors of garden flowers. Carbonate of soda reddens ornamental hyacinths, and superphosphate of lime alters in various ways, the hue or bloom of other cultivated plants.

To keep garlic and onions from sprouting, old time farmers dipped the heads of them in warm salt water.

It is declared that onions wax greater, if they be taken out of the earth, and laid a-drying 20 days, and then set again; and yet more if the outer-most peel be taken off all over.

Instinct has taught the deer, when ready to calve, to feed upon the wild parsnip.

Cows will feed freely on parsnip roots, which will cause them to give abundance of milk of a rich quality. In Germany they are sown for this purpose. Sheep when lambing, if fed with this root, produce much milk.

Let Geese Weed Your Farm and Garden

In this day of high wages, weeding has become a problem, especially near industrial areas. Many farmers, gardeners and nurserymen have overcome this situation and added to their profits by putting a flock of geese to work in their growing beds. Geese cannot be put in every type of garden, but they have been successfully used to keep down weeds in nurseries growing young trees, shrubs and evergreens. Geese have been used to weed cotton fields, strawberry and raspberry beds and even turned into Alfalfa fields. It is reported they eat only the weeds and brome grass.

Geese are also useful in keeping irrigation and drainage ditches from choking with weeds.

Old Time Repellents

To Destroy Spiders: After you have destroyed their webs, sprinkle the rooms with water wherein Plantain has been boiled, and smoke them with benzoin and frankincense, and none of them will ever appear there, at least, until the scent of these things is utterly extinguished—when the sprinkling may again be repeated, if it be found necessary.

To Drive Away Snakes: Burn Wallwort, Rue and Bay leaves, scatter the ashes and some fresh leaves in their haunts, and they will either immediately depart, or die in their holes or places of resort.

To Destroy Fleas: For the former, sprinkle the room with water wherein the roots of wild cucumbers and wormwood have been boiled; and lay between the mat and the bed, the herb Smartweed or Hound's-tongue, which grows in most ditches in summer.

To Destroy Moths: These usually infest clothes and hangings, and therefore prove very mischievous. If among clothes—to destroy them, make a powder of sassafras, the flowers of lavender, and the dried leaves of rue; lay these in small sprinklings amongst your woolens, silks, or linen, and scent your drawers or trunks well with them, and no moth will live in the scent of them.

But if they eat your hangings, or other things which you cannot order with this powder, then burn storax and sulphur in the room, the doors and windows being closed, and the scent will utterly destroy them, and the scent remaining in the hangings, will keep others from coming to them for 6 months, or as long as the scent remains in them, and then you may renew it.

Lambs Fatten Faster If Shorn of Wool

Lambs that have their wool removed will fatten faster, while requiring less feed, than will their coated cousins.

In a two-year study made by Cecil Pierce, an animal husbandman at the Oregon State College eastern Oregon branch experiment station in Union, Ore., he found that shorn lambs fed in both open lots and shelters, gained more than 17% a day over the wooled lambs.—Science News Letter.

Hogs were found to gain weight more quickly and more economically if they had plenty of fresh water during freezing weather.

A *cow* in the shade can be worth five in the sun; tests show that milk production can vary from 7.1 pounds in 105 degrees Fahrenheit temperature to 35.5 pounds at 51 degrees.

SLIPPERY ELM AS A GARGLE

"Slippery Elm boiled in water makes one of the best gargles for sore throat that can be supplied by the whole list of medicines. It should be sweetened with honey."—From Hills Family Herbal.

Tips from a Very Old Poultry Book

Chicken Lice: If your poultry be much troubled with lice, as it is common, proceeding from corrupt food, or want of bathing or fluttering in sand, ashes or such like—take pepper and mixing it with warm water, wash your poultry therein, and it will kill all sorts of vermin.

Sore Eyes in Chickens: In this case, take a leaf or two of Ground-Ivy—and chewing it well in your mouth, suck out the juice and spit it into the sore eye, and it will assuredly heal, as hath been often tried.

Making Chickens Tender: About an hour before you desire to kill them, pour down the throat of each, a spoonful of vinegar, and let them run about in the yard, and when they are killed, hang them up in their feathers, by the heels, in a smoky chimney; then pull and dress them, and they will be very tender.

If present occasion require them, when you have pulled and drawn them, heat a good pebble stone—wrap it up in a fine rag, and so put it into the belly of the foul, closing the vent to keep in the steam, and in half an hour they will be much tenderer than otherwise they would be.

To Fatten Fowl: Take Nettle leaves and seeds, gathered and dried in their proper season; beat them into powder, and make it into paste with wheat-bran or flour—adding a little sweet olive oil. Make this up into little cakes—coop them up, and duly feed them with it, giving them water wherein barley has been boiled, and they will be fat at or before the time proposed.

To Preserve Fowl: Take a large cask—knock out a board or two at the head, and in the others drive hooks to hang your fowls on, so as they may not touch each other, and cover the open places with the boards, leaving only the bung hole for an air vent; set them in a dry cool place, and they will keep as long again as in any other place. And thus you may keep flesh or fish.

"The growth of Wormwood should be encouraged in poultry walks—it being found beneficial to them."

"Rue leaves are sometimes gathered as a medicinal simple, and are also given to poultry having the croup."—London's "Encyclopaedia of Gardening," 1834.

"The pip or roupe is a common disease amongst their poultry, infecting one another with it. I conceive it cometh of a cold moisture of the brain. They will be very sleepie with it. The best cure for it is Garlic, and smoking of them with dryed Hysope."—John Josselyn, 1672.

Old chickens, or fowls lay well, and become fat and lively, when fed a mixture of Juniper berries and Ground Flax seed.

Old Recipes for Farm Stock

Recipe, which is excellent for horses that are stuffed up, and have a difficulty of respiration: Take powder of Licorice, and flowers of Brimstone, of each equal parts; mix them, and give from 2 oz. to 4 oz., according to the size of the horse, twice a day. This is a good medicine to cure broken-winded horses, taken at the beginning—or for short-winded or pursy horses, when the malady is confirmed.—Tournefort's 1725 "Compleat History of Drugs."

Parsley herb is good for sheep that have eaten a kind of wild ranunculus, which causes a worm to destroy their liver. It is also said to be an excellent remedy to preserve sheep from the rot, provided they are fed twice a week, for 2 or 3 hours each time, with this herb.—From Phillips "Kitchen Garden."

"When a cow is not well, and doesn't eat heartily, just give her a single handful of Poke root, cut fine."

"Cimicifuga racemosa—the infusion of the bruised root, is so generally regarded as a sort of panacea for stock (especially sick cows) that every farmer ought to know it, and be able with certainty to designate it."—From "Weeds and Useful Plants," 1859.

"Poke berries have done wonders for our cow. I tried medicines without much help. Poke berries have softened up the bag, and she has come back to her full amount of milk—which is 3 gallons to a milking.

"My father used Poke berries and a few bushes grew in the pasture. They were gathered if the cows didn't get them first, so that he would have a supply when needed."—S.W., Greeley, Neb.

"And the leaves of the trees were for the healing of the nations." (Rev. 22, 2.)

"And the fruit thereof shall be for meat, and the leaf thereof shall be medicine." (Ezek. 47, 12.)

"He causeth the grass to grow for the cattle, and herb for the service of man." (Psalm 104, 14.)

Man should observe kind Nature's laws, and from them learn result and cause.

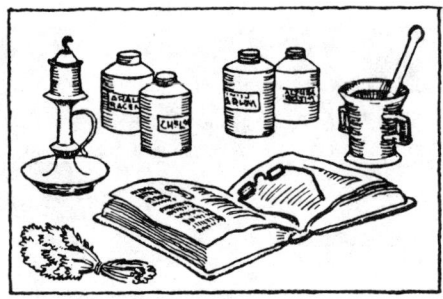

SECRETS OF AN OLD RECIPE BOOK

Beneficial Purpose to which the Juice of Aloes may be applied

In the East-Indies aloes are employed as a varnish, to preserve wood from worms and other insects; and skins, and even living animals are anointed with it for the same reason. The havoc committed by the white ants in India first suggested the trial of aloe juice, to protect wood from them; for which purpose the juice is either used as extracted, or in solution, by some solvent.

Efficacy of the Juice of Aloes on Ships Bottoms

Aloes have been found effectual in preserving ships from the ravages of the worm and the adhesion of barnacles. The ship's bottom, for this purpose, is smeared with a composition of hepatic aloes, turpentine, tallow, and white lead. In proof of the efficacy of this method, two planks of equal thickness, and cut off the same tree, were placed under water, one in its natural state, and the other smeared with the composition. On taking them up, after being immersed eight months, the latter was found to be perfect as at first, while the former was entirely penetrated with insects, and in a state of absolute rottenness.

To soften Ivory and Bones

Take sage, boil it in strong vinegar, strain the decoction through a piece of close cloth; and when you have a mind to soften bones or ivory, steep them in this liquor, and the longer they remain in it the softer they will grow.

Easy Method of discovering whether or not Seeds are sufficiently ripe

Seeds, when not sufficiently ripe, will swim, but when arrived at full maturity, they will be found uniformly to fall to the bottom; and fact that is said to hold equally true of all seeds, from the cocoa nut to the orchids.

On preserving Seeds of Plants in a State fit for Vegetation

Seeds of plants may be preserved, for many months at least, by causing them to be packed, either in husks, pods, etc., in absorbent paper, with raisins or brown moist sugar; or a good way, practised by gardeners, is to wrap the seed in brown paper or cartridge paper, pasted down, and then varnish over.

To facilitate the Growth of Foreign Seeds

Mr. Humboldt has found, that seeds which do not commonly germinate in our climate, or in our hot-houses, and which of course we cannot raise for our gardens, or hope to naturalize in our fields, become capable of germinating, when immersed for some days in a weak oxygenized muriatic acid. This interesting discovery has already turned to advantage in several botanic gardens.

To Prevent Blossom and Fruit Trees from being damaged by early Spring Frost

If a rope (a hempen one it is presumed) be intermixed among the branches of a fruit tree in blossom, and the end of it brought down, so as to terminate in a bucket of water, and should a slight frost take place in the night-time, in that case the tree will not be affected by the frost; but a film of ice, of considerable thickness, will be formed on the surface of the bucket in which the rope's end is immersed, although it has often happened that another bucket of water, placed beside it for the sake of experiment, has had no ice at all upon it.

Chinese Mode of propagating Fruit Trees

The ingenious people of China have a common method of propagating several kinds of fruit trees, which of late years has been practised with success in Bengal. The method is simply this: They strip a ring of bark, about an inch in width, from a bearing branch, surround the place with a ball of fat earth, or loam, bound fast to the branch with a piece of matting: over this they suspend a pot or horn, with water, having a small hole in the bottom just sufficient to let the water drop, in order to keep the earth constantly moist. The branch throws new roots into the earth just above the place where the ring of bark was stripped off. The operation is performed in the spring, and the branch is sawn off and put into the ground at the fall of the leaf. The following year it will bear fruit.

To Increase the Growth of Trees

It may be depended upon as a fact, that by occasionally washing the stems of trees, their growth will be greatly increased: for several recent experiments have proved that all the ingredients of vegetation united, which are received from the roots, stem, branches, and leaves, of a mossy and dirty tree, do not produce half the increase either in wood or fruit, that another gains whose stem is clean. It is clearly obvious that prop-

Secrets of an old recipe book—Continued

er nourishment cannot be received from rain, for the dirty stem will retain the moisture longer than when clean, and the moss and dirt will absorb the finest parts of the dew, and likewise act as a screen, by depriving the tree of that share of sun and air which it requires.

The Virtues of Hay Tea for Cattle

When there is a scarcity of hay, the following experiment will be found a valuable succedancum to the cattle, and a great saving to the farmer.

Boil about a handful of hay in 3 gallons of water (and so in proportion for any greater or smaller quantity) or if the water is poured boiling hot on the hay, it will answer nearly as well. Give it to the cattle and horses to drink when cold; or if the cattle or horses are any way ill, and under cover, give it to them blood warm.

This drink is so extremely nutritive that it nourishes the cattle astonishingly, it replenishes the udder of the cows with a prodigious quantity of milk, makes the horses stale plentifully, and keeps them healthy and strong; and by this method one truss or hundred of hay will go as far as eight or ten otherwise would do. The cattle and horses will not seem to like it at first, but if they are kept till they are very thirsty they will drink freely of it ever afterwards.

Farmers, and others, in Sweden, and other cold countries, who have cattle and horses, when they are in want of fodder, constantly pursue this method, and find the good effects of it; and there is no doubt but this method would have the same good effect on sheep in severe weather, when the sheep are housed, or the land covered with snow, especially if they were given a small quantity of salt, (a practice used in Spain to make the wool fine and soft,) to strengthen the sheep, and prevent the rot, for the stronger the sheep are the greater the quantity of wool they will produce, and which will be much finer and softer than when the sheep are lean and weak.

The hay, after being used as before-mentioned, and dried, may be used as a litter for horses or cattle; it makes very good manure, and saves straw, which will be a considerable advantage, especially when there is a scarcity of that article.

By a handful of hay, is meant as much as a person can grasp in his hand from a parcel of loose hay. And it is presumed and wished, as the above method is so easy and safe, that no person, who has cattle, cows, horses, or sheep, will neglect to try it.

This method was followed with a cow, which was kept in a large city, for the sake of the children, where no green food could easily be got in winter, except the refuse of the vegetables used in the family. Boiling water was poured into a tub half filled with hay, and the tub was covered till cold. But the cow eat the hay as well as the tea, seemed to be fond of both, and it was thought the milk was more plentiful. It was, in fact, a succedaneum for green food.

To Keep Crows From Corn

Take a quart of train oil, as much turpentine and bruised gunpowder, boil them together, and, when hot, dip pieces of rags in the mixture, and fix them on sticks in the field. About four are sufficient for an acre of corn. (This boiling process is dangerous. If tried, do it outside.)

Method of Destroying Insects on Fruit Trees

Make a strong decoction of tobacco, and the tender shoots of elder, by pouring boiling water on them; then sprinkle your trees with the same (cold) twice a week, for two or three weeks, with a small hearth brush, which will effectually destroy the insects, and the leaves will retain their verdure until the fall of the year.

If used early, as soon as the bud unfolds, itself, it will probably prevent the fly. The effect of tobacco has long been known, and elder water frequently sprinkled on honeysuckles and roses has been found to prevent insects from lodging on them.

The quantity to be made is from one ounce of tobacco to one gallon of water, with about two handfuls of elder. You may, however, make it as strong as you please, it being perfectly harmless to the plants.

The Good Effects of Elder in Preserving Plants from Insects and Flys

1. For preventing cabbage and cauliflower plants from being devoured and damaged by caterpillars.
2. For preventing blights, and their effects on fruit trees.
3. For preserving corn from yellow flies and other insects.
4. For securing turnips from the ravages of flies.

The dwarf elder appears to exhale a much more foetid smell than the common elder, and therefore should be preferred.

MORE SUNSHINE PUTS MORE SUGAR INTO APPLES

Apples have more sugar if they get more sunshine during the growing season. This was learned at Cornell's Agricultural Experiment Station in a long-time study aimed at correlating some of the factors like rainfall, amount of sunshine, and temperatures to the keeping quality of apples.

Another discovery was that the higher the temperatures during the last six weeks before harvest, the greater has been the amount of scalding in storage.—News Item.

HOW OUR FOREFATHERS HAD GREENS ALL WINTER

The roots of Chicory or Dandelion were taken up at the approach of winter, and stacked in cellars in alternate layers of sand, so as to form ridges, with the crowns of the plants on the surface of the ridge. Here, if the frost be excluded, they soon sent out leaves in such abundance as to afford a supply of salad during the winter. If light be excluded, the leaves are perfectly blanched, tender and succulent. Old-time sailing ships, that spent months at a time on high seas were provided with greens by similar methods. Sand was kept in barrels containing numerous holes, in which Dandelion or Chicory was grown. Soil was kept damp (NOT WET), with liquid fertilizers.

HOW GRANDPA FOOLED RATS

In or near the place frequented by these vermin, place on a slate or tile, one or two tablespoonsful of dry oatmeal. Lay it thin and press it flat, that you may easily ascertain what is taken away. The rats, if not interrupted, will come regularly there to feed. Supply them with fresh oatmeal for two or three days; and then mix in with about six tablespoonsful of dry oatmeal three drops of oil of anise seed, and feed them with this three days more; afterwards for one day give them but half the quantity of this scented meal, and next day the following mixture: To four ounces of dry oatmeal scented with six drops of oil of anise seed, add half an ounce of carbonated barytes, powdered very fine. Place this as before, and let the rats eat it without interruption for twenty-four hours. A few hours after eating it they will be seen running about as if drunk or paralytic; but they generally at last retire to their haunts and die. If only a small portion disappears, leave it for a day or two longer, and after that burn what remains, as a fresh mixture is prepared at a trifling expense. Be careful to keep the doors of the place where the poison is laid securely locked, so as to prevent danger to children or domestic animals by getting at it.

Another remedy: A number of corks, cut down as thin as a quarter, were roasted or stewed in grease, and then placed in the way of the rats. The dish was greedily devoured as a special delicacy, and, as was anticipated, they all died of indigestion.

Storing the *corn* plant in silos saves more of its food value than any other method of harvesting and storage.

KEEPING FARM TOOLS

Wipe them clean and dry, then hold them before a fire, and keep drawing them backward and forward until warm enough to melt wax—then take some bees-wax and rub it all over. Then put tool in a dry place, but not warm; it needs no other covering. The usual method is to wrap a dry hayband around, but in winter time this naturally contracts a moisture, or the damp air strikes in between the folds of the hayband.

OLD ENGLISH METHOD OF FATTENING POULTRY QUICKLY

The following plan for the fattening of poultry for immediate use, has been found, in the experience of one of the largest and best inns in the Kingdom, the speediest as well as the most effectual, both in the degree to which the fattening takes place and in the appearance, quality, and flavor of the fowls when dressed: Let the fowls be kept in a pen, perfectly dark, with the exception of one ray of light, which is allowed to enter through a small aperture and fall directly on the vessel containing the food. This food must be common rice which has become thoroughly soddened, penetrated and swollen by steeping in milk and keeping all night in a warm place. The poultry should have as much of this rice as they choose to eat, and in one week they will have attained their full perfection of fattening. As no advantage is gained by longer feeding, it will always be desirable to have such an arrangement in the time as shall allow only this period to elapse.

Another method is to put the fowls up to feed in warm places, and supply them with oatmeal balls (the meal being finely sifted): when the appetite grows palled, they are crammed.

OLD METHOD OF HATCHING CHICKENS

Take a small basket just large enough to hold as many eggs as you wish to hatch; wrap each egg in flannel, cover the top of the basket with dung, then bury them in a hotbed. In twenty-one days they will be hatched, then they must be kept in a basket close to the fire.

KEEPING CABBAGE

When the cabbages are cut, leave about two or three inches of the stalk, the pith of which is to be hollowed out, taking care not to cut or bruise the rind; tie the cabbages up by the stalks and then fill the hollow with fresh water daily. Thus, they will keep for several months.

I Shall Pass Through This World But Once.
Any Good, Therefore, That I Can Do,
Or Any Kindness That I Can Show
To Any Human Being,
Let Me Do It Now.
Let Me Not Defer It Or Neglect It,
For I Shall Not Pass This Way Again.

OLD TIME WEATHER-FORECASTING

Hints on How to Be Your Own Weather-Prophet

When standing on high ground and the horizon is unobstructed from all quarters, if the sky is absolutely cloudless, look for a storm within forty-eight hours.

If it starts to rain after seven o'clock in the morning it will continue to do so all day, and very often it is the indication of a three days' rain.

When it is raining and it brightens and darkens alternately you can count on an all-day rain, with a chance of clearing at sundown.

When the rain ceases and the clouds are still massed in heavy blankets one sure sign of clear weather is the patch of blue sky that shows through the rift large enough to make a pair of "sailor's breeches."

Another sign of continued rain is when the smoke from the chimney hovers low around the housetops. When it ascends straight into the air this indicates clearing weather

A foggy morning is usually the forerunner of a clear afternoon.

A thunder-storm in winter (usually in January or February) is always followed by clear, cold weather. It is not, as many think, the breaking up of winter.

People living near the seashore say a storm is "brewing" when the air is salty, caused by the wind blowing from the east.

A red or copper-colored sun or moon indicates great heat. A silvery moon denotes clear, cool weather.

The old Indian sign of a dry month was when the ends of the new moon were nearly horizontal and one of them resembled a hook on which the Indian could hang his powderhorn.

Many people troubled with rheumatism and neuralgia usually are excellent barometers and can predict changeable weather by "feeling it in their bones."

And the advice of the old weather-sage is "never go out during April month without being accompanied by your umbrella."

And then, for the special benefit of those who never can remember anything they read in prose, but do have a faculty for retaining jingles, the following important formulas are set out in verse:

> Red in the morning the sailor's warning;
> Red at night the sailor's delight.
>
> When you see a mackerel sky,
> 'Twill not be many hours dry.
>
> When the seagulls inland fly
> Know ye that a storm is nigh.
>
> A ring around the moon
> Means a storm is coming soon.
>
> When it rains before seven
> 'Twill clear before eleven.

PLANT WEATHER-FORECASTERS

Mushrooms and toadstools are numerous just before a rain.

"If the down flyeth off Dandelion when there is no winde, it is a sign of rain."

"Signs of a hard winter: Unusually large crop of nuts or acorns. Heavy moss on north side of trees. When sap of maple and sassafras go down early in the Fall. When leaves of grape turn yellow early in the season. Thick husks on the ears of corn.

When the flowers of pimpernel close during the day, it was believed to be a sure sign of rain. For this reason, the plant is also known as "poor man's weather glass."

INSECT AND ANIMAL WEATHER-FORECASTERS

Bees are sensitive to the increase in humidity that precedes a shower, and always return to the hive in time to escape a wetting.

Swallows fly low before a storm, because their prey—the insects—fly low at such a time.

It was an old custom to keep leeches in a jar or bottle, partly filled with water, to forecast weather. The leech is said to become very restless before storms, and its peculiar actions were supposed to indicate various phases in the weather to come.

It was a sign of a tough winter, when wooly caterpillars are dark from "stem to stern"; when hornets have triple-insulated nests, when wasps are sealing twice as many live spiders in the mud incubator tubes to feed their babies when they hatch.

It was also a sign of a tough winter when cattle get rough coats, and when rabbits and squirrels have unusually heavy fur.

Expect rain if fish bite and keep near the surface.

If a cat washes its face, look for fine weather. If it sits with its tail to the fire, look for bad weather.

Rain will follow if chickens wallow in the dust.

PENNYROYAL TEA

"It is good for the stomach, being warming and cleansing: If drank freely, will produce perspiration, and remove obstructions. In colds and slight attacks of disease, it will be likely to throw it off and prevent sickness. It is very good for children, and will remove pain in the bowels, and wind. In going through a course of medicine, a tea of this herb may be given for drink, and will cause the medicine to have a pleasant operation."
—Samuel Thomson, Botanic Physician—1831.

MOON LORE

And when the clear moon, with its soothing influences, rises full in my view from the wall-like rocks, out of the damp underwood, the silvery forms of past ages hover up to me, and soften the austere pleasure of contemplation.
—Goethe's "Faust".

Planting: The influence of the moon upon vegetation is an opinion hoary with age. In the Zend-Avesta we read, "And when the light of the moon waxes warmer, golden-hued plants grow on from the earth during the spring." An old English author writes:—

"Sowe peason and beanes, in the wane of the moone,
Who soweth them sooner, he soweth too soone,
That they with the planet may rest and arise,
And flourish, with bearing most plentiful wise."

Cucumbers, radishes, turnips, leeks, lilies, horse-radish, saffron, and other plants are said to increase during the fulness of the moon; but onions, on the contrary, are much larger and better nourished during the decline.

Harvesting: Husbandmen make haste to gather up their wheat and other grain from the threshing-floore, in the wane of the moone, and toward the end of the month, that being hardened thus with drinesse, the heape in the garner may keepe the better from being fustie, and continue the longer; whereas corne which is inned and laied up at the full of the moone, by reason of the softnesse and over-much moisture, of all other, doth most cracke and burst. It is commonly said also, that if a leaven be laied in the ful-moone, the paste will rise and take leaven better. Still in Cornwall the people gather all their medicinal plants when the moone is of a certain age.

Gathering mushrooms: In some parts it is a prevalent belief that the growth of mushrooms is influenced by the changes of the moon, and in Essex the subjoined rule is often scrupulously adhered to:—

"When the moon is at the full,
Mushrooms you may freely pull;
But when the moon is on the wane,
Wait ere you think to pluck again."

Tides: A writer of the sixteenth century says, "The moone is founde, by plaine experience, to beare her greatest stroke uppon the seas, likewise in all things that are moiste, and by consequence in the braines of man."
It is a common belief among many people living on coasts, that death mostly occurs during the falling of the tide. Every reader of the inimitable Dickens will be reminded here of poor old Barkis, whose life ebbed out with the tide.

Crop prediction: An old belief held that if Christmas comes during a waxing moon we shall have a very good year; and the nearer to the moon the better. But if during a waning moon, a hard year; and the nearer the end of the moon, so much the worse.

Weather signs: Another sage belief is that the condition of the weather is dependent upon the day of the week upon which the new moon chances to fall. We are told that "Dr. Forster declares that by the Journal kept by his grandfather, father, and self, ever since 1767, to the present time, whenever the new moon has fallen on a Saturday, the following twenty days have been wet and windy, in nineteen cases out of twenty." New moon on Monday, or moon-day, is, of course, everywhere held a sign of good weather and luck.

That a misty moon is a misfortune to the atmosphere is widely supposed. In Scotland it is an agricultural maxim among the canny farmers that—

"If the moon shows like a silver shield,
You need not be afraid to reap your field;
But if she arises haloed round,
Soon we'll tread on deluged ground."

Others say that a mist is unfavourable only with the new moon, not with the old.

"An old moon in a mist
Is worth gold in a kist (chest);
But a new moon's mist
Will never lack thirst."

At Whitby, when the moon is surrounded by a halo with watery clouds, the seamen say that there will be a change of weather, for the "Moon dogs" are about. At Ulceby, in Lincolnshire, "there is a very prevalent belief amongst sailors and seafaring men that when a large star or planet is seen near the moon, or, as they express it, "a big star is dogging the moon", that this is a certain prognostication of wild weather. I have met old sailors having the strongest faith in this prediction, and who have told me that they have verified it by a long course of observation.

Setting eggs—rooting trees: Classical authors counsel us to set eggs under the hen at new moon, and to root up trees only when the moon is waning and after mid-day.

Effect upon humans: Astrologers ascribe the most powerful influence to the moon on every person, both for success and health, according to her zodiacal and mundane position at birth, and her aspects to other planets. The

Moon Lore—Continued

sensual faculties depend almost entirely on the moon, and as she is aspected so are the moral or immoral tendencies. She has a great influence always upon every person's constitution.

Effect upon birth: Bacon wrote that children and young cattle that are brought forth in the full of the moon, are stronger and larger than those that are brought forth in the wane.

In Cornwall, when a boy is born in the wane of the moon, it is believed that the next birth will be a girl, and vice versa; and it is also commonly said that when a birth takes place on the "growing" of the moon, the next child will be of the same sex.

Maidens: In Berkshire at the first appearance of a new moon, maidens go into the fields, and while they look at it, say:—

"New moon, new moon, I hail thee!
By all the virtue in thy body.
Grant this night that I may see
He who my true love is to be."

Then they return home, firmly believing that before morning their future husbands will appear to them in their dreams.

Marriage: The ancient Greeks considered the day of the full moon the most propitious period for marriage. In Euripides, Clytemnestra having asked Agamemnon when he intended to give Iphigenia in marriage to Achilles, he replies, "When the full moon comes forth with good luck." In Pindar, too, this season is preferred.

Longevity: Galen, in the second century. taught that those who were born when the moon was falciform, or sickle-shaped, were weak and short-lived, while those born during the full moon were vigorous and of long life.

Dreams: Arnason says that in Iceland "there are great differences between a dream dreamt in a crescent moon, and one dreamt when the moon is waning. Dreams that are dreamt before full moon are but a short while in coming true; those dreamt later take a longer time for their fulfillment."

Fears: The Mexican moon-goddess is regarded in two entirely different aspects. She is held the beneficent dispenser of harvests and offsprings, as well as the goddess of the night, the dampness, and the cold; she engenders the miasmatic poisons that rack our bones; she conceals in her mantle the foe who takes us unawares; she rules those vague shapes which fright us in the dim light; the causeless sounds of night or its more oppressive silence are familiar to her; she it is who sends dreams wherein gods and devils have their sport with man, and slumber, the twin brother of the grave. So farther south, the Brazilian mother carefully shielded her infant from the lunar rays, believing that they would produce sickness; the hunting tribes of our own country will not sleep in its light.

THE HOG NEVER LOOKS HIGHER THAN HIS HEAD

More than to eat, the hog does not aspire;
To get and cram his food, he looks no higher,
Like men who only live to eat and drink,
Of Him who feeds us all they never think:
They heed not, they love not Him who dwells on high,
Like brutes they live, like brutish beasts they die—
The source of life, of hope, and heavenly love,
They care not for, they never look above.

CHIVES WILL GROW ON SILL, AND THEY IMPROVE MEALS

If you keep a pot of chives growing on your kitchen window sill, you can find many uses for them in summer dishes. Clip them into creamed cottage cheese, scrambled eggs, or add them to buttered noodles or elbow macaroni.

To catch a large number of fish, take the blood found in entrails of an ox or goat, with fat and marrow of sheep; mix with Thyme, Marjoram, Garlic, wine, yeast and flour. After thoroughly mixing, make into pills the size of marbles. Throw a few of these into the water where you intend to fish. If fish are in the area, these pills are supposed to attract them to your hooks.

TO CURE THE BITE OF A MAD DOG

Take raw onions, green rue, salt and the powder of Elecampane root, and beat them well together, and apply them to the wound. Renew it as occasion requires. Or take a wild pigeon, chicken or hen, open it, and lay it hot to the wound. It draws out the venom. Heal the sore with turpentine and hog's lard. Or scrape the wound and put mashed garlic and salt on it. It will draw out the poison.

Note: This is only offered as an emergency, where doctors are not immediately available. See a doctor as quickly as possible.

USEFUL PLANTS AROUND THE FARM

Bee or Wasp Sting: An old English recipe. Crush a handful of Rue leaves to a pulp and apply to sting.

Basil is used the same way. Culpeper said of it, "Being applied to the place stung by wasp or hornet, it speedily draws the poison to it. Old gardeners as well as modern also claim instant relief from stings by applying either Winter or Summer Savory. Basil and Summer Savory are annual.

Minor Cuts and Burns: In Europe the fat leaves of Houseleek or Healing Blade are crushed and applied directly to the affected parts. In the Mediterranean regions the crushed blades of Squills are used for the same purpose. Squills are house plants. Houseleek is winter hardy.

Sunburn, Minor Burns, Rash, etc.: Medicine Aloe is one of the most useful of all house plants. It is ornamental as well as useful. The thick blade contains a salve-like juice. One blade can be used for weeks. The severed end of the blade is self healing. The thin film can easily be broken with each use.

To Remove Stains from Hands: Beat Sorrel (Salad herb) to a pulp and rub mash over stained parts, then wash off.

Sprains, Swellings, Bruises, Cuts, Boils: Use fresh leaves, or better yet, the bruised roots of Comfrey. Apply as poultice.

HERBS FOR BEES

A bit of advice from an old herbal: "If a man put Bee Balm in bee hives, or else if the hives be rubbed therewith all, it keepeth bees together and causeth other bees to resort to their company."

Bee Balm or Melissa: Because bees are so fond of the nectar contained in this flower the ancient Greeks called the plant Melisphylla—the bee plant. Pliny wrote almost 2000 years ago regarding planting Melissa near hives: "When they (bees) are strayed away, they do find their way home by it (Melissa)." Melissa leaves as well as flowers have a honied lemony fragrance.

Bee Balm, American: This plant is entirely different and hardier than Melissa. It is a beautiful scarlet flowering native American mint. The foliage has a perfumy fragrance. The flowers are so popular with bees that the plant deserves the name American Bee Balm.

Balkan Sage: This plant sends up numerous tall slender stalks covered with a multitude of small purple flowers which attract many honey bees. Balkan sage adds beauty to any flower garden.

Borage: This is a self-seeding annual of vigorous growth. It is a light greyish plant brightened with lovely blue or pinkish star-like flowers which bloom from early summer until frost. Bees are very fond of Borage and it yields an excellent honey.

Hyssop: A bushy plant which blooms from early summer until late fall. The honey from hyssop flowers is well known for its odor and flavor. The plant is very hardy and requires no special care. Blue flowering varieties.   Pink or White varieties,

Anise-Hyssop: A handsome, tall plant native of the northwest. The attractive purplish blue flowers grow in dense spikes. Besides being interesting as a favorite bee plant, Anise-Hyssop has long been used by the Indians as a tea, for seasoning foods and for colds.

Moldavian Mint: An annual with spikes of many lovely blue flowers that bloom all summer. We have found that these blooms attract more bees than any other flower in our gardens (some 800 different plants). The flowers as well as leaves have a delicious lemony scent.

Rosemary: A wonderful bee plant but not winter hardy in northern states.

Sweet Basil: An old writer said of this herb, "It doth make the heart merrie." It seems to have the same effect on bees. They swarm wildly over the flowers as though the fragrance and nectar was intoxicating to them. The plant is a very useful culinary herb. The spicy fragrant leaves are used with sausages, stews, soups, vegetable salads, vinegar, pickles, sauces and most tomato dishes. The plant is an annual preferring sunny well drained location.

Thyme *(Thymus vulgaris)*: The world's sweetest and finest flavored honey is generally believed to be that which comes from Mount Hymettus near Athens where Thyme abounds. The plant is ornamental as well as useful as a culinary herb.

Wild Marjoram: This plant becomes covered with flowers in July and blooms until late fall. The profusion of flowers and the multitude of bees always make the Wild Marjoram bed a lively garden spot.

Winter Savory: A very hardy small shrubby plant which is covered with white flowers which bloom until late fall, long after plants have been killed by frost.

THE CURSED WEED

Standing on the side of a railroad track, a ragged half starved tramp was vigorously scratching his arm and violently cursing the tall weeds that caused this itching. Usually found growing near the cursed weeds is common Yellow Dock, whose leaves when crushed and applied as poultice offer a soothing relief from the burning itch. The juice of Nettle leaves itself is soothing for the nettle itch. The miserable tramp did not know this nor did he know that the irritating weed was potentially worth many dollars.

Like the tramp, not much more is generally known about this weed excepting that its common name is Stinging Nettle. Not only is it considered a useless weed but it is hated and often cursed for its rank growth as well as for the stinging hairs that cover the plant.

In Europe there is an entirely different opinion of Stinging Nettle. Folks of the Old World have learned through centuries of experience that Nettle is one of the most useful of all plants.

The young sprouts and tops are used in spring as a pot herb. Boiling renders the stinging hairs harmless. Nettle is a healthy and easily digested vegetable. It is slightly laxative.

In England a pleasant drink known as Nettle Beer is used especially by ailing aged folk. A tea of the dried herb is used medicinally. German soldiers were given mild Nettle Tea with sugar as a substitute for coffee and Oriental tea. The tea was also taken as a "spring tonic" and beverage during hot weather. An infusion made from the fresh leaves is applied to burns for its soothing effect.

Old Herbalists recommended combing the hair daily with the juice of fresh Nettle. Another old hair tonic was made by simmering a handful of dried herb in a quart of water for two hours. The infusion was applied to hair every other night.

When Nettle is cut and allowed to wilt, it loses its irritating sting, and the fodder becomes useful for livestock. It is said that cows will give more milk from Nettle fodder than when fed only on hay. In Germany dried Nettle herb is mixed with feed for thin horses suffering digestive troubles. Horse dealers mixed the seed of Nettle with oats and other feeds to give the animals a sleek coat. In Egypt oil from Nettle seeds is used for burning lamps.

Powdered Nettle herb is mixed with poultry feeds to fatten fowls and increase egg production. In Spring the tender green tops and sprouts of Nettle was chopped fine and mixed with bread to feed young turkeys, ducklings and goslings.

The Russians make a beautiful green dye for woolens from Nettle herb. The roots boiled with alum make a yellow dye. Nettle herb offers possibilities for manufacture of paper and insulation materials.

The tall stalks of Nettle yield a stronger and finer fiber than flax. The Germans used this in place of cotton in the last Great War. Nettle offers not only a superior substitute for cotton but several useful by-products as well. In spite of certain difficulties which have not been thoroughly overcome, there is evidence that the manufacture of Nettle will become a gigantic new industry in the future. Fabulous fortunes await those who find the key to nature's great wealth. The foolish will suffer for ignoring what took generations to learn.

Stinging Nettle is very common in moist ditches along railroad tracks. Here it often grows three or four feet tall. In drier soils, the plant is smaller. For experimental farming, Nettle would product best plants in muck soil.

Analysis of the fresh Nettle shows the presence of formic acid, mucilage, mineral salts, ammonia, carbonic acid and water.

OLD TIME HERBAL REPELLENTS

In Shakespearean times it was said, "When chamber is swept and Wormwood is thrown, no flea for his life dare abide to be known."

Another old saying regarding Wormwood, "The plant voideth away worms, not only taken inwardly but applied outwardly; it keepeth clothes from moths and wormes." Wormwood was used in considerable quantities by cloth manufacturers according to an old herbal.

Mugwort, related to Wormwood was also used to protect clothes from moths.

An old book said of the lemony scented Southernwood: "The perfume thereof driveth away all venomous beasts and so doth the herbe in all places where it is laid or strowen."

Powdered Fennel once was sprinkled around kennels and stables to drive off fleas.

In Old England, a bunch of Rue herb was kept on the bar to protect judges from diseases carried by prisoners.

Bunches of Rue were kept in the house and carried around by the peasants during plagues. The Rue was held in front of the mouth when they spoke to one another. Rue was planted because "the savour of Rue doth make serpents fly from the gardens and all other venomous beastes." The Schola Salernitana, compiled about 1100 says regarding Rue, "it putteth fleas to flight."

It was an old custom in French hospitals to burn Rosemary with Juniper berries to purify the air and prevent infections. Centuries ago peasants of latin countries carried a spray of Rosemary for protection against the "evil eye."

The sliced roots of fragrant Calamus were used to protect furs and woolens.

Pennyroyal is still used as a repellent for body lice and fleas. It was rubbed on the face and hands as a protection against mosquitoes.

Almost invariably one could find Catnip growing around buildings of old farms because of an old belief held that the odor of this plant drove off rats. The plants were set as a barricade around the buildings.

Lavender flowers were used for centuries to preserve linens from insects as well as to give them a fresh, clean odor. Lavender is still popular in sachets and potpourri.

Flowering Thyme and Woodruff are used like Lavender in central Europe. Thyme has a piny scent. Dried Woodruff has a refreshing scent of new mown hay.

Lavender Cotton or Santolina is a moth repellent of Colonial days.

Tansy leaves mixed with Elder leaves were sprinkled around bed posts to guard against would-be bed inhabitants.

Sprigs of fresh Tansy were used to drive off ants from pantries or wherever foods were kept. Tansy was also rubbed on meats to shoo off flies. Sage and Southernwood were also used like Tansy.

Banckes Herbal says of Rosemary, "'take the flowers and put them in thy chest among thy clothes or among thy bookes and mothes shall not destroy them."

Pliny wrote when Thyme was burnt "it puts to flight all venomous creatures."

When planted around dwellings, Feverfew was believed to purify the air and to ward off disease.

An old writer claimed that "when a garden is infested with moles, garlic or leeks will cause the moles to leap out of the ground presently."

Albertus Magnus advised using sulphur and garlic to drive out moles.

"The root stocks of the Yellow Water Lily, when bruised and infused in milk, will destroy beetles and cockroaches. The smoke of the same when burnt will get rid of crickets," from Herbal Simples.

It is said that fleas will not enter a room in which the herb Water Pepper is kept. (Fido would certainly appreciate this!)

From an English Herbal: (regarding Elder) The leaves when bruised, if worn in the hat or rubbed on the face, will prevent flies from settling on the person. Likewise turnips, cabbages, fruit trees or corn, if whipped with the branches and green leaves of Elder, will gain an immunity from all depredations of blight, but moths are fond of the blossoms."

Some 40 years ago, English nurserymen offered Basil seed for $1.25 per packet with a claim that it was mosquito repellent. Although the pests may not like this herb, we doubt that it did $1.25 worth of good.

NEW MEDICINES FROM WEEDS

Creeping Jenny (European bindweed) is not altogether bad. In the root of this plant is a substance that stops bleeding, and in wartime a medicine like that is vital.

This stop-bleeding substance was discovered by plant physiologist Arthur I. Bakke and hospital superintendent Norman D. Render, while they were studying the roots of this weed at a laboratory in Chariton, Iowa.

In chopping up the weed roots with sharp butcher knives, the men happened to nick their fingers, and suddenly noticed that although the cuts were deep, bleeding stopped instantly when the roots touched the wounds.

After processing the roots to obtain the vital substance, Dr. Render applied the dosage to volunteer patients at the Cherokee State Hospital, and found that the clotting of human blood was accelerated. Several pharmaceutical concerns are investigating production of the medicine in quantity.

Farmers will not be asked to grow bindweed to provide this material. It's already too plentiful.

WATERCRESS

Watercress is high in favor with nutritional advisers to the armed forces and our soldiers get it in soups and salads for the energy it produces. Dieters eat it because its carbohydrate content is low and because it makes more iron than any other leafy vegetable including spinach. It is fed to children with weak bones and soft teeth because of the amount of lime it contains and its high sulphur content is reflected in the cress tablets prescribed for eszema.

The Greeks had a word for it too! They referred to cress as a "wit-producing food."

TRAPPERS SECRET FOR GAME

A few drops of Oil of Anise, or Oil of Rhodium on a trappers bait will entice any wild animal into the snare trap.

The following secret applies to all animals, as every animal is attracted to a peculiar odor in a greater or less degree, but it is best adapted to land animals, such as foxes, minks, sables, martins, wolves, bears, wildcats, etc.: Take ½ pound strained honey, ¼ dram musk, 3 drams Oil of Lavendar, and 4 pounds tallow. Mix together thoroughly, and make into 40 pills or balls. Place one of these pills under the pan of each trap when setting.

MAKE HAY WHILE THE SUN SHINES

In Summer heat, when brightly shines the sun,
To make your hay, the proper time is come:
Spread round the new mown grass, and do it right,
Work while the sky is clear, and sun is bright.

WANTED! COON REPELLENT

Can you furnish, or advise a repellent to keep Coons from green corn, in mutton or roasting ear stage. They are devouring corn crops in certain areas adjacent to swamps, or wooded areas. An effective ingredient or artifice will be a boon to many farmers here. From—Meggett Seed Co., Hollywood, S.C.

The following letter was received in reply to this article.

"Here is a remedy to get rid of Coons. Get a good heavy wire, and make a snare. Catch one Coon, cut both ears off, and get a can of white paint, and paint the Coon white, then turn it loose and it will run all the Coons off the farm."—L.B., Anco, Ky.

Many customs and beliefs may easily be traced back to Indian and pioneer origin.

Eggs should be stored *large end* up to keep the yolks well centered.

TO REMOVE THE MUDDY TASTE FROM FISH

As this flavor exists only in the skin of fish, and becomes communicated to the body only on being first boiled, it will be sufficient, before dressing such as are taken from ponds or stagnant waters, to put them alive into a tub, and pour fresh water over them, adding half a handful of salt, stirring it up well among the fish, and finally rinsing them with fresh water.

TO DESTROY SLUGS, CATERPILLARS, ETC.

Put into an iron pot a pound of quicklime, and a pound of sulphur. Stir this up and add six pounds of water, and boil. Snails will immediately leave any place watered with this composition; and if trees are watered with it, any caterpillars upon them will die instantly.—From an old recipe book.

DESTROYING FLIES

Half a pint of boiling water poured upon a quarter of an ounce of quassia chips, and sweetened with sugar, will destroy flies—and is perfectly harmless if taken by children by mistake.

DESTROYING ROACHES

Slices or parings of cucumber strewed about the kitchen at night will destroy cockroaches.

FLEA CHASERS

Fumigate with pennyroyal leaves or brimstone, or tie up some of the fresh leaves in a bag, and place it in the bed.

Sprinkle the room with a decoction of bitter apple, briar leaves, or cabbage leaves—or fumigate with burnt thyme.

Place the leaves of tansy in different parts of the bed—under the mattress, between blankets, etc.

Rub the bed furniture with a decoction of elder leaves.

TO SAVE A WEAK SWARM OF BEES

Take an equal quantity of honey and brown sugar, mix them well together, put the mixture upon a plate, cover it with a large piece of silver paper, take it with a sheet to the hive, set it on the sheet upon the ground and place the hive over it, tie it up tight and carry it into a warm room, set it close to the heat, and leave it there all night. The bees will soon come down, pierce the paper, and take as much honey as will support them all the winter. Next day, place them in the coldest part of the garden, under a north wall; they will sleep until spring, when they should be moved to a south aspect. In this way, a weak swarm is better than a strong one, and will cast earlier in summer.—From an old recipe book.

TO CATCH FOXES

Take oil of amber and beaver's oil, each equal parts, and rub them over the trap before setting it. Set in the usual way.

TO CATCH MINK

Take oil of amber and beaver's oil, and rub over the trap. Bait with fish or birds.

TO CATCH BEAVER

In trapping for beaver, set the trap at the edge of the water or dam, at the point where the animals pass from deep to shoal water, and always beneath the surface, and fasten it by means of a stout chain to a picket driven in the bank, or to a bush or a tree. A flat stick should be made fast to the trap by a cord a few feet long, which, if the animal chanced to carry away the trap, would float on the water, and point out its position. The trap should then be baited with the following preparation, called—

THE BEAVER MEDICINE

This is prepared from a substance called castor, and is obtained from the glandulous pouches of the male animal.

The contents of five or six of these castor bags are mixed with a nutmeg, twelve or fifteen cloves, and thirty grains of cinnamon in fine powder, and the whole well stirred together with as much whiskey as will give it the consistency of mixed mustard. This preparation must be left closely corked up, and in four or five days the odor becomes powerful; and this medicine smeared upon the bits of wood, etc., with which the traps are baited will attract the beaver from a great distance, and wishing to make a close inspection, the animal puts its legs into the trap and is caught.

TO CATCH MUSKRAT

In the female muskrat, near the vagina, is a small bag which holds from 30 to 40 drops. Now all the trapper has to do, is to procure a few female muskrats and squeeze the contents of the bag into a vial. Now, when in quest of muskrats, sprinkle a few drops of the liquid on the bushes over and around the trap. This will attract the male muskrats in large numbers; and if the traps are properly arranged, large numbers of them may be taken.

In trapping muskrats, steel traps should be used, and they should be set in the paths and runs of the animals, where they come upon the banks, and in every case the trap should be set under the water, and carefully concealed; and care should be taken that it has sufficient length of chain to enable the animals to reach the water after being caught, otherwise they are liable to escape by tearing or gnawing off their legs.

SECRET ART OF CATCHING FISH

Put the oil of rhodium on the bait, when fishing with a hook, and you will always succeed.

THE HUNTER'S SECRET

The following secret applies to *all* animals, every animal is attracted by the peculiar odor in a greater or less degree; but it is best adapted to land animals, such as foxes, minks, sables, martins, wolves, bears, wild cats, etc.

Take one-half pound strained honey, one-quarter drachm musk, three drachms oil of lavender, and four pounds of tallow; mix the whole thoroughly together, and make it into forty pills, or balls, and place one of these pills under the pan of each trap when setting it. The above preparation will most wonderfully attract all kinds of animals, and trappers and others who use it will be sure of success.

TO CATCH FISH

Take the juice of smallage or lovage, and mix with any kind of bait. As long as there remain any kind of fish within yards of your hook, you will find yourself busy pulling them out.

A TIP FOR FISHERMEN

A board rubbed over a stake driven into the ground will drive earthworms to the surface.

TO CATCH ABUNDANCE OF EELS, FISH, ETC.

Get over the water after dark, with a light and a dead fish that has been smeared with the juice of a stinking gladwin—the fish will gather round you in large quantities, and can easily be scooped up.

CHINESE METHOD OF CATCHING FISH

Take Cocculus Indicus, pulverize and mix with dough, then scatter it broadcast over the water, as you would sow seed. The fish will seize it with great avidity, and will instantly become so intoxicated that they will turn belly up on top of the water by dozens, hundreds, or thousands, as the case may be. All that you now have to do, is to have a boat, or other convenience to gather them up, and as you gather them put them in a tub of clean water, and presently they will be as lively and healthy as ever.

This means of taking fish, and the manner of doing it, has, heretofore, been known to but few. The value of such knowledge admits of no question. This manner of taking fish does not injure the flesh in the least.

NOTE: American Indians used similar methods with native herbs.

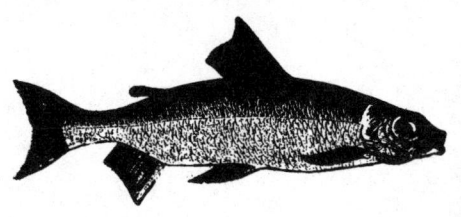

CATCHING MORE BULLHEADS

Here is an old, but good, stunt that will bring the bullheads in volume . . . in states where it is permissible, of course.

Place some chicken entrails in a burlap bag, tie the top and place in a lard can. With the lid off, let the entrails "age" on top of your garbage can. Usually, you can tell when they are ready by the way the neighbors complain. Now, put on the lid and take to your catfish hole.

Plant in a likely spot overnight and be on the job early the next morning. Catfish can follow a scent with remarkable ability and your reward will be a whopping big string of hungry bullheads. It's a "stinking" way to fish but one that's hard to beat, There is just one admonition—*don't*, for Pete's sake, dump the extra bait into the stream when you've got your catch! You'll want the bullheads you didn't catch this time to be alive and hungry when you come again.—From "Outdoor Indiana" magazine.

If you have swallowed a fish bone, it may be softened by drinking lemon-juice and also white-of-egg.

Bee Sting: Remove sting by squeezing—then bruise the green leaves of Plantain and rub over the sting. Pound some more leaves and bind it on. Relief is almost instantaneous. Plantain is generally available in any lawn or back-yard.

THE EUCALYPTUS AS A RIVAL OF COAL

An article in "Forest Leaves" states that the species of Eucalyptus have a remarkable capacity for storing the energy received from the sun. Experiments in south Africa have shown that a forest of these trees will each year produce twenty tons of fuel per acre. The dry timber is heavier than coal and gives out as much heat when burned. The trees thrive best in hot moist regions and it is asserted that if half the area capable of supporting the trees was planted to Eucalyptus forests, it would yield nearly three hundred times as much fuel per year, as the world now requires.—From The American Botanist.

RECIPE FOR FIRE PREVENTION

One tablespoonful of sulphur put in stove will stop instantly, the worst stove pipe fire or chimney fire. This does not destroy fire to cook on, but controls all danger. If a spoonful of sulphur is put in stove each week, the pipes on either heater or cook stoves, will rarely have to be taken down and cleaned. I place a spoonful in small pieces of paper—twist them up and place in a can—ready at all times for an emergency—keep cans close to stove to save hunting if pipes catch fire.
—Mrs. H.G. Alameda, Sask, Canada.

SPOTS AND STAINS

A satisfactory method of removing water spots from material is to dampen the entire material evenly and then press it while damp.

A fruit stain can be removed from white linen material by washing gently in warm chlorine water.

Fruit stains on white or fast color material, will usually disappear completely if the material is stretched over a bowl and boiling water is poured through it from a height of about three feet.

If boiling water is applied to stains containing protein, such as stains of milk and eggs, it coagulates the albumin and makes the stain extremely hard to remove.

Soap will aid in the removal of grease stains but will always set fruit stains.

Iron rust may be removed from white goods with sour milk.

Lemon juice and salt will remove rust.

Egg stains may be removed from silverware by rubbing with common salt.

Rubbing cloth well with turpentine will remove tar.

Raw potato rubbed on the hands will remove vegetable stains.

A raw potato rubbed on the soiled spots, is first aid when mud spots dry on the youngster's clothing.

Fresh ink stains may be removed if the material is immediately placed in sweet milk.

Forests help purify the air, preserve the water supply and prevent soil erosion.

USE CORN COBS FOR APPLE TREE MULCH

Corn cobs have given excellent results as a mulch for apple trees in Darke county, Ohio. Trees in a 17-acre planting have been given a 12-inch mulch as far out as limbs extend, over a period of several years. The bottom four or five inches of the mulch has the appearance of peat, and feeder roost have moved into this decomposed layer. Production has been good on soil so low in fertility it could produce only 10 bushels of corn per acre.

TO MAKE GAR FISH PALATABLE

This is a fish of very singular appearance, elongated in form, and with a mouth which resembles the bill of the snipe, from which circumstances it is often called the snipe-fish. Its bones are all of a bright green color. It is not to be recommended for the table, as the skin contains an oil of exceedingly strong rank flavour; when entirely divested of this, the flesh is tolerably sweet and palatable. Persons who may be disposed from curiosity to taste it will find either broiling or baking in a gentle oven the best mode of cooking it. It should be curled round, and the tail fastened into the bill. As it is not of large size, from fifteen to twenty minutes will dress it sufficiently. Anchovy sauce, parsley and butter, or plain melted butter, may be eaten with it.

TO PRESERVE DILL

Gather the dill while fine and pick it free from the stalks; next chop it as fine as you need it for sauces and put it in a chopping trough and put good butter on it. Rub the butter well into the dill and then pack it in glass jars, with some salt on top and over that a layer of cold sheep tallow. When using it, you take the butter with it, needing no other.

TO PRESERVE PARSLEY

Proceed exactly as with the dill, but with the difference that parsley must not be chopped before it is served. Pickle it whole.

TO SALT DOWN PARSLEY

Tie the parsley together in small bunches. These, together with a few bunches of celery, are put in layers, between which place salt. On top of all put a cover or something similar with some heavy weight on, to press the parsley. Rinse it well before using.

TO SALT DOWN DILL

Pick the dill as for pickle, but do not chop it. Put it in layers like parsley, with salt in between each layer. Then press it as above and do not forget to rinse it well when you want to use it.

TO PICKLE VARIOUS KINDS OF GREENS

Spinach, cabbage, cauliflower, peas or beans, asparagus buds, the fine green part of celery, all this may be placed in jars together with some cold, fresh butter, which has been melted and skimmed. Fill the jars, cover them well and keep them in a cellar or other cool place. These greens are used with great advantage for soups in the winter season. If small jars, use 1 at a time; but if they are large, put a layer of butter on the top, every time you have taken some.

ROASTED RABBITS

Remove the entire skin from 2 good sized rabbits, then the fine skin; cut off the head, open the belly, remove the insides, carefully separate the gall from the liver, wash and wipe the rabbit dry, lard with fine strips of larding pork, season with 1 even teaspoonful salt, lay into a roasting pan, put 2 ounces butter in small pieces over it, place in a hot oven, and roast, basting frequently till light brown; then add a little water and roast till done, which will take about 45 minutes; the meat should be juicy and rare on the bone. Lay the rabbit on a hot dish, garnish with shaved pink and white horseradish, and serve with celery-root salad and currant jelly.

TO PRESERVE VEGETABLES FOR WINTER USE

Green string beans must be picked when young; put a layer three inches deep in a small wooden keg or half barrel; sprinkle in salt an inch deep, then put another layer of beans, then salt, and beans and salt in alternate layers until you have enough; let the last layer be salt. Cover them with a piece of board which will fit the inside of the barrel or keg and place a heavy weight upon it. They will make a brine. When wanted for use, soak them one night or more in plenty of water, changing it once or twice until the salt is out of them, then cut them and boil the same as when fresh.

Carrots, beans, beet roots, parsnips and potatoes keep best in dry sand or earth in a cellar; turnips keep best on a cellar bottom, or they may be kept the same as carrots, etc. Whatever earth remains about them when taken from the ground, should not be taken off.

When sprouts come on potatoes or other stored vegetables, they should be carefully cut off. The young sprouts from turnips are sometimes served as a salad, or boiled tender in salt and water and served with butter and pepper over.

Celery may be kept all winter by setting it in boxes filled with earth; keep it in the cellar; it will grow and whiten in the dark. Leeks may also be kept in this way.

Cabbage set out in earth in a good cellar will keep good and fresh all winter. Small close heads of cabbage may be kept many weeks by taking them before the frost comes, and laying them on a stone floor; this will whiten them and make them tender.

Store onions are to be strung, and hung in a dry, cold place.

Culinary herbs

WEEDS AND ACORNS GOOD FOR YOU, SAY FOOD EXPERTS

Two Mayo Clinic nutritionists call upon the public to increase its food supply by eating foods usually considered unfit for human consumption.

Dr. Russell M. Wilder and Thomas E. Keys assert in the current Journal of the American Medical Association that weeds and acorns helped many Europeans stave off starvation during the war.

These are good sources of vitamins and minerals, it was pointed out.

Many weeds, such as milkweed, stinging nettle, summer mustard and sorrel are palatable, the nutritionists said.

Here's Ways in preparing them:

Dandelion Greens: Cut the stems from a half peck of dandelion leaves, and break each leaf into small bits, dropping these into cold water as you do so. Wash thoroughly, drain and lay in cold water for 15 minutes. Drain again, and put over the fire in a porcelain-lined saucepan, with enough salted water to cover them. Simmer for 15 minutes, while you make the following sauce: Cut together a tablespoon each of butter and flour, and pour upon them a pint of milk, in which a pinch of soda has been dissolved. Stir to a smooth white sauce. Drain the water from the dandelion leaves, and stir these into the sauce. Season to taste, and beat in very slowly, a whipped egg. Remove at once from the fire, and turn into a deep vegetable dish.

Dock Greens: Take the leaves and stalks of tender young narrow dock plants in early spring. Pick over, and wash carefully, cook in boiling salted water until tender, then drain, and season with butter and salt. Vinegar may be used if desired. Salt pork may be cooked with them, if liked, but they are more wholesome when seasoned with butter. Their chief value is for the water and alkaline salts which they contain. They need only a few drops of water to start them, then they cook in their own juice.

Lamb's Quarter Greens: This tender little plant, which grows so abundantly in some sections of the country, makes a very palatable dish when cooked with a piece of salt pork. Prepare and cook as any other kind of greens.

Poke Greens: The stalks and leaves of this plant make delicious greens in May before they become tough. They are at their prime in the South about the middle of April, and in the North the first of May. They will cook in 20 minutes.

Boiled Sorrel: Prepare and cook like spinach. If very large leaves, blanch for 10 minutes before cooking.

Lamb's Quarter Salad: Wash and dry the leaves of fresh Lamb's Quarter, line the salad bowl and cover with any left-over vegetable, meat, fowl, or fish desired. Add salad dressing, cover with another layer of Lamb's Quarter, garnish with hard-boiled eggs and nasturtium leaves. Serve with salad dressing.

Nasturtium Salad: Use the pods, leaves, flowers, or petals alone, or in combination in the proportions desired, and serve with salad dressing.

Pepper Grass Salad: Wash and dry the Pepper Grass. Line a salad bowl with crisp cress. Pile the Pepper Grass on this, and serve with salad dressing.

Dandelion Salad: Select the young green leaves of Dandelions; wash, throw them into cold water; drain, dry and serve with french dressing.

NOTE: Adding Water Cress improves this salad.

Tasty Salad with Herbs: With the heart of a head of lettuce, mix 1 handful of Sorrel, 1 teaspoon of chopped Chives, 2 sprigs of Chervil, 4 Tarragon leaves or Tarragon vinegar. Serve with dressing.

Spicebush: A handful of the twigs infused in a quart of boiling water, given in doses of a teacupful every hour or two, is a cooling beverage in fevers. A handful or two of the berries in a quart of spirits, forms a pleasant bitter.

NOTE: Spicebush berries have an aromatic mild peppery flavor.

PREPARING WILD DUCK

The common wild ducks are often unpalatable, caused by their disagreeable fishy flavor. In order to remove this flavor the ducks should be picked, singed, and drawn, then well washed inside and outside in cold water. Place a large kettle with boiling water over the fire, add 1 tablespoonful bicarbonate of soda, 1 carrot, and 2 onions; put in the ducks, boil 20 minutes; then take the ducks out and immediately plunge them into cold water, wash and rinse them thoroughly, and wipe dry; season with salt allowing 1 even tablespoonful for each duck, and ½ even teaspoonful white pepper, spread 1 ounce butter over each bird, and cover the breasts with a large thin slice of larding pork; set the pan in a medium hot oven, roast and baste frequently till light brown all over; then put a little boiling water in the pan, add a few slices of carrot and onion, and continue to roast and baste till done. Serve the ducks on a hot dish, free the gravy from fat, add a little broth, and strain it over the ducks; serve with celery-root salad and compote or jelly. Wild goose may be prepared in the same way.

AGRICULTURAL NOTES

Nitrogen applied to *peach trees* in California resulted in increased yields, but applied to prunes gave no results over a five-year period.

Beets need more sodium than they can get from most soils; therefore common salt is used by some beet growers as a fertilizer.

Soybean meal should not exceed 10 per cent of the total diet fed to hens producing eggs for hatching because a greater amount, it is found, may reduce the hatchability of the eggs.

Mature *corn,* which contains usually about 40 per cent moisture, loses about 21 pounds of water per bushel in drying to a 20 per cent moisture content when it is in condition to be put in storage.

Manure spread on the surface of garden beds as Winter cover can well be fresher and rawer than that which is to be applied and dug in in spring. However, raw manure should not be piled over the crowns of herbaceous perennial plants.

Heavy, sour garden soil can be made much more productive by liming to correct acidity and mixing in a two-inch covering of screened ashes from anthracite coal to improve soil aeration. Ashes can be spread on the garden during the Winter and dug in in Spring.

The strawberry bed should be covered two to four inches deep before night temperatures begin to drop below 20 degrees.

INDIAN TURNIP FOR POISON IVY OR POISON OAK

The common Indian Turnip or "Jack-in-the-Pulpit," as it is called is an excellent remedy when scraped and applied to the poisoned part. When the b l i s t e r s have flattened, apply cold cream to heal them sooner.

EARLY-CUT HAY BEST FOR MILK PRODUCTION

Largest amount of milk is produced on hay cut at the full-bloom stage, it has been found in experiments at Cornell University.

Early-cut timothy produced 95 per cent as much milk, and the late cut only 90 per cent as much.

Not only does hay made at the full-bloom stage of the grass have the greater milk-producing value, but it also has the greatest total yield to the acre—2.56 tons for the season as compared with 2.32 tons for the early cutting and 2.53 tons for the late cutting.

TO DRIVE RATS AWAY

Fill the rat holes with new slacked lime; repeat it a second time if necessary. It affects them in such a manner that they soon leave, very seldom requiring a repetition of the dose.

FISHING WITH HERBS

Take the juice of Smallage or Lovage and mix it with any kind of bait. Use half a dozen hooks on your line. Bait well, tying it firmly to the hooks. Now throw out your line and as long as there remains any fish within many yards of your hooks, you will find yourself kept very busy pulling them up. The root of Sweet Cicely steeped, is also excellent for the same purpose.

AUTUMN LEAVES

A very pretty way to ornament any plain article of furniture, a cabinet or paneled trinket cupboard, boxes, jars, trays, etc., is by the following simple process: Having collected the ferns and leaves in all their endless variety prepare them thus: Lay the leaves one by one on a piece of soft paper, wrong side up, and with a sharp penknife pare off the projecting veins, so that there will be as little roughness as possible, then place them in books with a heavy weight, and press them smoothly, leaving them there until you are ready to use them. Prepare the article by painting it black, using a fine brush for the purpose, because it will leave fewer traces. When this is perfectly dry and hard, give it a coat of fine, transparent varnish; and before it has become entirely dry, lay on the leaves and fern sprays in graceful groups, according to fancy, pressing them smoothly down, so that every part will adhere. When they are entirely dry, give it another coat of the same transparent varnish, going over the whole surface, leaves and all. If you wish to bronze the black ground in imitation of the Japanese lacquer ware, it can be done by sprinkling a little bronze powder over the sticky varnish after putting on the leaves, then rubbing it lightly with a soft rag to burnish it. These ornamentations are both permanent and effective.

TREES AND HEALTH

(*From a very old newspaper clipping.*)

Everybody knows that trees take the carbonic acid thrown out in the breath of men and animals, separate in into its component parts—carbon and oxygen—give back the latter to be used again, and work up the former into wood and fruit.

It is also coming to be generally understood that forest trees do important service in prompting rainfalls, and in helping to retain the surface water for springs, streams and general use.

It is also known that certain species, planted in malarial localities, help to render the latter healthy by somehow using up the deadly miasma.

IN THE GARDEN

HERBS AND GARDENS

Man's first garden was the Wild Garden. It was a paradise of Food Plants, Medicinal Herbs, and Raw Materials. In spite of this the inhabitants of this luxuriant garden endured hardships, suffering and starvation until his garden greens could be classified.

In the constant search for food, the primitive man found many plants of unusual odors and tastes. Some had peculiar effects upon him. With ages of actual contact with such plants (Medicinal Herbs) they began to realize that they were helpful in certain conditions which they were subjected to. Agreeable tasting or pleasant smelling plants (Culinary Herbs, Spices) were found to improve the flavor of not so tasty foods. This type of experimental work went on for thousands of generations until it was common knowledge just how plants could be best used.

The First Garden

With the development of clans and communities people found it more convenient to gather the seeds of useful plants from the wild garden and grow them nearer their gardens. For long ages after gardens retained their wild aspect because of the precarious life. A prosperous garden was too inviting to rival neighbors and marauding robbers.

As communities merged into great powers, gardens of rulers and influential became proportionately pretentious. Some included foreign plants as well as strange birds and animals. The beautiful villas of Roman Imperial times had classical formal gardens with elaborate fountains, trellises and ornaments comparable to the finest gardens of modern times. Ancient Egyptian Gardens of the Pharaohs resembled modern large estates.

With the inroads of barbarians and the fall of the great powers, gardens returned to a primitive state. Only behind the protective walls of castles was there any resemblance of order. Because of the limited space only the necessary medicinal and culinary herbs were planted.

The Monastery Garden

While people still busied themselves in strife at the time of the Middle Ages, monks worked quietly and diligently behind the protective walls of the monastery. These fortress-like colonies were usually perched on a hill like the walled castles, so they could also resist the assaults of would-be intruders. On the outside the monks terraced the steep hill and had vineyards, orchards and vegetable gardens. Within the walls was the cloister garden. In this garden the monks grew herbs for administering to ailing parishioners. They developed new varieties of valuable plants, established virtues of medicinal and culinary herbs and introduced new plants from far off lands. The writings of the ancients were studied and all was recorded for posterity. The monks deserve full recognition for their systematic effort in Horticulture and Herbal Materia Medica.

Ornamental Gardens

As peoples again became banded to large states, laws became more effective and strife became less frequent, allowing more time for general improvements. With the works and gardens of the monastery as inspiration and source of many new plants, gardens soon became a fascinating experiment for all people. The fortress-like castles gave way to elegant castles with impressive gardens replacing the fortified walls. The owners of great estates vied with each other until their gardens assumed entirely an ornamental aspect. The garden of useful herbs and vegetables became detached and confined to insignificant part of garden. The new type gardens developed distinctive designs such as Formal Gardens, Knot Gardens and Paterre Gardens.

Colonial Gardens

The early Colonial Gardens retained the simplicity and usefulness of the more humble gardens of the old world. They were given new color with the addition of native American herbs. The later Colonial Gardens reproduced the decorative designs of Europe in more modest scale.

With the establishing of physicians and apothecaries and the arrival of new spices and flavors the thousands of years old gardens of self-medication were crowded out with ornamentals. Some of these old time medicinals and pot herbs have returned to the wild state, some have spread over a large part of North America, others may still be found lingering near the old gardens of New England.

OLD GARDEN PLANTS

Clary Sage: Like many other herbs, this plant was brought to America in Colonial times. Being a native of moderate climates the plant never established itself well enough to continue in the wild state after the new gardens pushed out the "old timers." The plant forms clusters of large base leaves, then sends up tall stalks topped with large showy spikes of light blue, pinkish or white flowers. The bracts offsetting the flowers are tinged, giving the entire spikes a beautiful frosty appearance. The flowers as well as leaves have a strong piny camphoraceous fragrance. Centuries ago Clary was in considerable use medicinally. The herb is antispasmodic, balsamic, carminative, tonic, aromatic, aperitive, astringent and pectoral. The seeds soaked in cold water form a mucilage which is used to remove small irritating particles from the eyes. From this use the plant was called Clear Eye and See Bright. Culpeper advised using the mucilage from the seeds also for "drawing splinters and thorns out of the flesh." The fresh or dried leaves were used for cooking like garden sage. Culpeper also wrote, "the fresh leaves fried in butter, first dipped in a batter of flour, eggs and a little milke, serve as a dish to the table that is not unpleasant to any and exceedingly profitable." The Germans used Clary Sage to give Rhine wine a muscatel flavor. From this use the plant got the name Muscatel Sage. Clary is cultivated in Southern France today mainly for its oil which is used as a fixer of perfumes. Clary is biennial.

Clove Pinks: This is the Gillyflower of Medieval Europe. It was popular for its variety of color and sweet, spicy fragrance. Before Oriental spices became available to every one, the flowers of Clove Pinks were used with foods and for flavoring wine and vinegar. These lovely old fashioned pinks bloom from early summer until late fall and keep the air delightfully perfumed. Plants are winter hardy.

Costmary: More than a thousand years ago, Costmary was taken from its native home of India and brought to Asia Minor. From there it was carried to most parts of Europe and then to the New World. It was reared in New England gardens and brought westward to the Rockies with civilization. Here the plant seems to have reached the end of its journey as well as popularity. It is now found mainly in the wild state on very old farm sites. Costmary is a handsome, silvery yellow green plant with scent similar to Spearmint. The plant forms clusters of base leaves with slender stalks of daisy like flowers. Formerly the dried branches were tied with lavender and placed in chests and drawers as moth repellent and to give linens a fresh sweet scent. The leaves were used also to make "sweete washing water." Because of its taste and aroma, the herb was used to give ale a spicy flavor. For this reason, it was known also as Ale-cost. The herb was used medicinally and is mentioned in most old herbals. The minced fresh leaves were used in salads, pottage and flavoring.

Feverfew: The old fashioned Feverfew is generally found in the wild state near very old gardens while showy new forms have taken their place in the modern garden. The ancient magi ordered "Feverfew to be pulled from the ground with the left hand, and the fevered patient's name must be spoken forth, and the herbalist must not look behind him." Another old superstition held that when it was planted around dwellings it purified the air and warded off disease. The pungent odor of Feverfew is so disliked by bees that branches of it were carried around to hold them at a distance. The medicinal properties and uses of Feverfew are tonic, carminative, emmenagogue and stimulant. Although still used by country folk of Europe, the plant was long ago returned to oblivion in America. The plant forms grey green clumps brightened by a profusion of lovely creamy white daisy like flowers. A typical old fashioned plant.

Meadow Sweet: A typical old fashioned garden plant—not showy, but simply good looking. It has fernlike foliage and slender stalks, with clusters of small creamy white flowers. Leaves as well as flowers have a pleasant fragrance quite different from each other. It was a very popular strewing herb during the Middle Ages. The plant is native of England, but is found also near old New England gardens where it was transplanted in Colonial times. Other names for this lovely plant are Meadsweet, Queen of the Meadow, and Lady of the Meadow.

Pot Marigold: Centuries ago this plant was common in every garden. Today fancy new varieties have replaced the old fashioned plant. Not only is Pot Marigold a beautiful ornamental, but useful in foods, for coloring, as an adulterant for Saffron and in medicine. The dried flowers were so popular that grocers and spice-sellers kept barrels of it in stock. An old writer said: "No broths are well made without dried Marigold." Dairy maids used to churn the petals with their cream to give butter a yellow color. A strong infusion made from dried flowers was used to color hair for those "not beyinge content wyth the natural colour." Medicinally Marigold was used mainly as a local application. The dried flowers or fresh leaves boiled in lard make an excellent salve. The fresh flowers are said to relieve wasp or bee stings when rubbed on affected part. Pot Marigold is an easily grown annual that prefers a sunny location.

Southernwood is a little known herb in America, but a very old and common plant in Europe. There it is known by many names and put to many uses. The French call the plant "Garde robe" or guardian of clothes. Branches are placed in closets, chests, etc., to keep out moths. The English call the plant "Old Man," "Lad's Love" or "Boy's Love." Country lads made an ointment of the ashes and used it to promote the growth of a beard. The Italians use Southernwood to flavor fresh salads and cooked vegetables. It was an old custom for folk to take fresh branches of Southernwood to church. The refreshing scent was supposed to prevent drowsiness. The dried herb makes a pleasant, stimulating tea when prepared like Oriental tea. Medicinally, Southernwood is used as a tonic, emmenagogue, anthelmintic, antiseptic and deobstruent. Besides its many uses Southernwood is a fine garden plant. The upright growth and dense mass of fine leaves make it an excellent hedge plant. Planted along a walk or path the lemony fragrant foliage give clothes a pleasant scent with slight contact.

Tansy: Native of Europe, Tansy has made itself at home over a large part of North America. The entire plant has a strong aromatic and camphoraceous odor which no doubt attracted man's attention at a very remote date. Records show 2500 years of use. Tansy was popular as a culinary herb, household herb and medicinal herb. In Medieval Europe it became so common that it was used freely by the humble peasant in his valley hovels as well as by the lords of lofty castles. Although still in use as a home remedy the plant is cultivated today chiefly for its oil which is so powerful that its use is not recommended except by a practitioner.

Curled Tansy is similar to the rampant variety but quite rare. Its curly edged fernlike leaves make this a very beautiful garden specimen. Tansys have very deep green foliage and attractive golden button like flowers in clusters.

SIGNS OF RAIN

The hollow winds begin to blow,
The clouds look black, the glass is low;
The soot falls down, the spaniels sleep,
And spiders from their cobwebs creep.
Last night the sun went pale to bed,
The moon in halos hid her head.
The boding shepherd heaves a sigh,
For, see, a rainbow spans the sky;
The walls are damp, the ditches smell,
Closed is the pink eyed pimpernell,
Hark! How the chairs and tables crack;
Old Betty's joints are on the rack;
Loud quack the ducks, the peacocks cry;
The distant hills are looking nigh.
How restless are the snorting swine!
The busy flies disturb the kine;
Low o'er the grass the swallow wings.
The cricket, too, how sharp he sings.
Puss on the hearth, with velvet paws,
Sits wiping o'er whiskered jaws.
Through the clear stream the fishes rise
And nimble catch the incautious flies.
The glowworms numerous and bright
Illumed the dewey dell last night.
At dusk the squalid toad was seen
Hopping and crawling o'er the green.
The whirling wind the dust obeys,
And in the rapid eddy plays.
The frog has changed his yellow vest,
And in a russet coat is dressed.
Though June the air is cold and chill.
The mellow blackbird's voice is shrill,
My dog, so altered is his taste,
Quits mutton bones, on grass to feast;
And see yon rooks, how odd their flight
They imitate the gliding kite,
And headlong downward seem to fall
As if they felt the piercing ball.
"Twill surely rain"; I see with sorrow
Our jaunt must be put off tomorrow.

—From century old school book.

Here is a help: We gather bark, stems, leaves and seeds of long leaf eucalyptus, and make a decoration by boiling, which we use to spray plants affected with aphids. Plants can be eaten without harm after washing them well. Submitted by Mrs. W. H. M.

GARDEN ESCAPES

Brought to the New World by early Colonists—now considered weeds.

Burdock: This common European weed was brought to America as a medicinal plant. It soon became widely scattered, because the burdock seeds attached themselves to colonists' breeches, clothes and the fur of animals. Millspaugh wrote "the herb is so rank that man, the jackass, and the caterpillar are the only animals that will eat it."

Burdock root is a favorite blood "tonic" of herbalists. It was used as a decoction for rheumatism, gout and kindred affections. A decoction of seeds is still given to calm infants. The tea is sweetened and given warm.

Chicory: It would surprise many farmers to know that this weed, so common in barnyards and along waysides, was a highly regarded medicine of the ancient Egyptian and Arabian physicians. The plant was very common over most of Europe before America was discovered, and is still much used by people of modern times. The blanched leaves are used in salads—the baked roots as pottage, and the pulverized dried roots made into flour for bread. The roasted roots of Chicory was used to give body to coffee, or as a coffee substitute. Roasted Chicory imparts a rich flavor and smoothness when mixed with coffee.

Costmary: Forms thick clumps of silvery leaves. The plant is found lingering near ruins or sites of very old American houses. This relative of "Mums" was planted for its delightful mint scented leaves, which were placed among sheets, linens, in drawers, and in water in which clothes are washed. The plant was also popularly known as Bible-leaf, because of an old custom of using the leaves as page markers in Bibles. In Europe the plant was put into ale and negus, hence called Alecost. In France, the minced young leaves are used to give fragrance to salads and soups.

Dandelion: Nothing is more beautiful than a field of these golden heads—and nothing more aggravating than a lawn full of the plants. Dandelion was brought to the New World as a medicinal and garden green. Winds have carried the parachute-like seeds, until the plant is found in almost all parts of the northern hemisphere.

Lyle wrote that the root of Dandelion "is a mild, slow, relaxing and stimulating tonic hepatic, influencing slowly, the liver, alvine canal and kidneys. It assists digestion and assimilation. In its action on the liver, it is both secretory and excretory." Being mild, it needs to be given in large and frequently repeated doses. Its properties are greatly enhanced when used in conjunction with other agents. As a gastric tonic, it is very valuable in dyspepsia, and in irritation of the gastric and intestinal membrane, especially when there is torpor of the liver. The presence of Ginger renders it more diffusive.

Dandelion greens are still used by many folks. They are an excellent source of vitamins and minerals. Indians valued Dandelion greens highly. An old record states—"they scour the country for many day's journey, in search of sufficient to appease their appetites. So great is their love for the plant, that the quantity consumed by a single Indian exceeds belief."

Lamb's Quarters: Americans spend untold working hours to eradicate this old-time green from their gardens. Lamb's Quarters is distinguished by its upright growth, and the peculiar whitish bloom on its leaves.

Although discarded by the white man, Lamb's Quarters is a favorite among Indians. It is gathered by the Navajos, the Pueblo Indians of New Mexico, all the tribes of Arizona, the Diggers of California, and the Utahs, and boiled as an herb alone, or with other foods. Large quantities are also eaten in the raw state.

Plantain: American Indians called this weed "White Man's foot" because it seemed to follow his trail, no matter where he went. Although the Indian days are long past, the persistent weed still follows white man's foot—especially in his lawn.

The leaves of Plantain have been used for ages, as a poultice on wounds, cuts, bruises, etc. The leaves have a non-irritating rich chlorophyll content, with natural healing properties. Indians quickly adopted "White Man's foot" medicine. Some tribes carried the leaves around on hunting, fishing and war excursions, as a first aid measure.

Boerhaave, noted 18th Century physician, wrote that "in his own experience, he has found that fresh Plantain leaves, placed upon the feet, will ease the pain and fatigue engendered by long walks."

Purslane or Pigweed: This juicy prostrate plant was very popular as a vegetable in colonial times. The fat stems were mixed with salads, boiled like spinach, and pickled. Although long ago replaced by other vegetables, the plant persistently refuses to leave the garden. It can be hoed, chopped, spaded, etc., but will invariably come back.

Tansy: Goodrich wrote in his "Recollections of a Lifetime" that when he was a boy and clergymen visited his family "I went out behind the barn to gather Tansey for their morning bitters. Tansey bitters were esteemed a sort of panacea, moral as well as physical, for even the morning prayer went up heavily without it," and that "Every man imbibed his morning dram, and this was esteemed temperance. There is a story of a preacher about those days, who thus lectured his parish—"I say nothing, my beloved

GARDEN ESCAPES—continued

brethren, against taking a little bitters before breakfast, and after breakfast, especially if you are used to it—but what I contend against is this dramming, dramming, dramming at all hours of the day. There are some men who take a glass at 11 o'clock in the forenoon, and at 4 o'clock in the afternoon. I do not propose to contend against old established customs my brethren—rendered respectable by time and authority, but this dramming, dramming, is a crying sin in the land."

Yellow Dock: This plant is best known as a "troublesome weed." What most people do not know is that Yellow Dock has been used in medicine since ancient times, as a mild astringent, tonic, laxative and depurant—its use being similar to that of rhubarb and sarsaparilla. A decoction of the root has been found useful in dyspepsia, gouty tendencies, hepatic congestion and some forms of scabby eruptions. An ointment of the powdered root, with lard, has been considered very useful for the cure of itch. It is also considered an excellent dentrifice, where the gums are spongy. Yellow Dock roots are a rich source of vegetable iron.

The young leaves of Yellow Dock were much used as a pot herb in olden times.

WISDOM IS BETTER THAN STRENGTH

The man of giant size. with might and main
Tries hard to move the stone; 'tis all in vain:
The small, weak man, by his superior skill,
Applies a lever; moves it at his will.

Manhood is not measured by the size of the chest but by the quality of the heart.

Indians believed when the red-headed woodpecker made "a greater noise than ordinary at particular times, it is conjectured his cries then denote rain."

OLD EUROPEAN HERB IN COLONIAL GARDENS

In the colonial gardens were grown most of the family's foods—sweet flavoring herbs, medicines, as well as an assortment of plants used for scent, cosmetics, etc. One of the most popular of these "vanityes" was the lemony-pine scented Southernwood. Sprigs of this herb were carried by sensitive ladies when attending meetings or social gatherings, held in stuffy or badly ventilated colonial buildings. The herb was bruised slightly so that it emitted its pleasant aroma when fanned before the nose.

Southernwood was very popular as a remedy for "vanityes of the head." An old recipe advises "Take a quantitye of Sutherwood and put it upon kindled coales to burn and being made unto powder mix it with the oyle of radishes and anoynt a balde place and you shall see great experiences."

The lore of the Old World was transplanted with Southernwood. The plant was also known as Lad's-love because of its supposed powers as a love charm. A sprig placed in each shoe when in love, and worn through the day, was fancied also to bring about "great experiences."

SOAP FROM THE FIELDS

Bouncing Bet was brought to the New World more than 300 years ago, for its valuable saponin qualities. The plant is now neglected and forgotten, but may still be found along roadsides and near old homesites.

Bouncing Bet is a rugged perennial growing about 20 inches high, forming dense patches with its spreading habit. The carnation-like pink and white flowers cover the plant during its long blooming season. The fresh leaves stirred in lukewarm soft water produce a lather which was used for washing fine silks and woolens. It not only cleanses, but imparts a luster as well.

EARLY AMERICAN USE OF FENNEL

Every garden had its little patch of Fennel "for keeping old women awake in Church time. A sprig of Fennel was in fact the theological smelling bottle of the tender sex, and not infrequently of the men, who from long sitting in the sanctuary—after a week of labor in the field—found themselves too strongly tempted to visit the forbidden land of Nod, would sometimes borrow a sprig of Fennel, and exercise the fiend that threatened their spiritual welfare. — Deacon Olmstead himself, enthroned in the deacon's seat, was obliged now and then to take out his sprig of Fennel, in the very midst of the doctor's twelfthlies and fifteenthlies."—From Recollections of a Life Time, by S.G. Goodrich, 1856.

HOW GRANDFATHER MADE ROSES BLOOM TWICE A YEAR

1. Immediately after the first flowering, the shrub is to be deprived of every leaf, and those branches which have borne roses cut, so that only two or three buds shall remain. The cutting of the weaker branches may be in a less degree. If the weather be dry when the leaves are removed, it will be necessary to thoroughly water the stem, for several days, with the nose of the watering-pot: in this way the sap will not be arrested. 2. Then the brush is to be used, and the rose tree well cleansed by it, so that all mouldiness shall disappear: this operation is very easy after an abundant rain. 3. The earth about the rose tree is to be disturbed, and then twenty-four sockets of calves' feet are to be placed in the earth around the stem, and about four inches distant from it. The hoofs of young calves are the best, and give a vivid colour and agreeable perfume to the roses. These are to be placed with the points downwards, so that the cups shall be nearly level with the surface of the earth, and the plant well surrounded. This operation is to be repeated in the November following. These hoofs, dissolved by the rain or the waterings, form an excellent manure, which hastens the vegetation, and determines the reproduction of flowers. 4. Two waterings per week will suffice in ordinary weather, and they should be made with the nose of the watering-pot, so that the hoofs may be filled; but, if the atmosphere is dry, it will be necessary to water the plants every evening; and in the latter case it will be necessary, from time to time, to direct the stream of water on to the head of the tree.

TRANSPLANTING LARGE BUSHES AND SHADE TREES

In the autumn, before the frost comes on, dig a trench around the tree and cut the roots, but not too near the tree. Remove the tree through the winter, when the ground is frozen. Raise it up with the frozen earth adhering to the roots. The whole mass is easily raised with levers on to a strong sled, and can then be drawn erect by means of oxen or horses. Trees from 20 to 30 feet high can be moved by this method, and they will grow in the spring. Stake down trees until well established.

OLD METHOD FOR POISONED SHEEP

It is a fact well known to farmers, that sheep are frequently poisoned by eating common laurel (Kalmia latifolia). When you suspect this to be the case, give the sick animal a strong tea made of American Dittany (Cunila mariana), moderately warm. This simple remedy has been known to recover sheep in the last stages of the disorder.

It would be well for farmers whose cattle are in danger of being poisoned, to procure and dry a quantity of Dittany in the summer, and keep it by them through the winter, as it is in the latter season they are most likely to be affected. It may also be useful in other disorders incident to cattle—so much for the cure—as a prevention, destroy all the laurel on your farms.—From 1846 Recipe Book.

NOTE: American Dittany is a pretty native plant with a very fragrant smell similar to Marjoram. In late summer the plant is covered with small pink flowers that attract many bees. The dried herb was much used in pioneer days to make a grateful tea for colds and to excite gentle perspiration.

TO CLEAR HOUSES, BARNS, ETC., OF RATS AND MICE

Gather the plant Hound's Tongue, the cynoglossum officinale of Linnaeus, which grows abundantly in every field, at the period when the sap is in its full vigour, bruise it with a hammer, or otherwise, and lay it in the house, barn or granary, infested by rats or mice, and those troublesome animals will immediately shift their quarters.

NOTE: Hound's Tongue is an escape from early Colonial Gardens, being brought from the Old World for its medicinal properties. It is a greyish green plant with clusters of basal leaves and stalks bearing deep maroon colored flowers. The entire plant has a peculiar odor.

WASHES FOR VERMIN ON PLANTS

Tobacco Water: Infuse one pound of tobacco in a gallon of boiling water in a covered vessel, till cold.

For Lice on Vines: Boil ½ pound of tobacco in 2 quarts of water: strain, and add ½ pound of soft soap and ¼ pound of sulphur. Mix.

For Aphides: Boil 2 oz. of lime and 1 oz. of sulphur in water, and strain.

Poison for Plant Lice, and other insects: Boil 3½ oz. of quassia chips, and 5 dr. of powdered stavesacre seed in 7 pints of water, to 5 pints. Strain when cold, and use with a watering pot or syringe.

Cut Rose slips when signs are in the feet in November, plant deep, 6 inches or more in damp soil. Most all take root and bloom. This is good for other woody plants. March is also a good time if drought doesn't kill plants.
—Submitted by Mrs. Lola F. Lilly, MacArthur, W. Va.

HOW RUSSIANS PROTECT APPLE, CHERRY AND PLUM-TREES FROM FROST

The severity of the winters at St. Petersburg is so great that few fruit trees will survive it, even with careful matting; to prevent the loss which is thus usually sustained, the following mode of training has been attended with complete success. It consists in leading the branches of the trees on horizontal trellises only ten or twelve inches from the ground. When the winter sets in, there are heavy falls of snow, and as the frost increases, the snow generally augments, by which the trees are entirely buried, and receive no injury from the most intense frost.

Another great advantage of training trees in the above method, consists in the growth of the wood, it being of equal strength, and the fruit produced being all alike, the blooms come out much earlier, and the crop ripens sooner. The trees are always clean, and free from insects.

The only cherry that does not succeed in that way is the black heart; this is attributed to the damps which affect the early blossoms, but in a milder climate this injury would be obviated by placing the trellis higher from the ground. When the trellis decays under the apples, it is never renewed, as the trees keep always (from the strength of their branches) their horizontal position.

There are other advantages of treating fruit trees in this manner; they come sooner into bearing, and their fruit is not affected by high winds. The apples are never gathered, but suffered to drop off, for the distance they fall is not sufficient to bruise them.

SALT FOR TOMATO PLANTS

A market gardener of Lake County, Illinois, says that he has the most remarkable success in the use of salt upon his tomato plants. He applies it at various times during the season and in every case its effects are marked in the increased growth of both plant and fruit. In some cases he lays the roots of backward plants bare, sprinkling them with a tablespoonful of ordinary barrel salt, and covers with soil. Plants ordinarily treated in this way take an immediate start and develop the fruit.

TO RENOVATE OLD APPLE TREES

Take fresh made lime from the kiln, slake it well with water, and well dress the tree with a brush, and the insects and moss will be completely destroyed, the outer rind fall off, and a new, smooth, clear, healthy one formed and the tree assume a most healthy appearance and produce the finest fruit.

OLD GERMAN METHOD OF FORCING FRUIT TREES

With a sharp knife make a cut in the bark of the branch which is meant to be forced to bear, and not far from the place where it is connected with the stem, or, if it is a small branch or shoot, near where it is joined to the large bough—the cut is to go round the branch, or to encircle it, and penetrate to the wood. A quarter of an inch from this cut, make a second like the first, round the branch, so that by both encircling the branch, a ring is formed upon the branch, a quarter of an inch broad, between the two cuts. The bark between these two cuts is taken clean away, with a knife, down to the wood, removing even the fine inner bark, which immediately lies upon the wood, so that no connection whatever remains between the two parts of the bark, but the bare and naked wood appears white and smooth; but this bark ring, to compel the tree to bear, must be made at the time when the buds are strongly swelling or breaking out into blossom. In the same year a callus is formed at the edges of the ring, on both sides, and the connection of the bark that had been interrupted is restored again, without any detriment to the tree, or the branch operated upon, in which the artificial wound soon again grows over. By this simple (though artificial) means of forcing every fruit tree with certainty to bear, the most important advantages will be obtained.

TO SAVE FROST-NIPPED PLANTS

Before the plant has been exposed to the sun, or thawed, after a night's frost, sprinkle it well with water, in which common salt has been infused.

CENTURY-OLD METHOD OF PRESERVING FRUIT TREES IN BLOSSOM FROM FROST

Surround the trunk of the tree in blossom with a wisp of straw or hemp. The end of this sink by means of a stone tied to it, in a vessel of spring water at a little distance from the tree. One vessel will conveniently serve two trees; or the cord may be lengthened so as to surround several before its end is plunged into water. It is necessary that the vessel should be placed in an open situation out of reach of any shade, so that the frost may produce all its effects on the water by means of the cord communicating with it.

The fresh juice of Bloodroot is a rustic remedy for destroying warts.

HERBS and OLD SAYINGS

"Happy the age, to which we moderns give
The name of 'golden', when men chose to live
On woodland fruits; and for their medicines took
Herbs from the field, and Simples from the brook."

"If simple herbs suffice to cure,
'Tis vain to compound drugs endure."

"Angelica, the happy counterbane,
Sent down from heaven by some celestial scout,
As well its name and nature both avow't."

"Borage and Hellebore fill two scenes,
Sovereign plants to purge the veins
Of melancholy, and cheer the heart
Of those black fumes which make it smart;
The best medicine that God e'er made
For this malady, if well assaid."

"To enliven the sad with the joy of a joke,
Give them wine with some borage put in it to soak."

Wordsworth specially loved Celandine, and tuned his lyre to sing its praises:

"There is a flower that shall be mine,
'Tis the little Celandine;
I will sing as doth behove
Hymns in praise of what I love."

In token of which affectionate regard these flowers have been carved on the white marble of his tomb.

Pope praised the herb and flowers of Cowslip on account of their sedative qualities:

"For want of rest,
Lettuce and Cowslip wine—probatum est."

whilst Coleridge makes his Christabel declare with reference to the fragrant brew concocted from its petals with lemons and sugar:

"It is a wine of virtuous powers,
My mother made it of wild flowers."

Being a diminutive plant, with roots to correspond, the English Daisy, on the doctrine of signatures, was formerly thought to arrest the bodily growth if taken with this view. Therefore, its roots boiled in broth were given to young puppies so as to keep them of small size. For the same reason the fairy Milkah fed her foster child on this plant, "that his height might not exceed that of a pigmy":

"She robbed dwarf elders of their fragrant fruit,
And fed them early with the Daisy root,
Whence through his veins the powerful juices ran,
And formed the beauteous miniature of a man."

"Trefoil, Vervain, John's wort, Dill,
Hinder witches of their will."

A popular cure for nettle stings is to rub them with a Dock leaf, saying at the same time:

"Out nettle; in Dock,
Dock shall have a new smock."
or
"Nettle out; Dock in;
Dock remove the nettle sting."

Macer alleged that the use of Fennel was first taught to man by serpents. His classical lines on the subject when translated run thus:

"By eating herb of Fennel, for the eyes
A cure for blindness had the serpent wise;
Man tried the plant; and, trusting that his sight
Might thus be healed, rejoiced to find him right."

Milton says in *Paradise Lost*, Book XI:

"Thy savoury odour blown,
Grateful to appetite, more pleased my sense
Than smell of sweetest Fennel."

Fumitory was formerly much favoured for making cosmetic washes to purify the skin of rustic maidens in the Spring time:

"Whose red and purpled mottled flowers
Are cropped by maids in weeding hours,
To boil in water, milk or whey,
For washes on a holiday;
To make their beauty fair and sleek,
And scare the tan from summer's cheek."

"This is every cook's opinion,
No savoury dish without an Onion,
But lest your kissing should be spoiled,
Your onions must be fully boiled."

HERBS AND OLD SAYINGS—Continued

Concerning the cure of nervous headache by Garlic (and its kindred medicinal herb Asafoetida), and old charm reads thus:

"Give onyons to Saynt Cutlake,
And Garlycke to Saynt Cyryake;
If ye will shun the headake,
Ye shall have them at Queenyth."

Old Tusser tells us, in his *Husbandry for March*:

"Now Leeks are in season, for pottage full good,
That spareth the milch cow, and purgeth the blood."

And a trite proverb of former times bids us:

"Eat Leeks in Lide (March) and ramsons in May,
Then all the year after physicians can play."

"With vinegar, honey, and salt, the Orache
Made hot, and applied, cures a gouty attack;
Whilst its seeds for the jaundice, if mingled with wine,
—As Galen has said—are a remedy fine."

In Beaumont and Fletcher's *Faithful Shepherdess*, we read of:

"Black Horehound, good
For sheep, or Shepherd bitten by a wood-Dog's venomed tooth."

Shakespeare makes Perdita (*Winter's Tale*) class Lavender among the flowers denoting middle age:

"Here flowers for you!
Hot Lavender, Mints, Savory, Marjoram;
The Marigold, that goes to bed with the sun,
And with him rises, weeping: these are flowers
Of middle summer, and I think, they are given
To men of middle age."

Old Tusser says:

"Where chamber is swept, and Wormwood is strown,
No flea for his life dare abide to be known."

And again:

"What savour is better, if physic be true,
For places infected, than Wormwood and Rue."

"When the moon is at the full,
Mushrooms you may freely pull;
But when the moon is on the wane,
Wait till you think to pluck again."

"The meadow Mushrooms are in kind the best;
'Tis ill to trust in any of the rest."

"Sympathy without relief
Is like to Mustard without beef."

"Sinament, Ginger, Nutmeg and Cloves,
And that gave me my jolly red nose."

The Scarlet Pimpernel is named Anagallis, from the Greek anagleo, to laugh; either because, as Pliny says, the plant removes obstructions of the liver and spleen, which would engender sadness, or because of the graceful beauty of its flowers:

"No ear hath heard, no tongue can tell
The virtues of the Pimpernell."

The five graceful fringed leaflets which form the special beauty of the Eglantine flower, and bud, have given rise to the following Latin enigma (translated):

"Of us five brothers at the same time born,
Two from our birthday always beards have worn;
On other two none ever have appeared,
While our fifth brother wears but half a beard."

"You may break, you may ruin, the vase if you will.
But the scent of the Roses will hang round it still."

In some parts of England Rosemary is put with the corpse into the coffin and sprigs of it are distributed among the mourners at a funeral, to be thrown into the grave. Gay alludes to this practice when describing the burial of a country lass who had met with an untimely death:

"To show their love, the neighbours far and near
Followed, with wistful looks, the damsel's bier;
Sprigged Rosemary the lads and lasses bore,
While dismally the Parson walked before;
Upon her grave the Rosemary they threw,
The Daisy, Butter-flower, and Endive blue."

In early times Rosemary was grown largely in kitchen gardens, and it came to signify the strong influence of the matron who dwelt there:

"Where Rosemary flourishes the woman rules."

The *Schola Salernitana* says of Rue:

"Rue maketh chaste: and it preserveth sight;
Infuseth wit, and putteth fleas to flight."

A quaint old rhyme says of the plant:

"Noble is Rue! it makes the sight of eyes both sharp and clear;
With help of Rue, oh! blear-eyed man! thou shalt see far and near."

HERBS AND OLD SAYINGS
Continued

"He that would live for aye
Must eat Sage in May."

"Sage helps the nerves, and by its powerful might
Palsy is cured, and fever put to flight."

"Who the Sanicle hath,
At the surgeons may laugh."

"Cut your thistles before St. John,
Or you'll have two instead of one."

"They that will have their heale,
Must put Valerian in their keale."

"A woman, a donkey, a Walnut tree—
The more you beat them, the better they be."

She—"Fresh Woodruff soaks,
To brew cool drink, and keep away the moth."

"Betony is good for a man's soul or his body."—*Saxon Herbal.*

"Wood Betony is in its prime in May,
In June and July does its bloom display,
A fine bright red does this grand plant adorn,
To gather it for drink I think no scorn;
I'll make a conserve of its fragrant flowers,
Cephalick virtues in this herb remain,
To chase each dire disorder from the brain.
Delirious persons here a cure may find
To stem the phrensy and to calm the mind.
All authors own wood-betony is good,
'Tis King o'er all the herbs that deck the wood;
A King's physician rest such notice took
Of this, he on its virtues wrote a book."

"If they would drink Nettles in March
And eat Mugwort in May,
So many fine maidens
Wouldn't go to the clay."

"Also take sage and marjoram
Hit schall the kepe in savetee
Sounde and clene for to bee
Quyken the vaynes and the mynde
And all thy virtues kepe in kynde
Comfort the herte and kepe the sight
No man of erthe can telle his myghte."

"What savour is better, if physicke be true
For places infected than Wormwood and Rue?"
—Tusser, *Five Hundred Points of Good Husbandry*, 1580.

"In Health, if Sallet Herbs, you can't endure,
Sick you'll desire them, or for Food or Cure."

"Cold herbes now wholsom bee:
But let no blood in any wise:
By running stream and shadow tree,
Thy booke thou mayest well exercise."

HONEY SUPERSTITIONS

Honey was believed to have power over spirits because honey, one of the earliest foods, yields an intoxicating drink, has many good virtues. Old honey was and is still used for coughs from colds. Honey is used by the Hindus for washing their household gods. The Dekhan Brahman father drops honey into the mouth of his newborn child. Among higher class Hindus, especially among Brahmans, when a child is born honey is dropped into its mouth from a gold spoon or ring. Among Dekhan Hindus, when the bridegroom comes to the bride's house honey and curds are given him to sip. This honey-sipping is called madhuparka; its apparent object is to scare evil from the bridegroom. Honey is considered by the Hindus a great cleanser and purifier. It is also the food of their gods. In Bengal the Braham bride has part of her body anointed with honey. How highly the early Hindus valued honey appears from the hymn, "Let the winds pour down honey, the rivers pour down honey, may our plants be sweet. May the night bring honey, and the dawn and the sky above the earth be full of honey." This intense longing is probably for honey-ale, madhu, or mead. In Africa an intoxicating drink is made from honey. The Feloops of West Africa made a strong liquor out of honey, and the Hottentots are fond of honey beer. Mead made from honey was the favorite drink of the Norsemen. In England honeysuckle still keeps off witchcraft.—J. M. CAMPBELL in *Indian Antiquary*, Bombay, September, 1895.

GARLIC

The use of garlic in cooking and in raw salads is as old as time itself, but not every one knows that it is also available in tablet form for those who need it therapeutically but want to avoid the after-taste and odor.

Garlic is a food of antiquity and it was used for many ailments long before the advent of modern medicine. The father of medicine, Hippocrates, recommended garlic in intestinal disorders and upsets. Pliny in Rome used it widely. The Romans fed it to their soldiers and used it as an elementary antiseptic. Cheops (4500 B.C.) the builder of the pyramids, ordered his workers to eat garlic regularly so that they might have strength to keep fit. Heroditus tells of an early inscription on the Great Pyramid telling how many tons of garlic was consumed during its construction.

Garlic also stimulates the appetite and aids digestion by increasing the secretion of gastric juices and the secretion and discharge of the urine.

An old fashioned method of removing discoloration from teeth was to rub fresh strawberries on the teeth.

CATNIP USED AS RAT REPELLENT

One often finds Catnip growing around buildings of old farms because of an old belief held that the odor of this plant drove off rats. The plants were set as a barricade around the buildings.

HONEY BEE PLANTS

Anise Hyssop—*Agastache anethiodora*.
Balkan Sage—*Salvia sylvestris*.
Basil
Marjoram, Wild.
Meadow Sage—*Salvia pratensis*.
Moldavian Dragonhead — *Dracocephalum moldavica*.
Phacelia—*Phacelia tenacetifolia*.
Rocky Mountain Bee Plant—*Cleome serrulata*.

SKELETONIZING MAGNOLIA LEAVES

Soak the leaves in water for a long period or boil in soap and water until outer skin can be washed away. Then carefully cleanse and bleach in the sun.

KEEPS WOODCHUCKS AWAY

"Remove the head from an ordinary wooden barrel and place the barrel on its side in the middle of the garden. Then your trouble with woodchucks will be over."

Do not ask me why this works, because I have not the slightest idea about it. I only know that it does work.—C. S. Gifford, from *Horticulture*.

NO MORE CUTWORMS

My practice is to mix thoroughly one pound of arsenate of lead with two quarts or so of sand, and spread as evenly as possible over one hundred square feet of cultivated bed or border. Work it into the upper inch or two of soil with a rake. This rate of application is said to cause no damage to plants, and I can see none to mine. Quantities greatly in excess of this may damage some plants, therefore observe your measurements. Also tie on a dry handkerchief mask when mixing, and don't leave the poison within reach of children. After this compound has been mixed in the soil there should be no danger to persons. As the soil should remain poisoned for two or three years, do not repeat until needed. The application must be made in the fall or winter to catch the grubs in the ground.—By W. Terry.

CUTWORM BAIT

Cutworm control consisting of a bait, one part paris green or two parts calcium arsenate and 25 parts bran is effective in controlling these pests. The mixture should be moistened to make it flaky and then scattered around plants late in the evening.

RADISH ROOT WORMS

An easy way to prevent Worms in Radishes is to sow salt in the row when sowing the seed. Be careful not to use *too much*—just a light sprinkling, and brush it into the soil a bit before adding the seed. A sprinkling of any fine-cut brand of smoking tobacco is equally effective, and both require but one application. These treatments are equally good for worms in onions.

INDIAN POTATO BUG KILLER

Indians of the Great Lakes region made their own bug killer by boiling the herb and roots of common Mayapple in water. The strong decoction was sprinkled on potato plants. This was said to kill potato bugs as well as bug's eggs in the ground.

PARSLEY KEEPS BEETLES AWAY

Dear Editor—A couple of years ago I read that a few parsley plants grown among rose bushes keep away rose beetles. I have tried this for two seasons and, surprisingly enough, I have found that it works. I do not know whether the last two seasons have been generally freer of rose bugs everywhere, nor do I know why parsley should keep them away, but my experience may be useful to your readers.—L. F. Bachrach.

RED SPIDER IN GARDENS

Although a cold shower may be invigorating for most of us, it usually proves fatal to the red spider and is one of the leading controls for this minute pest. Wise gardeners will wash infested plants or shrubs with a stream of cold water, either early in the morning or late in the evening.

Not true spiders but rather minute mites, the so-called red spiders are primarily dry-weather pests. Few plants are exempt from the feedings of these little eight-legged animals. Their presence is indicated by a fine webbing and rusty appearance on the under sides of the leaves. Nearly impossible to see with the naked eye.

A GARDEN TIP

When slipping roses in the fall, I take a tin can, slit the sides and bottom, place earth in the can, then take a pencil to make a deep groove in the soil in the can, place sand in this, and then the slip in the sand, press firmly, place the can in the ground about an inch or so below ground level and cover with a glass jar, then draw soil up around the jar. In Spring when they appear to be well rooted, usually mid May, these may be moved to any location without disturbing the roots just lift the can and all, the same method may be used for Hydrangea slips.—Mrs. A. Schob.

Mice will never touch articles strewed over with Thyme.

LANGUAGE OF FLOWERS

WORMWOOD—Absence
Wormwood is the bitterest of plants; and absence, according to La Fontaine, is the worst of evils. Those in whose anxious breasts the "flame divine" is burning, will agree with the French author in his assertion. To be absent from one we love is to carry a vacant chamber in the heart, which naught else can fill.

If she be gone, the world, in my esteem,
Is all bare walls; nothing remains in it
But dust and feathers.

VIOLET—Modest Worth
The Violet has always been a favourite theme of admiration among visitors to Parnassus. Its quiet beauty and love of retired spots have ever made it the emblem of true worth that shrinks from parade. It is one of the first children of spring, and awakens pleasing emotions in the breast of the lover of the beautiful, as he strolls through the meadows in the season of joy. Ion, the Greek name of this flower, is traced by some etymologists to Ia, the daughter of Midas, who was betrothed to Atys, and changed by Diana into a Violet, to hide her from Apollo.

A woman's love, deep in the heart
Is like the Violet flower,
That lifts its modest head apart
In some sequestered bower.

LILY OF THE VALLEY—Modesty
The beautiful Lily of the Valley is the fit emblem of the union of beauty, simplicity, and love of retirement. It adds an indescribable charm to the spots where it blooms. Its snowy hues and general delicacy of appearance excite emotions of a kindred nature to those we experience in the company of one whose heart is free from guile, and whose manners are gentle and unpretending.

I had found out a sweet green spot
  Where a Lily was blooming fair;
The din of the city disturbed it not,
  But the spirit that shades the quiet cot
With its wings of love was there.
I found that Lily's bloom,
  When the day was dark and chill;
It smiled like a star in a misty gloom,
And it sent abroad a soft perfume,
  Which is floating around me still.

MIGNONETTE—Your Qualities Surpass Your Charm
The Mignonette was introduced into Europe from Egypt, in 1750. It flowers from the beginning of spring until the end of autumn. Linnaeus, who gave it the name of Reseda odorata, compares its perfume with that of ambrosia.

No gorgeous flowers the meek Reseda grace,
Yet sip, with eager trunk, yon busy race
Her simple cup, nor heed the dazzling gem
That beams in Fritillaria's diadem.

OAK—Nobility
The form of Oak tree, when grown fairly and naturally, is a perfect emblem of its qualities, so firm set, so massive, and strong. You may always know it instantly, whether as a wintry skeleton form, bare, and gnarled, and angular, or in its summer garb of rich and finely massed foliage, always the monarch of the woods.

How vain are all hereditary honours,
Those poor possessions from another's deeds,
Unless our own just virtues form our title,
And give a sanction to our fond assumption!

GRASS—Submission
According to the Greek historians, Grass was made the symbol of submission, because the ancient nations of the West gathered Grass and presented it to the conqueror, to show that they confessed themselves overcome. The grass is trodden under foot by imperial man; and, instead of returning to its former vigour with elastic spring, or punishing its violator like the nettle, yields to its fate—spiritless submission.

It grieves me to the soul
To see how man submits to man's control;
How overpowered and shackled minds are led
In vulgar tracks, and to submission bred.

NIGHTSHADE, OR BITTER-SWEET —Truth
According to the belief of the ancients, Truth was the mother of Virtue, the daughter of Time, and queen of the world. It is a frequent saying, that Truth lies at the bottom of a well, and that she always mingles some bitterness with her sweet blessings; and we have chosen for her emblem a plant which, like her, delights in the shade, and is evergreen. The Nightshade is the only plant in England which loses and reproduces its leaves twice a year.

Truth, crushed to earth will rise again,
  The eternal years of God are hers;
But Error, wounded, writhes with pain,
  And dies among her worshippers.

CACTUS—Ardent Love
The flower of the Cactus is chosen to signify ardent love, because of the glowing hues of the flower itself, and the heat of the climate in which the plant grows to the greatest size. The gorgeousness of the flower of the Cactus needs no eulogy. No fitter emblem could have been selected to represent the passion of love in its full flame.

I think of thee, when soft and wide
  The evening spreads her robes of light,
And, like a young and timid bride,
  Sits blushing in the arms of night:
And when the moon's sweet crescent springs
  In light o'er heaven's deep waveless sea,
And stars are forth like blessed things,
  I think of thee—I think of thee.

LESSONS IN FLOWERS

Flowers are one of the few noncontroversial things in life.

But they are certainly great teachers. They nourish our sensibilities, quicken our wonder over nature's magnificence and variety.

They prove to us, above all, that there is a power that defies mortal impatience, rebuffs wilfulness, induces serenity in a world that is largely aimless bedlam.

The best way to realize this, of course, is to grow them as well as buy them.

Even the posture required is healthily humbling, for most of a gardener's work is done upon his knees; hoping with love and reverence that what he does will be approved by the Master who rules the sun, the earth and air.

If he has faithfully followed His law, the result will be something human lives should resemble: A transitory and fragile existence under the compulsion of time, but leaving an unforgetable perfume, color and form to its successors.

The poor and the rich look upon labor as hardship and servitude. Hence the inspired writer prays: "Give me neither poverty nor riches"—for both relax the vital fibre and take away the strength and joy that spring from work well and gladly done.

If thou seekest truth seek it in thy own heart, and even there thou shalt not find it unless thou art a true man.

To be happy, we must be true to nature, and carry our age along with us.—Hazlit.

A comfortable old age is the reward of a well-spent youth; therefore instead of its introducing dismal and melancholy prospects of decay, it should give us hopes of eternal youth in a better world.—Palmer.

He who would pass the declining years of his life with honor and comfort, should when young, consider that he may one day become old, and remember, when he is old, that he has once been young.—Addison.

THE POOR MAN'S GARDEN

O'ershadawed by the bower,
  Grow southernwood and lemon-thyme,
Sweet-pea and gilliflower;
  And pinks, and clove-carnations,
Rich-scented, side by side,
  And at each end a hollyhock,
And an edge of London-pride.
  And here comes the old grandmother
When her day's work is done;
  And here they bring the sickly babe
To cheer it in the sun.
  And here on Sabbath mornings,
The goodman comes to get
  His Sunday nosegay, moss-rose bud,
White pink, and mignonette.
  And here on Sabbath evenings,
Until the stars are out,
  With a little one in either hand
He walketh all about.
  Yes! in the poor man's garden grow
Far more than herbs and flowers;
  Kind thoughts, contentment, peace of mind,
And joy for weary hours.
        —Mary Howitt.

DID YOU THINK TO PRAY?

When unexpected problems met you
At the break of day,
Finding you all unprepared,
Did you think to pray?
In the insecurity
Accompanying fright,
Did you think to breathe a prayer
That God would make things right?
Morning, noon, and night, God gives us
Help when-er we think to pray—
Let us ne'er forget the saying,
"God is just a prayer away."

To live is to acquire habits, and unless we fashion ourselves to virtue, we become the slaves of vice.

The old die amid the scenes of their childhood. Fathers and mothers and the long lost loved ones come back to them. The weary years of toil and trial have vanished; the wintry days have melted away and the spring of life blooms about them once more. They are become as tired children who having played a long while, hear a father's voice calling them home.

ANCIENT LEGENDS
How Flowers Got Their Names

These stories are reprinted in the quaint old English as they appeared in Henrie Lyte's 1586 translation of Dodoen's Herbal. Dodoen's information is evidently from very ancient Greek sources.

Story of Narcissus

These flowers tooke their name of the noble youth, Narcissus, who being often required and much desired of many brave ladies, because of his passing beautie he regarded them not; wherefore, being desirous to be delivered from their importunate sutes and requests, he went a hunting, and being thirstie, came to a fountaine, in which when he would have dronken, saw his owne favour and passing beauty, the which before that time he had never seene, and thinking it had been one of the amorous ladies that loved him, he was so wrapt with the love of himselfe that he desired to kisse and imbrace himselfe, and when he could not take hold of his own shadow or figure, he died at last by extreme force of love. In whose honor and perpetual remembrance, the earth (as the poets faine) brought foorth this delectable, and sweete smelling floure.

Story of Celandine

The Great Celandine is named in Greek, Chelidonium, that is to say, Swalow-herbe, because (as Plinie writeth) it was first found out by Swalows, and hath healed the eyes and restored sight to their yong ones, that have had harme in their eyes or have been blind.

The small Celandine was so called, because that it beginneth to spring and to floure, at the coming of the Swalowes, and withereth at their returne.

Story of Yarrow

This herbe had his name Achillea, of the noble and valient knight Achilles, whose valiant actes and noble Historie were described by Homer. They sayde Achilles used this herbe very much, and it was firste taught him by the Centaure Chiron. With this herb Achilles cured the woundes and sores of Telephus the sonne of Hercules.

Story of Centaury

Centorie was called in Greek Centaurian or Chironion, after the name Chiron the Centaure, who first of all found out these two herbes, and taught them to Aesculapius as Apuleius writeth. And as some other write they were so named, because Chiro was cured with these herbs of a certain wound which he tooke (beyng received as a ghest or stranger in Hercules house or lodging) by letting fall on his foote, one of Hercules shafts or arrowes as he was handling and viewing of the said Hercules weapon and armour.

Story of Ivy

Ivie is called in Greek, Cissos, because of a certain mayden or Damsel, whose name was Cissus, the which at a feast or banquet (whereunto the gods were al bidden) so danced before Bacchus, and kissed him often, making such mirth and joy, that being overcome with the same fell to the ground, and killed hirself. But assoone as the earth knew thereof, she brought foorth immediatelie the Ivy bushe, bearing still the name of the yoong Damsell Cissus, the which assoone as it groweth up a little, commeth to embrace the Vine, in remembrance that the Damesell Cissus was woont so to love and embrace Bacchus the God of wine.

Story of Myrtle

The Myrtell is called in Greeke Mursine bycause of a yoong maiden of Athens named Myrsine, who in beautie excelled all the maydens of that citie and in strength and activitie all the lusty laddes or brave yoong men of Athenes, wherfore she was tenderly beloved of the Goddesse Pallas or Minerva, who willed her to be alwaies present at tourney, and tilte, running, vaulting, and other such plaies of activitie or exercise, to the intent she should afterwarde as a judge give the Garlande or Crowne of honour to such as won the price and best deserved the same: but some of them who were vanquished, were so much displeased with her judgement that they slue her. The which thing as soone as the Goddesse Minerva perceived, she caused the sweete Myrtell to spring up, and called it Myrsine, after the name of the Damosell Myrsine, to the honour and perpetuall memorie of her, which tree or plant she loveth as much as ever she loved the yoong Damosell Myrsine.

The Story of Roses

The Rose is called in Greeke Rhodon, because it is of an excellent smell and pleasant savour, as Plutarch writeth.

Ye shall also finde this written of Roses, that at the first they were all white and that they became red afterward with the blood of the Goddesse Venus, which was done in this sort.

Venus loved the yoonker Adonis better than the warrier Mars (who loved Venus with all his force and might) but when Mars perceived that Venus loved Adonis better than him, he slew Adonis, thinking of this meanes to cause Venus not only to forgo but also to forget hir friend Adonis, and so to love Mars onely: of the which thing when Venus had warning how and where it should be accomplished, she was suddenly mooved and ran hastily to have rescued Adonis, but taking no care of the way at a sudden ere she was ware, she threw hir selfe upon a bed or thicket of white Roses, whereas with sharpe and cruell thorns, hir tender feete were so prickt and wounded, that the blood

ANCIENT LEGENDS (Continued)

sprang out aboundantly, wherewithall when the Roses were bedewed and sprinkled, they became all red, the which colour they do yet keepe (more or lesse) according to the quantitie of blood that fell upon them) in remembrance of the cleere and pleasant Venus. Some others write that for very anger which she had conceived against Mars, for the killing of hir friend the faire Adonis, she gave hir tender bodie willingly to be spoiled and mangled; and in despite of Mars, she threw hir selfe into a bed or herbor of prickly Roses.

Some also say, that Roses became red with the casting downe of that heavenly drinke Nectar, which was shed by Cupide that wanton boy, who playing with the Goddesse sitting at the table at a banket, with his wings overthrew the pot wherein the Nectar was. And therefore as Philostratus saith, the Rose is the flower of Cupid, or Cupids flower.

LINNAEUS' FLORA CLOCK

Linnaeus, the great Swedish naturalist, composed a flora clock to determine the time of day by opening and closing of certain flowers which he observed folded and unfolded their petals at regular hours. A few of these which served for the construction of his dial are enumerated here: Dandelion opens from 5 to 6 a. m. and closes between 8 and 9 p. m. Mouse-Ear Hawkweed opens about 8 a. m. and closes at 2 p. m. Yellow Goat's Beard opens at sunrise and shuts at noon with regularity. Smooth Sow Thistle opens at 5 a. m. and closes between 11 and 12 Noon. Cultivated lettuce opens at 7 a. m. and closes at 10. White Water Lily opens between 5 and 6 a. m. Mallow opens at 9 to 10 a. m. and closes at 1.

COAL ASHES RECOMMENDED FOR ROOTING PLANT SHOOTS

Anthracite coal ashes are an excellent material in which to set plant cuttings, while they are striking root, states Miss Mildred P. Mauldin of the San Antonio seed-testing laboratory of the U. S. Soil Conservation Service

Sifted hard coal ashes were used on a large scale for this purpose by her father, who for many years operated a wholesale cut-flower business in New York. Cuttings thus rooted were exceptionally free from diseases, especially from damping-off, a fungus plague that sometimes wipes out whole benchfuls of young plants. The ash-rooted cuttings, Miss Mauldin adds, produced large clumps of roots and carried throughout their lives much of the vigor with which they started.—*Science News Letter.*

Primula is said to be rendered of surpassing size and beauty by applications of raw meat near the roots.

ORNAMENTAL BERRIES, SEEDS AND PODS

Bittersweet: The scarlet seeds of this vine make this one of the showiest fall seeds. Bunches of Bittersweet are often sold along roadways in localities where it is found.

Canada Lily: The tall golden, candelabrum-like stalks and pods make excellent dry decorations. The plant with its tawny yellow flowers is a handsome addition to any garden.

Gas Plant: A lemony-scented old-time garden favorite. This plant exudes a gas which will make a tiny flash when lighted with a match on a still summer evening. The dried seed pods are star shaped. As a vase ornament they are most effective when painted with flat color. Gas plant is available in white or red flowering varieties.

Honesty: An old-time garden plant with lilac-like flowers. It is grown mainly for its very beautiful, large, silvery pods. It is often seen in florist shops.

Horsenettle: The lemon-colored, ball-shaped berries make very attractive table bouquets in the fall.

Motherwort: Tall stalks with series of clustered seeds. An interesting addition with other dry specimens.

Pampas Grass: Tall, blue-green grass bearing long spikes of fluffy plumes in the fall.

Wafer Ash: Golden brown flat seeds growing ball-like clusters. Very attractive in natural color or dyed.

Wild Yam: A vinebearing golden pods clustered like grapes. An interesting and beautiful decoration for the table.

Zebra Grass: A very handsome, tall growing grass that forms large clusters. The grass blades are beautifully spotted with yellow stripes. In the fall the plant bears fluffy plumes similar to Pampas Grass. They are fine dry ornaments for tall vases.

Any of the above plants are easily grown in the garden.

EXPERT ADVISES SULPHUR FOR AILING PLANTS

Champaign, Ill.—(UP)—Housewives being troubled by common flower garden troubles may find sulphur is something of a cure-all if properly used, Dr. F. F. Weinard, floriculture specialist at the University of Illinois, says.

Hollyhocks showing red pustules of rust on the underside of the leaves can be treated successfully with sulphur. To give proper treatment, Weinard advises, remove the first leaves which show rust, and dust the plants with sulphur. Snapdragons can be treated successfully the same way.

Weinard also urged the sulphur dust treatment for the perennial phlox.

The Juice of Aloes is fine for Burns, Itch, Sunburn.

OLD FASHIONED METHODS OF KEEPING FLOWERS

Any vegetable substance may be preserved moist in a solution of creasote, or in glycerine. The method of drying plants between sheets of paper needs no description. But the original form, and in many instances the color, of a fresh flower may be preserved by carefully immersing it in some fine dry material, and then rapidly drying in a baking oven. Millet seed has been used for this purpose, and may answer well for coarse specimens. For fine ones white river sand in equal grains must be used. To separate large grains it should be passed through a sieve; to remove fine particles it is copiously washed with water. While drying it is to be constantly agitated. It is further recommended that 1000 parts of this sand be intimately mixed with 1 of stearic acid and 1 of spermaceti, before using.

To Preserve Flowers in their Natural Shape and Color: Provide a vessel with a moveable cover. Fit to the top a piece of fine metallic gauze, and replace the cover. Pass through a sieve into an iron pot sand sufficient to fill this vessel, and heat it with ½ per cent of stearine, carefully stirring. Place the flowers on the gauze, and removing the bottom of the vessel, pour in the sand and stearine, so as to cover and envelop them. Place on the top of an oven for 48 hours. Remove the cover, invert the vessel, and the sand runs away through the gauze, leaving the flowers dried in their natural position. According to the Journal of Soc. Arts, fresh flowers may be preserved for some time in glycerine.

To Preserve Cut Flowers in Water: Add to the water a teaspoonful of salt, or a teaspoonful of charcoal. Flowers in pots may be watered with a weak solution of sulphite of iron.

HOW TO KEEP A BOUQUET OF FLOWERS FRESH AND FRAGRANT FOR WEEKS

The Japanese restore flowers by holding the end of the stems in the fire until they are completely charred. This may be done in the evening, and in eight hours they will be restored to vigor and freshness.

HOW TO FATTEN TURKEYS

It may be profitable for those having turkeys in their yards to know that pulverized charcoal mixed with meal and boiled potatoes will fatten those birds in a wonderfully short space of time.—From an old Recipe book.

HOW TO MAKE HENS LAY THE WHOLE YEAR

Give each hen half an ounce of fresh meat every day, and mix a small amount of red pepper with their food during the winter. Give them plenty of grain, water, gravel and lime.—From an old Recipe book.

HOW TO MAKE CUCUMBER VINES BEAR MORE CROPS

When a cucumber is taken from the vine let it be cut with a knife, leaving about the eighth of an inch of the cucumber on the them, then slit the stem with a knife from its end to the vine, leaving a small portion of the cucumber on each division, and on each separate split there will be a new cucumber as large as the first.—From an old Recipe book.

BETTER POTATOES

When planting potatoes wet them and roll in dry sulphur then plant. You won't be bothered with potato bugs and your potatoes will be clean and smooth. We have tried it for the last four years.—Submitted by Mrs. M. Bergdorf, Copley, Ohio.

TO SKELETONIZE LEAVES

Steep the leaves, seed-vessels, or other parts of the plant to be dissected, in rain water, until the whole of the soft matter is decomposed. Some require a few weeks, others several months. The rotted parts are now to be carefully removed by a fine brush, under the surface of water, or in a stream of water. A syringe is sometimes required. To bleach the skeletons soak them for some hours in a mixture of 1 oz. of strong solution of chloride of lime and a quart of distilled water. Lastly, wash thoroughly in cold water, and dry by exposure to air.

TRANSPLANTING SMALL SHRUBS WHILE GROWING

Dig a narrow trench round the plant, leaving its roots in the middle in an isolated ball of earth; fill the trench with plaster of Paris, which will become hard in a few minutes, and form a case to the ball and plant, which may be lifted and removed any where at pleasure.

TO DISPERSE BLACK ANTS

A few leaves of green wormwood, scattered among the haunts of these troublesome insects, is said to be effectual in dislodging them.

HOW GRANDFATHER FOUGHT INSECTS IN GARDEN

In some seasons the vegetables in our gardens are almost annihilated by worms of several species. Fall plowing or spading the ground just before frost sets in and strewing the ground with fine salt in the spring some time before the seeds are sown, are said to be the sovereign remedies against these petty but powerful depradators.

Set an onion in the center of a hill of cucumbers, squashes, melons, etc., and it will effectually banish the bugs.

If a tree or plant is affected with insects, tie up some flower of sulphur in a piece of gauze and dust the plants with it.

BED BUGS

Apply Sassafras oil in cracks and crevices —it is sure death for these pests.

WHO AM I?

I am more powerful than the combined armies of the world.

I have destroyed more men than all wars of the nations.

I am more deadly than bullets, and I have wrecked more homes than the mightiest of siege guns.

I steal in the United States alone over $300,000,000 each year.

I spare no one, and I find my victims among the rich and poor alike, the young and old, the strong and weak. Widows and orphans know me.

I loom up to such proportions that I cast my shadow over every field of labor, from the turning of the grindstone to the moving of every railroad train.

I massacre thousands upon thousands of wage earners a year.

I lurk in unseen places, and I do most of my work silently. You are warned against me, but you heed not.

I am relentless.

I am everywhere in the home, on the streets, in the factory, at railroad crossings, and on the sea.

I bring sickness, degradation and death, and yet few seek to avoid me.

I destroy, crush or maim; I give nothing but take all.

I am your worst enemy.

I AM CARELESSNESS.

The wages of sin is Death.
The wages of bad habits is also Death!

MISTLETOE IN FOLKLORE

Mistletoe figured in the folk lore tales and mythology of every country where it grew, and it was often of religious importance.

The power which the Mistletoe has of renewing itself when cut, was one reason why it was held in mystic honor. In all countries it was worshipped as the soul and embodiment of the holy forest. To the Norseman only the "mistil" could inflict injury on the Sun God, Baldur; to the Roman only the "viscum" could unlock the door of Hades for Aeneas to enter; to the English Druids only the "Misleta" cut from an oak by the light of the moon could give protection to man.

It is an evergreen shrub which clings to its host tree high up among the branches and gains its nourishment by penetrating the bark with its roots and purloining what sap it requires.

Mistletoe is peculiar in the manner of its growth. The branches turn always toward the object to which the plant is attached, a curious habit which made the ancients think of it as a visible god protecting its sacred tree and which aroused in all early peoples so much of wonder.

"When you are sick of the world of men, turn to the world of plants."—David Fairchild.

RESTORING FADING FLOWERS

Most flowers fade within four and twenty hours after they have been placed in water, but almost all can be preserved for a much longer period, if they be in the first instance placed in warm instead of cold water. When they begin to droop, the stems should be plunged into boiling water to about one-third of their length, and by the time the water is cold, the flowers will have regained their freshness. That part which has been in the boiling water must then be cut off, and the flowers replaced in cold water.

TO DRY FLOWERS AND PRESERVE THEIR NATURAL BEAUTY

Take some fine white sand, wash it repeatedly until all dirt is removed, and the water remains clear. Next dry it thoroughly, and fill a vase, a stone flower-pot, or a glass half full of the sand. In this stick fresh gathered flowers in their natural position, and afterwards cover them gently with the sand, taking care not to damage the petals. Now place the vessel in the sun, or in a room where a constant fire is kept, and let it remain until the flowers are perfectly dry. Then remove the sand carefully, and clean the leaves with a feather brush. You must gather your flowers for this purpose when they are dry, that is, after the dew has evaporated. The process succeeds best with single flowers, but the difficulty attending such double ones as pinks, carnations, etc., may be obviated by splitting the cup on each side; and when the flower is quite dry the incision made to adhere by means of gum water, or the cup may be pricked around with a pin to let out the moisture. Some flowers lose their natural lively color by this process, but it may be restored as follows:

Roses and other flowers of a delicate color should be exposed to a moderate vapor of brimstone; but crimson or scarlet flowers should be placed in a vapor of the solution of tin in spirits of nitre. The green leaves and stems are renovated by the vapor produced from a solution of steel filings in spirit of vitriol. When dried the scent of each particular flower may be artificially renewed by dropping into the middle of it some of its essential oil, thus oil of cloves will scent the pink, oil of roses the rose, oil of jasmine the jasmine, etc., and by this means a bouquet of flowers is obtained all through the winter months.

TO KEEP GERANIUMS FROM SEASON TO SEASON

When setting plant out, mulch soil well with peat moss. Dig plants before frost, shake off excess soil (not clinging peat moss) and hang upside down from hooks or strings in dark cool cellar or location.

MAKING HYDRANGEAS BLUE

Potted hydrangeas are often made to produce blue flowers by adding aluminum sulphate to the soil at the rate of a half pound to five gallons of water at weekly intervals. After two or three applications, it also seems to help to apply four ounces of ferrous sulphate per five gallons of water for a few weeks. This treatment is continued as long as it seems necessary to make and keep the soil acid.

TURNING HYDRANGEAS PINK

Blue flowered hydrangeas produce flowers that are of various shades of pink if they are grown in non-acid soil. A neutral or slightly alkaline soil will give the results you desire. Therefore, add sufficient lime to bring the pH of the soil to a figure somewhat between 6.7 and 7.2. The addition of the lime is best affected by lifting the hydrangea in fall, shaking the roots free of as much soil as is safely possible and then mixing the lime thoroughly with the soil before planting again. To be certain of the amount of lime needed to bring your soil to the required pH figure you must have the soil tested.

PARSLEY RICH IN VITAMINS

One ounce of the fresh herb contains over 30,000 international units of Vitamin A, 80 milligrams of Vitamin C (3 times as much as an orange) and 3 milligrams of Iron.

TIPS ON TREE AGES

It's easy to tell the ages of many trees if you know how. And the "know how" is simple—all you need to do is find the diameter of the trunk in inches at breast height and then multiply that by the correct number taken from the following table used by tree experts.

2½ for chestnut, white elm and tulip;
3, for black walnut, and 3½ for black oak;
4, for birch, sweet gum, chestnut oak, red oak, scarlet oak and sycamore;
5, for ash and white oak;
6, for beech, sour gum and sugar maple;
8, for shagbark hickory.

CEMENTING IRON TO STONE

If you have occasion to cement iron to stone or marble, the following mixture will be highly effective. It consists of plaster of paris, 30 parts, fine iron filings, 10 parts, and sal ammoniac ½ part, mixed with vinegar to form a fluid paste.

According to tradition Dandelion never grows where there are no human inhabitants. The early pioneers found no trace of them in America. After a few years up sprang a gray head and soon there were millions of them.

NITROGEN FOR YOUR SOIL

One great advantage of growing the Bean family is that colonies of nitrogen-fixing bacteria form on the roots. These organisms are able to take nitrogen gas from the air and convert it into nitrates, which remain in the soil for its good. Nitrogen is the central point in the elaboration of protein in plants. To encourage these minute creatures to manufacture nitrates appeals to me as far better than applying nitrogen-containing chemical manures. For one thing, they charge nothing for their work, while their own death serves to enrich the earth. Hence peas and beans should be grown on different parts of the kitchen-garden from year to year.

The entire family of *leguminosæ* has the same usefulness. Lupins and sweet peas, for example, are worth while in the flower bed for this reason. It will be clear from this fact that to burn the roots of leguminous plants when clearing the ground in autumn is wasteful. These should be broken up, with the haulm, and added to the compost heap.

When a tree is cut down, the *rings* in the wood visible on the stump tell not only the age of the tree but also indicates wet and dry years.

GOLD FISH

Allow not more than one fish to a quart of water, whether spring or river water. Change it daily in summer, every other day in winter. Use a deep vessel with small pebbles at the bottom. Keep them in the shade, and in a cool part of the room. Use a small net, rather than the hand, while changing the water. Feed them with cracker, yolk of an egg, lettuce, flies, etc., rather than with bread, and then only every third or fourth day, a very little at a time. Do not feed them at all from November to the end of February, and but little during the three following months.

YOUR GARDEN POOL

Algae or green slime can be controlled in a garden pool by potassium permanganate; a teaspoonful of a saturated solution of this chemical for each 3 gallons of water in the pool will not injure lilies or fish.

Parsnips are one of the few vegetables that contain bromine.

One reason that people like *radishes* in the early spring, it is said, is because they act as a spring tonic due to their sulfur and bromine content.

Bromine is essential to the adrenal glands and helps to build up physical courage.

LEAF SKELETONS

Plants, as well as animals, are organized bodies, and like them their parts may be dissected and decomposed by art, thereby unveiling to us their peculiarities of structure and habit, and enabling us more correctly to classify and arrange them. Among the various helps toward acquiring a knowledge of the anatomy of plants, one of the principal is the art of reducing to skeletons, leaves, fruit and roots; that is, of freeing them from their tender and pulpy substance, in such a manner as to allow us to survey alone the internal harder vessels in their entire connection. This has been done by various ways of decomposition.

Choose the leaves of trees of plants which are somewhat substantial and tough and have woody fibres, such as the leaves of orange, laurel, apricot, apple, oak, etc., but avoid such leaves as have none of the woody fibres which are to be separated and preserved by this method; such are the leaves of the vine, lime tree and some others. These are to be put into an earthen or glass vessel, and a large quantity of rain water to be poured over them; after this they are to be left to the open air and to the heat of the sun, without covering the vessel. When the water evaporates so as to leave the leaves dry, more must be added in its place; the leaves will by this means putrefy, but they require a different time for this; some will be finished in a month, others will require two months or longer, according to the toughness of their parenchyma. When they have been in a state of putrefaction for some time, the two membranes will begin to separate, and and the green part of the leaf will become fluid; then the operation of clearing is to be performed.

The leaf is to be put upon a flat white earthen plate and covered with clear water, and being gently squeezed with the finger, the membranes will begin to open, and the green substance will come out at the edges; the membranes must be carefully taken off with the finger, and great caution must be used in separating them near the middle rib. When once there is an opening toward this separation, the whole membrane always follows easily. When both membranes are taken off the skeleton is finished and it is to be washed clean with water, and then dried between the leaves of a book.

Fruits are divested of their pulp and made into skeletons in a different manner. Take for instance a fine large pear which is soft, and not tough; let it be neatly pared without squeezing it, and without injuring either the crown or the stalk. Put it into a pot of rain water, covered, set it over the fire, and let it boil gently until perfectly soft, then take it out and lay it in a dish filled with cold water; then holding it by the stalk with one hand, rub off as much of the pulp as you can with the finger and thumb, beginning at the stalk, and rubbing it regularly toward the crown. The fibres are most tender toward the extremities, and therefore are to be treated with great care there. When the pulp has thus been cleared off pretty well, the point of a fine penknife may be of use to pick away the pulp sticking to the core. In order to see how the operation advances, the soiled water must be thrown away from time to time, and clean poured on in its place. When the pulp is in this manner perfectly separated, the clean skeleton is to be preserved in spirit of wine.

This method may be pursued with the bark of trees, which afford interesting views of their constituent fibres.

These simple preparations not only form elegant ornaments, but they are extremely useful to the student in botany, more interesting and more readily comprehended than drawings of the anatomy of plants.

NOTE: Leaf Skeletons become very effective ornaments when sealed in transparent plastic, and have commercial possibilities.

CALENDAR LORE

"Monday for health,
Tuesday for wealth,
Wednesday the best day all.
Thursday for losses,
Friday for crosses,
And Saturday no luck at all."

FOR THE MONTH OF THE YEAR:
"Married in January's chilling time,
    Widowed you'll be before your prime.
Married in February's sleety weather,
    Life you'll tread in tune together.
Married when March winds shrill and roar,
    Your home will be on a foreign shore.
Married 'neath April's changeful skies,
    A checkered path before you lies.
Married when bees over May blossom flit,
    Strangers around your board will sit.
Married in queen rose month of June,
    Life will be one long honeymoon.
Married as July's flower banks blaze,
    Bitter-sweet memories in after days.
Married in August heat and drowse,
    Lover and friend in your chosen spouse.
Married in gold September's glow,
    Smooth and serene your life will flow.
Married when leaves in October thin,
    Toil and hardship for you begin.
Married in veils of November mist,
    Fortune your wedding ring has kissed.
Married in days of December's cheer,
    Love's star shines brighter from year to year."

The savour or sent of Mynte (Mint), rejoyceth man: wherefore they sow and strow the wilde Mynte in this countrie in places whereas feastes are kepte, and in churches—From Dodoen's 1586 Herbal.

Good Books Create Knowledge, Virtue and Happiness

The power of speaking to the eyes and heart,
Is great; and is indeed a wondrous art;
It might proves; it scorns the tyrant's power,
And will remain extant till earth's last hour:
An useful book may live from age to age,
And those unborn, may read its printed page.

ROSE PEARLS

Beat the petals of the red rose in an iron mortar for some hours, until they form a thick paste, which is to be rolled into beads and dried. They are very hard, susceptible of a fine polish and retain all the fragrance of the flower.

TO REVIVE WITHERED FLOWERS

Plunge the stems into boiling water and by the time the water is cold the flowers will revive. The ends of the stalks should then be cut off; and the flowers should be put to stand in cold water, and they will keep fresh for several days.

FLOWERS OF DIFFERENT COLORS ON THE SAME STEM

Split a small twig of the elder bush lengthways, scoop out the pith, fill each of the compartments with seeds of flowers of different sorts, but which blossom about the same time; surround them with mould, and then, tying together the two bits of wood, plant the whole in a pot filled with rich earth. The stems of the different flowers will thus be so incorporated as to exhibit to the eye only one stem, but a variety of flowers.

PROPAGATING PANSIES

Cuttings taken from the center of the plant are the best, but the side shoots and branches will also grow. Place these in a mixture of sand and loam, equal parts; shade from the heat of the sun; water occasionally. They will soon strike root and grow rapidly.

TO MAKE SEEDS START

Water with ammonia and oxalic acid once a week. Prepare a small bottle of each, and use only a teaspoonful in a quart of water.

CHARCOAL FOR FLOWERS

Powdered charcoal, placed around plants, has the effect of adding much to their richness.

SKELETON LEAVES

Fern leaves are pressed dry in a book, and then put into a tablespoon of chlorate of lime, to one quart of water. Other leaves must be simmered in water, with a little piece of yellow soap. As soon as the pulp will separate from the fibres put them in the chloride of lime, until bleached. When taken out of the lime dry them in an old writing book; place them in and lay something heavy upon them, and let them remain some days before disturbing them.

FLOWERS AND HEALTH

"Ozone" consists of highly electrified oxygen; the gas, when so electrified, has specially good qualities in regard to general health. A few of the ozone-producing plants are: cherry, laurel, clove, lavender, mint, fennel, lemon-tree; also, the narcissus, heliotrope, hyacinth, mignonette, and certain perfumes, such as cologne, oil of bergamont, extract of mille-fleurs, essence of lavender. The best sanitary agent is the common sunflower, in all districts where the atmosphere is liable to be corrupted.—From 1875 Cook Book.

FRESH-BLOWN FLOWERS FOR WINTER

Choose perfect buds of flowers, such as are latest in bloom and ready to open; cut them off with a pair of scissors, leaving to each a piece of stem about three inches long; cover the end of the stem immediately with sealing-wax, and then the buds will be a little shrunken and wrinkled; wrap each of them up separately in a piece of paper, perfectly clean and dry; put them away in a dry box or drawer. In Winter, or at any time you may wish for a blossom, take the buds over night and cut off the end of the stem sealed with wax, and put the buds in water wherein a little nitre of salt has been diffused; the next day you will have the pleasure of seeing the buds open and expand, and the flowers display their most lively colors and odors.

GERANIUM CUTTINGS

A florist gave this trick about starting slips. After you break them off the parent plant, lay them in the sun for a few minutes, until the broken ends are seared. They are less likely to rot.

If money be not thy servant, it will be thy master. The covetous man cannot so properly be said to possess wealth, as that may be said to possess him.

FALL GARDENING

To prevent insects from destroying your garden next year, you should start a sanitation program this fall and winter.

All vines and stalks in the garden should be piled and burned. Especially, you should destroy cucumber, bean and tomato vines, for they help insects and disease to carry over the winter. He also reminds gardeners that cornstalks are of little value in the average garden and they help the corn borer over the winter.

In the flower garden all tops of the peony, iris or dahlia should be burned, in fact any debris which might harbor borers should be burned. A soft-mulch of rotted manure, straw or peat-moss should be spread around roses and other perennials. The evergreens should also be mulched with peat moss.

Tree leaves should not be burned for, when rotten, they are equal to the same weight in manure.

NOVEMBER GARDEN

Plant bulbs; cut all peony stalks at the soil surface and burn them; protect hybrid tea roses by hilling the soil around the base of the plants; remove the tops of the hardy chrysanthemums and protect the basal shoots with a light mulch, or lift a few clumps of each variety and store in a cold-frame until spring.

FEEDING BIRDS IN WINTER

Any garden plant with large, open seed-pods can be turned into an effective bird-feeding station. Large hybrid mallows are among the easier plants to use. All one needs to do is to melt up some suet, stir in sunflower seed, millet, etc., then go out into the garden before the suet congeals and drop spoonfuls of the mixture into the empty seed-pods. The suet hardens as it cools, holding the seed firmly in place. Bird feeding by this method has only one disadvantage—the birds seem to prefer it. If one had previously had them coming to ordinary food trays by the twos and threes, they arrive by the dozens when the same food is displayed in these more natural containers.—From Missouri Botanical Garden bulletin.

Audubon, who is an authority on wild bird life, said of the wild turkey: "To prevent the disastrous effect of rainy weather, the mother, like a skillful physician, plucks the buds of the spicewood bush and gives them to the young."

If the grass grow in January, it grows the worse for it all the year.

If January calends be summerly gay
'Twill be winterly weather, 'till the calends of May.

DEEP WATERING IS ESSENTIAL FOR EVERGREENS

Evergreens retain their foliage throughout the Winter and require a good supply of moisture to prevent drying out. It is advisable to water them as long as the soil will absorb.

In the Winter, trees with deep-growing roots can secure their moisture from below the frost line. Not so with young evergreens, however. They not only need frequent and thorough watering before the real frigid weather descends but a protective mulch covering, as well.

Thorough soaking of the entire root system encourages growth downward. Roots tend to turn upwards seeking for moisture if there is an inadequate surface sprinkling. This, of course, makes for insecure root foundations.

One of the main causes of Winter injury in evergreens is the lack of adequate watering before the big freeze hits. Right after the cold snap, there may be sunny days. These, however, may not be warm enough to thaw out the ground. Thus, evergreens may evaporate a large amount of moisture and not be able to draw any water from below the frost line. Some time later, the Winter injury may be evidenced in the browning of the foliage.

HERBAL MOUTH WASH

For sweetening the breath—take ¼ ounce each of dried mint, thyme and lemon-thyme; ½ ounce of cloves, crushed; ½ nutmeg, grated; pour on to these ingredients ½ pint of any spirit and let the mixture stand together for 2 to 3 days, then strain off the tincture formed, and add 10 drops of oil of peppermint; it is then ready for use.

TO KEEP TOMATOES ALL WINTER

Pick when sound and ripe, not soft; leave the stems on; do not break or bruise them; lay them in weak salt and water for 48 hours; then pack in a jar without pressing; cover them with 2 parts water and 1 part vinegar, cold; put something over to keep them under the liquor. They will be as fresh as from the vine.

He who loseth wealth loseth much;
He who loseth a friend, loseth more,
But he that loseth spirits, loseth all.

WATERPROOF FOR LEATHER BOOTS AND SHOES

Linseed Oil, one pint; suet, eight ounces; Beeswax, six ounces; resin, one ounce. Melt together.

Go to friends for advice; to women for pity; to strangers for charity; to relatives for nothing.—*Spanish Proverb.*

TIPS FROM 270-YEAR-OLD TREATISE ON FRUIT TREES
Setting Out an Orchard

"Plant your tall trees in such places where you intend to make use of the land for grazing that they may be above the reach of cattle. But in such places where you can dispense with the absence of cattle, and use the land only for the scythe or spade, there it is best to plant dwarf or low grafted trees, for several reasons. You can plant more of them on a like quantity of land, because the shadow of the one tree does not reach the ground of the other, as the tall tree does. The low trees sooner attain to be fruit-bearing trees, and grow fairer than the tall; the sap in them wasting in its long passage, which in the shorter trees, expends itself soon in the branches. The lower and broad spreading tree is the greater bearer, by reason the blossoms in the spring are not so obvious to the bitter blasts, nor the fruit in the autumn to the fierce and destructive winds. Fruits are more easily gathered from a low than a tall tree."

"Any fruit on a low, well spread tree is better and fairer than on a tall tree, by the same reason that the tree is fairer, that is, that the sap is not so much wasted in the low and humble tree, as in the tall and lofty."

To Make Dwarf or Spreading Trees

"As the trees spring, and are apt to mount upwards, with the Nails of your Fingers may you nip off the tops of the aspiring Branches; which makes the side-boughs spread better, checks the Sap, and thereby causes the Tree to Fruitifie the sooner, and the better. This way of pruning in the Summer, is easier and better for the Tree than in the Winter, because the Sun heals the wound while the Branch is tender."

"In pruning Fruit trees, be cautious of cutting off the small Sprigs, which are the more apt to bear Fruit; it being too usual for ignorant Planters to beautifie their Trees by taking off the superfluous Branches, as they term them, whereby they deprive themselves of the Fruit."

Pruning Fruit Trees

"Prune the heads of some sorts of Trees that have but *small Pith*, as Apple-trees, Pear-trees, etc., when you remove them, to proportion the Branch and Roots as near as you can: but Wallnut-trees, Cherry-trees, Plum-trees, etc., that have a *large Pith*, are not to be topp'd, only some of the Side-branches may be taken away."

To Transplant a Tree in Summer

"Take of the Earth you digged out of the Foss (hole) you intend to plant your Tree in, and mix and temper it well with an equal part of Cow-dung, and as much water as will make it into a liquid Pap; fill the Hole almost with this, and then let the Root of the Tree gently sink into it; cover it over with dry Earth or Turf: This Tree will prosper very well."

"This is a good way to plant a Tree at other times withal, but then you need not use so much Cow-dung."

Swine in the Orchard

"Swine which are pernicious to all Gardens, yet are profitable in an Orchard. Therefore after your Trees have gained strength enough to bear the rubbing of these Cattel, you may keep your Swine in your Orchard all the Winter season unring'd by which means your Orchard will not only be thoroughly digg'd, but enriched by the Excrements of those diggers: in the Spring you may level it over again, which will exceedingly conduce to the fertility of your Plantation."

"Thus Swine, which never were accounted useful whillst alive, may now become the best improvers of your Orchards: repine not at the loss of your Grass, that will not be so much prejudiced as your Fruit meliorated."

Rabbits Love Obnoxious Weed

"Will you kindly tell me the botanical name of the enclosed weed. Here in Florida it is called Spanish Needle. Rabbits love it, and the large snails in my aquarium devour it. Is it good for humans, as a salad, and does it have medicinal properties?"—Mrs. E.C., Orlando, Fla.

Ans. Spanish Needle is known botanically as Bidens bipinnati. It is used as a pot herb by Africans. Succulent leaves may be used as a salad herb. We find no record of this plant being used as medicine.

SURE MEALYBUG KILLER

Steep one pint of quassia chips for an hour or more in a gallon of hot water. Add to this one pint of softened strong laundry soap and another gallon of water. Beat until you have strong suds. Add one teacupful of kerosene and emulsify thoroughly. Then add another two gallons of water and apply with a good brass syringe through a fine nozzle.

For Bugs Splattered on Your Car

Make a paste of baking soda and water Rub this on bug spots until they come off. This will not injure paint.

Maiden-Hair Ferns: A grand old lady in Barbados, B.W.I., grows magnificent maidenhair ferns. Her advice—keep camphor balls at the roots of the plants—it keeps them healthy and green.

The juice of Aloes is fine for burns, itch, sunburn.

Grow Your Own Green Onions

Plant onion bulbs in your garden in the early spring—as soon as the ground is workable—and you will have fresh green onions for table use.

Planting instructions: Work your ground and then plant bulbs in a row 2 inches apart with root end down. Do not plant too deep—just set firmly in row and cover with soil.

Onion bulbs are a "sure crop" and will grow in most any soil with little attention.

If you wish, you can let the bulbs grow in your garden the full growing season and harvest the dry, big onions.

CLEANING HOUSE PLANTS

Glossy leaved plants: Once a week wash with rubber bulb type sprayer or soft sponge in moderately warm water. If aphids are present, wash plants with soap-suds, then with clear water. White cottony patches on leaves and stems indicate that mealy bugs are present. They may be destroyed by dipping brush in alcohol and applying to mealy bug. Grayish or brownish leaves indicate red spider. This pest is controlled by dusting plant (underside of leaves) with sulphur.

Fuzzy leaved plants should be brushed with a small soft haired brush to remove dust.

Getting Rid of Old Tree Stumps

Bore holes in the stump with an auger and fill with a solution of saltpeter and water strong enough to hold up an egg. Let this dry and then pour coal oil on the stump and set it afire. The stump will slowly burn down to the roots. Or take a long pole chain, fasten to the stump, hitch a tractor to the pole chain and twist it out.

Home-Made Fertilizer

Save all your fallen leaves, lawn mower clippings, seedless weeds, etc. Pile and sprinkle occasionally with lime and soil. The fertilizer is ready for your garden when the leaves, grass, etc., have disintegrated. This is really wonderful for your flowers or vegetables.

DANGER!

Don't load your stomach, when you are excited, hot, or fatigued. Drink Yerba Mate —easy on the stomach and digestion.

It is a custom in the West Indies to sprinkle water in which Sweet Basil has been soaked, about stores, to attract buyers, and bring good luck to the merchants.

PLANT A TREE

Plant a tree. You found several here when you landed on this old earth and you've seen many cut down during your time. You have probably cut down a few yourself. The children who are born after you have passed on have a right to find a few trees standing. But they will not if every person who passes through this vale of tears cuts down a few and forgets to plant any. Plant a tree. Plant a dozen of them, and then you will have done something for the generations who follow you, even as some one did something for you ages ago.

LOVE OF NATURE

Welcome, silence! welcome, peace!
  O most welcome, holy shade!
Thus I prove as years increase,
  My heart and soul for quiet made.
Thus I fix my firm belief,
  While rapture's burning tears descend,
That every flower, and every leaf,
  Is moral Truth's unerring friend.

I would not for a world of gold
  That nature's lovely face should tire;
Fountain of blessings yet untold;
  Pure source of intellectual fire!
Fancy's fair buds, the germs of song,
  Unquickened 'mid the world's rude strife,
Shall sweet retirement render strong,
And morning silence bring to life.

Then tell me not that I shall grow
  Forlorn, that fields and woods will cloy;
From nature and her changes flow
  An everlasting tide of joy.
I grant that summer heats will burn,
  That keen will come the frosty night;
But both shall please, and each in turn
  Yield reason's most supreme delight.
      —From Songs of the Woodland,
      the Garden and the Sea.

Sing While You Drive

At 45 miles per hour, sing—
"Highways Are Happy Ways."
At 55 miles, sing—
"I'm But a Stranger Here, Heaven Is My Home."
At 65 miles, sing—
"Nearer, My God to Thee!"
At 75 miles, sing—
"When The Roll Is Called Up Yonder I'll Be There."
At 85 miles, sing—
"Lord, I'm Coming Home."

In an automobile accident in which some one is injured, chances of a death at 40 miles per hour are 1 in 16; at 55 miles per hour, 1 in 12; and at 65 miles per hour, the chances are 1 in 6.

Gardener working in a Sixteenth Century Herb Garden

THE PURSUIT OF NATURE

Working in the garden, or studying of plants calms the mind, and quiets the passions. Historical reseach produces unpleasant reflections, and in tracing the fate of kingdoms or individuals our feelings are often as much distressed as our minds are amused. Other branches of philosophy too often disgust us with the world, whereas the wonders of Nature display the power of the Almighty in the agreeable and tranquil manner.

"Go, mark the matchless workings of the Power
That shuts within the seed the future flower;
Bids these in elegance of form excel,
In colour these, and those delight the smell;
Sends Nature forth, the daughter of the skies,
To dance on earth and charm all human eyes"

The treasures of Nature are inexhaustible: there is enough for the most indefatigable industry, the happiest opportunities, the most prolix and undisturbed vacancies.

The vegetable world presents an almost infinite variety of objects, calculated not only to supply our numerous wants, but to gratify the senses, to delight the most refined taste and to elevate the mind to the God of Nature.

"Thus the men
Whom Nature's work can charm, with God himself
Hold converse, grow familiar day by day
With his conceptions; sit upon his plan,
And form to his the relish of their souls."

The charms of Nature have ever enchanted the sensitive soul of the poet, and inspired his verse. Courtier says, in his "Pleasures of Solitude."

"Though yet no cynic, still I must prefer
The works of Nature to the whims of Art:
THOSE speak their God—THESE oft from God deter;
THOSE to the soul true health and peace impart,
THESE oft pervert the head, and oft corrupt the heart."

Blackmore also invites us to this study:

"Your contemplation further yet pursue;
The wonderous world of vegetables view!
See various trees their various fruits produce,
Some for delightful taste, and some for use.
See sprouting plants enrich the plain and wood,
For physic some, and some designed for food.
See fragrant flowers, with different colours dyed,
On smiling meads unfold their gaudy pride."

"The Almighty work with man through Nature and when you defy Nature you are in reality defying your Maker."
—Elbert Hubbard.

YOU TELL ON YOURSELF

You tell on yourself by the friends you you seek,
By the very manner in which you speak;
By the way you employ your leisure time,
By the use you make of the dollar and dime.
By the spirit in which your burdens bear;
By the kind of things at which you laugh,
By the records you play on the phonograph.
You tell what you are by the way you walk,
By the things of which you delight to talk;
By the manner in which you bear defeat,
By so simple things as how you eat.
By the books you choose from the well-filled shelf,
By these ways and more, you tell on yourself;
So there is really no particle of sense
In an effort to keep up false pretense.
—Author Unknown.

"If you want to be happy for an hour, roast a pig. If you want to be happy for a year, marry. If you want to be happy for a lifetime, plant a garden."
—Old Chinese proverb.

To place ferns upon the window sill means their death, as they cannot live in a cold draft.

TO PRESERVE CUT FLOWERS: Put a little saltpetre in the water in the vase. Flowers will last as long as 14 to 20 days.

Dried Wormwood is an excellent protection against moths, when putting winter clothing away. It should be scattered lavishly between the folds, and each article wrapped in a newspaper before packing.

AROUND THE HOUSE

He That Is Warm, Thinks All Are So

Before a glowing fire, with slippered feet,
The full fed man sits on his cushioned seat;
When warm and smoking, then it is he's told
Of some poor people freezing with the cold;
He's quite surprised, and says he cannot see,
(Since he's so warm) how such a thing can be.

TO TAKE MILDEW OUT OF LINEN

Wet the linen which contains the mildew with soft water; rub it well with white soap, then scrape some fine chalk to powder and rub it well into the linen, lay it out on the grass in the sunshine, watching to keep it damp with soft water. Repeat the process the next day and in a few hours the mildew will entirely disappear.

QUAINT PROTECTION (?) FROM MOSQUITOES

Open windows wide and stretch across each one and across the door opening, a piece of red ribbon 2 inches wide. It is said that a mosquito will never pass a red ribbon. I almost wished for a visit from the little pests the past summer in order to test this. It is easily tried and well worth a trial.

HERBAL FLEA CHASER

Strip the leaves from the stalk of the pennyroyal, put into little bags made of muslin, sewed up all around, and place among the bedding. If more convenient, sprinkle with the oil or essence of pennyroyal.

OLD METHOD OF CUTTING GLASS

Make a small notch by means of a file on the edge of a piece of glass, then make the end of a tobacco pipe, or of a rod of iron of the same size, red hot in the fire, apply the hot iron to the notch, and draw it slowly along the surface of the glass in any direction you please, a crack will follow the direction of the iron.

In time of prosperity, friends will be plenty;
In time of adversity, not one among twenty.

WISE OLD SAYINGS

A good example is the best sermon.
A slip of the foot may soon be recovered; but that of the tongue may never.
As you make your bed, so you must lie.
Bear and forbear is good philosophy.
Beauty draws more than oxen.
By ignorance we mistake, and by mistakes we learn.
Call not the surgeon before you are wounded.
Care and diligence bring luck.
Diet cures more than the lancet.
Do all you can to be good, and you'll be so.
Do as the friar saith, not as he doeth.
Do unto others as you would be done unto.
Empty vessels give the greatest sounds.
Experience is good if not bought too dear.
Faults are thick where love is thin.
Foxes, when they cannot reach the grapes, say they are not ripe.
Good health is above all wealth.
Good words cost nothing, but are worth much.
He's my friend that speaks well of me behind my back.
Health is not valued 'till sickness comes.
He that eats till he is sick, must fast till he is well.
He must stoop, that hath a low door.
Home is home, be it ever so homely.
If thou canst not see the bottom, wade not.
Judge not of men, or things at first sight.
Keep thy shop, and thy shop will keep thee.
Knowledge in youth, is wisdom in old age.
Little minds, like weak liquors, are soonest soured.
Many come to bring their clothes to Church, rather than themselves.
Many go out for wool and come home shorn.
Prevention is better than cure.
One of these days is none of these days.
Sickness is felt, but health not at all.
Silence seldom doth harm.
Tell me the company you keep, and I'll tell you what you are.
That fish is soon caught who nibbles at every bait.
The first step to virtue, is to abstain from vice.
'Tis vain to learn wisdom, and yet live foolishly.
To err is human, to forgive divine.
Who looks not before, finds himself left behind.
Better ride on an ass that carries me, than a horse that throws me.
Eat to live, but do not live to eat.
When fortune smiles, take the advantage.
He liveth long that liveth well.
He that will enter into Paradise must have a good key.
Poverty parteth friends.
A long tongue is a sign of a short hand.
A young man idle, an old man needy.
He that would live for aye, must eat Sage in May.

OLD-FASHIONED PRESERVING METHODS

The following recipes were found in an 85-year-old cook book:

To Preserve Eggs: Sift some wood ashes through a coarse sieve, put them in a small cask or earthen pots, and as fast as you collect your eggs, put them in these wood ashes, with the small end down, taking care that they are entirely covered and do not touch each other.

Keeping Apples: Pack them in layers in dry sand, or in grain of any kind. The grain will not be injured a particle by using for this purpose.

To Preserve Potatoes: Have ready a large vessel of boiling water. Put a quantity of potatoes into a basket, and just immerse them in the water, and remove them instantly. This method is said to preserve them excellently.

To Keep Butter Sweet: Mix and reduce to a fine powder one part of sugar, one of purified saltpetre, and two of very pure sea-salt. Free the butter scrupulously from the buttermilk. Take one pound of butter out upon a clean board or marble slab, and knead into it one ounce of this mixture. Press it closely down into stone jars, leaving no spaces for the air. Tie the pots over with a clean buttered cloth and a bladder. Butter prepared according to this recipe will keep good several years.

TAMARIND WHEY

Mix an ounce of Tamarind pulp with a pint of milk, strain it and add a little sugar to the whey.

SWEET-POTATO-VINE GRAND FOR HOUSE

Anyone desiring a vine for the house, of rapid growth and good green color, should try the Sweet-Potato-Vine.

The best results are obtained if a medium sized potato is selected with tiny leaves, or sprouts, appearing on one end. Set the whole potato, leaves up, in a narrow container large enough to allow room for the first roots that will form. Pour water into the container until about two-thirds of the potato is submerged.

HOME-MADE MARSHMALLOWS

Dissolve one pound of gum arabic in one quart of water; strain; add one pound of refined sugar and place over the fire, stirring constantly until the sugar is dissolved and the mixture has become the consistency of honey. Next add gradually the whites of eight eggs, well beaten, stirring the mixture all the time, until it loses its stickiness and does not adhere to the fingers when touched. The mass may now be poured out into a pan slightly dusted with corn-starch. When cool divide into small squares.

RECIPES USED IN CIVIL WAR DAYS

Teeth: A mixture of honey with pulverized charcoal will make the teeth beautifully white without injuring the enamel.

Sea-sickness: Take as much Cayenne pepper as you can bear in a bowl of hot soup and, it is said, all sickness, nausea and squeamishness will disappear.

Tea Substitutes: Clean chopped meadow hay is said to be a very good substitute for tea, if used in the proportion of three to one. Also, strawberry and black currant leaves when carefully prepared, are very fragrant.

Elder Flower Tea: Infuse dried elder-flowers the same way as common tea is made; add a little acid to hide the sickly taste of the elder. Sweeten to the taste. This tea is excellent to promote perspiration.

Cough: Make a tea of equal proportions of flaxseed and coltsfoot, boil them well together, strain the liquor, and use it with honey. Use it many times in the day and night.

Chamomile Tea: Take twenty chamomile flowers, the rind of half a lemon peeled thin, and four cloves. Pour a cup of boiling water upon them, and let them stand closely covered all night. In the morning, strain off the liquor, and take a wineglassful before breakfast.

Strengthening Beer: Half an ounce orange peel, half an ounce Virginia Snakeroot, one ounce Peruvian bark. Put these into six quarts of water, and boil it down to four quarts. Add one pint molasses, one pint yeast; let it stand twenty-four hours and bottle it.

FRAGRANT CARPETING FLOWERS

The Thyme (serpyllum) may be called the most perfect plant for edging along pathways, between flagstones, in rock gardens or where ground covering plant is desired. Thyme forms solid masses of carpeting Most of the varieties are very free flowering. All have a delightful fragrance. No wonder they are so often refered to as CHARMING.

All Thymes like well-drained sunny location. Plants are winter-hardy.

Mother of Thyme: This is an old favorite. Forms loose mats of dark ever-green leaves and clusters of pink flowers. Plant has pine-like fragrance.

Golden Thyme: In spring the leaves are spotted with golden yellow. Plant is deliciously citron-scented.

Crimson Thyme: This is a plant gem, its tiny leaves forms solid carpet. When it blooms the carpet turns solid crimson. We believe this to be the freest flowering variety.

Lemon Thyme: Forms loose tufts of bright yellow-green leaves.

Carneus Thyme: A particular tough variety specially good between flagstones and path where trampling will release the pine-like fragrance. Flowers pink.

OLD FASHIONED HOUSEHOLD METHODS

To Protect Dried Fruit: Put it away with a handful or two of sassafras bark mixed with each bushel of the fruit, and it will save for years unmolested by those troublesome little insects.

To Keep Apples: Wipe every apple dry with a cloth, and see that no blemished ones are left among them. Have ready a very dry, tight barrel, and cover the bottom with dry pebbles. These will attract the damp of the apples. Then put in the fruit; head up the barrel; and plaster the seams with mortar, taking care to have a thick rim of mortar all around the top. Let the barrel remain undisturbed in the same place until you want the apples for use.

To Keep Hams for Summer Use: Tie them up securely in paper; cover closely with dry wood ashes in a box, and keep in a dry place. This keeps them sweet and protects them from all insects.

Another Method of Keeping Hams: Wrap them in good sweet hay, then enclose them in a tight bag, and hang in the granary. The nicest cold ham I ever saw was over a year old, and had been kept in the manner described.

To Keep Cucumbers: For one barrel use two pounds of alum, six quarts of salt and water sufficient to cover them. Pulverize the alum fine, and use coarse salt (solar salt such as is used for packing is best, as it contains no lime). Use only one-fourth the quantity to commence on as those put in first will take all the strength of the brine. Keep a weight on them and treat as ordinary salt pickles.

OLD FASHIONED REPELLENTS

To Keep Flies from Horses: Procure a bunch of smartweed and bruise it to cause the juice to exude. Rub the animal thoroughly with the bunch of bruised weed, especially on the legs, neck and ears. Neither flies nor other insects will trouble him for twenty-four hours. The process should be repeated every day. A very convenient way of using it is to make a strong infusion by boiling the weed a few minutes in water. When cold it can be conveniently applied with a sponge or brush. Smartweed is found growing in every section of the country. Usually on wet ground near highways.

To Clear a Room of Mosquitoes: A decoction of Pennyroyal, or some of the bruised leaves rubbed on the exposed parts will effectinually keep off those troublesome insects.

The root of Ginseng is chewed as a substitute for tobacco. The juice should be swallowed.

Fresh juice or a strong decoction of dried Elecampane root is useful as a wash for itch.

HOW GRANDMA KEPT GRANDPA FROM SNORING

Six drops of olive oil to a pinch of mustard, taken just before getting into bed. The function of the oil is that of a lubricant to the larnyx, while the mustard acts as a counter-irritant.

HOW OLD FOLKS FORECAST WEATHER

A ring around the sun or moon stands for an approaching storm, its near or distant approach being indicated by its larger or smaller circumference. When the sun rises brightly and immediately afterward becomes veiled with clouds, the farmer distrusts the day. Rains which begin early in the morning often stop by nine in place of "eleven," the hour specified in the old saw, "If it rains before seven."

On a still quiet day, with scarcely the least wind afloat, the ranchman or farmer can tell the direction of impending storm by cattle sniffing the air in the direction whence it is coming. Lack of dew in summer is a rain sign. Sharp white frosts in autumn and winter precede damp weather, and we will stake our reputation as a prophet that three successive white frosts are an infallible sign of rain. Spiders do not spin their webs out of doors before rain. Previous to rain flies sting sharper, bees remain in their hives or fly but short distances, and almost all animals appear uneasy.

SLEEP INDUCERS

Try sleeping with the head of the bed a foot higher than the foot.

A hot mustard foot bath is beneficial.

A hearty meal just before retiring, and a seat near the fire after a long, cold walk will usually cause a deep sleep.

A raw onion eaten before retiring will often induce sleep.

Try sleeping on a hop pillow. It often induces sleep.

HOME-MADE HARD LAUNDRY SOAP

5 pounds grease, 1 can lye, ½ cup powdered borax, ½ cup sugar, 3 pints cold water, 1 tablespoonful ammonia, 1 dessert spoonful baking soda. Put lye in earthen dish, pour on water, reserving one cupful, which put in a small dish—in this—dissolve the borax, sugar, soda. Put in ammonia. Warm and strain grease and when cool, add grease to lye. Stir this well with wooden stick, then add contents of smaller dish. Stir until thick and smooth, then pour into box or pan lined with heavy wax paper. Let harden and cut in cakes. After six weeks it is ready for use.

Ammonia Uses around the House

1 or 2 tablespoons ammonia added to a pail of water will clean windows better than soap.

A few drops in a cup of warm water, applied carefully, will remove spots from paintings.

Old brass may be cleaned to look like new by pouring strong ammonia on it, and scrubbing with a brush—then rinsing in clear water.

Keep nickel and silver ornaments bright by rubbing with a woolen cloth saturated in spirits of ammonia.

A dark carpet often looks dusty soon after it has been swept, and you know it does not need sweeping again; so wet a cloth or a sponge, wring it almost dry, and wipe off the dust. A few drops of ammonia in the water will brighten the colors.

For cleaning hair brushes it is excellent. Put 1 tablespoon ammonia into the water, having it only tepid, and dip up and down until clean; then dry with the brushes down, and they will be like new ones.

A few drops of ammonia water will take off grease from dishes, pans, etc. Does not injure the hands as much as the use of soda and strong chemical soaps. A spoonful in a quart of warm water, for cleaning paint, makes it look like new, and so with everything that needs cleaning.

No articles in the kitchen are so likely to be neglected and abused as dishcloths and dishtowels; and in washing these, ammonia, if properly used, is excellent. Put a teaspoonful into the water in which these cloths are washed; rub soap on the towels. Put them in the water; let them stand half an hour or so; then rub them out, rinse and dry outdoors in the sun.

Spots on towels will disappear with little trouble if a little ammonia is put into enough water to soap the articles, and they are left in it an hour or two, or overnight, before washing.

If the color has been taken out of silks by fruit stains, ammonia will usually restore the color.

When acid of any kind gets on clothing, spirits of ammonia will kill it. Apply chloroform to restore the color.

Grease spots may be taken out with weak ammonia in water; lay soft white paper over and iron with a hot iron.

Equal parts of ammonia and turpentine will take paint out of clothing, even if it be hard and dry. Saturate the spot as often as necessary, and wash out in soap suds.

Uses of Salt in the Kitchen

Damp salt will remove the discoloration of cups and saucers caused by tea and careless washing.

Brasswork can be kept beautifully bright by occasionally rubbing with salt and vinegar.

Salt dissolved in alcohol, gin, or ammonia, will take out grease spots.

Uses of Salt in the Laundry

Remove iron rust or ink spots by moistening the spots with salt and cream of tartar, or salt and lemon juice, exposing to full heat of the sun.

Mildew may be removed by rubbing common yellow soap on the article; then salt and starch over that; rub all in well and lay in the bright sunshine.

Salt—to Kill Weeds

For troublesome weeds, and for grass in sidewalks, driveways, etc., apply a dressing of coarse salt; this will kill all growth. Be careful not to put it on anything that should not be destroyed, however.

Miscellaneous Uses of Salt

Salt as a toothpowder keeps the teeth brilliantly white, and the gums hard and rosy.

If the feet are tired or painful after long standing, great relief can be had by bathing them in salt water. A handful of salt to a gallon of water is the right proportion. Have the water as hot as can be comfortably borne. Immerse the feet and throw the water over the legs as far as the knees with the hands. When the water becomes too cool, rub feet briskly with a towel.

If, after having a tooth pulled, the mouth is filled with salt and water, it will allay the danger of having a hemorrhage.

For those who have sensitive gums, inclined to bleed on the slightest provocation, a mouth wash of salt and cold water used once or twice a day will harden the gums and help relieve soreness by its hardening tendency.

Miscellaneous Uses of Soda

For scouring and brightening table and kitchen knives, use soda. Toilets, kitchen sink and laundry tubs can be kept sweet and clean with a generous use of soda and hot water.

Soda, moistened in milk or soapsuds, will remove fruit or tea stains on table linen or napkins.

Flowers can be kept fresh for a long time by putting a pinch of soda into the water in which they are held.

As a dentifrice for the teeth, soda is recommended as it neutralizes the acids which secrete themselves around the teeth, preventing thus their decaying effect. Use with a brush the same as tooth powder, or dissolve in water.

To clean jewelry, put in a flannel bag with soda and shake freely, or let it remain and it will become bright and clean.

Miscellaneous Uses of Borax

The scalp and hair need an occasional cleansing, and for this borax and water is excellent. After it has been well shampooed, wash it thoroughly with clear water, dry the hair and scalp well. Make the solution rather weak, and if the head is not naturally oily, a little cocoanut oil, or vaseline, can afterward be rubbed into the scalp.

A good pinch of borax in ½ glass of warm water makes a good wash for the mouth and teeth, or the powder can be sprinkled on the toothbrush and used in the usual way.

Borax cleanses, heals and removes odors of perspiration. 2 or 3 tablespoons of the powder may be dissolved in the bath water, or the solution may be added until the water feels soft. When you have done this, take your bath. It leaves skin soft, delicate and clear.

For all uses in the kitchen when cleanliness is the object, borax is good. For washing dishes, pots and pans, cleaning paint and sinks, the addition of borax will prove a great help. It is a foe to dirt and disease germs, hence can be used freely.

Spots and Stains

Iron rust may be removed from white goods by sour milk.

Mildew: Moisten the spot with clean water; rub on it a thick coating of castile soap mixed with chalk scrapings, rub with end of finger, then wash off.

Oil Marks on Wall Paper: Apply paste of cold water and pipe clay. Leave it on all night; brush off in the morning.

Paint Spots from Clothing: Saturate with equal parts of turpentine and spirits of ammonia.

Hands from Vegetable Stains: Rub with a slice of raw potato.

How to Remove Tar from Cloth: Rub it well with turpentine and every trace of tar will be removed.

How to Remove Egg Stains from Spoons: Rub with common salt.

Grass Stains: Wash in cold soft water without soap. Sometimes soaking in warm naptha soapsuds to which ammonia has been added is effective.

Aspirins and Vitamin C: If you must take aspirins, remember they cause your body to lose vitamin C more quickly. Balance this loss by taking more fresh fruits, salads, and leafy greens.

"Nothing is in the body that is not in the earth. The principle is to get into the diet of a Human Being the items which civilization tends to remove from the diet."

If you feel tired and worn out, it is possible you are not getting sufficient vitamins and minerals.

PEPPERMINT TEA LEAVES
Healthful Tea for Young and Old

Peppermint is an age-old health beverage enjoyed by our grandparents, their parents and many generations before them. Even the aboriginal peoples brewed teas from mints found growing in their native lands. Peppermint tea deserves a come-back because of its real merit as table tea. It deserves a place on the modern table because this high-speed and highly stimulated civilization needs soothing and healthful habits more than ever in the history of the human race. The use of Peppermint tea is so harmless that it can be given to babies with colic (one or two tablespoons of warm Peppermint tea, sweetened with sugar or honey). Peppermint tea may be used alone or made in various ways. Lemon may be added—sweetened if desired or added with other healthful tea herbs such as Alfalfa herb (vitamin rich), clover flowers (Indian used tea), Linden flowers (an old European tea).

Health Commandments

Help yourself to health. Form habits that will fight for you—not against you. Do not expect to have good health without effort. Health must be earned. Adopt the policy that an ounce of prevention is worth a pound of cure. Make food your servant, not your master. Eat for strength.

Breathe deeply, for air is life's first requisite and Nature's best tonic. Exercise for health, not for strength. Exercise sends clean blood to the brain. Seek sunshine, for sunshine and disease are always enemies.

Water—use plentifully daily; warm for cleanliness—cold for tonic. Keep a clear conscience, for true rest is mental as well as physical. Live cheerfully. Work planfully, read much, and play often. Play keeps premature old age at bay.

A healthy body is the guest chamber of the soul; a sick, its prison.—Francis Bacon.

Mysterious principle of life! by thee
We think, we feel, we move, we hear, we see:
Sailing awhile on thy uncertain wave,
The harbor that receives us is the grave.

    Papa is boss as everybody knows;
    But what mama says always goes.

FORGOTTEN MEDICINES

I have great faith in all Herb medicines, as my old Uncles and Great Uncles were Herb doctors. They raised their plants in their home gardens, and years after they were dead and their houses fallen down, the Herbs still grew in the gardens. I do wish more folks knew the value of these Herbs.—Writes Mrs. B. M., of Earlham, Iowa.

OLD TIME HOME RECIPES

Sleeplessness: Sleep upon a pillow made of Hops. Drink a cup of warm Hop tea before retiring. This often invites slumber.

Fever Sores: Make a decoction of half an ounce of Clover blossoms to one pint of water and boil about half an hour. Apply to fever sores three or four times a day.

Piles: Boil about a half ounce of Smartweed root with two ounces of lard and apply to piles three or four times a day. It may help to ease pain and itching.

Nausea: Chew a leaf or two of Mint or Sage (fresh or dried) to a tasteful pulp. See physician if appendicitis is suspected.

Toothache: Apply oil of cloves on a small piece of cotton and place in the cavity of tooth or rub gum lightly with oil of Sassafras. May help ease pain before seeing a dentist.

Hiccoughs: Put about a quarter of a teaspoonful of Cinchona bark, powdered, in two ounces of Peppermint water and give a teaspoonful every five or ten minutes. This often relieves.

Sick Headache: Make a strong decoction of Hop tea and take a wineglassful every half hour or hour as desired or according to response.

Aching and Tender Feet: Make a strong solution of White Oak bark and soak the feet night and morning.

Sore Throat due to Coughs, Colds: Hardly any remedy for sore throat proves more efficacious than the old fashioned plan of tying around the throat a slice of fat bacon on which is sprinkled black pepper.

A Good Liniment: For bruises on man or beast take equal parts of laudanum, alcohol and oil of wormwood. It reduces the swelling rapidly if inflamed, and relieves soreness like a charm. The sooner applied, of course, the better.

Baby Wash: A nice wash for the delicate skin of infants is made by obtaining maple twigs. Put a small lump of alum in and boil with the twigs. Wash the tender places with this in lieu of water.

OLD FASHIONED BITTERS AS STOMACHICS AND STIMULANTS TO THE APPETITE

Tonic Bitters: Cardamom, 4 parts; Nutmeg, 1 part; Cinnamon, 4 parts; Cloves, 2 parts; Ginger, 2 parts; Orange Peel, 1 part; Alcohol, 278 parts; Water, 278 parts; Sugar, 72 parts. Mix either by maceration or percolation.

Wild Cherry Bitters: Wild Cherry bark, 4 parts; Partridge berry, 1 part; Juniper berries, ½ part; Prickly ash, ¼ part; Exhaust with 40 parts water and after filtering add 8 parts of sugar and 6 parts alcohol.

German Bitters: Chamomile, 2 parts; Sweet Flag, 6 parts; Orris root, 8 parts; Coriander, 3 parts; Centaury, 1 part; Orange peel, 3 parts; Alcohol, 588 parts; Water 672 parts; Sugar, 24 parts.

Hop Bitters: Orange peel, 2 parts; Sweet Flag, 1 part; Pimpinella root, 1 part; Hops, ½ part, Alcohol, 320 parts; Water, 320 parts; Sugar, 20 parts. When otherwise completed this should be colored with burnt sugar.

Spiced Bitters: Poplar bark, 10 ounces; Pulverized Bayberry, 2 ounces; Pulverized Balmony, 2 ounces; Pulverized Golden Seal, 1 ounce; Pulverized Cloves, 1 ounce; Cayenne Pepper, ½ ounce; Sugar, 3 ounces; Water, 20 ounces; Alcohol, 28 ounces. Mix by either maceration or percolation; if by maceration, about the eighth day add six ounces of the best brandy and if by percolation add the brandy when through percolating.

Peruvian Bitters: Peruvian bark, 8 parts; Orange Peel, 8 parts; Cinnamon, ¼ part; Cloves, ¼ part; Nutmegs, ¼ part; Cayenne, ¼ part; Alcohol, 492 parts; Water, 492 parts. Mix either by maceration or percolation.

Stomach Bitters: Pulverized Gentian root, 1½ ounces; Orange Peel, 2½ ounces; Cinnamon, ¼ ounce; Anise seed, 4 drachms; Coriander seed, 4 drachms; Cardamon Seed, 1 drachm; Peruvian bark, 4 drachms; Gum Kino, 2 drachms; Best Alcohol, 1 pint. Macerate for one week and add one pound of sugar together with one quart of hot water, then filter.

Wine Bitters: Cinchona bark, crushed, 4 ounces; Gentian root, crushed, 2 ounces; Juniper berries, crushed, 1 ounce; Orange Peel, 1 ounce; California Port Wine, 4 pints; Alcohol, 1 pint; Water, 3 pints. Mix. Digest for one week; then filter, adding enough wine to complete one gallon. Dose: One-half to two tablespoonfuls for debility and loss of appetite.

Sweet Melissa makes an excellent tea in fevers, and when sweetened and acidulated with the juice of lemons or cream of tartar, forms a most grateful beverage.

CLEANING FABRICS

Milk Stains: Soak napkins or tablecloths a short time in cold water before washing, otherwise the spots will remain stiff.

Fruit Stains: Pour boiling water through the stains before the article is wet. Repeat if necessary. If this fails to remove the stain, dip in javelle water. (There is a tradition that old fruit stains can be removed by wetting them and laying them out on the grass in the season of fruit-tree blossoming.)

Ink or Fruit from Linen: To remove ink or fruit stains from linen, soak in kerosene as soon as possible and wash out in a strong suds of soap and water.

Ink Stains (In White Goods): Wet goods in clear water and rub on salts of lemon and place in the sun for a short time. Repeat if necessary. Be particular to rinse very thoroughly.

Ink Stains: Dip the garment in apple vinegar and rub with bicarbonate of soda.

Blood Stains: Rub coal oil on the spots two or three times, then wash out. Another Method: Make a thick paste of laundry starch and cold water. Plaster it over the stain on pillows, mats or mattresses. Let dry and if one application is not sufficient make a second.

Iron Rust: Pour boiling water into an earthen bowl and hold the cloth tightly over the top and drop some muriatic acid on the spot of rust. The steam will do the rest. In a minute drop the cloth into the hot water and the iron rust will wash out. Do not use soap. Another Method: Lemon juice and salt mixed together and put on iron rust will take it out. Keep it in the sun. If one application does not do it, try another. A solution of oxalic acid in water will also remove iron rust. Mix salt and cream of tartar, moisten with water; apply to the spot. Put in the sun. Repeat if necessary.

Mildew: Dissolve 4 tablespoons driest chloride of lime in ½ pint of water. Soak the article in this for 15 minutes. Take out and rub gently and put at once into a mixture of one part muriatic acid to 4 parts soft water. If the fabric is very delicate make the lime solution weaker and leave it in but five minutes.

Grease: Sponge a grease spot with 4 tablespoons alcohol to one of salt.

Scorch: Any article that has been scorched in ironing may be restored by laying it in the bright sunshine.

Removing Tar: Rub the spot with melted lard; then wash with soap and water. This applies to hands or clothing. Another Method: Rub the spot on the clothes with turpentine.

For Cleaning Woolen Dresses: Wash in gasoline—one gill of gasoline to a gallon of water. This will neither shrink the goods nor disturb the color, and the garment so washed will look like new.

For Cleaning Flannel: ¼ pound white Castile soap, 1 quart hot soft water; let cool and add: 1 ounce liquid ammonia, 1 ounce sulphuric ether, 1 ounce alcohol, 3½ quarts cold soft water. Excellent for cleaning all heavy woolen goods.

DO YOUR HOUSE PLANTS LOOK SICK?

Most house plants suffer from improper feeding. Plants should be fed continually just as house pets are. Even if the pot soil did contain all the necessary fertilizer when potted, it is continually consumed by the plant during its growth. Sooner or later, according to the type of plant, the pot soil is depleted of all plant food. Starved plants show different symptoms in different plants. Some stop growing. Flowering plants stop blooming or drop their blossoms before fully developed. Some plants become spindly, the leaves of others turn color and drop off. More sun will usually hasten the plant's death—more water induces rot. When the soil is exhausted the plant too will soon become exhausted and die.

TO PRESERVE PEACH TREES

The following mode of securing peach trees from injury, and promoting their bearing fruit plentifully, has been practised with uninterrupted success for many years.

As soon as the blossoms appear in the spring, fine ashes are scattered over them and the young leaves, by means of a tin box, perforated with holes, and fixed on the end of a pole. The process is easily performed, and is in the power of any one. It should be done, if possible, in a moist day, and when the wind is still.

Ginseng root is often chewed as a substitute for tobacco. The juice should be swallowed. An old fashioned cordial is made by steeping Ginseng root in wine or spirits.

HOW TO REMOVE ODORS FROM HOME FREEZER

First try washing all the interior surfaces of the freezer with plenty of soap and water. Then go over them with a cloth wrung from clear water. Wipe dry. If this does not dispel the odor, wash the freezer with soda water, using 1 teaspoon baking soda to each quart of warm water. If the odor persists, try vinegar, using about one cup to a gallon of water, or household ammonia in the same proportions.

But if none of these suggestions prove effective, don't give up. Try using heat to bring out the odor particles and get them into the air. To do this put something like a toaster or electric heater inside the freezer to heat it up. Then use an electric fan a couple of hours to blow the air out.

Activated charcoal, put into the warm freezer will absorb odors released by the heat. Or a commercial, wick-type air freshener may be put into the warm freezer for the same purpose.

If only traces of the smell remain, this is not likely to affect food frozen and stored in the freezer if care is taken to wrap the food securely. When a package is taken out remove the wrappings as soon as possible and dispose of them at once.

When the odor has been removed or reduced to where it is of no consequence, make a final washing of the inside surfaces of the freezer with soda water. Activated charcoal left in for a while will pick up any residual odor

OLD FASHIONED CLEANING BALLS

For removing grease spots from cloth: Take fuller's earth and dry it before the fire or in the sun, until it crumbles to powder, moisten it with strained lemon juice; add a small quantity of fine pearlash, and knead the whole up together until it acquires the consistency of stiff elastic paste. Mould it into any shape you desire, and dry the balls thoroughly in the sun; they are then ready for use, as follows: Moisten the spot on the cloth with water, then rub it with the ball, and place it in the sun to dry; next beat out the dust, wash the cloth with clean water, and the spot will disappear.

TO MAKE PAPER FIREPROOF

Nothing more is necessary than to dip the paper in a strong solution of alum water, and when thoroughly dry it will resist the action of flame. Some paper requires to imbibe more of the solution than it will take up at a single immersion, and the process must be repeated until it becomes thoroughly saturated. The alum will not injure the quality or color of the article, but on the contrary improve it.

Where tobacco plants are grown, women take several of the leaves to hang in clothes closets—it is said they effectively repel moths.

OLD FASHIONED WHITE PAINT

Whiting, 5 pounds
Skimmed Milk, 2 quarts
Fresh Slaked Lime, 2 ounces

Take a small quantity of the milk and put the lime in to form a cream-like consistency, add the balance of the milk and crumble the whiting upon the surface of the fluid, in which it gradually sinks. Stir or grind, as is usually done with other paints.

TO STAIN WOOD LIKE EBONY

Take a solution of sulphate of iron (green copperas) and wash the wood over with it two or three times; let dry, and apply two or three coats of a strong decoction of logwood chips; wipe the wood, when dry, with a sponge and water, and polish with linseed oil.

OLD FASHIONED GOLD VARNISH

Powdered Tumeric, 1 drachm
Powdered Gamboge, 1 drachm
Oil of Turpentine, 2 pints
Thin Mastic Varnish, 8 ounces
Powdered Dragon's Blood, 7 drachms

Digest with occasional agitation for fourteen days, in a warm place, then set it aside to fine, and pour off the clear.

NOTE: Excellent for antique furniture, etc.

REMOVING TIGHT RING

Thread a needle with a strong thread, pass the head of the needle with care under the ring, and pull the thread through a few inches toward the hand; wrap the long end of the thread tightly around the finger regularly to the nail to reduce its size. Then lay hold of the short end and unwind it. The thread repassing against the ring, will gradually remove it from the finger. This never-failing method will remove the tightest ring without difficulty, no matter how swollen the finger may be.

CRACKS IN STOVES

A paste of woodashes and common salt kneaded together, moistened with water, will fill up the crack, and become hard in a very short time.

COFFEE STAINS

Hold table-cloth over sink and pour boiling water over spot—then wash table cloth the usual way.

IF YOU CANNOT SLEEP

Try this: Lay on your back and inhale as much air as you can take, then hold as long as possible. Use same procedure when exhaling. This is said to be very effective on many people.

The perfume (scent) of Annise seede taken up into the nose cureth headache. — From Dodoen's Herbal.

Red Clover for Canaries

"I have found through my own experience that Red Clover tea is good for Canaries. My Canaries were shedding and would not sing. Two of my best singers did not have a feather on their head. I made a strong tea with 2 teaspoons of Red Clover, and ½ cup of hot water, allowing it to steep for 15 minutes. I gave them 30 drops a day in drinking water. In a month's time they were full of pep, singing again and all had a nice new coat of feathers."—Mrs. J.A.H., Oberlin, Kan.

Paprika Turns Canaries Red

Paprika is a rich source of vitamin C. Paprika fed to yellow canary birds, turns their plumage red, according to scientific reports. Paprika also improves the coloration of hatchery reared trout. Paprika is also called pimiento—but should not be confused with allspice, also called pimento. Note difference in spelling.

Canary Sings to Ripe Old Age

"My canary lived to be 15 years old. It sang every day. I fed it a few marigold petals when the plant was in bloom. Thanks." —Walter Schultz.

Herbs for Cage Birds

"Cage birds greatly enjoy plantain (plantago major) and its collection and sale, along with the equally well-known Chickweed and Groundsel, is a well recognized branch of street industry."

Parakeets Need Iodine, Too

This valuable element is good for your parakeet, chickens, cats, dogs, farm stock, as well as for you. Very little is needed, but it is important that we all get it. Offer iodine in its natural non-poisonous vegetable form with all the other vital trace elements that come with this valuable seaweed. Crush ½ kelp tablet in your parakeet's drinking water. Use whole tablet in drinking water for your pets. Use several tablets for your stock.

Safflower for Parrots

"Parrots eat the seed of Safflower with pleasure, and it has therefore been called Parrot's corn, being a wholesome food for that tribe of birds, although noxious to all other animals."
den."

To Make Seeds Start

Water with ammonia and oxalic acid once a week. Prepare a small bottle of each, and use only a teaspoonful in a quart of water.

Charcoal For Flowers

Powdered charcoal, placed around plants, has the effect of adding much to their richness.

Parakeets Require Lots of Vitamin B-2 to Breed

Parakeet fanciers who want to breed their birds should add lots of vitamin B-2, riboflavin, to the bird seed diet to insure good, hatchable eggs.

Scientists have found that breeding is most successful when twice the recommended amount of riboflavin is fed the birds. Parakeets need more of this vitamin than chickens.

One possible explanation for this is that parakeets waste a large amount of the fine-sized feed materials given them. It may also be that the birds have an unusually high requirement for riboflavin.

Another parakeet problem that can be attacked with improved diet is the poorly-feathered young bird. Such birds are called "runners," because they cannot fly to their perches.

Using experience in feeding other birds, the scientists added the vitamins, pantothenic acid and niacin, and several amino acids to the diet, adjusted the mineral content and used good quality proteins.

With this improved diet, no case of poor feathering was observed. The parakeet all-seed ration has to be supplemented with such fine material, the researchers state.

The food has to have enough of the necessary diet factors to keep the birds healthy even with the high waste. It is also important to keep the special nutrients in the ration throughout the bird's life. With an adequately supplemented food in the cage at all times, breeders do not have to switch to special nesting foods or other special diets at critical times.—Science News Letter.

Tames Wild Birds

"I love birds. It took me three years to tame a wild cat bird, but I finally accomplished it, after a great deal of patience. I would go out and call her, then she would fly to my outstretched hand, sit thereon, and feed and sing for me. She came back for five or six summers."

"The robins follow me all around the yard, and call me when they wish to be fed. Last winter one came back in January, and sat on my window-sill, and sang for me. The little thing looked half frozen—she endured the awful winter blasts to be with us. I named her Jan. I'll tell you a secret, if you care to tame birds, feed them raisins. I think Jan came back to get an extra share, before the others arrived, and believe me, she had plenty of them."—Mrs. G. Block, Canton, Ohio.

Bog Garden

HERBS USED AS REPELLENTS

Apple-of-Peru: The mashed fresh leaves placed in a saucer with water and some sugar, is an old-time fly killer. Harmless to pets.

Calamus: Sliced roots used in olden times to protect furs and woolens.

Castor Bean: A plant in the garden is said to keep away grasshoppers.

Costmary: Herb kept in linens for scent, and repellent.

Catnip: Old-time farmers set plants about farms to repel rats.

Feverfew: Fresh plant disliked by bees.

Herbal Mixture: Make strong decoction of Rue, Wormwood and Tobacco (equal parts) in water. Sprinkle or spray leaves and young branches of fruit trees every morning and evening, during the time the fruit is ripening. This will keep off caterpillars and chewing insects.

Lavender Flowers: Used to preserve linens, and give them a fresh clean odor.

Maiden Hair Tree Leaves: Used as markers, and to keep bugs out of books.

Mugwort: Dried herb used to repel moths.

Parsley: Plants grown around rose bushes to keep away rose beetles.

Pyrethrum (powdered): Used in sprays to kill many types of insects.

Quassia Chips: Half pint of boiling water poured upon a quarter ounce of Quassia chips, and sweetened with sugar, will destroy flies. Harmless to children and pets.

Rue: The Schola Salernitana, compiled some 800 years ago, states: "Rue putteth fleas to flight."

Santolina: Moth repellent of Colonial days.

Sassafras: A handful or two of Sassafras bark was mixed with each bushel of dried fruits to keep out insects, as well as add flavor to fruit.

Tansy: This herb was grown around peach trees in old-time gardens, as a means of preserving trees from insects.

Wild Mint: According to an old report from a Canadian farmer, "Wild Mint is a sure and reliable exterminator of rats." The herb was strewn around the walls or base of barns.

Woodruff Herb: Used to preserve and scent linens.

Wormwood: In Shakespearean times it was said, "When chamber is swept, and Wormwood is thrown no flea for his life dare abide to be known." Wormwood was used in great quantities by cloth manufacturers during the Middle Ages to protect woolens from moths.

DANGER OF NEW INSECTICIDES

Many of the new insecticides used to kill flies, mosquitoes and garden pests may be potentially dangerous to human beings.

Laboratory studies show that such poisons can be absorbed by the body. They are capable of causing damage to the liver, other organs, and nervous system.

Insecticides containing DDT, chlordane, parathion or selenium may produce in human beings toxic effects ranging from skin rashes to serious internal injuries from inhaling the poisons.

Although the Federal Food and Drug Administration has laid the groundwork for laws forbidding the use of dangerous insecticides, the government cannot legally act until cases of poisoning are definitely proven. Pressure exerted by the big food processors may lead to the banning of some of these new insecticides.

If you must use an insect-killer in the house or garden, buy one in which the active ingredient is pyrethrum or methoxychlor. These substances do not accumulate in the body and are not harmful to man or any other warm-blooded animal.

Do not eat unwashed fruit. To be entirely safe, peel apples and pears.

Dispose immediately of any fruits or vegetables, especially root vegetables that have a musty taste. They may have been contaminated by lindane or benzene hexachloride. Never use a spray containing selenium.

Warn your gardening neighbors against the dangerous sprays.

DOCTOR URGES OUTLAWING OF DDT

Dr. Morton S. Biskind believes the United States should outlaw DDT, parathion and certain other chemical insecticides.

He says food sprayed with them has caused an increasing number of fatal heart attacks among young persons.

FRESH CHIVES THROUGH THE WINTER

Fresh minced chive leaves add a delicious onion flavor to cottage cheese, sandwiches, salads, soups, meats, gravies, etc.

Take up your plants in the fall, and divide them into small clumps (if old and large). Place broken red clay pots or rocks in the bottom of planting pot for drainage. Place moss over drain material and set your chives in any fair soil. Keep soil moist but not soaking, and keep in sunny location.

Like water cress, potted chives offer market possibilities if you live in or near a city.

HOME HEALTH HINTS

Fresh air, sufficient exercise, plenty of sleep, simple foods and daily bathing are requisite to good health.

Elderly people should form the habit of emptying the bladder thoroughly. In late life more effort is required to evacuate the bladder. Negligence in this matter is apt to induce a mild form of paralysis, making evacuation even more difficult.

When moles or other smooth growths begin to roughen or scale, they should be given attention for it generally means the beginning of cancer. See your doctor.

Flowers of Sulphur sprinkled in the shoes and stockings are recommended to keep chiggers off. In severe cases of chigger bites on the body, diluted Tincture of Iodine touched to the irritated spot gives relief. Hot strong salt water or a super-saturated solution of common baking soda will sometimes give relief.

During the summer months one's diet should consist principally of fruits and vegetables. Eat moderately and avoid stomach troubles.

There is very little danger of drinking too much water. Most of us do not drink half the quantity we should. The system requires more water during the summer than during winter. Form the habit of drinking a glass of water every hour or so during the day and your health will be better for it.

If your urine is darker than clear amber you may need to drink more water.

A very pleasant, healthful and nutritious drink may be made for fever patients from thoroughly washed apple peelings. They may be used fresh, or dried in the oven for future use. Steep the peelings for a few minutes in boiling water and add lemon or orange juice or peppermint or other flavor as desired.

The pain of varicose veins or ulcers of the leg, which are especially troublesome at night after retiring, can be greatly relieved by the patient sharply elevating the feet 15 to 30 minutes. This position empties the veins and rests the vein walls, affording much comfort and inducing restful sleep.

A mixture of the tincture of capsicum and a small quantity of the mucilage of acacia or glycerine painted over a surface, which is discolored by a severe bruise, will remove the discoloration. If applied early it will prevent discoloration.

A remedy for stye on the eye is to make a poultice of fresh tea leaves moistened with water and applied to the stye.

For nausea or sickness of the stomach, try cinnamon tea. Put one teaspoonful of ground cinnamon into a teacup and pour over it a half cupful of boiling water. When it settles it is ready for use.

DRUNKENNESS

"Bacchus" might remove the effects produced by an excess of wine, etc., by drinking a wineglassful of olive oil. It will prevent the hurtful fumes from rising. It will have the same effect if taken before an intended debauch—from an old recipe book.

BLEEDING NOSE

This may be stopped by raising the arm on the same side as that of the nostril from which the blood flows.

SEASICKNESS

Take as much Cayenne pepper as you can rightly bear in a bowl of hot soup, and the nausea will disappear.

Also, it has been observed that ladies wearing long corsets, or girdles, are sometimes perserved by them from seasickness. An instance is given of a seaman who escaped this malady for many years, by wearing a belt on account of some injury he had received in his side.

HICCOUGH

Take about a teacupful of cold water at nine sips, and the involuntary cough will cease.

FRAGRANT ODOR FOR SICK ROOMS

A few drops of oil of sandalwood, dropped onto a hot plate, will be found to diffuse a most agreeable balsamic perfume throughout the atmosphere of sick rooms, or other confined apartments.

WHEN CHILDREN ARE BILIOUS

First give a mild laxative, Senna Pods, figs, or prunes, then ½ cupful of warm Peppermint tea; then rest—and no food for about 12 hours.

RECIPE FOR SUN BATHING

Reinforce your blood with iron-rich foods, or iron-rich herbs, such as Yellow Dock, Strawberry leaves, Burdock root, and Salep—you will tan more easily and evenly.

VITAMIN B FOR THE IRRITABLE

Lack of patience, lack of stamina for emotional trials, may be caused by nutritional deficiencies. Insufficient Vitamin B may be one cause. This can easily be checked by adding Vitamin B to your diet.

Harmless Herbal Carminative Recipe Used For Easing Menstrual Periods, Nausea, Etc.

Anise seed, finely ground, 6 parts
Chamomile, finely ground, 3 parts
Peppermint, finely ground, 4 parts
Fennel seed, finely ground, 3 parts
Cinnamon, powdered, 3 parts
Ginger, powdered, 2 parts

One teaspoonful of this formula to a cup of water. Boil 2 minutes—cover and let stand 5 minutes. Strain. Sweeten if desired with honey. Drink hot.

RECIPES FOR INSECT BITES AND STINGS

There are certain odors and substances which most insects dislike, as they appear to go very much by smell. Some people find certain of them more effective than others. It is a good idea to try out a few to discover which suits best. The use of lavender water, for instance, has been proved most efficient by some people. Others find oil of Citronella, oil of Geranium, or oil of Eucalyptus useful for rubbing exposed parts. Smokers also say that smoke helps to repel the pests.

Here is a recipe against mosquito bites that has been proved very effective. Half fill a tumbler with Epsom salts, pour in just enough very hot water to melt it, add 20 drops of glycerine, and then rinse very lightly in the solution, two pieces of clean linen about 9 inches square, and put them in a waterproof bag or old tobacco pouch. When in the open, pat all exposed flesh, especially well up the back of the head and wrists, and let it dry on. Repeat if out long. It shows slightly on the face, but is good for the complexion.

To repel gnats, put a handful of Quassia chips into a bowl of cold water, leaving for 12 hours or longer. Bottle, and for use, sponge the exposed skin with the liquid. The bitter taste is a preventive.

Ant bites are not uncommon, and their irritation may be allayed by eau-de-Cologne. For bites of spiders, centipedes and scorpions —suck the wound and apply vinegar, ammonia or tobacco juice. (Do not suck wound if you have a mouth sore.)

It is important that no wound should be scratched, although there is a temptation to do so. If some soothing application is at hand, apply it at once in order to relieve the itching. Glycerine, smelling salts, ammonia, washing soda, are usually effective. Another way of relieving the pain is by bathing in salt water, then applying some such oil as Peppermint or Menthol. If the bites are very aggravating this method can be tried as an alternative to others mentioned before.

With bee stings the first and essential thing is to remove the sting. This can be done with a small pair of forceps or a sterilized needle or blade of a pen knife, or even with a clean finger nail. The wasp does not leave his sting in the victim's skin.

The stinging Hymenoptera have both acid and alkaline poisons, and that is perhaps why what seem curiously contrasted remedies appear to be at least semieffective. With wasps the alkaline substance seems to predominate; with bees the acid appears the stronger. Therefore with the first acid is often more useful, with the latter an alkali, in order to neutralize it. Here is a valuable tag to remember: AB and VW, which, when translated, means: Ammonia for bees and horse flies, and vinegar for wasps.

Strong ammonia, therefore, dabbed onto a bee sting is most useful. If the sting looks fiery and is beginning to swell, the best thing to do is to poultice it. Use a cloth or cotton wool damped with lime water or a strong solution of bicarbonate of soda.

With wasp stings one cannot beat using a weak acid such as lemon juice or vinegar, or damp tea leaves which are effective with bee stings, too). Epsom salts in a dry condition also give relief, and another simple and effective cure is to rub the place with a moistened aspirin tablet. Tincture of Calendula stops any irritation from wasp or bee stings, or those of other insects almost immediately; if in the mouth, a drop or two obviates any dangerous swelling. Rubbing with a Clove or Garlic is valuable for wasp stings and so is an onion. If stung in the back of the mouth—a most dangerous happening—eating a piece of onion is sometimes all that can be done.

There is an old French remedy which the peasants swear by, valuable not only for bees and wasps, but all insect stings. It consists of Aloes dissolved to saturation point in tincture of tolu. The pain of the sting is completely allayed in a very few minutes and all after-effects diminished to a vanishing point. It is usually sufficient to smear the bite firmly two or three times with the wet cork.

Finally, two homely remedies. First, for a wasp sting, rub it with slices of raw potato. This is often useful when working in the garden. If done at once there will be hardly any swelling. Or, rub the place with a handful of damp earth. This remedy is universal among the peasants of Russia when they are stung by a wasp or bee. The pain stops almost immediately and neither irritation of the skin nor swelling ensues. Evidently the acids and alkalis in the earth neutralize the venom of both insects equally well.

NOTE: *Above refers to non-venomous insect bites. If bitten by a Black Widow spider, Scorpion or other poisonous venoms, see Physician at once.*

LIGHT PERFUME

Electric lights and light perfume can work together to make a whole living room fragrant. Toilet water or cologne sprayed on electric light bulbs will do the job. When the lights are switched on, their heat will diffuse the scent through the room and provide a subtle fragrance.

STOP NAGGING!

This is one of the most vicious habits of the entire human race. It is vicious because it appears to be harmless. Nagging is actually like slow torture—the cruelest form of punishment of ancient China and the Middle Ages.

No one is perfect—no, not even you. Everybody is entitled to some little habit that actually does not harm or concern anyone. These habits can easily be overlooked by diverting your own attention to some useful and healthful hobby, such as gardening, raising house plants, studying nature, church work, etc.

Kindness and cheer cost nothing, and go a long way. Try this in your own household—you will be surprised how contagious good words and deeds are.

Nagging can affect your health, and everyone associated with you. It can affect your entire life, and others about you.

WORK KILLS WORRY

Worry wears worse than work. Worry destroys; work produces. Worry wastes energy; work utilizes it. Worry subtracts; work multiplies. Worry dwarfs, depresses, confuses, kills; work kills worry. Don't worry—cheer up and go to work!

DON'T

pamper your child
make him feel inferior
be too severe
frighten him
make him jealous
worry him or worry over him
talk about sickness
boss him too much
say "don't" to him all the time
compare him with others
lie to him
glorify his temper tantrums
bribe him
overexcite him
get angry at him
show favoritism
exhibit authority for its own sake
humiliate him

HABITS

The greatest iceberg once was just
  A tiny flake of snow,
And flake on flake adhered to it,
  And it did slowly grow.

And so it is with habits good,
  Or habits very bad;
In time they'll give you lots of joy,
  Or make you very sad.

HEALTH MAXIMS

Early to bed and early to rise make a man healthy and wealthy and wise.

When you are well, let yourself alone; you can never be better than well.

The almost universal cause of dyspepsia is eating too fast, too often, and too much.

Never take a cold bath while tired, nor less than two hours after a regular meal.

Sameness of food is a great drawback to health, for nature craves a variety of elements.

That woman lives longest who wisely divides the occupations of life between brain and muscle.

Never eat when you are not hungry, nor drink when you are not thirsty; it imposes on nature.

Marriage is the natural condition of man, and without it no man nor woman ever feels settled in life.

To be always well is an attainable blessing—the uniform result of self-denial, temperance, and an industrious life.

Either cold feet or constipated bowels attend a large majority of human ailments, the cure of which would be effected by their removal.

The three great elementary principles of every healthy community, as well as of individuals, are pure air, perfect cleanliness, and well-cooked food.

Little Things Worth Knowing

That warm borax water helps remove dandruff.

That salt should be eaten with nuts to aid digestion.

That it rests you in sewing, to change your position frequently.

That a hot, strong lemonade, taken at bedtime, will break up a bad cold.

That tough meat is made tender by lying a few minutes in vinegar water.

That a little soda water will relieve sick headache caused by indigestion.

That a cup of strong coffee will remove the odor of onions from the breath.

That a cup of hot water drank before meals will prevent nausea and dyspepsia.

That well-ventilated bedrooms will prevent morning headaches and lassitude.

That one in a faint should be laid flat on her back; then loosen her clothes and let her alone.

That fever patients can be made cool and comfortable by frequent sponging off with soda water.—From an old Health Book.

"My son, if you would be wise, open first your EYES, your EARS next, and last of all, your MOUTH, that your words may be words of wisdom, and give no advantage to thine adversary."—Proverb of North American Indians.

OLD-FASHIONED HOUSEHOLD HINTS

To Make Canaries Sing
A piece of rock candy as large as a filbert, put in the drinking water of a canary, will cause it to sing.

To Remove Ink Spots
Melt a piece of mould candle of the best quality, and dip the stained linen in the melted tallow, then wash thoroughly.

To Keep Out Red Ants
Place in the closet, or wherever they appear, a small quantity of green sage.

To Expel Fleas
Strip the leaves from the stalk of the Pennyroyal, put into little bags made of muslin, sewed up all around, and place among the bedding. If more convenient, sprinkle with the oil or essence of Pennyroyal.

To Remove Iron Rust
Mix salt with lemon juice and apply to the spots.

To Remove Iron Rust from White Goods
Soak the stains in a weak solution of tincture of chloride and rinse immediately after with much water. The tincture of salt is more reliable in removing iron rust and quicker in its action than oxalic acid.

To Wash Feather Pillows
Choose a bright windy day; fill the wash tub with hot suds and plunge the pillows (with feathers) in them. Put them through several waters, shaking them out briskly, then hang on the line in the open air. When perfectly dry, shake well, and they will be light, fresh and sweet. After they have been washed in this way, they ought to be hung out in the warm, fresh air every day for a week, but they must never be put directly in the hot sun, as the heat draws the oil out of the feathers and gives them an unpleasant odor.

Home-Made Furniture Polish
Bees' wax, half a pound, and a quarter of an ounce of alkanet root, melt together in an earthen pot until the former is well coloured. Then add linseed oil, and spirits of turpentine, of each one-fourth pint, strain through a piece of coarse muslin.

Pleasant Perfume and Preventive Against Moths
Take cloves, caraway seeds, nutmeg, mace, cinnamon and Tonquin beans, of each one ounce; then add as much Florentine Orris root as will equal the other ingredients put together. Grind the whole well to powder, then put it in little bags among your clothes.

TO KEEP TOMATOES FRESH
Take one teacupful of salt to one pail of water, and put the ripe tomatoes into it with a weight on them. You can use them any time in the winter by soaking them in water and changing it till they are fresh enough to cook any way you choose, or they are nice right from the brine with a lunch.

POT MARIGOLD
Centuries ago this plant was common in every garden. Today fancy new varieties have replaced the old fashioned plant. Not only is Pot Marigold a beautiful ornamental, but useful in foods, for coloring, as an adulterant for saffron and in medicine. The dried flowers were so popular that grocers and spice-sellers kept barrels of it in stock. An old writer said, "No broths are well made without dried Marigold." Dairy maids used to churn the petals with their cream to give butter a yellow color. A strong infusion made from dried flowers was used to color hair for those "not beyinge content wyth the natural colour." Medicinally Marigold was used mainly as a local application. The dried flowers or fresh leaves boiled in lard make an excellent salve. The fresh flowers are said to relieve wasp or bee stings when rubbed on the affected part. Pot Marigold is an easily grown annual that prefers a sunny location.

TO FATTEN FOWLS IN A SHORT TIME
Mix together ground rice, well scalded with milk, and add some coarse sugar. Feed them with this in the day time, but not too much at once; let it be pretty thick.

PROTECTION AGAINST MOTHS
Pfleider, a German inspector of passenger cars, states that a single stem of hemp, with the leaves and blossoms, mixed with the stuffing of a car seat, will protect it from moths for years, and that hemp for this purpose should be gathered just when in blossom, dried rapidly in the shade, and kept in covered wooden vessels in a dry place.

NUTS EASILY CRACKED WHEN SOAKED IN SALT WATER
Nut shells, particularly those of pecans, become soft and easy to crack when soaked in salt water for a few hours. The nut meats can then be easily removed whole, agriculture extension agents in Mississippi have found.

HAIR OIL
Olive Oil ½ pint, oils of Rosemary and Origanum of each ⅛ of an ounce. Apply freely.

LONGER LIFE THROUGH DIET

This is one of the most neglected, as well as most important factors in preserving health and long life. We give more attention to the diet of our house pets and stock, than we do to ourselves, simply because the animal span of life is so much more noticeable than human life.

Diet should be adjusted and varied according to health condition, climate, work or sedentary habits, and changed as one becomes older.

Foods for weak and sickly should be different from healthy... People employed in heavy physical labors, require plenty of milk, cheese, eggs and meats, while people employed in light clerical or office work, require less of these foods, and more of salads, vegetables and fruit. As a person becomes older, the diet should become more and more restricted—with stress on easily digested vitamins and mineral-rich foods.

* * * * *

A classic example of diet regimen is the case of Thomas Parr, the Englishman who lived to be 152 years old. As Parr became older, his diet became more restricted to easily digested energy foods. His great age came to the attention of nobility, who wanted to know the secret of his long life. They hoped, also, to attain his great age without changing their own dissipating mode of living. Parr was invited to sit at one of the sumptuous meals of these would-be long-lifers. The meal promptly ended Parr's long life. He was buried in Westminister with the epitaph:

"Thomas Parr, the man who lived the longest, died at the age of 152 years, of an intestinal disease, the result of a too copious meal."

Parr's royal friends of course, went on eating their heavy rich meals, which rewarded them with painful ailments, and an early grave.

LOW FAT DIET CUTS BRITISH DEATH RATE

The most serious form of hardening of the arteries is being partly controlled in England by the "austerity diet," a British authority on heart blood vessel diseases, says.

Dr. George Pickering said that since rationing began in 1939 and England went on a low fat diet, deaths from arteriosclerosis have decreased especially in elderly victims of diabetes. "The same thing happened in World War I after the submarines hit our food supply," Pickering told a news conference.—News Item.

TO BE FAT IS TO BE OLD

Many Americans eat three good sized meals per day, nibble something between them, then end the day with a snack or "night cap." If you are one of these persons, you are not much different than Thomas Parr's royal friends—your inevitable end will be the same as the royal indulgers.

Over-eating kills more people than all the wars man ever stirred up in his history. When you are 50 years old, every pound of overweight means one per cent off your life expectancy. If you weigh 50 pounds too much, your life expectancy is reduced by 50 per cent! You can get a fair idea what your heart must bear with overweight, by carrying a bag of sand (5 or 10 pounds) from the moment you arise, until you are back in bed again at night. You will think the sand bag increased in weight many times before the day is over. It is true that overweight is more equally distributed, and apparently less tiring, nevertheless every ounce of excess "baggage" is wasted energy, and fat impedes healthy functioning of organs.

Fat kills by promoting disease and by making various diseases more deadly. Among overweight people there is more heart disease, more kidney trouble, more diabetes, far more cancer, and three times as much high blood pressure as among people of average weight. Fat people have more falls and other accidents, than people of normal weight.

The safest way to reduce is to eat less of fattening foods, such as butter, cheese, cream soups, gravies, pastries, pies, carbonated soft drinks, and alcoholic beverages. Satisfy hunger with salads, fruits, and Peppermint tea.

"Man's first disobedience, and the fruit
Of that forbidden tree, whose mortal taste
Brought death into the World and all our woe With loss of Eden"—Milton.

Treat your body as you would a machine, if you expect to get long years of service from it. As it gets older, it should be given more and more considerate care. Off the super-highways we often see an ancient Model-T Ford purring along like a kitten. In the big cities, we often find a brand new car completely worn out, or "shot" in a very short period of time. Cars, and human lives, are what their drivers made them.

A FATHER'S ADVICE

A father, sending his boy out into the world, gave him the following rules. He said he could never hope to get on in life without meticulously observing them:

Tell the truth—lies are hard to remember.

Shine the heels as well as the toes of your shoes.

Don't lend money to your friends—you will lose both.

Don't watch the clock. It will keep going—you do the same.

You do not need clean cuffs every day, but you will need a clean conscience all the time.

Don't borrow money, unless you positively have the wherewithal to pay.

TO MARRIED FOLK

Once there lived a sage, venerable in age and of sound judgment and prudence, who spent his days administering admonition to young married folk. His wisdom has been passed down the ages and is summarized in the following points. It is well to suggest that the older married folk, perhaps, are not too old to read and learn as well.

Don't ever both get angry at the same time.

Never talk at one another, either alone, or in company.

Never speak loud to one another, unless the house is on fire.

Let each one strive to yield oftenest to the wishes of the other.

Let self denial be the daily aim and practice of each.

Never find fault unless it is perfectly certain that a fault has been committed, and always speak lovingly.

Never taunt with a past mistake.

Neglect the whole matter rather than one another.

Never allow a request to be repeated.

Never make a remark at the expense of each other—it is a meanness.

Never part for a day without loving words to think of during absence.

Never let the sun go down upon any anger or grievance.

Never let any fault you have committed go by until you have frankly confessed it and asked forgiveness.

Never forget the happy hours of early love.

Never sigh over what might have been, but make the best of what is.

THE WORLD'S GREATEST NEED

"The greatest want of the world is the want of men,—men who will not be bought or sold; men who in their inmost souls are true and honest; men who do not fear to call sin by its right name; men whose conscience is as true to duty as the needle to the pole; men who will stand for the right though the heavens fall."

I Shall Pass Through This World But Once.
Any Good, Therefore, That I Can Do,
Or Any Kindness That I Can Show
To Any Human Being,
Let Me Do It Now.
Let Me Not Defer It Or Neglect It,
For I Shall Not Pass This Way Again.

CHILD TRAINING

Rule yourself before attempting to rule your child.

Remember always that our most effective lessons are given by personal example.

So far as possible be what you would have your children be. If you are peevish, fretful and complaining, disliking to do this duty and despising that, etc., do not be surprised if you find the same disposition cropping out in your children.

If, on the other hand, you are cheerful and happy regarding the duties of life as your greatest pleasure; if you are thankful for such things as you have in the present life . . . the little ones round your feet will quickly discern and catch your happy, thankful, energetic and helpful spirit, and thus half the victory will be accomplished.

Never by word or example encourage idleness; children are better off if they have some care and responsibility; they will develop more nearly perfectly if they have some time and opportunity to work out their own original ideas; not too many toys, else there will be no room for ingenuity.

Play should always be secondary to real service. Prompt and cheerful obedience should be expected and enforced, not by repeated urging to duty, but by a single showing to duty. There should be a penalty of some kind for its non-performance.

Do not lower your dignity by working yourself up into a nervous excitement. Train your children to be sensitive to the approval of God, of parents, and of their own conscience. This is one of the fine points that will require skill and ingenuity. You will need to study the disposition of your child; to watch for opportunities to instruct and impress him and to let none of them slip. You will need to watch the little things in his deportment, to express your affectionate approval of his good points, and your pain and displeasure at his errors and failures. Let him feel that God's eyes and your eyes are over him, just as we feel that God's eyes are over us.

Teach children to be generous, to prefer one another, and to be watchful for one another's interest. The table is a good place for cultivating good manners.

Cultivate acquaintance of your children. Be young with them, but give them the advantage of your years of experience. Hold your own standpoint, but sympathize with theirs, and do not forget your feelings and experiences at their age.

BEAUTY AND SCENTS

GRANDMOTHER'S BEAUTY AIDS

Yes, Grandmother too was glamorous in her day despite the fact she had no beauty shops or drug store cosmetics. Women of the past made their own preparations with ingredients from the kitchen or garden. Many of these old-time concoctions have been used for generation after generation—back to early American times—and to old Europe where they are still being used. Some of these recipes form the basis of modern preparations.

COMPLEXION WASHES

A teaspoonful of the flour of sulphur and a wine-glassful of lime-water, well shaken and mixed; ½ wine-glass of glycerine, and 1 wine-glass of rose-water. Rub it on the face every night before going to bed. Shake well before using.

Take a small piece of gum benzoin and boil it in spirits of wine until it becomes a rich tincture. In using it pour 15 drops into a glass of water, wash the face and hands and allow it to dry.

The whites of four eggs boiled in rose-water; ½ ounce of alum; ½ ounce of sweet almonds; beat the whole together until it assumes the consistency of paste. Spread upon a silk or muslin cloth, to be worn at night.

The following reads like a cooking recipe. It was intended "to stimulate and give tone to the skin": ¼ ounce powdered long peppers; ½ ounce powdered cinnamon; 1½ ounces aromatic spices; ⅜ ounce powdered cardamon seeds. Mix all throughly in 1 quart of alcohol and allow to stand several days. Apply to the skin as a wash at least once a day.

A rather messy recipe—but said to be good: Mix 1 teaspoonful of the best tar in a pint of olive oil or almond oil, by heating the two together in a tin cup set in boiling water. Stir until completely mixed and smooth, putting in more oil if the compound is too thick to run easily. Rub this on the face when going to bed, and lay patches of soft cloth on to keep tar from rubbing off. The bed linen must be protected by cloth folded and thrown over the pillows.

This recipe dates back to thousands of years before Grandmother's day: Bathe the face and shoulders—or if you can afford more —take a leisure bath in sweet milk. Allow milk to dry on the skin for an hour before washing off. Sweet cream was used as a facial. It was applied to the face with gentle rubbing "in the direction of the wrinkles." Another method: Rub on as much cream as the face will stand—then powder with fine starch mixed with small amount of alum (1 teaspoonful alum to 1 pound of starch). Allow to remain on face 15 to 20 minutes before washing off with clear water.

A home-made cream for whitening the neck can be made from cucumbers. Cut one cucumber into half-inch slices and place in a heat resisting receptacle. Pour over the cucumber, two ounces of almond oil. Allow this mixture to simmer for several hours. If you have a double-boiler sauce-pan it would be ideal to use it for this purpose. Pour off the liquid and measure it. To each ounce of the liquid add just under an ounce of lanolin and less than half-ounce of white wax. Warm this mixture together and stir throughly. Add some lavender essence before putting into jars.

SKIN PREPARATIONS

To Soften Skin: Mix ½ ounce of glycerine with ½ ounce alcohol, and add 4 ounces of rose-water. Shake well together and it is ready for use.

Cold Cream: 5 ounces oil of sweet almonds; 3 ounces spermaceti; ½ ounce of white wax, and 3 to 5 drops of attar of roses. Melt together in a shallow dish over hot water. Strain though a piece of muslin when melted, and as it begins to cool, beat it with a silver spoon until cold and snowy white.

FRECKLES (NON-PERMANENT TYPE)

Gather 1 or 2 handfuls of common chickweed; add small quantity of soft water, and make a mash. Apply mash to freckles and allow to remain on 5 or 10 minutes morning and evening. Wash afterward with clear water. If the above recipe was not satisfactory, there were several others to choose from: Make a wash with strong decoction of dried Elder flowers and boiling water. Apply when cool—morning and night.

Others—1 oz. of honey with luke-warm water. Apply when cold as often as convenient.

Carbonate of potassa—20 grains; milk of almonds—2 oz; oil of sassafras—3 drops. Mix and apply 2 or 3 times a day.

1 oz. alcohol; half a dram salts tartar; one dram oil bitter almonds. Let stand for one day and apply every second day.

SURFACE CAUSED PIMPLES ON THE FACE

1 tablespoonful of borax to ½ pint of water is an excellent remedy for cutaneous eruptions.

Grandmother's Beauty Aids—Continued

Another—pulverize a piece of alum the size of a walnut. Dissolve it in 1 oz. lemon juice, and add 1 oz. of alcohol. Apply once or twice a day.

Or—10 grains camphor, 20 grains powdered acacia, 2 drachms precipitated sulphur, 2 oz. lime water, 2 oz. rose-water. Apply to the face with a soft cloth at bed time. Allow to dry and brush off excess powder.

BLACKHEADS

The following was used to soften blackheads, so that they may easily be squeezed out: 1 dram boracic acid, 1 oz. alcohol, 2 oz. rose-water.

PREMATURE WRINKLES

Dissolve the following in 8 oz. of alcohol. 32 grains each of powdered benzoin and powdered gum arabic. When throughly dissolved, add 46 grains pwd. sweet almond, 16 grains pwd. cloves, and 16 grains ground nutmeg. Allow to stand 48 hours, shaking occasionally. Add ½ oz. of rose-water, then strain whole through coarse cloth. Apply to wrinkles every night before retiring.

Another method: Mix equal parts of alcohol and white of egg. Apply to wrinkles every night before retiring.

DOUBLE CHIN

This was reduced by dipping a piece of linen in pure vinegar, rinsing it out thoroughly, then placing it under the chin, letting it extend from ear to ear, and keeping it in place with a long bandage reaching to top of head. This was left on for 2 hours at a time. If the application caused redness or irritation, starch or other soothing powder was applied to skin.

HEAVY EYES

Gather fresh Elder leaves with flowers when possible; steep a handful in 1 or 2 quarts of boiling water. When this is cool, lie down and place steeped Elder across the forehead and eyes, keeping leaves in place with soft cloth bandage. The effect is very soothing, as well as clarifying to the mind.

Irritated eyelids: Take a slice of stale bread—cut as thin as possible, toast both sides well, but do not burn it—when cold, soak it in cold water, then put it between a piece of old linen and apply, changing when it gets warm.

LIP SALVE

Melt in a jar placed in a basin of boiling water—¼ oz. each of cocoa butter and spermaceti, 15 grains pwd. benzoin, and ½ oz. oil of almonds. Stir until mixture is cool. Color red with alkanet root.

NAIL CARE

If finger nails are hard or brittle, immerse then in warm olive oil every night or apply small amount of vaseline upon them.

TEETH AND GUM CARE

The ashes of stale bread, throughly burned was a popular old-time dentifrice. Common salt was much used to clean teeth. The mouth was generally rinsed with water containing a few drops of tincture of myrrh in it. Powdered charcoal was also used to clean the teeth as well as to sweeten the mouth and breath. For convenience, the powdered charcoal was placed in a bottle of water. When used it was shaken and a few drops placed on the tooth brush.

The stem of common garden Althea bush was used for whitening the teeth. Cut a small branch from the bush and crush the cut end; rub this end vigorously on the teeth. It will make them brilliant white, without the slightest danger to the enamel, according to an old recipe.

Flour of sulphur was used especially for discolored teeth. It was brushed on the teeth and gums with a rather hard tooth-brush.

Another recipe recommends equal parts of cream of tartar and salt—pulverize and mix. Wash the teeth in the morning and rub them well with this powder.

Vinegar was used instead of water on teeth, to remove tartar.

The following was intended to keep gums healthy: Gargle made of 1 oz. of ground Peruvian bark, steeped in ½ pint of brandy for 2 weeks. Put a teaspoonful of this into a tablespoonful of water, and gargle the mouth twice a day.

Another—take 1 oz. pwd. gum myrrh, 2 tablespoonfuls of honey, and a little pwd. garden sage; mix together and wet the teeth and gums with a little, twice a day.

HAIR PREPARATIONS

The following recipe is intended for dark hair: Take 1 oz. of common green tea and 1 oz. garden sage leaves. Place in a graniteware container with 1½ quarts of water. Boil down to ⅓ of original quantity—then allow to stand for 24 hours. Strain, bottle, and use it morning and night, rubbing it well into the scalp.

Hair Oil: Mix equal parts of olive oil and spirits of rosemary, and add a few drops of oil of nutmeg. Rub scalp every evening with a few drops of this mixture. The author of this century old recipe believed it would "promote the growth of hair."

Egg Shampoo: Mix the white and yellow of an egg throughly in 1 oz. of water. Apply to hair and massage scalp vigorously with rotary motion of the hands. After the operation rinse the hair thoroughly with clear water.

Keeping hair in curl: Take a few quince seed, boil them in water, and add perfume if you like. Wet the hair with this and it will keep in curl. It is also good to keep the hair

Grandmother's Beauty Aids—Continued

in place on the forehead, or going out in the wind.

REDUCING WITH SASSAFRAS TEA

The following recipe was taken from a 70 year old recipe book: "A strong decoction of Sassafras, drunk frequently, will reduce the flesh as rapidly as any remedy known. A strong infusion is made at the rate of 1 oz. of Sassafras to a quart of water, boil it ½ hour, very slowly, and let it stand until cold, heating again if desired. Keep it from the air."

Note: We find no other printed or authoritative record of Sassafras being used for above mentioned condition. Medicinally, Sassafras bark is reputed to be aromatic, stimulant, diaphoretic and alterative.

CAMOMILE TEA

Put about ½ ounce of Camomile flowers into a jug, pour a pint of boiling water upon them, cover up the tea, and when it has stood about ten minutes pour it off from the flowers into another jug; sweeten with sugar or honey. A cupful of it in the morning will strengthen the digestive organs. A teacupful in which is stirred a large dessertspoonful of moist sugar and a little grated ginger, is an excellent thing to administer to aged persons a couple of hours before dinner.

DECOCTION OF CAMOMILE

Take 2 ounces of Camomile flowers and 1 ounce of fennel seeds; pour over them 4 pints of boiling water; let them boil, and strain perfectly clear.

HOP TEA

Pour a quart of boiling water upon half an ounce of hops, cover this over and allow the infusion to stand for fifteen minutes; the tea must then be strained off into another jug. A small teacup may be drunk in the morning, which will create an appetite and also strengthen the digestive powers. It is an excellent medicinal drink.

FLAXSEED TEA

Wash 2 ounces of Flaxseed by putting them in a small strainer and pouring cold water through it; take the yellow rind of half a lemon, as thin as possible; to the Flaxseed and rind add one quart of water; let it simmer for an hour and a half. Strain away the seeds and to each half pint of tea add a teaspoon of sugar.

OBESITY

Drink Mate Tea frequently between meals. Step up vitamin foods—salads, fruits, etc., and cut down on heavy starchy foods, especially breadstuffs.

LIME WATER

Lime, 4 ounces
Water, 1 Gallon

First slack the lime with a small portion of the water, then add the remainder and stir them together and cover the vessel immediately; in about 3 hours it is ready for use. Always keep in a well stoppered bottle.

ROSE WATER

Oil of Rose, 15 drops
Carbonate of Magnesia, 1 teaspoonful
Distilled water, 1 pint

Rub the oil first with the magnesia, then with the water gradually added, and filter.

AROMATIC HERB WINE

Two drachms each of—Wormwood, Peppermint, Thyme, Hyssop, Sage, Lavender, Sweet Marjoram, and 2 pints of Port Wine: Macerate for several days, transfer to percolator and displace. Uses:—As a mild stimulant tonic, and in simple flatulence distress of the stomach. Dose—½ wine-glass as needed.

CINNAMON WATER

Oil of Cinnamon, ½ teaspoonful
Carbonate of Magnesia, ¼ teaspoonful
Distilled Water, 2 pints

Rub the carbonate of magnesia throughly with the oil of cinnamon, and gradually add the water.

FENNEL WATER

Oil of Fennel, ½ teaspoonful
Carbonate of Magnesia, ¼ teaspoonful
Distilled Water, 2 pints

Rub the oil with the magnesia, then gradually add the water and filter.

PEPPERMINT WATER

Oil of Peppermint, ½ teaspoonful
Carbonate of Magnesia, ¼ teaspoonful
Distilled Water, 2 pints

Rub the oil with the magnesia, and then add the water gradually and filter through paper.

A GOOD OLD-FASHIONED LINIMENT

3 oz. Spirits Camphor
2 oz. Olive Oil
1 oz. Oil Peppermint
1 oz. Chloroform

Shake well before using. Apply whenever pains occur, rub well into the skin.

OLD FASHIONED FRUIT AND VEGETABLE BEAUTY AIDS

Beauties of other days were noted for their delicate baby-like skin. Most of the old time beauty aids were for whitening or bleaching effects upon the skin.

Apples: In Gerard's time an ointment made of pulp of apples, swine's grease and rosewater was sold in shops to beautify face and take away roughness of skin. The juice of sour apple was rubbed on warts to remove them.

Cucumber: Cucumbers are still used as a beauty aid. Lotion: ½ pint juice of cucumbers; 1½ ounces deodorized alcohol; 3¼ ounces oil of Benne; 1 drachm powdered Castile soap; 1¾ drachms blanched Almonds. Work soap into cucumber juice, beat up almonds in a clean stone mortar and gradually work in cucumber liquid with soap. Strain through a clean muslin strainer, then return to mortar and while stirring gradually work in alcohol in which oil of Benne has been previously dissolved. Use in massaging the face and throat as it not only whitens the skin but also tones relaxed tissues. It may also be used to cleanse skin.

Juice Lotion: Cut cucumbers into small pieces, pound them into a paste, then extract the juice by straining through a jelly bag. Apply to skin twice or three times a day. Cucumbers may, of course, also be used in raw state by merely dicing them and rubbing the skin briskly with diced parts.

Lemon: As a wash, dilute lemon juice with water. For neck and shoulders the sliced lemon may be applied directly, allowing the juice to remain on the skin for several minutes, then washing off with soap and water. The hands may be made white and soft and supple by daily sponging them with fresh lemon juice which further keeps the nails in good order.

Oranges: Common oranges, cut through the middle while green, and dried in the air, being afterwards steeped for forty days in oil, are used by the Arabs for preparing an essence famous among their old women because it will restore afresh dark or black colour to gray hair.

Pineapple: If applied to horny excresences on the skin, such as corns, or warts, the fresh juice is powerfully solvent; so that if a thin slice of Pineapple be kept in close contact with a corn for 8 hours the corn will become so soft as to admit easy removal.

Potato: Hair Dye: Pare a dozen potatoes, cover them with cold water and let them boil in an iron pot until soft. Strain the water off and leave it to cool, being careful that it touches nothing, lest it stain. Make a thorough application of it to the hair and then, in order to set the color, let the hair dry in the sun.

Rhubarb: To keep light hair light, take equal parts of rhubarb stalks and honey; steep in three parts of white wine. Allow to stand 36 hours, strain and thoroughly wash hair with the mixture and allow it to dry on.

Spinach: Skin Whitener and Beautifier: Wash spinach and boil two heaping handfuls in two quarts of water. Add 15 grains each of powdered alum, powdered borax and pulverized camphor. Use twice daily—always shaking the bottle before using.

Strawberries: To make a lotion, take fresh, ripe strawberries, pick and wash them carefully; mash the berries to pulp, strain through linen cloth; dilute strained juice with an equal quantity of water; soften it by adding a pinch of powdered borax. This lotion is excellent for whitening the skin. Another Method: Take 4 pounds Strawberries and 1 quart of rectified spirits and boil together in a strong solution of salt water until nearly dry or pasty. Apply paste to arms or neck. It is a whitener and astringent.

Ancient Roman beauties used crushed strawberries mixed with milk as a skin beautifier. (This recipe makes my mouth water).

French ladies simply crush strawberries in clear water.

Fresh Strawberries are also rubbed on teeth to whiten them.

Tomato: This bleaching recipe originated in Paris (where everything is tried). Cut tomato into thin slices; rub well upon hands, neck or shoulders; let it remain for five minutes; wash off with water mixed with borax (teaspoonful powdered borax to quart of water). The application is said to bleach out sunburn and whiten the neck.

Watermelon: Yes, even this was used as a skin beautifier. At least it was simple to use. Take a good size piece (with plenty of the red part attached) and rub the face, neck and arm briskly until pulp of melon has worked off almost to the rind. It is said to remove or moderate wrinkles. The juice of Watermelon may be strained off and applied with the fingers—the massaging effect probably is also important for results.

OLD TIME HAIR PREPARATIONS

The following recipes are reprinted exactly as they appeared in newspapers or magazines some 80 or 90 years ago. It must be realized that in those days many claims made have since proved very highly exaggerated. Such words as "to prevent," to "to restore," "tonic," etc., were often used indiscriminately.

Hair Wash: Take two or three ounces of Rosemary leaves and put them into a jar with half a pint of cold water. Place the jar near the fire and let the contents simmer gently for an hour or two. When the water is somewhat reduced, the infusion will be sufficiently strong. Then add half a pint of rum and let it stand for several hours. When cold, strain the liquid from the leaves and keep it in a bottle to be ready for use. Apply it to the roots of the hair with a small sponge or a soft brush. Egg wash for the hair is made by beating up the yolk of a raw egg and add it to rosemary infusion made as above.

Growth of Hair Increased and Baldness Prevented: Take four ounces of Castor Oil, eight ounces of good Jamaica rum, thirty drops of oil of lavender, or ten drops of oil of rose. Anoint occasionally the head, shaking well the bottle previously.

Lotion for the Hair as Recommended by Dr. Locock: Aqua ammonia, oil of sweet almonds, of each two drachms; spirits rosemary, one ounce; oil of mace (essential) one-half drachm; rose water, two and one-half ounces. First, mix the almond oil with the ammonia, then, having added the oil of mace to the rosemary shake them up with the oil and ammonia; and finally add the rose-water by degrees and mix well. To be used as a lotion, applied once a day with a soft hair-brush.

Gray Hair: A good application on the hair turning gray is the following: Distill two pounds of honey, a handful of rosemary and twelve handfuls of the tendrils of the grape vine, infused in a gallon of new milk; about two quarts of water will be obtained from this, which apply to the hair frequently.

Tonic Wash for the Hair: When the hair is falling off, the following tonic wash will be found very useful: Take half a fluid ounce of tincture of quinine, one drachm of bicarbonate of ammonia and five and a half ounces of rose water; first dissolve the ammonia in water then add the tincture. Apply it gently to the roots of the hair twice a week or oftener if found to be beneficial.

To Color Human Hair Black: and not stain the skin, it is asserted that a liquid may be made by taking one part of bay rum, three parts of olive oil and one part of good brandy by measure. The hair must be washed with the mixture every morning and in a short time the use of it will make the hair a beautiful black without injuring it in the least. The articles must be of the best quality mixed in a bottle and always shaken before applied.

What Causes the Hair to Turn Gray: An English writer has asserted that an undue proportion of lime in the system can be a contributory cause of premature gray hair, and advises to avoid hard water, either for drinking pure or when converted into tea, coffee or soup, because hard water is always strongly impregnated with lime. Hard water may be softened by boiling it; let it become cold and settled and then use it as a beverage.

Perfume for Hair Oil: Oil of Bergamot, 1 ounce; Oil of Rosemary, 1 drachm; Oil of Cassia, 5 drops; Oil of Cloves, 5 drops; Oil of Rose Geranium, 10 drops. Alcohol sufficient to make 4 ounces. Mix.

Bald Heads: A most valuable remedy for promoting the growth of the hair is an application once or twice a day of wild indigo and alcohol. Take four ounces of wild indigo and steep it about a week or ten days in a pint of alcohol and a pint of hot water, when it will be ready for use. The head must be thoroughly washed with the liquid, morning and evening, application being made with a sponge or soft brush.

Hair Tonic: A tea made of pouring one pint of boiling water on two tablespoonfuls of dried rosemary leaves with a wineglassful of rum added is excellent.

Jaborandi Hair Tonic: Glycerine, 2 ounces; Jaborandi, 4 drachms; Cinchona Bark, 1 ounce; Alcohol, 2 ounces; Bay Rum, 2 ounces; Rose Water, 10 ounces. Reduce the Jaborandi and cinchona to a moderately fine powder and exhaust them by percolation with the alcohol, bay rum and water, mixed together. To percolate add the glycerine and filter.

HENNA
Nature's Own Dye

Herbs are the least harmful hair dye in the world. Most manufactured hair dyes are of coal tar, or metallic origin, which are often irritating or actually dangerous to people of susceptible constitutions. Chemical dyes have been known to eat away the hair, penetrate the scalp, and poison the entire body.

No two hair requirements are exactly alike. In the privacy of your own home, you can learn to henna your hair according to the way it "takes" and according to your personal taste. You can learn to give your hair new color and life, as well as giving yourself a youthful appearance. *No one in the world will take better care of your hair than yourself. Your own method can be the envy of your friends.*

Tips on Using Henna

Henna gives the hair golden red shades. It is *BEST* applied to brown types of hair. Chamomile, Sage, Walnut hulls, Logwood, and mixtures are used for other types of hair.

DO NOT use plain henna on white or gray hair—it will turn a gaudy orange or pink.

WHEN dyeing hair, be sure the scalp is healthy and free from lesions, eczema, psoriasis, etc. It is generally believed hair dyeing is not successful during pregnancy and menstrual periods. Systemic conditions sometime influence hair dyeing also. Best results from henna are obtained when the hair has not been previously dyed with chemicals.

Some hair "takes" henna more quickly than others, so it is advisable to test a lock of hair to be dyed *before* dyeing the entire head to determine henna requirements and shade desired. <u>*When dyeing, consider color of your eyebrows, complexion, etc., in order to get a harmonizing and natural appearance. Henna dye shows the color MORE after the second day of application.*</u>

Shampoo Hair Before Using Hair Dye

Shampoo the hair thoroughly just before dyeing. When necessary, the addition of a small portion of carbonate of soda will do much to remove the grease from the hair. Give 2 soapings if necessary. It is important than the hair be free of all oil, otherwise it will prevent the dye from taking evenly. After shampooing the hair, rinse with hot water only. A cold water rinse may leave lime or iron deposits which would affect the henna coloring. Do not dry the hair before applying henna.

Materials

Use china bowl and wooden spoon for mixing henna, as metal may cause chemical reaction. It is most important, also, to have a good quality herb. Many henna powders are actually nothing more than siftings containing considerable sand and dirt.

Henna Rinse

Henna rinse is generally used on lighter shades of brown hair because it is easier to acquire the color desired. It is also advisable for a novice to use the rinse until the "taking" nature of henna is understood. If the first rinse is too light, it may be repeated until the desired shade is obtained. (Do not forget to shampoo hair before application.)

Rinse: Steep ½ oz. of henna in one quart of boiling water for 20 minutes. Strain liquid, and pour over hair, allowing it to remain on 5 to 15 minutes—then rinse with clear water. Dry hair by combing. Castile soap will remove scalp stain after dye is set.

Henna rinse may be made with less coloring and applied gradually over a period of a week so people will not notice the dye effect immediately.

Henna Paste

In order to apply evenly, one should be assisted when using Henna paste.

Henna paste is used to get bright red shades, and used on dark brown hair where it is more difficult for color to show. Henna paste is made by mixing hot water (not boiling) to henna. Thickness of henna paste is determined by the color desired, and according to darkness of hair to be dyed. A thin paste is sufficient for medium dark and a heavier paste for dark brown hair. After the hair has been parted into strands, apply henna paste quickly from roots to ends, and so on, strand by strand, all over the head. A brush may be used when applying thin paste—thick paste should be applied with the hands—protected with rubber gloves to avoid staining. Be sure to saturate both sides of the parting—and the thickness of applications must be equal, in order to obtain an even shade. When the hair is covered with the paste, wrap a cloth wrung from hot water, around the head. Keep

HENNA—continued

it moist, *as the action of henna stops when the paste becomes dry.* Leave on according to shade desired: Medium shades about 10 minutes; dark hair about 30 to 45 minutes. Wash off all henna thoroughly with hot water —using no soap.

If the hair becomes redder than desired, saturate the scalp and hair with a good quality of olive oil—let it remain on for some time—then shampoo with castile soap and hot water.

Cut leaves are generally used for rinse, and powdered leaves for paste.

Miscellaneous Tips

Henna paste is greenish at first—then turns golden, and finally dark the longer it stands.

Wear old clothes, and do dyeing where there is no danger of staining. Have clean combs, brushes, towels, etc., within easy reach when dyeing.

Dye stains may be removed from the skin with olive oil, alcohol, cleansing cream, lemon juice, or ordinary soap and water.

Ancient Egyptians stained their fingers and toenails, as well as their hair and beard— their horses' manes, tail, etc.

Remove Hair Dyes before Getting Permanent

Vegetable hair dye may be removed by applying a 10 per cent solution of iodine evenly over the hair. Next use a 20 per cent solution of ammonia as a rinse. Then shampoo in the usual way.

Hair Dye Mixtures

Test, on clipped hair locks, should be made before dyeing.

One or more tablespoonfuls of ground cloves mixed with henna will darken the resulting shade.

A dark brown shade may be obtained by mixing one part henna to 3 parts indigo. Avoid touching scalp.

A generous pinch of Logwood chips, added to henna, gives a deeper shade of red. A tiny pinch of copperas is necessary, with this mixture, to set the dye.

Black walnut hulls, or black chinese tea, are also used for dyeing hair. Boil ingredient (one or the other) in 1 quart water. Allow to steep until a very dark brew is obtained. Add copperas, the size of a pea, to set dye. Strain and use like rinse. Repeat rinses until desired shade is acquired.

Sage Dye for Dark Hair: Place 4 oz. Sage with 2 quarts of water, in an *iron kettle.* Let it simmer until reduced to 1 quart. Allow to stand covered for 24 hours—strain and apply evenly to the hair, with a brush—the same as if you were applying henna paste.

Sage Rinse: Prepare like henna rinse. This adds life and darkens dark hair.

A Favorite Recipe of English Beauties: Use henna rinse, follow with Chamomile rinse. This gives some types of hair a marvelous sheen.

STYLES IN HAIR COLOR SHOW FALL TREND TOWARDS REDHEAD

Redheads are coming back. Hair experts say that before the snow flies, you'll have a yen to be a redhead.

The red trend is becoming increasingly obvious at beauty shows and in national surveys of beauty experts.—News Item.

Tonic for Dry Hair

Sweet almond oil, 3 oz.; oil of Rosemary, 1 oz.; oil of Bergamot, 10 drops, or oil of Orange, 20 drops.

Tonic for Light Hair

Take 1 oz. strained honey, 1 oz. rhubarb stalks and 3 oz. white wine. Steep the mixture over a slow fire. Let it stand for 24 hours in a cool place. Strain. Apply as a lotion, rubbing it well into the scalp and wetting the hair. Wipe the hair with a soft towel, but allow the mixture to dry in.

Tonic for Prematurely Gray Hair

Mix 3 oz. alcohol with 1 oz. Castor oil and ½ drachm oil of Bergamot.

Salve for Faded Hair

Mix 3 oz. oil of Almonds with 1 oz. oil of Rosemary, and 35 drops oil of Mace. Rub into scalp every other night.

Curling Fluid for Fine Oily Hair

One tablespoonful of bruised Quince seed and 1 pint of distilled water. Boil gently until reduced to one half; strain; then add 1½ oz. alcohol and 1½ oz. cologne.

Chamomile Rinse for Blond Hair

This rinse brings out the highlights of blond hair. Use 3 or 4 tablespoons of dried flowers to a pint of water. Boil from 20 to 30 minutes—strain when cool. Hair should be shampooed before rinse is applied, as hair must be free from all oil. Apply rinse by pouring over the hair while the head is held over the basin. Dip a brush in rinse, which has dropped into the basin, and work into the hair by parting hair. Rinse may be poured over hair several times and brushing repeated. Dry hair the usual way.

Mousy Blond Hair

The following is an inexpensive shampoo that keeps blond hair from turning a mousy shade—keeps hair shiny—cleanses the scalp and helps keep scalp free of dandruff. Take ¼ oz. of Chamomile flowers and ¼ oz. of Quassia chips. Boil together for 10 to 15 minutes in enough water to make a reasonable rinse. Use once or twice a week.

The Indians of New Mexico and Arizona regions are very proud of their hair and take good care of it. The hair is usually washed once a week and after performing dirty work, after a journey and before taking part in ceremonies. The hair wash was made with the roots of native varieties of Yucca (Yucca glauca, Yucca baccata, etc.). Suds were made by allowing roots to steep in water for several minutes. It was then stirred until a good lather is worked up. The roots were removed and lather was ready for use. It was applied and rinsed out like other shampoos.

HERBS USED FOR HAIR

Recipes from Old English Herbals:

"A tea made with Wormwood with a few drops of the essential oil of Wormwood will serve as an astringent wash to prevent the hair from falling off when it is weak and thin."

"An ounce of dried leaves and flowers (Rosemary) treated with a pint of boiling water and allowed to stand until cold makes one of the best hair washes known. It has the singular power of preventing the hair from uncurling when exposed to damp atmosphere. An infusion of the herb (Rosemary) mixed with Poplar bark and used every night will make the hair soft, glossy and strong." (Rosemary is still used in many hair preparations.)

A very popular recipe used for hair was made with Common Stinging Nettle. The infusion was made by boiling a handful of dried Nettle in one quart of water for two hours. The infusion was strained and bottled when cold. It was applied to the scalp every other night. This was said to prevent falling hair and make the hair soft and glossy. Another method: Boil a handful of Stinging Nettle with vinegar and water. Add Eau de Cologne after cooling and straining. Old herbalists also recommended combing the fresh juice of Stinging Nettle into the hair daily.

Gerard made this fantastic claim regarding Maidenhair Fern: "It maketh the hair of the head and beard to grow that is fallen and pulled off."

Culpepper said of Southernwood, "The ashes mingled with old salad oil helps those that have their hair fallen and are bald."

Bancke also wrote: "The ashes (Southernwood) meddled with oil restoreth where any man lacketh hair."

HERBS USED FOR TINTING HAIR

In the days when there were no beauty shops and drug store preparations, elegant ladies made their own hair treatments. Women of nobility and wealth maintained laboratories with "chemists" supplied with domestic, foreign and secret ingredients. Women of lesser means had to content themselves with inexpensive common herbs. While all the elaborate preparations have passed to oblivion, the simple herbal recipes survived time and fashions. Many are now used in the most modern beauty shops either in natural form or concealed under a fancy name, label and deceiving scent. Among the herbs still used for the hair are Chamomile, Sage, Henna and Mullein flowers.

An infusion made with Chamomile flowers is used to bring out the lustre and highlights of blond hair. It is simple to make. Use three or four tablespoonfuls of dried flowers to a pint of water. Boil from twenty to thirty minutes, strain through fine strainer when cool. The hair should be shampooed before the rinse is applied as hair must be free from oil. Apply the rinse by pouring over the hair while the head is held over a basin. Dip a brush in the rinse, which has dropped into the basin and work into the hair by parting hair. The rinse may be poured over the hair several times and the brushing repeated. Dry the hair the usual way.

Henna is not only the oldest known hair rinse in the world but is the most widely used as well. It is used to tint hair an auburn shade. Different shades are made by mixing Henna leaves with Sage, Indigo or other herbs. It is made and applied like Chamomile rinse.

Sage is used to darken hair. It is not a dye and may be removed by shampoo. Sage rinse is made by placing the contents of two 1 oz boxes of herb in a quart of water and boiling thirty minutes or longer. The more it is allowed to boil, and the more herb used, the darker the rinse will be. Strain through a fine strainer after it has cooled. Apply like Chamomile rinse. Remove all traces of Sage rinse before a permanent as it is apt to streak when heat is applied.

An old herbal said of Mullein, "An infusion of the flowers was used by the Roman ladies to tinge their tresses of the golden colour so much admired in Italy; and now in Germany a wash made from Mullein flowers is valued as highly restorative." The infusion and application is like Chamomile rinse.

Although no longer in popular use, Marigold flowers were also used for tinting blond hair for those "not beyinge content wyth the natural colour."

In American Pioneer days ladies had to give up their Old World preparations upon their severance with civilization. They were not handicapped long, however; as nature offered many substitutes for things that could not be brought to the wilderness home. Walnut hulls were not only found to be excellent for darkning the hair but the trees were quite common over a large part of the country.

ARE YOU NERVOUS?

Cut out tea and coffee and try this herbal combination: equal parts of Mistletoe, Scullcap, Valerian and Wood Betony. Use one ounce of mixture to one pint water. Boil for ten minutes, strain when cool. Drink a cupful three times a day.

ROSEMARY POMATUM

Strip from the stem, two large handfuls of recently gathered Rosemary. Boil it in a copper saucepan, well tinned, with half a pound of hog's lard, until reduced to four ounces. Strain it, and put it into a pomatum pot.

HAIR POMADE

Take of extract of Yellow Peruvian bark, fifteen grains; extract of rhatany root, eight grains; extract of Burdock root and oil of nutmegs, of each, two drachms; camphor (dissolved in spirits of wine) fifteen grains; beef marrow, two ounces; best olive oil, one ounce; citron juice, half a drachm; aromatic essential oil as much as sufficient to render it fragrant; mix and make into an ointment. Two drachms of Bergamot, and a few drops of otto of roses would suffice. This is considered a valuable preparation.

MILK OF ROSES

Bitter Almonds, 4 ounces; distilled water, 3 ounces; elder flower water, 2 ounces; make an emulsion and add oil of tartar, 1½ ounce; tincture of benzoin, 1 drachm. Cosmetic. Beautifies and renders the skin smooth.

FRENCH MILK OF ROSES

Rose water, one pint; Tinctures of Benzoin and Storax, of each, half an ounce; spirits of roses, two drachms; rectified spirit, one ounce. Mix. A cosmetic wash.

RECIPE FOR SUN BATHING

Reinforce your blood with iron-rich foods or iron-rich herbs, such as Yellow Dock, Strawberry leaves, Burdock root and Salep. You will tan more easily and evenly.

LOZENGES FOR BAD BREATH

Gum Catechu, 1 ounce; white sugar, 2 ounces; orris powder, ½ ounce. Make them into a paste with mucilage, and add a drop of Neroli. One or two may be sucked at pleasure.

SOMETHING IN YOUR EYE?

If a cinder or any foreign substance gets into the eye, take a single Flax or Clary Sage seed, moisten it on the tongue and put it under the lid, close the eye for a moment, and the substance will adhere to the seed and come out with it. The seeds are absolutely harmless.

NAUSEA

Chew a leaf or two of Mint or Sage (fresh or dried) to a tasteless pulp. Remedies that sick sinking feeling.

WRINKLES

Take barley water, strain it through a fine cloth, and add a few drops of oil of balm of Gilead. Place in a bottle and let stand for from ten to twelve hours—shaking the bottle occasionally until the balsam is entirely mixed with the water. This mixture improves the complexion and preserves the appearance of youth. If used only once a day, it removes wrinkles and gives the skin a surprising lustre. Wash the face before using this fluid.

OLD FASHIONED VIOLET PERFUME

Drop 12 drops of the oil of rhodium on a piece of loaf sugar; powder this well in a glass mortar, and mix thoroughly with three pounds of orris root. This will resemble violet perfume. If more oil is added, a rose perfume will be produced.

COSMETIC WASH FOR THE FACE

Pound a lump of Benzoin gum and put it into a decanter, which fill with spirits of wine, sixty degrees above proof; as soon as the gum is dissolved, add more until the alcohol is thoroughly saturated. A few drops to this tincture in either pure water or rose water is an admirable cosmetic wash for the face.

ROUGH HANDS

Melt a quarter of a pound of fine white wax with an ounce of oil of St. John's Wort, and apply this to the hands as often as you conveniently can, persevering for several weeks until the roughness disappears.

St. John's Wort oil is made by simmering the dried herb in olive oil until herbs have become softened and diffusive. Do NOT strain. Cork and use as required. Strength of this oil is determined by amount of herb and oil used.

Recipe for Dull Dark Hair

Take ¼ oz. of Rosemary, ¼ oz. of Southernwood and ¼ oz. of Quassia chips. Boil together for about 10 minutes in sufficient water to make a rinse.

Premature Grey Hair

Hair that has become prematurely grey may often be restored to its natural color by a good sulphur hair massage. Sprinkle flowers of sulphur over the scalp and massage it into the skin. Do this fairly often to begin with, until the condition of the hair has improved; then once a week will be sufficient to keep the hair in good health. This treatment, together with careful washing and brushing, should definitely improve matters and prevent increasing greyness. It will also strengthen weak and falling hair, although this is often caused by ill health, and a good general tonic may be necessary before a cure can be effected.

Egg Shampoo

Rub the yolks of 2 eggs into the hair, and let stand for 15 or 20 minutes. Shampoo with lukewarm water. Soap is not necessary, as the yolks of eggs will make lather. Use small amount of vinegar or lemon juice in rinse water. Follow with clear water. Egg shampoo is especially useful when hair tangles easily after a permanent.

Recipe for Dandruff

Be sure your comb and brushes are kept scrupulously clean. Brush hair thoroughly night and morning. Use a blunt-edged, large-toothed comb. Apply the following lotion: 3 tablespoonfuls Borax, 3 oz. Rosemary. Steep mixture in 1 quart of boiling water. When cold, add ½ oz. glycerine and 30 drops cologne. If the hair be moist or oily, use one tablespoonful of borax in a two- or three-times weekly shampoo.

A Simple Hair Tonic

1 oz. alcohol, 4 oz. Bay Rum and 10 drops oil of Mace. Shake bottle each time used.

Medicated Oil for Scalp

Mix 1 pint of good grade olive oil with 2 oz. castor oil, 1 oz. sulphur and 1 dram oil of Tar.

Dry Shampoo Powder for Light Hair

Powdered Orris root shaken into the hair from a container with perforated top, and then brushed carefully out, is as good as any other dry shampoo. If the hair is very oily and damp, the powder will absorb the oil and dampness, and make the hair quite dry.

GOLDEN BROWN HAIR

"I tried the recipe for the Golden Brown hair preparation as was told in the Herbalist Almanac, and was very pleased with the result."—Mrs. D. E. C., Barberton, Ohio.

This is the article that appeared in the Herbalist Almanac:

"If your locks are fading and you'd care for a head of lovely golden brown hair with all the highlights of nature's own, try this simple homemade recipe. There's nothing in it that can possibly harm you in any way and the results will prove better than you could reasonably expect. I've been using it for years, and continually have compliments on the beauty of my hair.

"Take a handful of Sage and steep in 1 pint of water for several hours (the longer the darker the tea). Measure 2 rounding teaspoons henna in dry bowl and add 1 teaspoon Ground Cloves, stirring until mixed. Add enough of the Sage tea to this to make a thin paste, stirring until smooth. After shampooing your hair, and rinsing, partially dry it and then cover your scalp with the henna paste mixture, using all it will take. Tie a cloth around the head and leave the paste on for about one-half hour, or longer if a darker shade is desired. Remove cloth and rinse hair in tepid water to remove the paste. A lovely reddish brown head of hair will result, with golden highlights. For a dark brown I sometimes use the liquid from boiled Walnut hulls instead of cloves—but personally, I prefer the lighter shade.—Submitted by R.E.S., Star, Idaho.

Snarly Hair: Add a little hair oil to your hair; then comb out one small strand at a time—or apply alcohol with a piece of cotton, then comb out.

Self-love, my liege, is not so vile a sin as self-neglecting.—Shakespeare.

Perfume Was a Sign of a Higher Culture

With the advent of civilization and the beginning of culture, the ancient art of alchemy sprang up from learning to manipulate various substances. The religious rituals, the art of healing and the art of compounding were closely related in those days.

The various odoriferous substances, domestic and from far off countries, commanded the attention of the ancient compounders, the Egyptian priests and sorcerers, masters of the secret art. These materials consisted, according to the Papyrii of Old Egypt, of various aromatic substances, such as balsams, gums, frankincense, barks, seeds, leaves, flowers, and were used in making of Temple Incense, Perfumes, for baths and ointments.

Perfumes existed in Pharaoh's time. The earliest records of Perfumery art were found in Egypt, dating back to King Menes, about 5000 B. C., and the formula for an Egyptian perfume named "Kyphi" consisting of various gums, olibanum, mastic, aromatic woods, etc., was preserved and occasionally used in various rites for fumigation through centuries up to our time. Perfumes were used for diverse purposes: as offerings to Deities, for esthetic purposes, for a positive stimulating effect on the nervous system and as agents for embalming.

The Greeks, Romans and Arabs excelled in the art of Perfumery. Avicenna, an Arab Physician, in the tenth century was preparing fragrant waters from leaves and flowers of various plants.

Later on this art was rediscovered in the Orient by the invading Crusaders, who brought it back to Europe, where it flourishes namely in the Mediterranean regions since. The credit for actual invention of perfumes as we know them today is given to Mauritius Frangipanni who discovered the process of extracting the odour from aromatic substances with alcohol.

PERFUMES OF OTHER DAYS

(Taken from an 80-year-old scrap book)

Rose water: Put roses into water, add to them a few drops of acid; the vitriolic acid seems to be preferable to any. Soon the water will assume both the color and perfume of the roses. *Another:* Take two pounds of rose leaves; place them on a napkin tied around the edges of a basin filled with hot water, and put a dish of cold water upon the leaves; keep the bottom water hot and change the water at the top as soon as it begins to grow warm. By this kind of distillation you will extract a great quantity of the essential oil of the roses by a process which cannot be expensive and will prove very beneficial.

To Collect the Odors of Flowers: Roses and all flowers containing perfumed oils, may be made to yield their aromatic properties by steeping the petals or flower leaves in a saucer or a flat dish of water and setting it in the sun. The petals should be entirely covered with water, which, by the way, should be soft or rain water. A sufficient quantity should be allowed for evaporation, and the vessel should be left undisturbed for a few days. At the end of this time a film will be found floating on the top. This is the essential oil of the flower, and every particle of it is impregnated with the odor peculiar to the flower. It should be taken up carefully and put in tiny vials, which should be allowed to remain open until all watery particles are evaporated. A very small portion of this will perfume glove boxes, apparel, etc., and will last a long time.

Scented Powder: A charming recipe for scented powder, to be used for wardrobes, boxes, etc., far finer than any mixture sold at the shops, is the following: Coriander, orris root, rose petals, calamus, each one ounce; lavender flowers, two ounces; rhodium wood, one-fourth drachm; musk, five grains. These are to be mixed and reduced to a coarse powder. This scent on clothes is as if all fragrant flowers had been pressed in their folds.

Sachets or Scent Bags: This mixture placed in silk bags or ornamental envelopes is agreeable to smell of and also economical for imparting a pleasing odor to linen and clothes as they are packed away in drawers for they prevent moths. For heliotrope powder, take half a pound of orris root, a quarter pound of ground rose leaves, two ounces of powdered tonquin bean, one ounce vanilla bean, one-half drachm grain musk, two drops otto of almonds; mix it all by sifting through a coarse sieve. This is one of the best sachets ever made and perfumes tablecloths, sheets, pillow cases and towels deliciously. For lavender powder, take one pound of powdered lavender, a quarter pound of gum benzoin and a quarter of an ounce of oil of lavender. For patchouli, use one-half pound of partchouli ground fine and a very little of patchouli oil. Sandalwood sachet is good and consists of the wood ground fine. Cedarwood, when ground, forms a body of other sachet powders and will keep moths at a distance. Dried fennel, when ground, is also used for scenting bags and ground nutmeg is liked for this purpose.

Useful Perfume: A very pleasant perfume, and also a preventive against moths may be made of the following ingredients: Take of cloves, caraway seeds, nutmeg, mace, cinnamon and Tonquin beans, of each one ounce; then add as much Florentine Orris root as will equal the other ingredients put together. Grind the whole well to powder and then put it in little bags among clothes, etc.

HERB LORE

NINON DE LENCLOS was that famous beauty of the old French Court who retained her youthful charms to such a miraculous degree that one of her grandsons fell in love with her when she was seventy. The circumstances were peculiar. He had never seen her before and everything ended most respectably when he found out who she was. What I'm getting at is the news that French historians claim they have discovered the secret formula Ninon used to keep herself looking young. She took Herb baths, and this is how she concocted them: "Take a handful of dried Lavender Flowers, a handful of Rosemary Leaves, handful of Dried Mint, Handful of Comfrey Flowers, and one of Thyme. Mix all together loosely in a muslin bag. Place in your bath, pour on enough boiling water to cover and let soak ten minutes. Then fill up tub. Rest fifteen minutes in the magic water—and think virtuous thoughts."—Submitted by O. M., Columbia, S. C.

Scented "Cakes" for the Wardrobe

After melting 1 oz. paraffine and 2 oz. white petrolatum, mix 10 grains heliotropin. Now add 5 drops oil of Bergamot, 5 drops Oil of Lavender and 2 drops Oil of Cloves, stirring the whole "mass" until cool. After it has settled, cut into small squares and wrap in tin foil until used.

To use, rub on handkerchiefs, clothing, etc.—it not only perfumes the wardrobe but kills moths.—Submitted by Mrs. M. B. Copley, Ohio.

ORRIS
Perfume of Grandmother's Day

Grandmother's favorite perfume was a violet-like scent derived from the roots of Orris—known as Fleur de Lys, or Florentine Iris. The finest scented Orris is grown in the vicinity of Florence, Italy. The roots acquire their violet scent upon drying—the aroma improving and mellowing with age.

Modern perfumes are complicated processes of man's own manipulations. The delicate natural scent of Orris is simply acquired by placing the roots among clothes in closets, drawers, desks, etc.—the roots being put into handkerchiefs, sachets or fancy bags. A variety of scents may be made by mixing with other aromatic botanicals. The root was also much used to scent dry shampoos, dentifrices, and cosmetics.

Orris bags, sachets, etc., offer business opportunity and occupational pastime for convalescent and elderly folks. Bits of lace, silk, cheese-cloth, or other inexpensive materials can be used to make delightful gifts—using plain or mixed Orris.

The following recipes represent a few of the finest of Grandmother's day:

(*Recipes may be simplified or changed to suite taste.*)

Sachet Powders
For sachet-bags, handkerchief cases, bureau pads

Heliotrope: Powdered Orris, 2 oz.; powdered Rose leaves, 1 oz.; Cassia flowers, 1 oz.; Tonka beans, ½ oz.; Vanilla beans, ½ oz.; Oil of Bitter Almonds, 8 drops. Grate the beans, or pulverize in a metal mortar; crumble the Cassia flowers and mix well.

Jockey Club: Cassia flowers, 2 oz.; Rose leaves, ½ oz.; Orris root, ½ oz.; Tonka Beans, ¼ oz.; Vanilla beans, 1 drachm; Musk, 3 grains; oil of Jasmin, 10 drops; Oil of Rose, 10 drops.

Potpourri: Ground Rose leaves and ground Lavender flowers, each 2 oz.; Orris root, 1 oz.; ground Cloves, Alspice and Cinnamon, each 2 drachms.

Perfume Powder: 1 oz. Lavender flowers, 2 drachms powdered Orris root, ½ oz. bruised Rosemary leaves, 5 drops oil of Rose. Mix well.

Frangipanni: Take of powdered Orris, 3 oz.; cut khus-khus root, 2 drachms; ground Sandalwood, 2 drachms; oil of Rose, neroli and sandalwood, each 5 drops.

Triturate oils with Orris: An ounce of white sand assists in blending.

Violet: Wheat starch, 4 lbs.; powdered Orris, 1 lb. Mix together and add attar of Lemon, ¼ oz.; Oils of Bergamot and Cloves, each 1 drachm.

Many people prefer plain Orris in sachets. Orris may be tinted in shades of violet or pink.

Poudre d'Iris: Powdered Orris, 6 lbs.; powdered Bergamot peel and Acacia flowers, each 4 oz.; powdered cloves, ¼ oz. Mix and sift.

Toilet Powder

Corn and rice starch, ½ lb.; Orris root and chalk, each 1 oz.; Oil of Lemon, and Oil of Bergamot, each 15 drops; Oil of Neroli, 10 drops; Oil of Bitter Almonds and Oil of Verbena, each 2 drops. Mix well in a mortar, and pass through a very fine sieve.

Sprinkling Orris powder in gloves counteracts excessive perspiration.

Orris Face Powder

Powdered Orris root, ½ oz.
Rice flour, 3 oz.
Rice starch, 3 oz.
Carbonate of Magnesia, 1½ oz.
Powdered Boric acid, ¼ oz.
Essence of Bergamot, 15 drops.

Orris Foot Powder

A dainty foot powder should be in every woman's toilet dresser, especially if her feet perspire freely:

Powdered Orris root, 1 oz.
Powdered Alum, ½ oz.
Rice powder, 3 oz.

Another Orris Foot Powder Formula

Powdered Orris root, 20 grams
Starch, 20 grams
Alcohol, 2 grams

This should be sprinkled in shoes or stockings, to avoid offensive perspiration odors.

INCENSE OF ANCIENT TIMES

Incense ingredients of ancient civilization and early Christians: Frankincense galbanum, myrrh, mastic, rosemary, opopanax, storax.

Incense ingredients of Oriental nations: Cinnamon, cloves, camphor, dragons blood, galbanum, sandalwood, star anise.

Incenses associated with superstitions: Myrrh, Orris and Sandalwood generally are a part of all such mixtures.

No. 1—Charcoal 5 parts, frankincense 4 parts, sandalwood 3 parts, myrrh 1 part, cinnamon 1 part, orris 1 part, patchouly leaves 1 part, saltpeter ¼ part.

No. 2—Charcoal 8 parts, olibanum 4 parts, sandalwood 2 parts, cinnamon 2 parts, myrrh 1 part, orris root 1 part, saltpeter ½ part.

No. 3—Charcoal 8 parts, winters bark 4 parts, sandalwood 4 parts, orris 2 parts, patchouly 2 parts, myrrh 2 parts, olibanum 2 parts, saltpeter ½ part.

FRENCH RECIPES

French recipe: Charcoal 6 oz.; benzoin 2 oz.; balsam of Tolu ½ oz.; yellow sanders ½ oz.; labdanum 1 dr.; nitre ¼ oz. Mix pulverized ingredients with paste made with gum tragacanth. Form into small cone-shaped pastilles and set out to dry.

Dr. Paris' recipe: Benzoin 1 oz.; cascarilla 1 oz.; myrrh 8 scruples; oil of nutmeg 5 drops; oil of cloves 5 drops; nitre ½ oz.; charcoal 6 oz.; enough tragacanth to make a paste. Form into pastilles.

From an old Apothecary book: Styrax 2½ oz.; benzoin 12 oz.; musk 15 grains; burnt sugar ½ oz.; frankincense 2½ oz.; gum tragacanth 1½ oz.; rosewater sufficient to form pastilles.

A la vanilla: Benzoin, storax and olibanum each 6 oz.; nitre 5 oz.; cloves 4 oz.; vanilla beans ½ pound; charcoal 2 pounds; oil of cloves ½ oz.; essence of vanilla 7 or 8 oz. This is an expensive but good mixture. It may be cheapened by cutting ingredients, or adding more charcoal and substituting deer tongue herb for expensive vanilla beans. Deer tongue has a fine vanilla like aroma, and is used in flavoring tobacco.

The following recipes are from "A Practical Guide For The Perfumer" printed in 1868:

No. 1—Sandalwood 8 oz.; cascarilla 4 oz.; benzoin 4 oz.; khus-khus or vetivert 1 oz.; nitrate of potash 1 oz.; musk ⅛ drachm. All ingredients should be fine ground. If pastilles are desired mix ingredients with paste made of tragacanth, and form into cones. All to set on wax paper until dry.

No. 2—Charcoal 8 oz.; benzoin 6 oz.; Tolu 2 oz.; vanilla 2 oz.; cloves 2 oz.; oil of santal 1 drachm; oil neroli 1 drachm; nitre 1 oz.; mucilage of tragacanth. Prepare pastilles as in recipe No. 1

BELIEF IN THE POWER OF ODORS

"Physicians might (in my opinion) draw more use and good from odors than they do. For myself have often perceived, that according unto their strength and qualities, they change and alter, and move my spirit, and work strange effects in me, which makes me approve the common saying—that invention of incense and perfumers in Churches, so ancient and so far-dispersed throughout all nations and religions, had an especial regard to rejoice, to comfort, to quicken and to arouse and to purifie our senses."—Montaigne.

HIDDEN SECRETS OF NATURE AND SCIENCE

Excellent herbs had our fathers of old
Excellent herbs to ease their pain,
Alexanders and marigold,
Eyebright, orris, and elecampane.

Basil, rocket, valerian, rue
(Almost singing themselves they run),
Vervain, dittery, "Call me to you,"
Cowslip, melilot, rose-of-the-sun;
Anything green that grew out of the mould,
Was an excellent herb to our fathers of old.
—Rudyard Kipling.

HERBS FOR PILLOWS

Scented pillows were popular in old England. The delicate fragrance of herbs was released when pressure was put to the pillow. Each pillow may be made with a different scent. The herbs may be mixed with the pillow stuffing, used entirely as a stuffing, or put into sachet bags, and placed inside the pillow. Scented pillows may be made with practically any fragrant botanical. Some of the most popular ingredients were: Calamus; Khus-Khus or vetivert; lavender flowers; lemon verbena; meadow sweet; orris root; rosemary; rose geranium; sweet fern; vanilla leaf; woodruff; etc.

Scented pillows were also used for the sick room, for their soothing influence. Dr. Fernie wrote in 1914: "A pillow stuffed with hops, was successfully prescribed by Dr. Willis for George The Third, when sedative medicines had failed to give him sleep; and again for our late King Edward VII."

(Note: We do not claim this will invite slumber in everyone.)

Pillows stuffed with white pine needles are still popular in Europe, for their fragrance. Rosemary, or summer or winter savory are sometimes added with the white pine needles.

In India pillows are stuffed with the aromatic leaves of vitex.

In Colonial America, pillows were stuffed with native life-everlasting, for its delicate and soothing aroma. Millspaugh wrote that the dried herb was "recommended as a filling for pillows."

PILLOWS FOR ANIMALS TOO!

Dogs enjoy better sleep on cedar pillows, as the odor repels fleas.

Cats love pillows with valerian roots, thyme or cat mint.

WONDROUS SCENT FROM AUTUMN FIELDS

"Perhaps the herb Everlasting, the fragrant immortelle of our autumn fields, has the most suggestive odor to me of all those that set me dreaming. I can hardly describe the strange thoughts and emotions that come to me as I inhale the aroma of the pale, dry, rustling flowers. A something it has of sepulchral spicery, as if it had been brought from the core of some great pyramid, where it had lain on the breast of a mummied Pharaoh. Something too, of immortality in the sad, faint sweetness lingering so long in its lifeless petals. Yet this does not tell why it fills my eyes with tears, and carries me in blissful thought to the banks of asphodel that border the River of Life."—Oliver Wendell Holmes.

INCENSE

Incense was used since remote ages. It was important in ceremony among pagans and all civilizations. Myrrh probably was held in the highest esteem of all incense ingredients. Sacred history teaches us that Eastern nations looked on Myrrh as one of the most precious productions of the earth. In Moses' time, and before, it was burned on altars, mixed with benzoin. Myrrh was one of the presents brought by the three Kings to Christ at the time of His birth.

The odor of incense was thought to dispose the mind to devotion, produce an elevated mental state, or in some way affect the psychic body.

Incense was probably most widely used during the Middle Ages, when it was put to every imaginable use. Incense was used as a protection against dreaded plagues, as an air purifier, and various ways as a remedial agent. It was burnt at feasts, weddings and sorrowful occasions. Special mixtures were used in black magic and to read the signs of the sun, stars and moon. Mixtures were burnt to gather together the spirits and "chaseth" away evil ones. Mixtures were made for successful business undertakings, love ventures, and a variety of others to strengthen the mind, to make prophetic dreams, to conquer, for good luck, etc. (Note: we do not make supernatural claims for our incenses.)

In the days of the French aristocracy, incense was sometimes important as family emblems. Aristocrats ordered, or made, their own personal concoctions, which were burnt in their private rooms. Clothes were fumigated with the same scent, and even the person became known by his or her particular incense scent.

SCENTED HERBS AS MEDICINE

The odor of fresh picked ripe apples makes our mouth water with desire to eat them.

The smell of pine-woods makes us want to fill our lungs "to the gills" with its refreshing fragrance.

There are countless number of scents that react on us in as many different ways. For ages herbalists believed scented herbs were beneficial to certain mental as well as physical conditions. Old herbals reveal quaint and interesting beliefs. Even the secret of longevity was attributed to inhalation of certain scented herbs. Rycharde Banckes wrote more than 400 years ago that if one would smell often of Rosemary it "shall keep thee youngly." Another herbalist believed that smelling Wild Marjoram frequently would help in staving off old age. Many centuries earlier, Pliny wrote that Anise seed tied in a bag and suspended to the pillow and smelled by the sleeper, it would preserve youth and prevent disagreeable dreams as well.

The pleasing and delicate fragrance of Lavender inspired Turner to write in 1551, "Lavender flowers quilted in a cap and dayly worne are good for all diseases of the head that come of a cold cause and that they comfort the braine very well." The scent of Lavender oil is said to be beneficial for nervous headache. The scent of Lavender water is claimed to powerfully affect lions and tigers. The animals will become quite docile under its influence.

Not all scented herbs are agreeably fragrant as Marjoram, Rosemary and Lavender. The very old and once popular herb, Meadow Sweet, was strewn about because of its peculiar delicate and indescribable odor. It was a favorite strewing herb of Queen Elizabeth. Gerard wrote: "The leaves and flowers of Meadowsweet excel all other herbes for to deck up houses, to strew in chambers, halls and banqueting houses, in the summer time; for the smell thereof makes the heart merrie and delighteth the senses."

German Rue has a powerful and penetrating medicinal odor. Centuries ago in England bunches of Rue were kept upon the bar in criminal courts in belief that it preserved judges from being infected with jail fever which was so prevalent among prisoners brought before them.

Another old belief held that if Sweet Melissa was sewed up in linen (with silk thread) and worn under one's dress it would make the wearer beloved by all. Probably some of our own ancestors used this old and harmless recipe: "Dry roses put to the nose to smell do comfort the brayne and herte and quickeneth the spyryte."

A 300-year-old quill-written note in the Indiana Botanic Garden's copy of *Dodoen's Herbal* states: "Willows brought into chambers and sett about the bede of those that bee sick of agues, doe mightiliy coole the heate of the aire, which thing is wonderfull refreshing to the sick patiente."

In Europe to this day folks make up scented pillows of hops to sleep upon for mania and restlessness. In pioneer American settlements one may still find pillows made of delicate sweet-scented Life Everlasting, white pine needles or fragrant Sweet Fern.

The American Indians also employed scented herbs. Indians of British Columbia made a bedding of the spicy Northern Wild Ginger for infants when they were restless or ill. It was said to make them quiet or well.

Writers as well as herbalists believed in the efficacy of scents. Lord Bacon once wrote: "The heart receiveth benefit or harm most from the air which we breathe, from vapors, and from affections." On a visit to the India House of Amsterdam, Sir William Temple stated that the aromas of numerous spices had a definite tonic effect upon him. John Evelyn proposed to make London the healthiest and happiest city of the world by planting hedgerows of Rosemary, Jasmine and other sweet-scented herbs about the city.

IMPORTANCE OF BREATHING

It is calculated that the area of the walls of the air cells of the lungs in the average healthy person is around 1,800 to 2,000 square feet! From this fact one can form an idea of the great imporance of keeping the thin sensitive walls of the air cells in our lungs healthy and vigorous.

A healthy person requires about 300 cubic inches of air in each inhalation. He usually takes only about 100. Thus, besides this inefficiency of air supply, there always remains a considerable volume of stagnant air in the bottom and the upper parts of the lungs. What happens to all stagnant water, the same law applies here, too. Where there is no life, or sufficient activity, decadence and dissolution of the tissues take place. This is the beginning of T. B., of all other lung ailments and of many other diseases of the human body.

LAVENDER, LAVENDULA VERA

This is the variety made so famous for its sweet essences by the English. In Roman times lavender was already used in considerable amounts for perfumes, bath waters and toilet unguents. It is a beautiful grayish green bush-like plant with slender spikes of small bluish-purple flowers. The flowers are used medicinally, as linen and dresser perfume, sachet, bath water, etc.

THE COLD SITZ-BATH

For disorders of the stomach and bowels, as also for some ailments common to women, the hot or cold water sitz-bath is without equal. This is taken night and morning, or three times daily, by sitting in a foot-bath or zinc bath containing a few inches of cold water, for from 5 to 15 minutes at a time. The upper parts of the body, together with the legs (which are kept outside the bath) must be kept covered, only the lower abdomen and buttocks being immersed. If the whole body is made cold the benefit will be lost. After the bath the parts must be rubbed and warmed immediately.

HIP BATHS IMPROVE VISION

The cold hip baths produce striking temporary improvement in visual functions involving binocular vision, in visual acuity and in critical fusion frequency. They also produce temporary improvement in the rate at which a person can tap a telegraph key and in eye to leg muscle reaction time as shown by automobile driver reaction tests.

Men who took the baths regularly reported feeling exhilarated. Some said that the visual field appeared brighter, that black objects looked blacker and white ones whiter.

To take the bath, the subject sits on a chair with feet resting on another chair or stool and sprays water over his lower abdomen and hips. For the first three to five minutes increasingly hot water, to the limit of comfort, is used. This is gradually changed to tap coldness (45 to 65 degrees Fahrenheit) and the cold water is continued for five to 15 minutes.

PINE BATH

A pine bath is really an age-old practice, but it has recently been revived in the United States. It immediately makes a hit with anybody who tries it because pine has a number of healthful effects, being applicable to many parts of the body. The soothing effect of pine, its restful quality and the pleasant effect on the nose and throat are what have caused the location of sanitaria near pine forests.

The pine bath is simple to prepare. Boil or steam white pine needles and buds until you have a brew which is sufficiently aromatic that when added to the bath water it gives the desired effects.

Perhaps the most striking effect of the pine bath is in a general state of fatigue. It is slightly rubefacient, that is to say, it causes a redness and increased circulation of the skin, and this, in conjunction with the odor and the clearing of the nasal passages and the nose, produces a wonderfully relaxing and stimulating effect. Little rheumatic pains or stiffness of the joints are also favorably affected by this rubefacient quality.

To anyone who is engaged in a nervous and continually high-strung occupation, the use of a pine bath after returning home in the afternoon is an experience which can hardly be adequately described.

The full value of a bath as a pick-up is not felt unless one takes it slowly and luxuriously. At least 20 minutes should be given to it, with thorough rubbing of the skin afterwards so that you feel as if your skin were tingling with vitality.

(See Special Notice, Page ¶)

TURKISH BATH

This bath cannot be recommended for every individual; it is too heroic for feeble people. Persons who are reasonably strong, and who have a well-balanced circulation, may take the Turkish bath with no serious effects during or after it; perhaps with benefit, especially where the dietetic habits are bad, and the skin is greasy. But those who live hygienically, the skin being unobstructed and depurating freely, will seldom or never require this bath; and where the heart's action is feeble, or there is a tendency to congestion in the brain or other organs, a treatment so heroic would be dangerous.

REFRESHING HERBAL WASH

The following recipe makes a delicious, refreshing and cooling wash for the sick room:

Take of Rosemary, Wormwood, Lavender, Rue, Sage and Mint a large handful of each. Place in a stone jar, and turn over it one gallon of strong cider vinegar, cover closely, and keep near the fire for four days; then strain and add one ounce of pounded camphor gum. Bottle and keep tightly corked.

There is a French legend connected with this preparation called VINAIGRE a QUATRE VOLEURS. During the plague at Marseilles, a band of robbers plundered the dying and the dead without injury to themselves. They were imprisoned, tried and condemned to die, but were pardoned on condition of disclosing the secret whereby they could ransack houses infected with the terrible scourge. They gave the above recipe. Another mode of using it is to wash the face and hands with it before exposing one's self to any infection. It is very aromatic and refreshing in the sick-room; so, if it can accomplish nothing more, it is of great value to nurses.

SCIENTISTS APPROVE GRANDMA'S REMEDIES

Philadelphia—(INS)—Science has proved that grandma really knew her vegetables when she fumigated the disease-laden air of a sick room by boiling a pot of onions.

Russian chemists have learned that onion vapors have bactericidal properties which can be used to heal infected wounds, according to Edward F. Kohman, a Philadelphia chemist.

Onions were one of grandma's stock household remedies whether for curing a common cold or a baby's fever.

FANCIFUL BEAUTY AIDS OF THE PAST

Herbals of the Elizabethan period claim that an ointment made from Cowslip flowers and hog's grease "taketh away the spots and wrinkles of the skin, and doth add beauty exceedingly, as divers ladies, gentlewomen and she citizens whether wives or widows."

From an old English herbal: "Fumitory was formerly much favoured for making cosmetic washes to purify the skin of rustic maidens in the springtime":

"Whose red and purpled mottle flowers
Are cropped by maids in weeding hours,
To boil in water, milk and whey,
For washes on a holiday;
To make their beauty fair and sleek,
And scare the tan from summer's cheek."

Brunswyke wrote in 1527, "I have heard that if maids will take Wild Tansy and lay it to soake in buttermilk for a space of nine days and wash their face therewith, it will make them look very faire."

Culpepper wrote of Southernwood: "Boiled with barley-meal it removes pimples and wheals from the face or other parts of the body." Of Water Cress he wrote: "The leaves bruised or the juice is good to be applied to the face or other parts troubled with freckles, pimples, spots or the like at night and washed away in the morning."

In Galen's time the distilled water of Solomons Seal was used by ladies as a cosmetic for removing pimples and freckles from the skin.

In the Middle Ages, Fennel seed was chewed during fasting days as it was supposed to dull the appetite. An old recipe "for to make one slender: Take Fennel and seethe it in water, a very good quantity, and wring out the juice thereof, when it is sod, drink it first and last, and it shall swage either him or her."

Gerard wrote, "The gentlewomen of France do paint their faces with these roots (Alkanet)." Alkanet root has been used since very ancient times.

An old fashioned method of removing discoloration from teeth was by rubbing fresh strawberries on them.

From Banckes' Herbal: "Boyle the leaves (Rosemary) in white wine and washe thy face therewith and thy browes and thou shalt have a faire face."

Mary: "I can't marry him, Father. He's an atheist and doesn't believe there's a hell."
Father: "Go ahead and marry him, Mary; you'll convert him."

OLD HOUSEHOLD USE OF HERBS

In olden times sophisticated folk rubbed fresh mint on furniture for its oily content and its refreshing aroma.

In the Middle Ages, fresh Tansy herb was wrapped around meats as a preservative and to discourage insects.

From "Herbal Simples": "The juice from the bulbs of Garlic can be employed for cementing broken glass or China by force of its mucilage."

Scouring Rush is still used in Europe for cleaning greasy and burnt crusted pots and pans. A smaller and finer blade variety of Rush called Pewterwort is used for polishing pewter utensils, other metals, wood utensils, cabinets, etc. Pewterwort is better known as Horsetail Grass in this country. The American Indians used Horsetail Grass to polish off their arrow shafts.

Before the days of insulation and cooling systems, Gerard wrote of Woodruff: "hanged up in houses, in the heat of summer, doth very well attemper the air, cool and make fresh the place, to the delight and comfort of such as are therein."

Gerard wrote in regards to Herb Twopence, (Lysimachia), "The smoke of the burned herbe driveth away serpents and killeth flies and rats in the house."

SKAAL

Jean Hersholt told us of the true meaning of the Danish toast—"Skaal." You will recognize it because it is close to a similar word, with slight variations in spelling, in other Scandinavian countries.

Each letter in the word *"Skaal"* means something. For instance, the Danish word for *health* starts with an "s;" *love* begins with "k;" *old age* with "a;" and "a" also stands for—*many talents*. The Danish word for *luck* starts with an "l" as does our word. Put together these letters spell s-k-a-a-l . . . SKAAL. So, when a Dane raises his glass and toasts a friend he means—

"Here's to your health and to your love; may your old age be happy; may you have many talents, and may you have good luck!"

KITCHEN CONCERNS

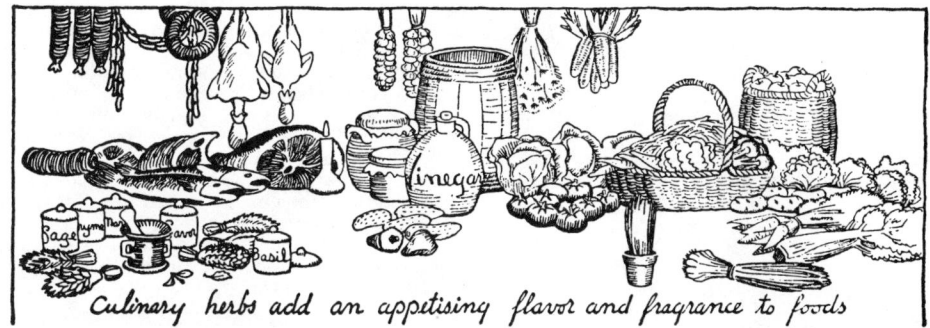
Culinary herbs add an appetising flavor and fragrance to foods

CULINARY VINEGARS
Tarragon Vinegar
Put fresh Tarragon leaves into a stone jar and pour on them a sufficient quantity of the best wine vinegar to cover them. Set the jar in a warm place for 14 days; then strain through a jelly bag. (In the same way may be made elder-flower, basil, green mint, and burnet vinegars. Cress and Celery vinegars are made with ½ oz. of the bruised seed to a quart of vinegar. Horseradish vinegar, with 3 oz. of the scraped root, 1 oz. of minced shallots, 1 dr. of cayenne, to a quart of vinegar. Garlic vinegar is made with 2 oz. of minced garlic to a quart of wine vinegar. Shallot vinegar in the same proportion. Chilli vinegar, with 50 English chillies, cut or bruised (or ¼ oz. cayenne pepper), to a pint of the best vinegar; digest for 14 days.)

Camp Vinegar
Take 12 chopped anchovies, 2 cloves of garlic minced, 1 dr. of cayenne, 2 oz. of soy, 4 oz. of walnut catsup, and a pint of the best vinegar; digest for a month and strain.

Or

Vinegar a quart, walnut catsup a pint, mushroom catsup 3 tablespoonfuls, garlic 4 heads, cayenne ½ oz., soy 2 tablespoonfuls, port wine 2 glasses, 3 anchovies, and a tablespoonful of salt; put them into a bottle, shake daily for a month, and decant.

Curry Vinegar
Infuse 3 oz. of curry powder in a quart of vinegar, near the fire, for 3 days.

Raspberry Vinegar
Macerate 2 lb. of fresh raspberries with a pint of the best vinegar for 14 days and strain. Or to a quart of the juice add 2 oz. of strong acetic acid, or enough to render it sufficiently acid.

French Spice Vinegar
Take Basil, Thyme, Rosemary, and Tarragon, a handful of each—two handfuls of Marjoram, Balm, Mint, Curled Mint and Bay leaves together, two spoonfuls crushed dill seed, one spoonful black pepper and allspice mixed, and finally pounded cloves. Put all this in a large bottle with a wide neck and pour on to it good vinegar, and let it stand in a warm room 2 or 3 weeks; then strain the vinegar and keep it well covered. A little of this used in steak sauces and ragouts imparts a fine taste and saves much spicing. This vinegar has the special merit of communicating its flavor immediately.

MIXED SPICES AND SAVORY HERBS
Italian Tamara
Coriander seed, cloves, and cinnamon, of each 8 oz.; anise and fennel seeds, of each 4 oz.; mix.

Sweet Spice
Equal weights of cloves, mace, nutmegs, cinnamon, and sugar.

Ragout
Salt 16 oz., pepper 8 oz., nutmeg, ginger, and allspice, each ¼ oz., lemon peel 8 oz., mustard flour 8 oz., cayenne 2 oz., mix.

Sausage
Pepper 5 lb., cloves 1½ lb., nutmegs 1½ lb., ginger 2½ lb., anise seed ½ lb., coriander seed ½ lb. Mix.

Savoury Ragout
Salt 2 oz., mustard, black pepper, and grated lemon peel, of each 1 oz., allspice, ginger and nutmeg, of each ½ oz., cayenne ¼ oz.

Soup Herb Powder, or Vegetable Relish
Dried parsley, winter savoury, sweet marjoram, lemon thyme, of each 2 oz., dried lemon peel and sweet basil, of each 1 oz.: mix. They should be carefully dried in a Dutch Oven, powdered, passed through a hair sieve and kept in closely-covered bottles. For sauces, soups, etc.

Peas Powder
Pound together in a marble mortar 2 oz. each of dried mint and sage, ¼ oz. each of celery seed and black pepper, and rub them through a hair sieve.

Horseradish Powder
Take up the roots in November or December, dry them carefully with a gentle heat, and reduce to powder.

Soup Herb and Savory Powder
Mix three parts of "Soup Herb Powder, or Vegetable Relish" with one part of "Savoury Ragout."

CULINARY HERBS

Thyme
Flavor: Mint with mild, pine-like fragrance.

Chopped fresh leaves or ground dried herbs used with beef, pork, mutton, game, poultry, stews, soups, dressings, sauces, gravies, pickles, vegetables, etc. Dishes which require long cooking should not be flavored with thyme until about an hour before the food is finished cooking.

Garden Marjoram
Flavor: Similar to thyme; aromatic, peppery.

Chopped fresh leaves, ground dried herb often used in dishes with thyme or used alone in dishes listed under thyme. It should not be cooked too long.

Summer Savory
Flavor: Peppery coriander seed-like taste.

Fresh or dried herb used sparingly on lima beans, dried beans, string beans, peas, veal, pork and poultry dressing. Cook herb with foods.

Sweet Basil
Flavor: Spicy, clove-like.

Sprinkle the minced, fresh leaves on soups and stews just before taking from the fire. Basil may be used in sauces, salads, tomato dishes and making spicy vinegar. It is often used with Tarragon. In dry form it is used in flavoring sausage. For soups and stews, Basil in dry form may be put in a small cloth bag so that it can be removed before serving.

Tarragon
Flavor: Piquant.

Tarragon Vinegar is made from this herb. Its flavor is perfect for sauces and pickling. Used also in meat, stews, soups and salads.

Sage
Flavor: Aromatic.

Minced fresh leaves or ground dried herb used for pork, sausage, poultry dressing and tomato dishes. Cook with hot dishes.

Garden Burnet
Flavor: Like Mild Cucumber.

Fresh chopped leaves used in green salads.

Garden Sorrel
Flavor: Sour.

Chopped fresh leaves used in soups and salads.

Herba-Barona
Flavor: Like Caraway Seed.

Sprig of fresh herb on beef roast. This is a famous old English dish.

CHIVES
Chives contain a large amount of mustard oil which gives them their sharp "taste." They are claimed to "stimulate the appetite, help secrete the gastric juices by stimulating the digestive organs," and "exercise a strong diuretic effect." They are referred to as "digestive stimulants, exciting the flow of saliva and gastric juice." They are said to "aid in dissolving phlegm in catarrh." Because of their *strong diuretic action*, "it is commonly believed that these vegetables are particularly beneficial as a blood cleanser."—*Dr. Shelton's Hygienic Review*.

IRISH STEW
Take 2 or 3 pounds of the neck of mutton and cut it into chops; pare 3 pounds of potatoes, cut them into thick slices, put them into a stew pan with a quart of water, 2 or 3 carrots, turnips or onions may be added (the last seldom omitted); salt and pepper the mutton when added to the gravy; let it boil or simmer gently 2 hours and serve very hot.

ONION OMELET
Cut some onions into slices, give them a few turns over the fire; when nearly done, moisten them with cream and season with salt and pepper; mix this with 4 or 5 eggs; beat the whole up well and fry the omelet in butter or bacon fat.

TARRAGON VINEGAR
Place 1 box (two boxes for stronger) of our French Tarragon in one quart of good cider vinegar. Cover and allow to stand 14 days. Strain. One tablespoon of Tarragon vinegar with two tablespoons of salad oil, plus salt, makes a very fine French dressing for green salads. Tarragon vinegar adds piquant flavor to meat sauces, stews, pickles, etc.

SPONGE LOAF CAKE
Especially good for Strawberry Short Cake.
Time: 45 to 50 minutes.

1 cup pastry flour 3 tablespoons cold
1 cup sugar water
4 eggs 1 teaspoon vanilla

Measure flour after sifting once. Sift again with sugar 5 times. Separate eggs and beat yolks until thick and lemon colored. Add water and continue beating. Add vanilla then fold in flour and sugar. Lastly, fold in the stiffly beaten egg whites. Bake in an ungreased 7-inch tube pan at 350 degrees.

TO CURE HAMS
Eight pounds coarse salt, 4 gallons water, 4 ounces salt petre, 2 pounds brown sugar; boil, stirring well to dissolve the ingredients; skim, and when cold pour over the meat, which must always be kept well covered with the pickle. Hams to remain in pickle 1 month, or a few days longer if very large. This recipe, if carefully prepared, never fails to make delicious hams.

SPICES AND FLAVORS

Allspice. An aromatic berry used for flavoring cakes, frostings, puddings, soups, jellies, sauces, pickles, chow-chow, piccalilli, etc. It is often used with cloves, nutmeg and cinnamon.

Arrow Root. This West Indian plant tuber contains a starch which is very nutritive. It is very easily digested and used in puddings, cookies for babies and in the diet for those recuperating as it is nourishing.

Bay Leaves. Used with soups, stews, beef roasts, gravies, sauces, pickles, etc.

Boteka. A popular leaf seasoning in the Nuevo Leon section of Mexico. Whole leaves are used like Bay leaves. They are particularly fine with steaks and beef roasts. The cut leaves are used as a tea for indigestion and tonic.

Canella Bark. A very pleasing aromatic bark used as a condiment. It is often known as "white cinnamon" and used similarly.

Cloves. Used in cooking apples, apple pie, ham, spiced fruits, chow-chow, piccalilli, watermelon rind, cucumber pickles.

Cassia Buds. Used in pickling and potpourris.

Cayenne. A pinch will "pep up" barbecues, sauces, etc. Whole dried pods or powdered.

Cinnamon. Powdered cinnamon used in apple sauce, apple and pumpkin pies, cakes, bread, toast, rolls, spiced fruits, etc. Whole sticks used in pickling.

Dill Herb. Used for pickling, in beef sauce, boiled fish, bean soup, etc. Young leaves are used for seasoning salads, also stirred in mayonnaise.

Fennel Herb. Used alone or with Thyme in flavoring foods. Particularly good with baked fish. Tender fresh leaves used in salads and stirred in mayonnaise.

Garlic. Adds a delicious mild flavor to salads when rubbed on salad bowl. Excellent with pork or beef. May be rubbed on meat or small pieces may be inserted.

Jamaica Ginger. Powdered root used in cakes, bread (ginger), baked fruits, relishes, pumpkin pies and spiced pears, etc.

Mace. This is more delicate in flavor than Nutmeg. It is the outer covering of the nutmeg kernel. Used like nutmeg.

Nutmeg. Used in baking, spicing fruits, etc.

Paprika. This gives that sweet flavor to so many Hungarian dishes.

Peppercorns. One or two berries used with beef, pot roast, corned beef, gravies, in pickling, etc.

St. John's Bread. A long pod with sweetish honey and nut-like flavored pulp. In the Mediterranean and Balkan regions delicious tarts, cookies and cakes are made from the ground St. John's Bread.

Tumeric. Powdered roots used as condiment, in curry powders and as yellow coloring. Whole root used in pickling.

TO MAKE GRAVY WITHOUT MEAT

Slice three onions, and fry them in a little brown butter. Add to them two teacups of water and the same of beer, salt to taste, a little fine lemon peel, pepper, ketchup, a pinch of Marjoram and a pinch of Savory, and a slice of toasted bread. Simmer it in a saucepan 20 minutes, skim off the fat, and strain it. It tastes exactly as though made with meat.

APPLE BREAD

Stew or grate some apple, and mix it well with wheat flour. Add a little sugar, and yeast enough to raise it. Prepare it the same as wheat bread. It requires a little longer baking.

RICE AND WHEAT BREAD

Simmer a pound of rice in two quarts of water till it is perfectly soft. When it is lukewarm, mix it very well with four pounds of flour, three cakes of compressed yeast dissolved in a pint of water, a little salt, as for other bread. When well kneaded, set it to rise before the fire. Bake as other bread. This is a very nutritious, healthful and economical bread.

POTATO BREAD

Boil 12 mealy potatoes, work them with a small piece of butter and as much milk as will cause them to pass through a colander. Take half a pint of yeast, and the same quantity of warm water, mix it with the potatoes and pour the whole on five pounds of flour; add salt, as usual and, if necessary, to knead it well, more milk and water; then let it stand to rise before the fire.

SPICES FOR SEASONING ALSO PREVENT FOOD RANCIDITY

Certain spices prevent food's edible fats from turning rancid according to scientists of the National Chemical Laboratory in Poona, India. Previously it has commonly been assumed that spices were added to foods, particularly in tropical countries, to cover up rancidity or decay. They report that Cumin, Caraway or Fennel seeds, Cinnamon, Nutmeg, Cloves, Pepper, Turmeric and red Chillies are among the spices that will preserve fats even under very severe oxidation tests.

SPICED CITRON PRESERVES

Grate the yellow rind from the fruit, cube and parboil the white inner rind. The fruit is then placed in a sirup made of one cup of sugar to one cup of water and cloves and cinnamon are added to the boiling mixture. Seal in jars.

SPICED VINEGAR FOR PICKLES

1 gallon of vinegar
1 pound of sugar
2 tablespoonfuls of allspice
2 tablespoonfuls of mustard seed
2 tablespoonfuls of celery seed
2 tablespoonfuls of salt
1 tablespoonful of turmeric powder
1 tablespoonful of black pepper
1 tablespoonful of mace
2 nutmegs, grated
3 onions
1 handful of grated horseradish

SPICED SALT

¼ ounce of thyme
¼ ounce of bay leaf
¼ ounce of pepper
⅛ ounce of marjoram
⅛ ounce of cayenne pepper
½ ounce of cloves
½ ounce of nutmeg, grated

Dry, powder and sift these, thoroughly mixed. To every four ounces of this mixture add one ounce of salt. Keep in an air-tight box or can. This is an excellent seasoning for soups, dressings, veal loaf, etc. One ounce to three pounds of dressing is sufficient.

MULLED WINE

Boil some spices, cloves, nutmeg, cinnamon, or mace, in a little water; then add a wineglass of sherry, or any kind of wine, and some sugar; bring it to the boiling point, and serve with toast. If claret is used, it will require a good deal of sugar.

GINGER SNAPS

1 cup of molasses
½ cup of butter or shortening, heated and put in the molasses
¼ cup of water
1 teaspoonful of soda
1½ teaspoonsful of ginger

Flour enough to roll rather soft. Bake in a quick oven.

TOMATO MUSTARD

One peck of tomatoes and one teaspoonful of salt. Boil in a preserve kettle half an hour; strain it through a colander, and return it to the kettle with the following:
1 dessert-spoonful of ground cloves
1 dessert-spoonful of allspice
1 dessert-spoonful of black pepper
1 dessert-spoonful of ginger
1 dessert-spoonful of cayenne pepper

Let it boil down considerably; then strain it through a sieve, and add flour of mustard until the proper thickness is obtained, and simmer for a short time. Bottle for use.

FRENCH MUSTARD

Slice up an onion in a bowl; cover with good vinegar, and leave two or three days. Pour off the vinegar into a basin, and put into it
1 teaspoonful of pepper
1 teaspoonful of salt
1 tablespoonful of brown sugar, and
Mustard enough to thicken

Smooth the mustard with a little of the vinegar as you would flour for gravy. Mix it, set on the stove and stir until it boils, then remove and use it cold.

AROMATIC MUSTARD

6 tablespoonfuls of ground mustard
1 tablespoonful of flour
2 tablespoonfuls of sugar
1 teaspoonful of salt
1 teaspoonful of pepper
1 teaspoonful of cloves
1 teaspoonful of cinnamon

Mix with vinegar in which one onion has been boiled. Let stand before using.

BOILED TOMATO CATSUP

Put half a bushel of tomatoes on the fire and boil gently for one hour, then press through a sieve. Return the juice to the kettle and boil very low; add a quart of strong vinegar and boil half an hour; then add—
¼ of a pound of sugar
½ a teacup of salt
1 ounce of black pepper
1 ounce of allspice
½ ounce of cloves
¼ teaspoonful of cayenne pepper
And stir until well mixed

Put a small pinch of powdered assafoetida in a glass, with two tablespoonfuls of vinegar, pour in the kettle and stir until it boils. Take up, bottle and seal.

RED PEPPER CATSUP

Take four dozen red peppers; put on the fire in a quart of vinegar and water each, with two roots of horseradish, grated, and six onions, sliced. Season with salt, pepper, mustard seed and spice. Boil ten minutes and strain. Then add a teacup of brown sugar, two ounces of celery seed and one of mace, with a pint of strong vinegar. Boil one hour.

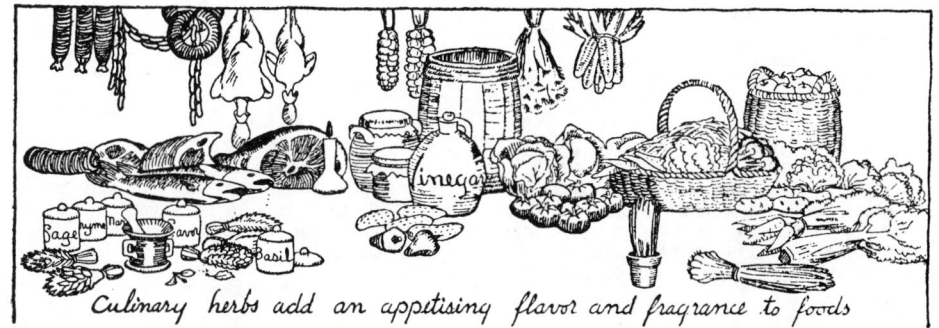
Culinary herbs add an appetising flavor and fragrance to foods

SPICED VINEGAR

This is a very useful article to keep on hand to use with fish, oysters, or cold meats sliced. None but the nicest quality of pure cider vinegar should be used for the purpose. Any flavor may be used by itself, or several together. Gather such herbs as you prefer, and let them remain a long time in a jar of vinegar, until the flavor is extracted. Mint, Sage, and sweet marjoram, in equal parts, import a good flavor. Celery seed pounded and soaked in vinegar is very fine.

HONEY VINEGAR

One pint of strained honey and two gallons of soft water. Let it stand in a moderately warm place. In three weeks it will be excellent vinegar.

LIKES TARRAGON FLAVOR

"Some time ago I sent for a box of Tarragon leaves and I must say I never had anything that blended so good with vinegar. I love the taste of it."—Mrs. W. S. P., Shelbyville, Ind.

Tarragon vinegar is simple to make. Directions with each box. Once you have tried Tarragon vinegar you will always use it.

A SPICY HERB

Mother Nature offers us an unlimited assortment of pleasantly scented and flavored plants. Outstanding among these plants we find Sweet Basil one of the most agreeable. This herb has a sweet spicy clove-like fragrance. It is used in many ways to impart its flavor in foods. A few fresh leaves are added to soups or stews just before food is taken from the fire. In dry form, the herb is put in small cloth bags so that it can be removed when proper flavor is obtained. The dried herb is used in sausage, sauces, salads, tomato dishes and making of spicy vinegar. Sweet Basil and Tarragon herb form a very good flavoring combination.

ONION VINEGAR

Chop six large onions and sprinkle over them one tablespoonful of salt. Then set away to stand six hours. Dissolve a tablespoonful of white sugar in one quart of best cider vinegar, scald and turn hot over the chopped onions. Cover the vessel and let it stand two weeks, then strain out the liquor and bottle for use.

GARLIC VINEGAR

Steep an ounce of garlic in two quarts of the best white wine vinegar; add a nutmeg scraped. This vinegar is much esteemed by the French.

HERB SAUCE

Parsley, celery leaves, chives, borage, 1 tablespoon thick, sour cream, 1 of olive oil 1-2 of vinegar, mustard, salt, pepper.

Take desired quantity of herbs, chop fine, and mix with the other ingredients; season to taste.

Note: 1-2 hard-boiled, chopped eggs, and 1 chopped onion will greatly improve the sauce.

PIQUANT GRAVY

One tablespoon lard, one heaping tablespoon flour, 1 large or several small onions, cut fine, water and meat gravy, or bouillon, pepper, allspice, salt, sugar bay leaves dill, vinegar, Chili sauce, whole mustard, celery seed.

Melt the lard, brown the flour in it, add the onion; when this begins to brown, pour in the water and meat gravy or rich bouillon, add the spices, vinegar and sugar to taste; boil ½ hour; when done it must be like thick cream; add the Chili sauce and serve.

Excellent for sliced remnants of beef roast or sliced soup meat, which must be simmered in the gravy 20-30 minutes. Also very nice with plain boiled potatoes instead of gravy.

When flavoring foods with herbs—the taste and flavor of foods SHOULD predominate. The flavoring herbs should ONLY give foods a touch of nature's fragrance.

SAVORY SEEDS

The general uses mentioned with savory seeds are by no means complete. They may be used with any food where the flavor of a particular seed is desired.

Anise—Used in flavoring cookies, pastries, soup, beets, salads, liqueurs and cordials.

Caraway—Used in flavoring roast goose, duck and pork; bakery, black bread, salt rolls and sticks; Kuemmel and liqueurs, cottage cheese, cheeses, sauerkraut, roast apples, Hungarian goulash, etc. Caraway may also be used with Thyme, Marjoram and Savory.

Cardamon—Used in flavoring cookies, cakes, candies, curry powders and liqueurs. It is said the Syrians use one or two of these highly aromatic (whole) seeds with coffee.

Celery—Used in flavoring catsup, pickles, soups, French dressings, salads, sauces, gravies, cabbage and beet dishes. Also used with spicy herbs, Basil, Tarragon, Marjoram.

Coriander—Used in flavoring bakery pastries, confections, sausage, pickles, cordials, liqueurs, etc. Also used with Savory, Marjoram and Thyme.

Cumin—Used in flavoring liqueurs, pastries, baking, soups, salads, meats, cheese, sauerkraut and spicy dishes. Fine with culinary herbs.

Dill—Used in flavoring vinegar, pickles, sauces, gravies, soups, fish, etc.

Fennel—Used in flavoring, black bread, sauerkraut, soups, fish, and sauces. Fennel is also used with culinary herbs.

Mustard—*Black or White*—The Black Mustard Seed is stronger than White. They are used in sauces, pickles and curry powders. Ground Mustard Seed is particularly fine with Sage when rubbed on pork roast.

Poppy—Used on cookies, cakes, bread, rolls, etc.

"By chase our long lived fathers earn'd their food;
Toil strung the nerves, and purified the blood:
But we their sons, a pamper'd race of men,
Are dwindled down to threescore years and ten.
Better to hunt in fields, for health unbought,
Than fee the doctor for a nauseous draught;
The wise, for cure, on exercise depend;
God never made his work for man to mend."
— *John Dryden.*

PRESERVING PORK SAUSAGE

Take fresh made sausage, make it into balls as for the table, cook it slowly, but well done; then lay it evenly in a tin can or earthen jar, pouring all the grease that fries from the meat over it, as each layer is placed in the can. When done cooking the meat should be entirely covered with lard to exclude the air.

SEASONING FOR PORK SAUSAGE

To 10 pounds of meat, add 4 ounces of salt, 2 of black pepper, and 1 ounce of sage. Mix thoroughly.

INDIAN METHOD OF COOKING CLAMS

Wash them clean, place them point downwards upon the earth, or on the hearth; put over them burning coals and cinders, and roast till they incline to spring open. They are most delicious in this way, eaten directly from the shells.

Three Bay Leaves

The Bay leaves we all are familiar with come from the Mediterranean regions. The aromatic leaves are used in pickling, spiced vinegars, stews, beef roasts, consomme, purees, croquettes, tomato casserole, canned tomato soup, etc. A single leaf is used in soups, also in water to boil potatoes.

Besides the imported Bay, there are two other varieties which are used in the same way in localities where they are found. These native American varieties have distinctive flavors of their own. Each deserves a trial. You may prefer them to common Bay.

Indian Bay, also known as California Laurel, is a native of California, and was formerly much used by the Indians for flavoring food as well as for medicine. Indian Bay leaves have a flavor similar to common Bay, excepting that its leaves are decidedly more fragrant and have a peppery tang.

Another variety of Bay, found growing in the Monterrey regions of Mexico, is better known as Boteka. This variety has a cool, mild fragrance. Boteka is also used to make a very pleasant tea.

CHIVES (SCHNITTLAUCH)

The chopped blades of Chives add a delicious flavor when sprinkled on cottage cheese, potatoes, salads, sandwiches, soups, stews, meats, gravies, etc. Chives may be planted in a pot for winter use.

PAPAYA USED FOR BURNS

A new aid in the treatment of burns may come from a tropical fruit, it appears from the report of Dr. G. R. Cooper and Dr. J. W. Beard of Duke University, before the meeting.

Papaya juice, from the fruit and leaves of the tropical American papaw or papaya tree, contains an enzyme, papain, which helps remove damaged tissue in the burned area, the scientists found. Papain by itself is not too effective but when combined with an amino acid, cysteine, its action is increased. Addition of sodium salicylate, close relative of aspirin, makes the injured tissues more susceptible to the papain-cysteine action—From *Science News Letter.*

Ginger Tips

Ginger should NEVER be boiled, as boiling dissipates its strength and destroys the aromatic flavor. Ginger tea is generally made by pouring ½ pint of boiling water over 1 teaspoonful of the cut root, and allowed to steep several minutes. When using the powdered root, a paste should first be made by adding a small amount of cold water with powder, stirring until thoroughly mixed; then add hot water. Place a saucer over steeping tea in order to preserve its aromatic properties.

Ginger is grown in India, China, Japan, Africa and the West Indies. The world's finest Ginger, however, comes from the mountains of Jamaica— supply is obtained DIRECT from Jamaica growers. This SEASONAL FRESH stock is kept in air-tight containers and kept whole until used, because few botanicals deteriorate more rapidly than this root. Exposed to the air, it shrinks to a hard, useless wood, as the oils contained in the wood are extremely volatile. Much of the Ginger offered today stands or is shoved around in warehouses by buyers, handlers and manufacturers. As the roots arrive in gunny sacks, much is lost by the time the consumers get the article.

Chilled?

Try hot milk with a good pinch of powdered Ginger.

WHY GINGER IS POPULAR IN THE TROPICS

CAUTION: Too much Ginger hinders digestion.

A small quantity of Ginger used as a seasoning, or a bit taken at the close of a meal, aids digestion, in preventing unnatural fermentations from springing up and overpowering the natural, weaker ones. For this reason, Curry powder, or fresh or ground Ginger, are a constant ingredient in meat dishes, in the very hot climates. They stimulate digestion. If spices and high seasonings are ever to be recommended, it certainly is in hot weather, when the digestion is rather sluggish. Adding a pinch of Ginger to foods is far better than drinking artificially-flavored, synthetic-colored iced drinks, pops, etc.

As no two constitutions are alike, discover for yourself the right size "pinch" of Ginger you need. Begin sparingly and add more according to taste and need.

Caribbean Ginger Drink

To each pint of cold water, add ⅓ cup of good vinegar, 2 teaspoonfuls of ground Ginger, and 6 teaspoonfuls of granulated sugar. Keep covered in cool place. A thirst satisfier —used in summer on some of the Caribbean islands.

Flavoring Extract of Ginger

Take 4 ounces of ground Jamaica Ginger, 1 pint of grain alcohol. Macerate the ginger in the spirits (in a closed vessel) for a fortnight or more; then filter it through a little cotton-wool placed in the neck of an ordinary tin funnel. Repeat the percolation three or four times, adding enough alcohol to bring the extract up to the full measure.

This extract is intended to be used exclusively in the kitchen; though if one wishes he may of course use it also "for the stomach's sake."

Aromatic Extract of Ginger

Take 4 ounces of powdered Jamaica ginger, 1 ounce finely ground Cardamon seeds, ½ ounce each of powdered Cinnamon and Cloves, ⅛ of an ounce of Oil of Peppermint, 1 pint pure grape brandy. Macerate the Ginger, Cardamon seed, cinnamon and cloves in half the brandy one week; then filter it through a little cotton-wool placed in the neck of an ordinary tin funnel. Repeat the percolation three or four times. To the clear liquid add the Oil of Peppermint. Bottle tight and shake well until the oil is well cut.

While this extract imparts an excellent flavor to some kinds of cookery, gingerbread, spice cakes and the like, its highest value consists in adding a few drops of it to a glass of sweetened water, to form a healthful beverage, etc.

Add a pinch of ground ginger to French dressing the next time you toss up a salad.

SPICY MEDICINE of the AGES

Ginger hath a warming concocting power, mollifying of the belly gently, and good for ye stomach.—Goodyer's translation of 1900-year-old Herbal.

Ginger tea is an excellent stimulant and carminative in flatulency of the stomach and bowels, caused by eating green fruit, or irritating articles of diet.

Dyspeptic patients from hard drinking have been known to receive considerable benefit by drinking 1 or 2 cupfuls of Ginger tea for breakfast.

Gout Medicine in Early 1800's

"Many gouty patients have been in the habit of taking a teaspoonful of Ginger powder, mixed in any liquid, an hour before dinner, and they declare with considerable advantage."—Robt. Thorton, M.D., 1814.

Ginger as a Stimulant

Hot Ginger tea is an emergency medicine in cases in which brandy or whisky is given to produce an immediate stimulating influence. From half a teaspoonful to a teaspoonful will produce greater stimulation than half an ounce of brandy.

Ginger tea stimulates the stomach actively, producing a pleasing sense of warmth. It relieves flatulence, and quickly helps flatulent colic. In atonic conditions of the stomach and intestinal tract, it stimulates the structure to renewed activity, and materially assists in the restoration of normal tone. It helps relieve pain from any cause, *except inflammatory action, when this remedy must be avoided.*

Ginger for Coughs

The infusion of Ginger root has been used with benefit in cases of simple bronchial catarrh, such as aged persons are subject to.

The powdered root mixed with honey or molasses, or the root chewed and swallowed, is often useful for coughs.

"The Garden of Health," printed in 1633, advises eating Ginger-flavored roasted apples for cough. As heat dissipates properties of Ginger, the powder should be sprinkled over the sugared apples just before removing from fire.

Ginger root is chewed for increasing the flow of saliva, for relieving toothache, and in hoarseness, loss of voice, relaxation of the uvula and tonsils, and paralysis of the muscles of the tongue and fauces.

Ginger Used Externally

Ginger is used in England in baths, fomentations, and as a substitute for mustard poultice. If the patient has a very delicate skin, it is better to prepare the poultice of crushed flaxseed, and then sprinkle it thickly with powdered Ginger.

Grandma's Favorite Ginger Recipes

Ginger tea was taken to cause sweating whenever colds threatened. The warm tea was taken freely when going to bed. The patient generally takes a hot mustard foot bath while the body, prepared for bed, is wrapped in warm blankets. During the foot bath, which lasts about 20 minutes, the patient should slowly drink the warm Ginger tea. After the foot bath, the patient should get into a warm bed, still wrapped in blankets, and allow the sweating thus induced to continue for from half an hour to an hour, slowly and carefully removing excess clothing until perspiration subsides.

Warm Ginger tea was also taken for menstrual cramps, due to suppression from exposure to cold.

If warm Ginger tea is given at the beginning of an hysterical attack, it will often drive away or lessen the attack, and produce quiet and restful sleep.

Miscellaneous Old Fashioned Ginger Recipes

Recipe used in colic, pain in the stomach and dyspepsia: Mix 1 oz. of powdered Gentian root with 1 teaspoonful of powdered Ginger. Take a spoonful in molasses every morning.

Doctor J. Reitch wrote in 1842 that "Ginger is the finest of all stomachics. It fortifies the stomach, assists digestion, excites appetite, and dispels flatulency. It is rather suited, however, to old persons and cold constitutions, than to the young and bilious." He further states that the small granulated Ginger mixed with sugar is "a very agreeable mode of taking Ginger medicinally. What are called digestive pills, and which are taken before dinner, and at night, are made chiefly of Rhubarb root and Ginger, and are the most wholesome of all preparations for aiding digestion. The tincture or essence of Ginger, which may be substituted in all cases for the powder, is made by infusing an ounce of the powder in 3 oz. of spirits of wine, and leaving it for some days, occasionally shaking the bottle, then allowing it to settle and filtering it. A few drops of this in tea, or any liquid, makes a fine stomachic."

Ginger in Medicines

Ginger root is often employed as a corrective with rhubarb and other drastic purges, to help prevent gripings of the bowels, and it stimulates them so as to require a less dose to act upon them.

Ginger root has been used in combination with other agents, in diarrhea and dysentery. Prepared with rhubarb in the form of a cordial or syrup, few articles are more valuable. A syrup made of Ginger, Rhubarb and Cranesbill is very useful for summer complaint.

Ginger root is a valuable addition to tonics. The root is used to disguise unpleasant taste in bitter or saline compounds.

Ginger in Food & Beverage

Great quantities of Ginger root are used in pies, cookies, cakes, biscuits, gingerbreads, essences, liquors, ginger beer, ginger ale, ginger champagne, pickling spices, liver sausage, mince-meats, curry powders, etc., etc.

Ginger Beer

This beverage, which was formerly so popular in England, under the name of Ginger Pop, is made as follows: Take of loaf sugar, one pound; cream of tartar, one ounce; bruised ginger, two ounces. Add two gallons of boiling water, and ferment for 24 hours with yeast.

Ginger Beer Powders

These are prepared in the manner of soda powders. One and one-third dram of pulverized loaf sugar, five grains of pulverized ginger, and twenty-six grains of bicarbonate of soda are put into a blue paper—and thirty grains of tartaric acid into a white paper. Each powder is dissolved in ½ pint of water, and the solutions mixed, which form a pleasant effervescing draught.

Ginger Wine

Take of bruised ginger, six pounds; water, five gallons. Boil for half an hour, and add 14 pounds of sugar; continue the boiling until this is dissolved, then cool, and add seven lemons, sliced, and 1½ pints of brandy. Ferment with a little yeast, confine in a tight cask for 3 months; then bottle.

Ginger Ale Recipes

One ounce Ginger, sliced; one teaspoonful essence of lemon; ¾ of a pound of granulated sugar; six quarts boiling water; infuse the ingredients in the boiling water until cold; then strain and ferment it with three or four spoonfuls of fresh yeast; then bottle.

Another method: One ounce sliced Ginger; ½ ounce dried orange peel; tie them up in a piece of muslin and boil with eight quarts of water; strain and add one ounce of citric acid, a teaspoonful of essence of lemon, and 1½ pounds of granulated sugar. When cold, add 2 tablespoonfuls of yeast; let it work for 12 hours; then bottle it.

COFFEE GINGERBREAD

2 cups enriched flour, 1 teaspoon salt, 1 teaspoon soda, 1 teaspoon ginger, 1 teaspoon cinnamon, ½ teaspoon cloves, ¼ cup sugar, ½ cup shortening, 1 cup molasses, 1 egg well beaten, ½ cup double-strength hot coffee. Sift dry ingredients together and cut in shortening until mixture is in fine crumbs. Stir in molasses and egg; then beat in hot coffee. Bake 45 minutes, or until done, in a 9-inch square cake pan, at 350 degrees.

CREAMY PUMPKIN PIE

Make pastry for 9-inch one-crust pie. Beat together with rotary beater, 1¾ cups mashed cooked pumpkin, ½ teaspoon salt, 2 eggs, ¾ cup sugar, 1½ cups undiluted evaporated milk, 1¼ teaspoons cinnamon, ½ teaspoon ginger, ½ teaspoon nutmeg. Pour into pastry-lined pie pan. Bake 45 to 50 minutes in hot oven 425 degrees, or until silver knife inserted into filling's side comes out clean. Soft center will "set" later.

HONEY GINGERBREAD

½ cup brown sugar, ½ cup honey, ½ cup shortening, 2 scant cups flour, ½ cup buttermilk, 1 egg, 1 teaspoon baking powder, ½ teaspoon cloves, ½ teaspoon salt, 1 teaspoon cinnamon, 1 teaspoon ginger, ½ teaspoon soda dissolved in 2 tablespoons water. Cream the sugar, shortening and honey together. Sift the flour, baking powder and spices together; then add to the first mixture alternately with buttermilk. Add the egg, then the soda mixture. Bake ½ hour in a 350- to 375-degree oven.

GINGER AND MOLASSES COOKIES

¾ cup shortening, 1½ cups molasses, 5 tablespoons boiling water, 4 cups sifted flour, 2 teaspoons soda, 1½ teaspoons ginger, ½ teaspoon cinnamon. Cream shortening, add molasses and hot water, and blend. Mix and sift dry ingredients and add them. The dough will be very soft. Chill it thoroughly and roll out to a fourth-inch thickness. Cut and bake on a floured cookie sheet at 350 degrees.

Ginger Syrup

Take of Ginger root, bruised, three ounces; boiling water, a pint; steep for 24 hours, strain, add 3 pounds of loaf sugar, and dissolve with a gentle heat, so as to form a syrup. This is used to give a pleasant flavor to drinks, and is frequently employed to cover the taste of nauseous medicines.

Ginger Jelly

To any fruit jelly, add shreds of thin-sliced preserved stem Ginger *before* the jelly sets (heat destroys Ginger flavor). Ginger gives jellies a new piquant flavor.

PUERTO RICAN HERB STALLS

Tucked in a corner of Caribbean market places, one can always find the native herb dealers with their assortment of leaves, barks and roots tied up in neat little bundles.

In San Juan we found the usual herb stall selling Old World—Rue, Basil, Marjoram and Thyme, with native herbs of early Borinquén Indians and Spaniards. Herbs are offered for practically every ailment. Many being used simply in "get well" baths—and as teas, lotions or amulets. The efficacy of some botanicals depends upon prayers and faith the user will have in the medicine.

Of all the aromatic botanicals offered, the refreshing scent of Khus-Khus invariably attracts first attention in the herb stall. Khus-Khus is an amber colored long fibrous root used in dressers to give linens and underclothes a delicate fresh scent. It is kept in rooms to keep out cucarachas (roaches) and other insects.

Opposite the herb seller, we found a special stall for superstitious folks.* Number 7 apparently is considered THE LUCKY number, as powders, oils, and lotions bear this number. One could purchase "Lovers Oil" to aid amorous intentions; "Attraction Oil," a sort of bait for the opposite sex; "Fast Luck Oil," "Lodestone Oil," etc. In a large bottle was a yellowish liquid labeled "Hot Foot Oil." This mixture is supposed to throw off scent and deceive the sheriff's bloodhounds when they are hot on your trail.

On the dusty shelves were also mason jars filled with botanical curios. Tonka beans and Star Anise were sold as good luck charms; Adam and Eve, and Orris roots were sold as lovers charms. "High John," "Southern John" or "Lesser John the Conqueror" roots are supposed to give bearer fantastic physical or financial powers.

*According to some authorities, the idea that seven is an important number is older than the ancient Greeks. It is based, not on mystical theories of the perfect number derived from the seven planets known to the ancients, but on cycles in nature. The sun's activity, weather changes, fever crises, egg incubation and gestation, the menstrual cycle—all may be measured in halves or multiples of the week. And eminent scientists report that periods based on seven make up a fundamental time pattern of mind and body in matters where both health and disease are concerned.

TREE "BLEEDS" ON GOOD FRIDAY

This rare phenomena has been repeatedly reported from wide sources. The following account comes from a lady living in Kingston, Jamaica, where the tree or bush is quite common:

"It is a fact that the Physic Nut Tree bleeds on Good Friday. If cut on any other day in the year the stain that comes out is white. I should know, because I have tried it. Moreover, if the tree is cut early on Good Friday morning the latex is white and does not get red until around mid-day."

NOTE: This writer found the same beliefs among peasants of Haiti and the Dominican Republic.

EGG SUPERSTITIONS

There is another egg superstition connected with Good Friday, but as I have never tried it, I can only speak from hearsay. The white of a very fresh egg is poured carefully into a glass of water in the very early morning, then placed in the sun as soon as it rises. At twelve o'clock the results are read, and various people see outlines according to the extent of their imagination. Some tell of seeing wedding cakes, which means imminent marriage; others see coffins, and know there'll be a death in the family; still others see ships which foretell a future voyage.

As a child I longed to be able to read my fate, but was not allowed to indulge in what my father termed "heathenish practices," and as an adult I have never been tempted to try what I now regard as childish.

I have heard, too, that rainwater caught on Good Friday is a sure cure for any ailment, especially if it is closely bottled and allowed to stand for a year; but again I have to admit that I have never tried it.—R.P.—*The West Indian Review.*

DON QUIXOTE'S EAR TREATED WITH ROSEMARY

Don Quixote having tilted with a Biscayan (not a windmill that time) had lost half an ear and he and his squire had come upon a camp of goat herds, who made them welcome and fed them. Don Quixote then told his squire to lie down and sleep if he wished to do so, saying—"yet stay and dress my ear before thou goest, for it pains me extremely."

The following is quoted verbatim from the book: "Thereupon one of the goat herds, beholding the wound as Sancho offered to dress it, desired the knight not to trouble himself for he had a remedy that would quickly cure him; and then fetching a few rosemary leaves, which grew in great plenty thereabout, he bruised them and mixed a little salt among them, and having applied the medicine to the ear, he bound it up, assuring him he needed no other remedy, which in a little time proved very true."—Sent by H.G., Kokah, Minn.

ESSENCES FOR MEAT

ESSENCE of GARLIC: Chop up a quarter of a pound of lean ham, an onion, a carrot, and 2 cloves of Garlic; put them into a saucepan with a bunch of sweet herbs and some pepper, and nutmeg; add 3 cupfuls of consomme, and simmer until it is reduced one-half; then strain through a sieve. It is used with roasted and broiled meats.

ESSENCE of HAM: Slice 6 ounces of the leanest ham; put them into a saucepan with 2 onions, 2 sliced carrots, a bunch of sweet herbs, half a glass of champagne wine, 2 cupfuls of consomme, and 2 cupfuls of plain veal jelly; simmer until reduced one-third; then add another half glass of champagne wine; let these boil, and then strain through a fine sieve. This is a good essence for broiled meat and game.

ESSENCE of FINE HERBS: Put into a saucepan 2 tablespoonfuls of Tarragon vinegar, 4 cupfuls of consomme, a bunch of fine herbs, and a little pepper; reduce these one-half over a very slow fire; then take out the bunch of fine herbs, and add a tablespoonful of Chervil and Tarragon, chopped very fine; simmer again for a few minutes, then squeeze in the juice of a lemon. This is used with steaks and chops of any kind.

ESSENCE of LEMON with OIL: Put into a little pan, a tablespoonful of chopped Parsley and Tarragon, a little salt and pepper, 2 tablespoonfuls of Tarragon vinegar, six tablespoonfuls of Olive Oil, and the juice of a lemon. This essence is used for broiled poultry, and game, and fish.

ORANGE ESSENCE: Put into a stewpan, 6 ounces of ham, a little Nutmeg, a small bunch of sweet herbs, half the peel of an orange, a cupful of plain veal jelly, and two cupfuls of consomme; simmer until reduced one-half then add the juice of an orange, and strain through a sieve. This essence is recommended for Wild duck and ducklings.

The man who is waiting for something to turn up might begin with his shirt sleeves.

Vanilla Recipes From an Old Cook Book

VANILLA EXTRACT: Cut and chop fine two or three pods and pound fine in a mortar; rub or pound into them a little powdered sugar; put in a pint bottle, add a tablespoonful water and let stand over night. The next day pour on a cup of spirits of wine, cork well and let stand for a month, shaking every day.

VANILLA FLAVORING: Split four beans and clip in bits with scissors; put seeds, husks and all into a bottle and pour over it one pint of brandy or whiskey; cork tightly, shake frequently for the first four or five weeks. It is then ready for use and will keep for years.

VANILLA FUDGE: Put into a shallow porcelain lined pan a heaping tablespoonful butter, a coffee cup granulated sugar, a third of a cup of condensed milk and water mixed in about equal parts, and a tiny pinch of salt. Set over the fire and stir constantly. Cook eight minutes from the time the mixture begins to boil, or until the mixture thickens so as to scarcely drop from a spoon. When it reaches this stage remove at once from the fire. Now add a scant teaspoonful of Vanilla and stir briskly until so thick that stirring becomes difficult. This will be in about ten minutes. Turn on a buttered pan and when nearly cooled mark into squares. This is delicious either fresh or when several days old.

VANILLA PARFAIT: Cook a half cup each sugar and water over the fire until it threads. Do not stir after the sugar has dissolved. Beat the whites of three eggs until very stiff, pour the syrup slowly over it, beating constantly. Flavor with Vanilla, and when cold fold in a pint of cream whipped stiff. Pour into a mould and pack.

VANILLA PODS: Many professional cooks prefer to use the pods themselves in flavoring, declaring that the flavor imparted is more delicate. When making a cream or pudding, the pod is stirred in the substance to be flavored. It is then removed, washed in two waters and reserved for future use. If care is taken a pod will last for a long time.

KITCHEN TIPS

Instead of shelling peas, throw them, pods and all, into a kettle of boiling water, after washing and discarding all spoiled ones. When they are done the pods will rise to the surface, while the peas will stay at the bottom of the kettle. Peas cooked in this manner have a fine flavor.

Before trying to break a coconut put it in the oven to warm. When heated a slight blow will crack it, and the shell will come off easily.

If you want nicely flavored butter, with the buttermilk well worked out, try putting in a teaspoonful of clear honey to about three pounds of butter. You cannot taste the honey but it improves the butter.

Wash and slice ten stalks of rhubarb, cut and core three medium sized apples, then stew apples and rhubarb together. Hang up in a jelly bag. For every pint of juice take a pint of sugar; boil till it jellies and pour into tumblers.

Before cooking mushrooms I always distinguish them from poisonous fungi by sprinkling salt on the spongy part, or gills. If they turn yellow, they are poisonous; if black, they are wholesome.

Buttermilk is excellent for cleaning sponges. Steep the sponge in the milk for some hours, then squeeze it out and wash in cold water.

In icing cakes dip the knife frequently into cold water.

Clean oil cloths with milk and water; a brush and soap will ruin them.

Tumblers that have had milk in them should never be put into hot water.

A small piece of charcoal in the pot with boiling cabbage removes the smell.

If your coal fire is low, throw on a tablespoonful of salt and it will help it very much.

A spoonful of stewed tomatoes in the gravy of either roasted or fried meats is an improvement.

When cooking onions, set a tin cup of vinegar on the stove and let it boil, and it is said you will smell no disagreeable odor.

Salt will curdle new milk, hence in preparing porridge, gravies, etc., the salt should not be added until the rest of the dish is prepared.

A carelessly kept coffee-pot will impart a rank flavor to the strongest infusion of the best Java. Wash the coffee-pot every day and twice a week boil borax and water in it for fifteen minutes.

Cayenne pepper blown into the cracks where ants congregate will drive them away. The same remedy is good also for mice.

Broil steak without salting. Salt draws the juice in cooking. It is desirable to keep this in if possible. Cook over a hot fire, turning frequently, searing on both sides. Place on a platter. Salt and pepper to taste.

Fish may be scaled much easier by first dipping into boiling water about a minute.

Salt fish are quickest and best freshened by soaking in sour milk.

Milk which has turned or changed may be sweetened or rendered fit for use again by stirring in a little soda.

Always boil vegetables in salted water.

When peeling onions, keep your hands and the onions under water.

After feathers have been plucked from fowl, soak it in salted cold water for a short time. The pin-feathers can be removed easier.

FRENCH ROLLS

Take a tablespoonful of lard or butter, three pints of flour, a cup of yeast and as much milk as will work it up to the stiffness of bread; let the mixture rise until very light and make up in small rolls; bake to a light brown color.

FRENCH BREAD

Two quarts of flour; scald one pint of it; butter half the size of an egg, mix with cold water; two-thirds cup of yeast; when mixed, knead fifteen minutes, using as little additional flour as possible. Let rise twelve hours; cut and work with a knife ten minutes before putting into the pan to bake.

VIENNA BREAD

For four pounds of flour, take one and three-quarter ounces of Fleischmann's Yeast, half an ounce of salt and three pints of milk and water in equal proportions. Dissolve the yeast and salt in the liquid, and make a very thin sponge in the middle of the flour. Let it stand three-quarters of an hour, then stir in the rest of the flour. Let it stand two and a half hours, then take it upon the board and cut it into pound pieces, knead a little, then cut each pound piece into twelve pieces, form into circular balls of dough and bake fifteen minutes in a very hot oven.

ITALIAN PUDDING

Take half a quart can of peaches, three ounces of bread or cake crumbs, a half cup of milk, two eggs and an ounce and a half of sugar and a teaspoonful of fresh lemon juice. First put the crumbs through a sieve, put on a flat dish a layer of the peaches and sprinkle over half of the crumbs; put over this another layer of peaches and sprinkle over them the remainder of the crumbs; put the milk in a small saucepan and allow it to come to the boiling point; put in a small bowl the yolk of two eggs and half an ounce of sugar, mix and pour into the boiling milk, adding the lemon juice; then pour the mixture over the crumbs and peaches and place the pudding in an oven for ten minutes; add to the white of the eggs a small pinch of salt and whip to a very stiff froth; add the remaining sugar, mixing with the whites of the eggs, and sugar very roughly over the top, and place the pudding in the oven for a moment to firm the eggs.

MEAT TIPS

Great care must be taken in the selection of meats. If the beef is bright red it may be regarded as good and fresh.

Veal should be clear and firm and the fat white.

Mutton should be fat, and the fat clear, hard and white.

Lamb should be light red and fat.

Pork, the lean, fine grained and both fat and lean very white.

Tongues of any kind should be thick, firm and have plenty of fat on the under side.

Boil mutton 15 minutes to a pound, ham 20, corned beef 20.

For roasting mutton allow 12 minutes to a pound and 12 over, veal 15-17, pork 20 and 20 over, beef 15 and 15 over.

Fresh meats that are to be boiled should always be put in boiling water to set the juices, corned meats or ham in cold water to extract the salt and when done left in the water until cold to make them nice and juicy.

Steaks are best cut thick and best broiled. Never add salt or pepper until a steak is done, and not to a roast until half roasted.

Never turn a roast nor add any water to it, unless the butter, of which a liberal supply should be used, threatens to burn, and then use it only sparingly. Baste frequently, after the roast has been in the oven 20-30 minutes, with the drippings to keep the meat juicy.

Butter is better than lard for all roasts, and should, as stated before, be used liberally, excepting with fat pork; a fat goose or fat ducks. To these add only a little water before putting in the oven.

If meat is tough wash it in water with a little vinegar, or, when boiling it, add a little to the water but not to soups. Much washing must, however, be avoided, as it impairs all meats, and steaks, chops, etc., must never be washed.

Beef is often tough because it is used too fresh. It should always hang in a refrigerator for several days at least to give it the tenderness, which alone makes it palatable. Veal should always be used fresh.

When fresh meat must be kept longer than expected and no ice is at hand, sprinkle it with black or red pepper or powdered charcoal, which wash off when it is used. Such meat is only suitable for stews.

Have you lost your appetite because you must abstain from harsh spices and condiments? Why not try culinary herbs? They have been used for ages before the harsh spices were introduced to Europe.

HUNGARIAN LIVER

1 cup lard
1½ pounds sliced onion
2 green peppers diced
1 tablespoon paprika
2 teaspoons salt
1 pound liver, floured and seasoned

Melt lard and simmer onions and pepper in it. Sprinkle with salt and paprika while cooking. Remove before onion is browned, skimming out vegetables and leaving fat in pan. Brown liver quickly in same fat. Place on platter and top with onions and green pepper, and serve with garnish of tiny, parsley buttered, new potatoes.

ROAST PORK

A small loin of pork, three tablespoons of bread crumbs, one onion, half a teaspoon sage, half teaspoon salt, half teaspoon pepper, one ounce chopped suet, one tablespoon drippings. Separate each joint of the loin with the chopper, and then make an incision with a knife into the thick part of the pork in which to put the stuffing. Prepare the stuffing by mixing the bread crumbs together with the onion which must have previously been finely chopped. Add to this the sage, pepper, salt and suet, and when all is thoroughly mixed, press the mixture snugly into the incision already made in the pork, and sew together the edges of the meat with needle and thread, to confine the stuffing. Grease well a sheet of kitchen paper, with drippings, place the loin into this, securing it with a wrapping of twine. Put to bake in a dry baking pan in a brisk oven, basting immediately and constantly as the grease draws out, and roast a length of time, allowing twenty minutes to the pound and twenty minutes longer.

LAMB CHOPS WITH CREAM

Ingredients: A little butter, a little water, enough potatoes to fill a small dish, 1 teacupful of cream.

Lamb chops are excellent cooked this way. Put them in a frying pan with a very little water, so little that it will boil away by the time the meat is tender; then put in lumps of butter with the meat and let it brown slowly. There will be a brown, crisp surface, with a fine flavor.

A GERMAN DISH

Ingredients: A tender fowl, salt, pepper, mace, flour, yolk of 1 egg, hot lard, liver, gizzard, parsley.

Quarter a tender fowl, season the pieces with pepper, salt and mace, flour and then dip them in the beaten yolk of an egg; fry a golden color in hot lard; dish them, garnished with the liver and gizzard fried separately, and with fried parsley. Serve either with a salad garnished with hard-boiled eggs or tomato sauce.

Man Thinks Himself Wise, Till God Shows Him His Folly

A man was wondering why the acorn small,
Should grow on oaks so mighty, and so tall.
While on the slender pumpkin vine abound
Much larger fruits than on great oaks are found;
But soon an acorn chanced to rattle down,
Which hit the foolish fellow on the crown:
Had pumpkins grown upon the oak instead,
He, doubtless, would have got a broken head.

MOCK TURTLE SOUP

Black beans, 1 pint; 2 onions; 2 bunches celery; marrow bone of beef; 1 tablespoonful of catsup; 1 lemon; 2 eggs; pinch of thyme; 1 teaspoonful of salt; 1 teaspoonful of cloves; 1 teaspoonful of pepper.

The beans should be soaked over night. In the morning, pour off the water, and to the beans add four quarts of fresh water, the onions and celery chopped fine, and the seasoning. Add the beef and boil several hours; then set aside until the next day, for the fat to rise. Remove the fat, add the catsup and let the soup come to a boil. Just before serving, add the lemon and hard-boiled eggs, chopped fine.

TOMATO SOUP

Cut small the red part of 3 large carrots. 3 heads of celery, 4 large onions, 2 large turnips. Put them in a soup kettle with a good sized piece of butter, and ½ pound lean ham; then add a little broth, from meat that was boiled the day previous. Add a quart can of tomatoes, let boil 1½ hours; season with pepper and salt; strain it through a sieve. Can be served on bits of bread, fried.

FLEMISH SOUP

Slice 6 onions, 12 potatoes, 2 heads celery, into a jar or pot, as you choose, to bake or boil your soup; add 2 or 3 pounds of beef, with bones well cracked; bake four hours closely covered, or boil 3 hours slowly; rub through a sieve; add ½ pint boiled milk, pepper and salt, and serve hot.

BEEF SOUP

A shin of beef, cold water, 6 quarts; 1 onion, 1 turnip, 3 potatoes, all chopped fine; 1 cup of raw tomatoes; salt, pepper and sage, enough.

Put the meat in the pot in the morning, and cover with the water. Just before the water boils, skim carefully, let it simmer, and as it boils away add more water. About noon, add the seasoning, and the other ingredients. Then boil an hour, strain off, and thicken with a spoonful of flour. This will make just three quarts of soup; and when carefully prepared, is most delicious.

VEGETABLE SOUP

Put a large lump of butter in a stew pan; have ready a small quantity of cabbage, sorrel, 2 onions, 2 carrots, 3 potatoes, a few peas, beans, turnips, parsley, lettuce, cucumbers, artichoke bottoms, and asparagus — all chopped fine. Let them stew in the butter until quite tender, stirring to prevent burning. Season with a very little cayenne, salt, pepper, and ketchup—celery seed and some good meat broth. Boil all together. Any of the vegetables may be omitted but the greater variety the better.

OKRA SOUP

Two pounds of the round of beef, 4 sliced onions, 4 quarts water, a dozen tomatoes, 1 teacup sliced okra, 1 green pepper; boil slowly five hours; put it through a colander. Serve with small pieces of toasted or fried bread.

BEAN SOUP

Soak 1 quart of beans overnight, in lukewarm water. Put them over the fire the next morning, with cold water enough to cover, four or five hours before dinner. Let them scald up, and throw off the water. If not soaked overnight, scald in two or three waters Then put them in cold water, with a piece of salt pork. Boil slowly for three hours, keeping the pot well covered. Season with anything you please—cayenne, celery, or slices of lemon. Some prefer sliced carrot, sliced onion, and a little chicken broth. Boil 4 hours, and then strain through a colander to remove skins.

VEGETABLE SOUP

1 sliced turnip; 1 sliced carrot; 2 sliced onions; 4 ounces cut celery; ½ ounce of flour; 3 ounces of butter; 3½ quarts of water; 2 tablespoonfuls of salt; 1 teaspoonful of pepper; a sprig of parsley.

Put all the ingredients in two quarts of water, and boil until they are tender; then rub through a sieve, add 3 pints of water and when it boils, stir in the butter rubbed smooth with the flour; salt and pepper. Let the whole boil two or three minutes; then serve.

PREPARING FISH

Fresh Fish of all kinds, after being thoroughly cleaned and washed, should be placed in cold water, well salted, for a half hour before being fried, boiled, baked or broiled.

Frying: Dry it with a cloth and dredge well with flour or corn meal. Fry a few pieces of salt pork and then put in the fish, and fry to a nice brown. It must be well done. Salad oil gives it the finest color, for those who prefer it.

Broiling: Split the fish open, have the bars of the gridiron rubbed with a little lard, to prevent their sticking. Put the inside down first, and let it nearly cook before turning it. Butter the skin side before turning it down. Broil slowly and butter when put on the platter which must be warmed. Shad, mackeral, etc., are much nicer broiled.

Boiling: Do not cut it open. Pin it in a cloth, as it is easier to take it up. Put in a kettle and nearly cover with boiling water. One half hour's boiling will usually cook any moderate-sized fish. Serve with egg sauce.

Baking: Wash and wipe them, and lay them head and tail, in a baking dish, the bottom of which has been spread over with a little butter or drippings. Add a very little vinegar and water. Season with salt, chopped onions and parsley, if liked. Shake plenty of dried and grated bread crumbs over them, and bake. A hot oven, and a good-sized fish, will take ¾ of an hour. Garnish with a fringe of curled new parsley, or hard-boiled egg.

TIPSY OYSTERS SHED SHELLS IN RECORD TIME

Fish and Wildlife Service experiments point the way to more rapid shucking of oysters. In laboratory tests the oysters were soaked in carbonated water for five minutes.

The carbon dioxide intoxicated the bivalves to the point where the large muscle holding the shells closed relaxed and the oysters were easily opened. In one test, a novice opened 150 drunken oysters in twenty minutes, a speed difficult for the most experienced oyster shucker to attain with sober oysters. Neither flavor nor quality of the oysters was affected.

LEFTOVER FISH

By the following plan, a good dish may be made from cold fish which has been left from dinner of the previous day. Any kind of fish will be suitable. Free the fish from the bone, and cut it into small pieces. Season this with onions and parsley chopped, and salt and pepper. Beat two eggs well with a spoonful of catsup. Mix the whole together with the fish and put it in a baking dish with two or three small slices of bacon over it. Bake before the fire in a dutch oven. Serve with oyster sauce or melted butter.

If your job requires hard muscle work, you need Vitamins, Minerals, and energy foods to keep up your strength.

SAVORY CLAM CHOWDER

To make really savory clam chowder, add a small pinch of thyme, a bay leaf and a few caraway seeds. The seasoning is as important to good chowder as the clams.

A little marjoram mixed with the salt and pepper rubbed on a steak before broiling adds appetizing flavor.

Take stuffed eggs, season the mashed yolk mixture with a combination of sage and marjoram—not too much of each.

Flavorful meats are yours for the spicing. Add a pinch of dill to the chicken soup, marjoram to the basting liquor for the roast, tarragon and thyme to fish dishes and sauces, and pickling spices to a stew. And next time you make beefburgers add 1 teaspoon garlic vinegar and ½ teaspoon dry mustard to each pound of hamburger.

HOW TO TELL FRESH FISH

When you select fresh whole fish at the market, look for those that have bright, clear, bulging eyes, gills that are reddish pink. Also, the fish must be free from slime and without odor. Make sure, too, that the flesh is firm and elastic . . . that it will spring back when you press it.

DRY BREAD MADE FRESH

Any dry or old bread, such as light bread, biscuit, corn bread, or even cake, which you desire to serve may be easily freshened. Place it in a paper bag, or wrap it in brown paper or light bread paper; close tight, and set in the oven. The bread will become very soft and appetizing. Do not dampen. Or a loaf of new light bread put into the oven before being unwrapped will be made far better than without such treatment. Try it. You will be surprised.

To remove the smell of onions from the breath: Parsley eaten with vinegar will remove the unpleasant effect of eating onions.

To conceal taste of castor oil: Beat the castor oil with the white of an egg, until both are thoroughly mixed.

Do you have a lot of colds? Try building up your resistance with Vitamins, Minerals, or energy foods.

Calf's-Foot Jelly

Cut across the first joint, and through the hoof, place in a large sauce-pan, cover with cold water, and bring quickly to the boiling point; when water boils, remove them, and wash thoroughly in cold water. When perfectly clean put into a porcelain-lined sauce-pan, add cold water in the proportion of three pints to two calf's feet, put sauce-pan over fire, and when water boils, set aside to a cooler place, where it will simmer very slowly for five hours; strain the liquor through a fine sieve, or a coarse towel, let it stand over night to set, remove the fat that has risen to the top, dip a towel in boiling water, and wash the surface, which will be quite firm. Now place in a porcelain-lined sauce-pan, and melt, add juice of two lemons, rinds of three cut into strips, one-fourth pound of cut loaf-sugar, ten cloves, and one inch of cinnamon stick. Put the whites of three eggs, together with the shells (which must first be blanched in boiling water) into a bowl, beat them slightly, and pour them into the sauce-pan, continuing to use the egg-beater until the whole boils, when the pan should be drawn aside where it will simmer gently for ten minutes, skimming off all scum as it rises. While simmering, prepare a piece of flannel by pouring through it a little warm water; and when the jelly has simmered ten minutes, pour it through this bag into a bowl, and repeat the process of straining until it is perfectly clear, then add a half gill of sherry (or brandy, or brandy and sherry mixed in equal proportions), stir well, pour into moulds, and place upon ice or in a cool place until jelly sets and becomes firm enough to turn out and serve.

CHICKEN FEET SOUP

Cut off feet at the usual joint, wash and throw into boiling water, and after a little while draw off their skins and scales and boil them. Their gluten is a delicious base for sauces or soups. Boil with the feet, the head, wing tops and neck of the chicken, and a delicate broth, impossible to make from other parts of the bird, is produced.

MILK SOUP WITH CHERVIL

Boil with salt and pepper one quart of milk and pour it in the tureen over browned bread. Sprinkle chopped chervil on the top, and serve.

NOTE: The delicate flavor of Chervil is fine in soups, salads, meats, etc.

Are you nervous? Cut out tea, coffee, cocoa and stimulants—use Mate tea, Parsley leaf tea or Alfalfa and Mint tea often.

VEAL SOUP

Take a knuckle of veal, crack the bone, wash, and put it on to boil in more than sufficient water to cover it. After boiling some time, pare, cut, and wash two onions, five or six turnips, and put in with the meat. When this has boiled one hour, add some sweet marjoram, rubbed fine, with salt and cayenne pepper to taste. Then take flour, which mix with cold water to the consistency of cream, and add to the soup while boiling. Care must be taken not to make it too thick. Then pare and cut into small pieces six or eight potatoes, which add about half an hour before being served; and about ten minutes before sending to table put in a few dumplings. As veal makes a white soup, the color is much improved by adding a tablespoonful of burnt sugar. This soup may be thickened with rice, if preferable.

CORN MUSH

Put four quarts fresh water in a kettle to boil, salt to suit the taste; when it begins to boil stir in one and a half quarts meal, letting it sift through the fingers slowly to prevent lumps, adding it a little faster at the last, until as thick as can be conveniently stirred with one hand; set in the oven in the kettle (or take out into a pan), bake an hour, and it will be thoroughly cooked. It takes corn meal so long to cook thoroughly that it is very difficult to boil it until done without burning. Excellent for frying when cold. Use a hard wood paddle, two feet long, with a blade two inches wide and seven inches long, to stir with. The thorough cooking and baking in oven afterwards takes away all the raw taste that mush is apt to have, and adds much to its sweetness and delicious flavor.

PIGS'-FEET SOUSE

Cut off the horny parts of feet and toes, scrape, clean and wash thoroughly, singe off the stray hairs, place in a kettle with plenty of water, boil, skim, pour off water and add fresh, and boil until the bones will pull out easily; do not bone, but pack in a stone jar with pepper and salt sprinkled between each layer; cover with good cider vinegar. When wanted for the table, take out a sufficient quantity, put in a hot skillet, add more vinegar, salt, and pepper if needed, boil until thoroughly heated, stir in a smooth thickening of flour and water, and boil until flour is cooked; serve hot as a nice breakfast dish. Or, when the feet have boiled until perfectly tender, remove the bones and pack in stone jar as above; slice down cold when wanted for use.

PORKSTEAKS

Fry like beefsteaks, with pepper and salt; or sprinkle with dry powdered sage if the sausage flavor is liked.

CARAWAY COOKIES

1 cupful butter	1½ teaspoonfuls baking powder
2 cupfuls sugar	½ teaspoonful salt
3 cupfuls flour	2 tablespoonfuls Caraway seed
4 eggs	

Cream the butter and add half the sugar. Beat the yolks, add the remaining half of the sugar and beat with the butter, then add the beaten whites. Mix the baking powder, spice and salt with the flour and stir into the butter mixture. Take a teaspoonful of the flour and stir into the butter mixture. Take a teaspoonful of dough, make into a ball with floured hands, place the balls in a pan, press or flatten into a round cake and bake ten minutes.

KENTUCKY CORN CAKES

Take one quart of cornmeal and two tablespoonfuls of common wheat flour (whole wheat); add salt to taste, and mix thoroughly with a sufficient quantity of buttermilk to form a batter. Next melt a heaping tablespoonful of lard, stir in with the batter well, bake on a hot griddle, pouring them thin.

NEW ORLEANS MOLASSES CAKE

Two cups of molasses, one of butter, four eggs, half a cup of cold water, one-half teaspoonful of soda, one teaspoonful of ginger, four cups of prepared flour, heat the molasses before mixing and stir the butter in while hot; let it cool before you put the eggs in; this will make the cakes, as they should not be very thick; bake one-half hour in quick oven.

GINGER ICE BOX COOKIES

¾ c. molasses	½ tsp. salt
¾ c. melted fat	¼ tsp. cloves
1 egg, beaten	1 tsp. ginger
3 c. sifted enriched flour	1 tsp. cinnamon
	½ tsp. soda

Combine molasses and fat. Add beaten egg and stir until blended. Add combined sifted dry ingredients; stir until smooth. Shape dough into a roll, wrap in waxed paper. Store in refrigerator. Slice ⅛-inch thick, and bake on greased cookie sheet in moderate oven (375° F.) 10 min. If desired, sprinkle cookies with coarse white sugar before baking.

SPICE CAKE

4 teacups flour	1 teaspoon soda in 1 cup of sour milk or cream
1 teacup butter	
3 teacups sugar	
4 eggs	½ teaspoonful each of Nutmeg, Allspice, Mace, Cinnamon and Cloves

Cream butter and sugar. Break the 4 eggs over it and beat. Add milk and soda and put in gradually flour and the spices. Drop with spoon in pans and ice with white icing and flavor with lemon.

TEXAS CUP CAKES

Two cups of sugar, one cup cream, half cup cold water, three and a half cups of flour, half a cup of butter, six eggs, yolks and white beaten separately, one teaspoon vanilla flavor; bake in tins—cups are best. This is a very light and delicious cake, and certain of being good if properly made.

VIRGINIA APPLE CAKE

Take one cup of bread dough; put one and a half cups of sugar into it, roll it about an inch thick, put it in a long pan, then slice good baking apples thin, and put smoothly over the dough; sprinkle sugar, butter and cinnamon over it and bake. This is very nice indeed, and much used in Virginia for a tea cake as it is a general favorite.

PEPPERMINT CANDY

2 teacups white sugar	and ¼ teaspoon soda
1 tablespoon butter	½ cup boiling water
1 tablespoon vinegar	

Set on stove and stir until throughly dissolved. Cook till brittle. Remove from the stove, flavor with 3 or 4 drops of oil of peppermint, and beat till creamy. Pour on slab and cut in squares.

Slice unpeeled tomatoes fairly thick. Dust with salt, pepper and Sweet Basil Herb. Dip in egg and crumbs and fry—tasty!

HERB SOUP

1 cupful finely shredded spinach	3 teaspoonfuls salt
½ cupful shedded sorrel	4 tablespoonfuls butter
¼ blanched and sliced leek	1 tablespoonful chervil
White heart leaves head lettuce	2 quarts boiling water
4 potatoes	½ pint croutons

Have the sorrel, spinach and lettuce fresh, tender and free from tough midribs. Wash and shred. Cut the washed leek into thin slices. Put in the stewpan with the butter and cook fifteen minutes, being careful not to brown. Now add the potatoes, salt, and boiling water. When the soup begins to boil, draw the stewpan back where the contents will cook gently for one hour. At the end of this time, crush the potatoes with a fork, add the chervil and simmer five minutes longer. Turn into the soup tureen, add the croutons and serve. If preferred, the soup may be rubbed through a puree sieve, returned to the fire, and when boiling hot be poured on the yolks of two eggs which have been beaten with two tablespoonfuls of milk. This soup may be varied infinitely. Any number of green vegetables can be employed in making it, care being taken to use only a small quantity of those of pronounced flavor.

ICELAND MOSS JELLY

Wash and bruise Iceland or Irish moss and soak it all night; dry and boil it, putting an ounce to a quart of water until it is reduced to one-half the quantity; strain it through a sieve. Take it with milk or wine or flavor to taste. It may be boiled in milk and turned into a shape when cold.

ORIENTAL DISH

Wilt thoroughly a few fine cabbage leaves; mix with one cup of well chopped raw beef, one-quarter of a cup of uncooked rice, a small onion chopped fine, and a good sized tomato; add salt; roll compactly within a piece of wilted leaf one-half tablespoonful of this mixture, folding in the ends snugly; place in rows in a flat bottom sauce-pan with a little water at first, and uncovered; fifteen minutes later add more water and cover; boil an hour.

CHINESE SOUP

Two young fowls or one full grown; half pound of ham; one gallon of water. Cut the fowls into pieces as for fricassee; put these with the ham, into the pot with a quart of water, or enough to cover them fairly; stew for an hour if the fowls are tender; if tough, until you can cut easily into the breast; take out the breast, leaving the rest of the meat in the pot; add the remainder of the water boiling hot; keep the soup stewing slowly while you chop up the white meat you have selected; rub the yolks of four hard boiled eggs smooth in a mortar or bowl, moistening to a paste with a few spoonfuls of the soup; mix with these a handful of fine bread crumbs and the chopped meat and make it into small balls. When the soup has boiled—in all two hours and a half—if the chicken is reduced to shreds, strain out the meat and bones, season with salt and white pepper and chopped parsley, drop in the prepared force meat, and after boiling ten minutes, to incorporate the ingredients well, add, a little at a time, a pint of rich milk thickened with flour. Boil up once and serve. A chicken a year old would make better soup than a younger fowl.

FRENCH STEAK

1 porterhouse steak	1 teaspoonful lemon juice
½ teaspoonful finely chopped shallot	1 teaspoonful meat extract
1 tablespoonful tarragon vinegar	½ teaspoonful horse radish
⅓ cupful butter	
Yolks of 2 eggs	

Wipe a porterhouse steak, broil, and serve with sauce made as follows: Cook shallot in vinegar five minutes. Wash ⅓ cupful butter and divide in thirds. Add 1 piece butter to mixture with yolks of eggs, lemon juice and meat extract. Cook over hot water, stirring constantly; as soon as the butter is melted, add second piece, then a third piece. When the mixture thickens add horse-radish. The time for broiling the steak depends, of course, on how you like it; if it is wished rare, five minutes over a hot fire or under the flame of a gas stove will cook it sufficiently. When you wish the steak well done, give it from six to eight minutes.

SPANISH SAUCE

4 tablespoonfuls butter	2½ tablespoonfuls lean raw ham
4 tablespoonfuls flour	1 carrot
2 cupfuls white stock	1 onion, sliced
	1 stalk celery
	2 cloves

Melt butter in saucepan, add flour, and stir over a gentle fire until nicely browned; mix with white stock, ham, carrot, sliced onion, celery, cloves, a pinch of salt and pepper; stir until beginning to boil, then simmer gently on back of stove for one hour; skim off grease before serving.

FRENCH SORREL SOUP

2 pints boiling water	1 teaspoonful salt
3 tablespoonfuls butter	Yolk 2 eggs
⅓ cupful shredded sorrel	½ cupful bread cut in dice and dried in the oven or fried in butter.
3 tablespoonfuls milk	

Tear the tender green parts from the midribs of the cultivated sorrel; wash in cold water and shred very fine. Put half the butter in a stew pan and add the shredded sorrel. Place on the fire and cook five minutes, stirring frequently. Now add the boiling water and salt, and boil ten minutes. Beat the yolks of eggs well, add the milk, pour into the soup tureen, and add the remaining half of the butter cut into bits. Gradually pour the boiling soup in the tureen, stirring all the while to combine the hot mixture with the egg yolk. Add the bread dice and serve.

PIQUANTE SAUCE

4 tablespoonfuls butter	1 blade mace
1 small carrot	3 allspice berries
6 shallots	4 tablespoonfuls vinegar
1 bunch savory herbs	½ teaspoonful sugar
½ bay leaf	1 cupful stock
2 slices lean bacon	Cayenne and salt to taste
2 cloves	Parsley
6 peppercorns	

Put the butter into a saucepan with the carrot and shallots cut into small pieces, add the herbs, bay leaf, spices and bacon minced fine; let these ingredients simmer slowly until the bottom is covered with a brown glaze; keep stirring and put in remaining ingredients, simmer gently fifteen minutes, skim off every particle of fat. This is an excellent recipe when a sharp but not too acid sauce is required.

SPANISH STEW

1 chicken
2 pounds veal
1 can mushrooms
1 can pimientos
¼ pound butter
1 can cream
1 teaspoon salt
¼ teaspoon black pepper
Dash of cayenne pepper.

Boil chicken and veal together until tender; cut from bone. Chop meat, mushrooms and pimientos fine. Add one quart of stock to meat; add other ingredients and cook slowly until mixture thickens. Serve hot.

ARABIAN STEW

Select as many pork chops as there are people and place chops in an iron frying pan. Cover each chop with uncooked rice, sliced raw onions, green peppers, sliced; then pour over all this two cans tomatoes. Season and simmer for about 1½ hours or until pork is thoroughly tender.

FRENCH STEW

2½ pounds veal (inexpensive cut) cut in 1-inch pieces.
Sear, stirring often, for 10 minutes, in
3 tablespoons butter
2 cups hot water
1 large onion, finely diced
2 cups raw diced potatoes
6 medium carrots, diced
2 teaspoons salt
½ teaspoon pepper
½ teaspoon paprika

Cover and cook over low heat 1 hour or until meat is quite tender.
Blend, then add to meat:
4 tablespoons flour
1 small can cream of mushroom soup.
Continue cooking on top of stove, stirring constantly, 5 or 10 minutes.

ORIENTAL LAMB STEW

2 pounds lamb chunklets
2 tablespoons chopped onion
1 No. 2½ can tomatoes
1 tablespoon curry or chili powder
8 ripe or green olives
⅛ teaspoon lemon juice
Salt
Cereal squares

Buy lamb chunklets of two-inch lean cubes of lamb shoulder. Remove excess fat from meat. Brown meat in hot pan. Add onion. Add tomatoes and curry or chili powder. Cover and simmer until meat is tender, about one hour. Just before serving, add chopped olives, lemon juice and salt to taste. Pour into center of platter and surround with cereal squares. For the cereal squares, chill cooked cereal until very firm. Unmold and cut into slices about one-half inch thick. Dip in flour and fry golden brown. Serves 6 to 8.

CREOLE BEEF STEW

1½ pounds lean beef
2 cups tomatoes
1 large onion
1 green pepper
1 cup string beans
3 ears or 1 can corn
2 carrots—sliced
Flour, Worcestershire sauce and potatoes as indicated.

Place 1½ pounds of lean beef in a casserole or deep iron skillet. Around the beef place as many potatoes as needed, tomatoes, onion, green pepper, string beans, corn, carrots. Sprinkle well with salt and pepper, partially cover with water and place in a slow oven to cook until the meat is done. More water may be added to prevent meat from drying out too much. Remove from pan and place on serving platter and garnish with the vegetables. Add flour to thicken the meat juices and make gravy, using chopped parsley and Worcestershire sauce for the final flavoring.

AMERICAN BEEF STEW

2 pounds beef from chuck
2 tablespoonfuls of fat
4 medium size onions (chopped)
½ No. 2 can tomatoes
1 green pepper
4 carrots diced

Melt fat in bottom of kettle, add chopped onions until slightly browned, then add meat cut in small cubes. Add tomatoes and green pepper cut in strips. Add enough boiling water to cover ¾ of contents, then add salt and pepper to taste. Cover kettle and let simmer for 1½ hours. Then add diced carrots, and continue simmering for one hour longer or until meat and carrots are tender. Replenish the boiling water if necessary for sufficient gravy. Thicken gravy.

PAPRIKA VEAL STEW

2 lbs. veal steak, 1 inch thick
1 teaspoon salt
⅛ teaspoon pepper
1 peeled clove garlic
2 tablespoons oleomargarine
2 cups hot water
¾ cup sweet or sour cream
1 teaspoon paprika

Cut veal into 2-inch pieces and sprinkle with the salt and pepper. Cut gashes in the garlic and cook in the fat in a covered skillet for 3 minutes or until delicately browned. Add the meat, and sear on all sides until light brown. Add the water, cover and simmer very gently until meat is tender, or about 1 hour. Add the cream and paprika, reheat, remove garlic and serve. Serves 6.

FRENCH LAMB STEW

This is a recipe that my mother, who seemed to know how to feed our family of eight most economically, always used when I was growing up in France.

- 3 pounds lamb shoulder, cut in stewing size pieces
- 3 carrots
- 3 pieces celery
- 2 medium sized tomatoes or 1 cup, canned
- 1 quart boiling water
- 2 eggs
- Cracker meal
- 1 clove garlic
- 1 bay leaf
- 1 clove

Roll meat in cracker crumbs, after first dipping in beaten egg. Repeat this twice. Brown in fat in saucepan, add water and other ingredients and allow to cook slowly for about 1 hour or until thoroughly tender.

OYSTER STEW

- ½ pint small oysters
- 4 tablespoons butter or margarine
- 3 cups milk
- 1 cup cream
- Salt and pepper to taste

Look over the oysters and remove any small pieces of shuck which may cling to them. Do not wash and do not discard the juice.

Combine milk and cream and heat in a double boiler. Melt butter in a saucepan or kettle, add the oysters and juice and cook and stir until the edges of the oysters curl. This will take a very few minutes. Add the hot milk and cream at once, season and serve at once in hot soup bowls. This will make four servings.

BOLOGNA SAUSAGE

Take a pound of beef suet, a pound of pork, a pound of bacon fat and lean, and a pound of beef and veal. Cut them very small. Take a handful of sage leaves chopped fine, with a few sweet herbs. Season pretty high with pepper and salt, take a large well-cleaned gut and fill it. Set on a saucepan of water, and when it boils, put it in, first pricking it to prevent its bursting. Boil it one hour.

ENGLISH SAUSAGE

Take 1 lb. of young pork, fat and lean, without skin or gristle, 1 lb. of beef suet, chopped fine together; put in ½ lb. of grated bread, half the peel of a lemon shred, a nutmeg grated, 6 sage leaves chopped fine, a teaspoonful of pepper, and 2 of salt, some thyme, savory, and marjoram, shred fine. Mix well together and put it close down in a pan until used. Roll them out the size of common sausages and fry them in fresh butter of a fine brown, or broil them over a clear fire, and send them to table hot.

SAUSAGES AND SAUERKRAUT

Cook 3 pints of sauerkraut in a saucepan over the fire, cover with 1 quart boiling water, add 2 ounces pure leaf lard or beef fat, and cook 1½ hours; then dust over ½ tablespoonful flour, stir and cook a few minutes. 15 minutes before serving, wash 1½ pounds of Frankfurter sausages in cold water, lay them on top the kraut, cover tightly, draw the saucepan to side of stove, let it remain 10 minutes; then remove the sausages; grate 1 large peeled raw potato, add it to the kraut, stir and boil 5 minutes; then serve.

PIGS' FEET

They should be thoroughly cleaned and thrown into salt water over night, then boiled until almost in pieces. While cooking drop in the water a small red pepper pod, a few whole cloves and allspice. When done, and well drained, put the feet one by one into a jar and cover with good clear vinegar, and in two days they will be ready for the table.

PARSLEY SAUCE

Melt in a saucepan 2 ounces of butter; add 1 tablespoonful of flour; stir this over the fire a few minutes; then add ½ pint boiling milk; season with ½ teaspoon salt; boil 3 minutes; remove from the fire; add 1 tablespoonful fine-chopped parsley, and serve.

OLD FASHIONED HASH

Chop very fine some cold cooked corned beef and cold boiled potatoes, 1 pint of each. Place a saucepan with 1 tablespoonful butter and 1 gill fine chopped onion over the fire, cook slowly 5 minutes without browning; add 1 tablespoonful flour, stir and cook 2 minutes, add ½ pint of stock or broth (if neither of them are handy add ½ pint of boiling water, and ½ teaspoonful beef extract); stir and cook 3 minutes; add the hash, stirring and cooking over fire 6 minutes, season with ¼ teaspoonful pepper, and salt to taste; then serve.

POTTED SPARE RIBS

Take 3 pounds fresh spare ribs, wash and wipe dry; then season with 1 even tablespoonful salt, 1 even teaspoonful pepper. Place a saucepan with ½ tablespoonful lard and ½ tablespoonful butter over the fire, put in the meat, and cook till the spare ribs begin to brown, turning often; add ½ cupful boiling water, cover and cook till done; if the water boils away, add more water (they require about one hour's cooking). When done transfer the ribs to a hot dish; remove the fat from the gravy, mix ½ tablespoonful cornstarch with 1 gill of cold water, add it to the gravy, stir and cook 2 minutes, then add sufficient boiling water to make 1 pint of sauce; strain and serve with the meat. Serve with plain boiled potatoes, and apple sauce.

HERB BUTTER SAUCE

For asparagus points up the flavor for this bland vegetable. Soften 4 tablespoons of butter or margarine and add 1 egg yolk (uncooked) and beat up together. Add a tiny pinch each of rosemary, thyme, tarragon and mix. Then add lemon juice a drop at a time, mixing as you add, until the mixture is fluffy. Add 1 tablespoon mixed parsley and a dash each of salt and pepper. Chill, then serve a spoonful over each serving of hot cooked asparagus.

MINT SYRUP

2 cups sugar
1 cup water
1 tablespoon dried or fresh mint leaves chopped fine

Stir together and simmer until sugar is completely dissolved. Cover and let stand 1 hour. Strain and use in the place of ordinary syrup for fruit beverages, gelatins and fruit cups.

MINT SALAD DRESSING

1 tablespoon mint syrup
2 tablespoons olive oil
1 teaspoon lemon juice
¼ teaspoon salt
⅛ teaspoon paprika

Beat the syrup into the oil, add lemon juice and beat, then seasoning and beat. This dressing makes an entirely new dish out of ordinary Waldorf salad, goes well with romaine and makes a wonderful combination with pineapple and cream cheese salad.

SAVORY HERB BAGS FOR WINTER USE

Soup and stew days may seem a long way off, but now is the time to get ready for them by making the bags of savory herbs which will flavor them to perfection. Make 2-inch square bags of washed cheesecloth, fill them with a tablespoon of mixed dry herbs, sew up the fourth side, and they will be ready to savor the boiled meals that are so popular on wintry days.

To make the herb mixture, take 1 tablespoon each of dried, crushed thyme, summer savory, marjoram, bay leaves, celery seed, rosemary and sage. Mix them together, then measure out a tablespoon of the mixture for each herb bag. These bags may be made in quantity and if they are stored in a covered box or jar they will retain their full strength until used.

SAGE JELLY FOR MEAT DISHES

1¼ cups boiling water
2 tablespoons sage
¼ cup vinegar
3 cups sugar
Yellow or green vegetable coloring
½ bottle fruit pectin

Pour boiling water over sage, cover, and steep for 15 minutes. Strain and measure 1 cup. Add vinegar and sugar and bring to a boil; add coloring to give desired shade. As soon as mixture boils, add fruit pec', stirring constantly. Bring to full rolling boil and boil hard for half a minute. Remove from heat, skim, and pour quickly. Paraffin at once.

TARRAGON WITH TURKEY

Snip off a handful of tarragon leaves and mince them fine. When the turkey is out of the broiler, strain the drippings. Turn drippings into a little saucepan and, while heating, add the minced tarragon. Serve a bit of this sauce over the turkey and enjoy the exotic taste.

ONIONS WITH HERBS

Prepare a quart of small white onions, throw them into boiling water, add 2 sprigs of parsley, 1 of thyme, a clove, a bay leaf, a dash of nutmeg, a small clove of garlic, salt and pepper. Boil 20 minutes, drain onions and discard seasoning. Put a heaping teaspoonful of butter in a saucepan and, when melted, blend in a level tablespoonful of flour. Then add the onions, cover with half broth and white wine, or white grapejuice with lemon, and simmer slowly until all cooked and sauce is reduced, and serve.

VEAL STUFFING

Using dried sweet herbs, you can give your roast of veal a delicate difference. One and one-half cups bread crumbs, small piece of butter, juice of 1 lemon, 1½ teaspoons finely chopped sweet herbs, 1 egg, pepper and salt to taste. Melt butter in pan, stir in bread crumbs, salt and pepper. Remove from heat and mix in bowl with herbs and lemon juice. Then stir in well beaten egg, press mixture into pocket in veal, and roast.

BERNAISE SAUCE FOR SIRLOIN STEAK

Two shallots finely chopped, good pinch of thyme, ½ bay leaf, 10 peppercorns crushed, 3 tablespoons vinegar, 12 green tarragon leaves, 1 cup Hollandaise sauce, ½ tablespoon tarragon in leaves minced, ½ tablespoon parsley minced. Cook shallots, thyme, bay leaf, parsley, crushed peppercorns and tarragon leaves with vinegar until quantity is reduced to half. Strain, add Hollandaise sauce and stir in finely chopped tarragon leaves and the chopped parsley.

ENGLISH MUSTARD SAUCE

Sauce for cold meats and cold vegetables. Combine two teaspoons of grated onion with 1 tablespoon of prepared mustard. Rub in 1½ teaspoons sugar, 2 teaspoons olive oil, and 2 teaspoons tarragon vinegar. These must be smoothly and thoroughly blended, and set in the refrigerator to chill before serving.

TAMARIND BEVERAGE

Boil three pints of water with a teacup of tamarinds, a few currants and raisins until it has evaporated one third. Strain and cool it.

TO ROAST AN OLD FOWL

Dress and soak in cold water for 2 hours. Boil until tender, put into roaster and stuff with a sage dressing. Spread 2 tablespoons of flour mixed with butter over the chicken. Put in oven and bake until a nice brown.

SOUTHERN FRIED CHICKEN

Prepare chicken, cut up, and allow to stand over night in salt and water; when about to cook, dry, sprinkle with pepper and roll thoroughly in sifted flour. Take equal parts of lard and butter, and when boiling hot in the frying pan, drop in the chicken, turning constantly. Cook fast, at first, then slowly, until well browned. For gravy, dredge in flour and add a little water, allow to simmer. Cut a bunch of parsley up fine and stir in, at last add 1 pint of cream.

OLD-FASHIONED BOILED DINNER

Procure brisket of corned beef (or if pork is preferred, a large piece of salt pork), put into the pot over a brisk fire with enough cold water to cover it; let it come to a boil, then skim, in ½ hour set the pot back on the fire and boil slowly until tender. About ¾ of an hour before dishing, skim the liquor free from fat; put a portion of it into another kettle with 1 cabbage, cleaned and cut in 4 quarters, ½ dozen peeled white turnips of medium size, cut in halves, and 4 carrots, scraped, and the same number of scraped parsnips, each cut in 4 pieces; boil until tender. Put into the kettle containing the meat, ½ hour before serving, as many medium-sized peeled potatoes as desired. Serve all together, meat and vegetables from 1 dish. Boiled beets, cooked separately, sliced hot, with vinegar over them, should also be served as a side dish. Cooking the cabbage in another dish prevents them from tasting of this vegetable when cold.

CORN BEEF

Put four gallons of fresh water, ½ pound of coarse brown sugar, 2 oz. saltpetre, seven pounds of common salt, into a boiler; remove the scum as it rises, and, when well boiled, leave it to get cold. Put in the meat in the pickle, lay a cloth over it, and press the meat down with weight.

LAMB WITH PEAS

Cut the scrag, or breast of lamb, in pieces and put in a stewpan with water enough to cover it. Cover the stewpan closely and let it simmer or stew for fifteen or twenty minutes; take off the scum, then add a tablespoonful of salt and a quart of canned peas; cover the stewpan and let them stew for half an hour; work a small tablespoonful of wheat flour with a tablespoonful of butter, and stir it into the stew: add pepper to taste; let it simmer together for ten minutes.

POTATO SALAD

Ingredients: Shallot, some cold boiled potatoes, 3 parts of oil to one part of tarragon vinegar, pepper and salt to taste, and a small quantity of any of the following: Powdered sweet herbs, mint, parsley, chervil, tarragon or capers.

Rub a dish with shallot; dispose on it some cold boiled potatoes cut in slices; beat together three parts of oil and one part, more or less according to the strength of it, of tarragon vinegar, with pepper and salt to taste. Pour this over the potatoes, and strew over all a small quantity of any of the following: powdered sweet herbs, mint, parsley, chervil, tarragon or capers, or a combination of them all, finely minced.

LAMB WITH HERBS

Braise a piece of breast of lamb in a stewpan with a little water and some onions, carrots, celery, whole pepper, salt, cloves, parsley, and sweet herbs to taste. When sufficiently cooked to allow it, pull out all the bones, and put the breast between two dishes with a heavy weight on it. The breast being quite cold and flat, cut it out into small cutlets; egg and breadcrumb them, then fry them a nice color in lard, and serve with puree of peas in the center of the dish.

KENTUCKY STYLE POTATOES

Slice potatoes thin on a slaw cutter placed over a pan of water, and let stand ½ an hour, which hardens them; put them in a pudding dish or dripping pan, with salt, pepper and about half a pint of milk; bake for an hour, take out and add a lump of butter ½ the size of an egg cut in small bits and scattered over the top. The quantity of milk cannot be exactly given; enough to moisten the potatoes, with a little left as a gravy.

STEAMED BROWN BREAD

Two cups corn meal; one cup flour; two cups sweet milk; one cup sour milk; two-thirds cup molasses; two level teaspoons soda; one tablespoon salt. Steam for three hours.

SUET PUDDING

One cup chopped suet; one cup molasses (New Orleans); one cup chopped raisins; one cup sweet milk; three cups sifted flour; one teaspoon soda dissolved in milk; spices to taste. Steam three hours. Serve with sauce made as follows: One cup of sugar; one-half cup of butter; one egg—cream well. Cook by pouring boiling water and stirring constantly.

Fenugreek Tea is really wonderful. I am very fond of boiled cabbage, but it used to give me gastric indigestion. By taking Fenugreek Tea before meals, I can now enjoy the cooked cabbage, and feel no ill effects afterward.—Mrs. R. P. W., of St. Petersburg, Fla.

CULINARY ESSENCES, TINCTURES, ETC.

Lemon Flavour
Fresh lemon peel, cut thin, 3 dr., essence of lemon 1 dr., alcohol 3 oz. (Another method is to rub a lump of sugar on clean, dry lemons, till the yellow rind is taken up by the sugar; then scrape off the saturated part of the sugar, and keep it in a closely covered pot for use.)

Tincture of Cinnamon
Bruised cinnamon 3 oz., a bottle of Cognac brandy; digest for a fortnight, and strain. (Tincture of Allspice, Nutmeg, Cloves, in the same manner.)

Essence of Cinnamon
Bruised cinnamon 2 dr., oil of cinnamon 1 dr., highly rectified spirit 3 oz.; digest, and strain.

Essences of Nutmeg, Mace, Cloves, Allspice, etc.
These are made from the spices and their essential oils, as Essence of Cinnamon.

Essence of Celery
Celery seed ½ oz. to 1 oz., brandy 4 oz.; digest for 8 to 10 days, and filter.

Essence of Caraway
Bruised caraway seed 1 oz., rectified spirit 8 oz., oil of caraway ¼ oz., brown sugar ¼ oz.; digest for 8 or 10 days, and filter.

Aromatic Essence of Ginger
Fresh grated ginger 3 oz., fresh thin lemon peel 2 oz., brandy 1½ pint; macerate for 10 days.

Essence of Cayenne
Put ½ oz. of cayenne pepper into half a pint of brandy; let it steep for a fortnight, then pour off the clear liquor.

Spirit of Savoury Spices
Black pepper 1 oz., allspice ½ oz., nutmeg ¼ oz. (all pounded); infuse in 16 fluid oz. of brandy for 10 days.

Spirit of Soup Herbs
Lemon thyme, winter savoury, sweet marjoram, sweet basil, each 1 oz., grated lemon peel and shallots, each ½ oz., celery seed 1 dr., infuse in a pint of brandy for 10 days.

Spirit of Savoury Spices No. 2
Salt 1 oz., mustard, black pepper, and grated lemon peel of each ½ oz., allspice, ginger and nutmeg, of each ¼ oz., cayenne ⅛ oz. Infuse in a quart of brandy for 10 days.

Soup Herb and Savoury Spice Spirit
A mixture of equal measures of "Spirit of Soup Herbs" and "Spirit of Savoury Spices No. 2."

Rosemary is for remembrance
Between us daie and night;
Wishing that I might alwaies have
You present in my sight.

Cream of Curry Soup
2 pints chicken stock, 2½ tablespoons flour, 2 tablespoons butter, 1 good teaspoon Curry powder, ½ cup cream, 2 egg yolks, fried croutons, salt, cayenne pepper. Blend flour and melted butter and chicken stock; cook for 15 minutes, adding salt to taste and a pinch of cayenne pepper. Moisten Curry powder with some stock and add beaten egg yolk and blend with cream and stir into soup which should not be allowed to boil further. Serve at once, garnished with butter croutons.

Curried Corn and Tomatoes
Brown 1 medium-sized onion in 2 tablespoons butter or margarine. Add 2 tablespoons flour and 1 teaspoon Curry powder. Blend well. Add 1½ cups canned tomatoes, 1 teaspoon salt and 1½ cups whole kernel corn. Cook over moderate heat until slightly thickened.

Lamb Curry on Rice
1½ cups cubed cold lamb, 2 tablespoons butter or margarine, ¾ cup chopped onion, ¼ green pepper (if desired), ½ cup diced celery, 1 clove garlic, 1 teaspoon Curry powder, 1½ teaspoons salt, 1 tablespoon Worcestershire sauce, 2 cups stock (or 2 bouillon cubes and 2 cups water), 2 tablespoons flour. Brown the onion, pepper, celery, and garlic in fat. Add the meat, Curry powder, salt, Worcestershire sauce and stock (or bouillon). Cook for about 30 minutes over slow heat. To thicken, mix flour with ¼ cup cold water and add to mixture. Cook for 10 minutes more. Serve in a ring of boiled rice.

Curried Rice and Onions
(*With Peas and Tomatoes*)
4 oz. rice, ½ lb. onions, 2 oz. fat, 1 cup cooked peas, tomato and peas for garnishing, seasoning, 1 teaspoon Curry powder. Wash the rice; then drop it into 2 quarts of boiling water and cook 17 minutes, after which drain well. Meanwhile simmer the thinly sliced onions in a little water until tender. Now mix the cooked rice, cooked onions, margarine, seasoning to taste, and the Curry powder, and make hot over a low heat. Turn on to a hot dish, border with the hot peas and garnish with sliced tomatoes either fried or grilled.

Egg Curry
2 tablespoons butter, 2 tablespoons flour, 1 teaspoon Curry powder, ⅛ teaspoon paprika, ½ tablespoon finely chopped onion, ½ teaspoon salt, 1⅓ cups scalded milk, 4 hard-cooked eggs, 1 cup cooked rice. Cream the butter and flour together. Add the Curry powder, paprika, chopped onion and salt. Stir well; add the scalded milk and cook until mixture thickens. Chop the whites of the eggs and add them with the cooked rice to the above mixture. Serve in patty shells, and garnish with grated yolks of eggs.

Too Many Cooks Spoil the Broth

To make good broth how busy all we see,
To join their skill they all as one agree:
First one into the broth the salt will throw,
Next one peppers it well, and thus they go:
To make it better still, we see a third
Puts into the seething pot some savory herb;
They stir it round and round, while hard it boils,
'Tis vain; by many cooks the broth it spoils.

HOREHOUND CANDY

Prepare a small decoction by boiling two ounces of the dried herb in a pint and a half of water for about half an hour, strain this and add three and one-half pounds of brown sugar, boil over a hot fire until it reaches the requisite degree of hardness, when it may be poured into flat tin trays, previously well greased, and marked into sticks or squares with a knife, as it becomes cool enough to retain its shape.

OLD FASHIONED APPLE JELLY

Take twenty large, juicy apples, pare and chop; put into a jar with the rind (yellow part) of four large lemons, pared thin and cut in bits; cover the jar closely and set in a pot of boiling water; keep water boiling all around it until the apples are dissolved; strain through a jelly-bag, and mix with liquid the juice of four lemons; to one pint of mixed juice one pound sugar; put in kettle and when sugar is melted set it on the fire, and boil and skim about twenty minutes, or until it is thick, fine jelly.

SUCCOTASH

Take equal quantities of corn, cut from the cob, and lima beans; 1 or 2 pounds of salt pork. Wash the pork, and put on to boil. When about half done, put in the vegetables. Boil all until tender. Take out the pork, and add a little milk—and a little more salt if needed. Give it one good boil.

BEEF STEW WITH WINE AND HERBS

(Serves six to eight)
2 pounds boneless beef stew meat; flour; salt; pepper; 1 clove garlic, minced (or less); 1 large onion, sliced; ½ teaspoon marjoram; ½ teaspoon thyme; 2 tablespoons chopped parsley; 1 cup dry red wine; water; 3 carrots, sliced thick; 3 medium potatoes, peeled and quartered. Meat should be cut into small pieces. Roll in flour which has been seasoned well with salt and pepper, and brown on all sides in bacon drippings or beef suet, fried out. Add garlic and onion, let cook in fat with meat for 5 minutes, very slowly. Add herbs, wine and one cup water. Cover and let simmer very gently for three hours, or until meat is tender. Add carrots and potatoes and more salt during last half or three-quarters of an hour of cooking. Add more water from time to time as it cooks off.

The wine may be omitted and water used in its place. That will still give you an elegant stew. Plenty of freshly ground pepper goes a long way to make the seasoning perfect.

BOILED ONIONS

It is a good plan to boil onions in milk and water, it diminishes the strong taste of this vegetable. It is an excellent way to chop them up, after they have been boiled, and put them into a stewpan with a little milk, butter, salt and pepper; let them stew about fifteen minutes; this gives them a fine flavor, and they can be served very hot.

SAVORY POTATO PANCAKES

Quarter of a pound of grated ham, one pound of mashed potatoes and a little suet, mixed with the yolks of two eggs, pepper, salt and nutmeg. Roll it into little balls or cakes and fry it a light brown. Sweet herbs may be used in place of ham. Plain potato pancakes are made with potatoes and eggs only.

JENNY LIND CAKE

One cup of sugar, small piece of butter the size of a small egg, 1 cup milk, 1 teaspoon soda, 2 teaspoonsful cream of tartar in 2 cups flour, ½ pound chopped raisins. Lemon or vanilla flavoring.

SOFT MOLASSES CAKE

One cup butter, 1 cup sugar, 1 cup molasses, 4 cups flour, 3 eggs, 2 scant teaspoons soda; ½ tumbler of milk, butter, sugar and molasses beaten together; add eggs, flour and the milk with the soda dissolved in it; rub the top with the white of an egg, molasses or a little butter when it comes from the oven.

LEMON SUGAR

Rub the rind of some fresh lemons upon a large piece of sugar, and as it discolours the part upon which it is rubbed, scrape it off with a knife; when you have obtained a sufficient quantity, dry a little in the screen and bottle for use when required. Orange sugar may be made in the same manner, substituting very red oranges for lemons.

VANILLA SUGAR

Chop a stick of well-frosted vanilla very small, and put it into a mortar with half a pound of lump sugar, pound the whole well together in a mortar, sift through a hair sieve, and put by in a bottle or jar, corking it up tight and using where required.

LEMON SUET PUDDING

To eight ounces of finely grated breadcrumbs, add six fresh beef kidney suet, free from skin, and minced very small, three and a half of pounded sugar, six ounces of currants, the grated rind and the strained juice of a large lemon, and four full-sized wellbeaten eggs; pour these ingredients into a thickly buttered pan, and bake the pudding for an hour in a brisk oven, but draw it towards the mouth when it is of a fine brown colour. Turn it from the dish before it is served and strew sifted sugar over it; two ounces more of suet can be added when a larger proportion is liked. The pudding is very good without the currants.

OLD FASHIONED CREAM SUBSTITUTE

Beat two eggs, one ounce of sugar and a small piece of butter, with one pint of warm milk, then put it into hot water and stir it one way, until it acquires the consistence of cream. Instead of eggs as above, use a spoonful of arrowroot, if you like, first beaten with a little cold milk.

LEMON CREAM

Cream, one pint; yolks of three eggs; powdered sugar, six ounces; the yellow rind of one lemon, grated, with the juice; mix, apply heat and stir until cold. If wanted white, the whites of the eggs should be used instead of the yolks.

ORANGE FLOWER RECIPES

Macaroons: Have ready two pounds of very dry white sifted sugar. Weigh two ounces of the petals of freshly-gathered orange blossoms after they have been picked from the stems; and cut them very small with a pair of scissors into the sugar, as they will become discoloured if not mixed with it quickly after they are cut. When all are done, add the whites of seven eggs and whisk the whole well together until it looks like snow; then drop the mixture upon paper without delay, and send the cakes to a very cool oven. It is impossible to state with accuracy the precise time required for these cakes, so much depends on the oven; they should be very delicately coloured and yet dried through.

Candy: Beat in three quarters of a pint (or a little more) of water, about the fourth part of the white of an egg and pour it on two pounds of the best sugar broken into lumps. When it has stood a little time, place it over a very clear fire, and let it boil for a few minutes, then set it on one side, until the scum has subsided; clear it off and boil the sugar until it is very thick, then strew in by degrees three ounces of the petals of the orange blossoms, weighed after they are picked from their stems. Continue to stir the candy until it rises into one white mass in the pan, then pour it into small paper cases, or on to dishes. The orange flowers will turn brown if thrown too soon into the syrup; it should be more than three parts boiled when they are added. They must be gathered on the day they are wanted for use, as they become soon discoloured from keeping.—From an old recipe book.

ORANGE SYRUP

Select ripe and thin skinned oranges. Squeeze the juice through a sieve; to every pint add a pound and a half of sugar; boil and skim as long as any scum rises. You then may take it off; let it grow cold and bottle it. Be sure to secure the corks well. Two tablespoons of this syrup, mixed in melted butter, makes an admirable sauce for a plum or batter pudding, and it also imparts a fine flavor to custards.

LEMON JUMBLES

One teacup sugar, ½ teacup butter, 3 teaspoons milk, 1 teaspoon cream of tartar, ½ teaspoon soda, 1 egg, 2 small lemons—the juice of one and rind of two. Mix rather stiff and roll out.

MARMALADE

Can be made from all kinds of fruit, by thoroughly cooking them; strain through a colander or coarse sieve, adding 1 pound sugar to 1 pint fruit after it is strained; boil until it is a thickened mass, taking care that it does not scorch; when cool put in glass jars.

WORCESTERSHIRE SAUCE

To a gallon of ripe tomatoes, washed and cut up, take 3 quarts of water and let it boil down half; stir occasionally to prevent tomatoes from sticking. After boiling thus, press the tomatoes through a sieve; add 2 tablespoons of ginger, 2 tablespoons black pepper; 2 tablespoons salt; 1 tablespoon cloves, and 1 tablespoon red pepper. Boil all down to a quart, and add a tumbler of vinegar; strain, bottle and cork tight. At this last boiling the kettle had better be placed over the fire in a pot of water to prevent scorching. Another, and more pungent recipe, is a gallon of tomatoes; 5 tablespoons salt; 2 tablespoons cayenne pepper; 2 tablespoons black pepper; 1 teaspoon mace; 1 teaspoon cinnamon; 1 teaspoon allspice; ½ teaspoon cloves; 2 large onions chopped; 1 quart of cider vinegar, and 1 tablespoon ground mustard. Some folks like a little garlic. Simmer gently four hours. Be careful not to scorch. Stir frequently. Strain through a sieve when cool. Bottle with new corks.

HERB STUFFING

Two teaspoons dried sage, 1 teaspoon dried savory, 2 teaspoons dried parsley, 1 teaspoon celery leaves, 1 teaspoon dried thyme, salt, pepper and onion to taste, 1 egg (beaten), 15 slices buttered toast. Pour warm water over toast—break slices with fork—add all other ingredients and mix thoroughly. I add prunes to this as my family enjoy them. Use ½ recipe for a large chicken.

MINCE MEAT FOR PIE

Two pounds of beef, boiled, and chopped fine; 1 pound of suet—chopped; if eaten cold, pork is better than suet; chopped fine; 5 pounds of apples, chopped; 2 pounds raisins, seeded; 2 pounds currants, well washed; ½ pound citron, or candied lemon peel, cut fine; 2 tablespoons cinnamon; 1 tablespoon grated nutmeg; 2 tablespoons mace; 1 tablespoon cloves; 1 tablespoon allspice; 1 tablespoon salt; 2½ pounds brown sugar; 1 quart cider, boiled, or sherry wine; 1 pint of best brandy. This will keep all winter, in a stone jar, well covered, in a cool place. If too dry when used, add a little more cider.

GRAVY FLAVOR

Salt, 12 parts; Ginger 2 parts; Cinnamon, 1 part; Black Pepper, 1 part; Allspice 1 part; nutmeg, 1 part; Cloves ¼ ounce. Grind and mix thoroughly. A dash of any or all of the following herbs will add zest and aroma to mixture; Thyme, Marjoram or Savory.

CELERY SAUCE

Wash 2 heads of fine white celery—cut it into small pieces, and put it into a quart of milk and simmer about an hour. Then rub it through a fine sieve. Beat the yolks of four eggs with ¼ pint of cream. Mix all together and stir over a gentle fire five minutes, or until it thickens. Serve on fish.

HORSE RADISH AND CELERY SAUCE

Prepared as pepper sauce, with the addition of a little salt and no sugar. Let stand for a week or two and bottle.

PEPPER SAUCE

Take 6 or 8 red peppers, 1 ounce black pepper corns, 2 tablespoons granulated sugar in 1 quart vinegar, scalded and poured over peppers. Strain and put into bottles in about a week. Eaten with raw oysters, boiled fish, or salad.

CURRIE POWDER

Coriander seed powdered, three ounces: Cayenne pepper, three drachms; turmeric three-quarters of an ounce; cumin seed, three quarters of an ounce, foenugreek seed, three quarters of an ounce; Cardamoms, a quarter of an ounce. All should be powdered. A quarter of an ounce of cloves is sometimes added to the above.—Recipe of an English Duke.

SAGE AND ONION SAVOURY

Mix together 2 tablespoons chopped onion, 1 teaspoon sage, 6 ozs. breadcrumbs, 2 ozs. oatmeal, 2 ozs. chopped beef suet, and seasonings of salt, pepper, etc., to taste, and add enough milk to make a soft mixture. Put in a greased tin and bake one hour in a moderate oven. Cut into squares and serve with gravy or parsley sauce.

TAMARIND MARMALADE

One quart shelled tamarind nuts, water, sugar. Boil tamarinds in plenty of water until soft. Put through sieve, to remove seeds and fibers. Measure equal parts of sugar and pulp and simmer slowly, stirring constantly until the mixture thickens enough to coat a silver spoon. Pour into sterilized jelly glasses and seal with wax.

Jelly for Invalids. Boil one ounce of cut Agar Agar in 20 ounces of water for 10 minutes. Strain before liquid becomes cool. Jell may be sweetened and flavored with lemon or orange peel.

Arrowroot is one of the most easily digested nutritives and for this reason it is of special value to dyspeptics.

TAPIOCA APPLE

One teacup of tapioca soaked in 1 quart of warm water. Peel 6 or 8 tender and tart apples, halve them, take out the cores, lay them in a dish with the core side up; sprinkle in each hollow some cinnamon and sugar, or a little lemon juice. Sweeten the tapioca before pouring it over the apples. Bake about 1 hour. A soft custard with this is very nice, poured over it at the table.

OLD FASHIONED SWEET JOHNNYCAKE

1 cup of coarse chopped suet
1 cup of sour milk
1 cup of sugar
1 teaspoonful of soda
A pinch of salt

Corn meal enough to make a thin batter. Bake in a long pan for half an hour.

CORN MEAL MUFFINS

2 cups corn meal
1 cup of flour
2 teaspoonfuls of molasses
1 teaspoonful of baking powder
2 cups of milk
1 salt-spoonful of salt

Bake half an hour. These may be fried as griddle cakes.

COCOANUT DROPS

6 eggs, whites beaten to a stiff froth
½ pound of pulverized sugar
1 pound of grated cocoanut

Drop on buttered pans and bake.

HOME-MADE CRACKERS

Take enough light bread dough for a loaf of bread; work into it about a ½ teacupful of shortening, either lard or butter, and a ¼ teaspoon of soda. Knead in flour enough to make very stiff, and pound and cut it for half an hour. Roll and cut into cakes; prick and let stand to rise. After baking, leave in a slow oven until perfectly crisp.

NEW JERSEY CREAM CAKE

One and a half cups of cream, 1½ cups sugar, 1 egg, small piece of butter the size of a small egg, 2 tablespoons of molasses, ½ teaspoon soda, 1 teaspoon cinnamon, ½ teaspoon cloves, and a little nutmeg; a few raisins chopped; flour enough to stir a stiff batter.

CUSTARD PUDDING

Boil one pint of milk, with a small piece of lemon-peel and half a bay-leaf, for three minutes; then pour these on to three eggs, mix it with one ounce of sugar well together, and pour it into a buttered mould, and steam it twenty-five minutes by standing the dish in a stewpan containing about half a pint of water, that is, the water should be about half way up to the rim of the dish; set the stewpan (covered close) upon the fire and let it slowly boil. When the pudding is properly set turn out on a plate and serve.

FRITTERS

3 eggs
2 tablespoonfuls of sugar
1 pint of sour milk
1 teaspoonful of soda
A pinch of salt
Flour enough to make a stiff batter

Beat thoroughly. Drop a large spoonful in hot lard. Fry brown and roll in powdered sugar when done.

CHEESE FRITTERS

Slice thin, half a dozen large, tart apples and prepare half as many thin slices of cheese. Beat up one or two eggs, according to the quantity required, and season high with salt, mustard and a little pepper. Lay the slices of cheese to soak for a few minutes in the mixture. Then put each slice between two slices of apples, sandwich style, and dip the whole in the beaten egg. Fry in hot butter and serve hot.

HOMINY FRITTERS

1 egg
½ cup of sweet milk
1 tablespoonful of flour
1 quart of boiled hominy
A pinch of salt

Roll into oval balls with floured hands; dip in a well-beaten egg and then in dried bread crumbs, and fry in hot lard.

SAUCE FOR FRITTERS

1 heaping tablespoonful of butter
2 heaping tablespoonfuls of flour, rubbed together
1½ cups of boiling water, and cook five minutes
1½ cups of brown sugar
1 salt-spoonful of ginger
1 even teaspoonful of cinnamon, or, if preferred, juice of
½ a lemon
½ a nutmeg

Stir until the sugar is all melted. Serve hot.

NEW ORLEANS CORN BREAD

1½ pints of corn meal
½ pint of flour
1 tablespoonful of sugar
1 teaspoonful of salt
2 heaping teaspoonfuls of baking-powder
1 tablespoonful of lard
1¼ pints milk
2 eggs

Sift together corn meal, flour, sugar, salt and baking powder; rub in lard cold, add eggs (beaten) and the milk; mix into a moderately stiff batter; pour from bowl into a shallow cake pan. Bake in rather hot oven thirty minutes.

SWISS CAKES

Mix a quarter of a pound of fine flour, two ounces of sifted sugar, the grated peel of a lemon, and half a pound of butter, to a paste, with the white of an egg, and a little milk. Roll it thin, cut into biscuits, and brush them over with the yolk of an egg, over which sift the fine sugar; bake them on tins.

GERMAN HONEY CAKES

One pound honey, 1 pound syrup, 1 pound rye flour, 1 pound wheat flour, 1 even tablespoonful of soda, 1 teaspoon cinnamon, ½ teaspoonful cloves, ¼ teaspoonful cardamon (each pulverized and sifted), ¼-½ pound blanched split almonds, 2 ounces citron, 2 ounces candied orange peel, ¾ cup sweet, white lard.

Let the honey and syrup come to a boil, then remove from the stove, and when partially cooled add the flour and lard. Mix thoroughly, cover the crock well and stand away in some warm place for at least a week. After the lapse of that time, roll out the dough on the baking board and add the soda dissolved in a little cold water, also the spices, fruit and almonds, knead well after adding each ingredient, until all is perfectly mixed. Again roll out the dough about ¼-inch thick, wash with sweet milk and bake in dripping pans until done, which will require fully 15 minutes, in quite a hot oven. When done cut them any shape or size desired, spread with frosting and put an almond on each cake, return to the oven until the frosting is dry, but do not let it scorch.

VIENNA ROLLS

One quart flour, 2 teaspoonfuls baking powder, butter size of an egg, ½ teaspoonful salt, boiled cooled milk.

Sift the flour 2-3 times with the baking powder, rub into this the butter and salt, then stir all to a stiff dough with milk. Take small pieces of the dough, roll them into small round lumps, cut them across slightly in opposite directions from side to side with a sharp knife, set them in tins not touching each other, brush them over with milk or melted butter and bake.

ANGELS' FOOD CAKE

One and one-half cups sifted, granulated sugar (scant measure), 1 cup flour sifted four times, whites of 11 eggs, 1 teaspoonful vanilla, 1 even teaspoonful cream of tartar.

Beat the whites with the cream of tartar, when half beaten add the sugar lightly, then the flour. Add the flour gradually sprinkling spoonfuls into the egg and sugar. After all is added, flavor, but do not stop beating until ready for the pan. Do not grease the pan, bake 40 minutes and when done treat the same as all sponge cakes.

Note: Do not cut angel's food the same day it is baked, it is always lighter and finer when it is a day or two old. Chopped almonds or other nuts will be found a delicious addition if added just before putting the dough into the pan. Candied cherries chopped very fine and added in the same way have the appearance of rubies imbedded in the snow.

SUNSHINE CAKE

Yolks of 10 eggs, 1 cup sugar, ½ cup butter, ½ cup milk, 1½ cups flour, ½ cup corn starch, 3 teaspoonfuls baking powder, 1 teaspoon vanilla, pinch salt.

Beat the yolks to a cream, add the butter and sugar creamed together, then the milk, the vanilla and salt, follow gradually with the flour, corn starch and baking powder sifted together. Bake immediately.

ORANGE MARMALADE

This is a very elegant preparation, but requires the most careful attention. Rub a few tender and juicy oranges with a flannel cloth, and remove any defective parts. Put the oranges whole into a good quantity of cold water, and boil them gently till a pin's head will easily pierce them. Then cut them in quarters and pick out all the seeds. With a very sharp knife, slice them very thin, skin and all. Dissolve the sugar in a very little water, and clarify it thoroughly. Boil the syrup till it begins to thicken, then add the sliced oranges, and boil fifteen minutes. This should not be used for six months, and will then be found perfectly transparent and delicious.

LEMON MARMALADE

Pare off the thin rind, then the white pith, cut the lemons in two and extract the seeds. Squeeze the juice and chop the pulp, together with the thin rind, very fine. Break the sugar very fine, dissolve it with water in which the pith has been boiled a few minutes to extract its strength. Allow half a pint of this water to a pound of sugar. When the syrup is well prepared, as before directed, add the juice and chopped rind with the pulp. Boil fifteen minutes. The syrup should be quite thick before adding the juice; it is also necessary to allow a pound and a quarter of sugar to a pound of lemons on account of their extreme sourness. This should be put in a wide-mouthed jar, and sealed when cold. It is better for keeping, not being at all adapted to immediate use.

USE OF LEMON LEAVES

Lemon seeds, if planted and treated as house plants, will make pretty little shrubs. The leaves can then be used for flavoring. Tie a few in a cloth and drop in apple sauce when boiling and nearly done. It is cheap essence.

STEWED BEEF

Ingredients: 1 tablespoon of butter, 2 sliced onions, 12 whole cloves, allspice, ½ teaspoonful of black pepper, 1 pint of cold water, 2 or 3 pounds of tender beef, a little flour, a few sprigs of sweet basil.

In a stew-pan place a large tablespoonful of butter in which fry until quite brown two sliced onions adding, while cooking, 12 whole cloves; the same of allspice; half a teaspoonful of salt and half that quantity of black pepper; take from the fire, pour in a pint of cold water, wherein lay two or three pounds of tender lean beef cut in small thick pieces; cover closely and let all stew gently two hours, adding, just before serving, a little flour thickening. A few sprigs of sweet basil is an improvement.

PORK CHEESE

Ingredients: About 2 lbs. of cold roast pork, a dessertspoonful of chopped parsley, 5 sage leaves, pepper and salt, a bunch of savory herbs, 2 blades of mace, a little nutmeg, ½ teaspoonful of minced lemon peel, sufficient gravy to fill the mould.

Cut the pork into pieces, but do not chop; there should be about a quarter of fat to a pound of lean; sprinkle with pepper and salt, pound the spices thoroughly and mince as finely as possible, the parsley, sage, lemon peel and herbs; then mix all this nicely together. Place in mould and fill with gravy. Bake a little over an hour. When perfectly cold, turn out.

ITALIAN SPAGHETTI SAUCE

Cook 2 cups of chopped onion until transparent in ½ cup of oil—salad or olive. Add 2 cloves of garlic, finely minced, and ½ pound of mushrooms, sliced. Simmer over low heat until the mushrooms and onions are browned a little. Now add 2 cups of water and 2 or 3 teaspoons of meat paste, 1 teaspoon of salt and 4 cups of canned tomato sauce. Add ¼ teaspoon of mixed herbs and simmer for about one-half hour.

Keep in refrigerator and reheat as you need it.

GREEN TOMATO SALAD

Perfectly smooth, spotless tomatoes, onions, pepper, salt, sugar, vinegar olive oil.

Wash the tomatoes perfectly clean, remove the stem end and slice.

Dressing: Equal parts of vinegar and water, sugar, pepper and salt to taste, and a liberal quantity of oil. Mix with the tomatoes and serve with or without the onions.

Garnish with red or yellow tomatoes.

When using herbs for flavoring give foods only a nip or touch of sweet herby fragrance. Foods should NEVER be saturated with definite flavor of herb.

GREEK SOUP

Ingredients: 4 lbs. of lean beef, 1 lb. of lean mutton, 1 lb. of veal, 4 ozs. of lean ham, 4 carrots, 4 onions, 1 head of celery; a little soy, a few allspice and a few coriander seeds, some pepper and salt, 10 quarts of water.

Cut up the beef, mutton and veal into small pieces and throw into a stewpan with 10 quarts of cold water; add a little salt, and then place on the stove to boil; take off the scum, add a little cold water, and take off the second scum; then cut up the carrots, onions and celery and throw in the pot; add a little more salt, a few allspice, and coriander seeds; let it simmer six hours, color the soup with a little soy, and strain it through a fine cloth; take off any fat that may be on the soup with a sheet of paper; before sending to the table boil the soup, and place in the tureen a little fried lean ham cut into small pieces.

HERBS FOR SOUP

Gather and dry in a moderate stove-oven such articles as you may be able to obtain such as sage, sweet marjoram, lemon thyme, winter savory, sweet basil, celery seed and others. When perfectly dry, break them into a mortar, pound them fine and sift through a hair sieve. Put them in bottles, closely stopped, and they will retain their fragrance and flavor for many months. This composition of the fine aromatic herbs is an invaluable acquisition, when the fresh herbs cannot be had. The delicate flavors of the several herbs combine and blend into each other so as to form most delicious seasoning. In the whole form herbs may be used as bouquet garni, that is place in a cloth bag so it can be removed after desired flavor is obtained.

SPANISH SOUP

Ingredients: Chives, cucumber, some water, pinch of salt, some lemon juice, some oil, crumbled bread, chopped marjoram.

Put some chopped chives and cucumber cut up in the shape of dice into a large salad bowl, add a small quantity of water, a pinch of salt, lemon juice and oil. Throw in some crumbled bread, which must be able to float. Finally sprinkle some finely chopped marjoram over the whole, and your "gaspacho" is ready.

HERBS ADD FLAVOR

Add a pinch of herbs with bread crumbs when breading chops or cutlets—it does wonders! Use sage with pork—Thyme or Marjoram with veal.

LEMON CANDY

Steep the grated peel of 1 lemon in the strained juice of 2 lemons for an hour; strain, squeezing the cloth hard to get out all the strength; then pour three cups of clear water over 6 pounds of white sugar and when dissolved, set over the fire in a bright tinned or porcelain sauce-pan, and bring to a boil. Boil briskly until a little of the candy becomes hard and brittle when thrown into water. Stir in the lemon juice; boil one minute and add a teaspoonful of dry soda, stirring well. Instantly turn out upon broad shallow dishes. Pull as soon as it may be handled and cut into lengths.

VANILLA CANDY

Prepare in the same way as above, but substitute, for flavoring the vanilla extract.

PINEAPPLE, BANANA, RASPBERRY AND STRAWBERRY CANDIES

These candies are made likewise as above, with the requisite flavors.

PEPPERMINT, WINTERGREEN, SASSAFRAS, CINNAMON, ROSE, ANISE, CLOVE, ETC., CANDY

Make in the same way but flavor with a few drops of the essential oil instead of with the essence or extract.

PEPPERMINT DROPS

Take one pound of dry granulated sugar and place it in a lipped sauce-pan; add enough water to form a stiff paste, say two ounces. Set over the fire until it begins to boil and remove it at once. Keep stirring and when a little cool, add extract of peppermint to suit the taste. Color if desired, and drop on sheets of white paper.

MOLASSES CANDY

Take equal quantities brown sugar and Orleans molasses (or all molasses may be used), and one tablespoon sharp vinegar, and when it begins to boil skim well and strain, return to the kettle and continue boiling until it becomes brittle if dipped in cold water, then pour on a greased platter. When cool enough, begin to throw up the edges and work, by pulling until bright and glistening like gold; flour the hands occasionally, draw into stick size, rolling to keep round, until pulled out and cold. With a greased knife press nearly through them at proper lengths, and they will easily snap; flavor just before pouring out to cool.

LIQUID MEASURE USED IN THIS BOOK

2 teaspoonfuls equal 1 tablespoonful.
4 tablespoonfuls equal 1 ounce.
16 ounces fluid equal 1 pint.
64 tablespoonfuls equal 1 pint.
128 teaspoonfuls equal 1 pint.

COUGH CANDY

Steep 2 ounces of boneset (thoroughwort) and ½ an ounce of blood root in 1½ pints of water, for half an hour. Strain, and add this to 3½ pounds of brown sugar, and proceed as for horehound candy.

BERTIE'S COOKIES

1 cup sugar; 3 eggs beaten light; ½ cup of butter; 1 cup of sweet milk; 4 cups prepared flour; nutmeg and cinnamon. Cream the butter, spices and sugar; add the egg yolks, then the milk, whites of the eggs and flour alternately: Cut out and bake quickly.

COASTING COOKIES

1 pound of flour; 8 ounces of butter; ½ pint of molasses; 1 tablespoonful of soda, beaten hard in the molasses; 1 tablespoonful each of coriander and caraway seeds, powdered; ginger to taste. Soften the butter, stir in the molasses, ginger, seeds and flour. Roll thin, cut and bake in a quick oven.

FAMILY COOKIES

½ pound butter; 1½ pints sifted flour; 1 pint light brown sugar; 1 gill sour cream; 2 teaspoonfuls of caraway seeds; 1 teaspoonful of soda dissolved in hot water; 1 egg. Soften the butter and stir in the sugar, cream, egg, soda, seeds and flour. Roll, cut and bake in a quick oven.

GINGERBREAD

One-half cup of molasses; one-half cup of sugar; one-half cup of butter; one-half cup of sour milk; one and one-half cup of flour; two small eggs; one-half teaspoon of soda; teaspoonful of cinnamon; ginger; and one-half teaspoon of cloves, a little nutmeg.

CORN CAKE

One pint of milk; half a pint of corn meal; four eggs, a scant tablespoonful of butter; salt; and one teaspoonful of sugar. Pour the milk boiling on the sifted meal. When cold, add the butter (melted), the salt, the sugar, the yolks of the eggs, and, lastly, the whites, well beaten. Bake half an hour in a hot oven. It is very nice baked in iron or tin gem pans, the cups an inch and a half deep.

RECIPES AND REMEDIES OF EARLY ENGLAND

(Taken from book under same title by Violet and Hal W. Trovillion of Herrin, Illinois.)

The Queen's Ordinary Bouillon: "A Hen, a handful of Parsley, a sprig of Thyme, three of Spearmint, a little Balm, half a great Onion, a little Pepper and salt and a clove; as much water as would cover the Hen and this boyled to less than a pinte, for one good pottinger full."

A Very Rich Cherry-Cordial: "Take a Stone Pot that has a broad Bottom and a narrow Top and lay a Layer of Black Cherries and a Layer of very fine powdered Sugar; do this till your Pot is full; Measure your Pot and to every gallon it holds, put a quarter of a Pint of true Spirit of Wine. You are to pick your Cherries clean from Soil and stalks, but not wash them. When you have thus filled your Pot, stop it with a Cork and tie first a Bladder, then a leather over it, and if you fear it is not close enough, pitch it down close and bury it deep in the Earth for six Months or longer; then strain it out and keep it close stopped for your Use. 'Twill revive, when all other Cordials fail."

To Candy Flowers with their Colours: "Take Gum Arabick and steep it in Rose-Water all night, the next day take what Flowers or Herb you please and dip them well in that Gum water and swing them well from it, then strew them very thick with Sugar beaten fine on every side, and lay them upon plates to dry in the sun and when you find they begin to dry turn them on clean plates, and if you find sugar wanting supply it."

To Make An Apple Hash: "Take ye largest apples you can get, pare ym and cut ym in round slices. Dip ym in wheat meal and fry ym until they begin to brown. Be carfull in turning for fear they break. So lay ym up on your dish. Melt butter and Sack (white wine) and Sugar wit a sprig of romary (rosemary). So put it upon ym and Sinimond (cinnamon) upon them. Serve ym up for the second course (in early times, the main course.)"

Perfume for Pipes: "Take Balm of Peru half an ounce, seven or eight drops of oyl of Cinamon, Oyl of Cloves, five drops, Oyl of Nutmegs, of Thyme, of Lavender, of Fennel, of Aniseeds (all drawn by distillation) of each a like quantity, or more or less as you like the Odour and would have it strongest; incorporate with these half a dram of Ambergrease; make all these into a paste which keep in a box, when you have filled your pipe of Tobacco, put upon it about the bigness of a pins Head of this Composition. It will make the smoak most pleasantly odoriferous, both to the Takers and to them that come into the Room; and ones Breath will be sweet all days after. It also comforts the Head and Brains."

Against a Woman's Chatter: "Against a woman's chatter; taste at night fasting a root of radish, that day the chatter cannot harm thee."

To Make Love Powders: "Take of the Female Fern root a quart of an ounce, dry it well, powder it with the seed of Lupins and burnt Peach stone, make them into a fine powder, give it in a Glass of Water or other liquor, and if you be anything taking or pleasing in person or behavior doubt not but the party to whom you give it will soon be loving and kind, though before never so coy or averse to Love."

A Never Failing Recipe to Cure Love: "Take two ounces of Spirit of Reason. Three ounces of the powder of Experience. Five drams of the juice of Discretion. Six ounces of the powder of Good Advice and two spoonfuls of the Cooling Water of Consideration, make it into pills and drink a little. Continue after therein. One dose clears the head of the Maggots and Whimzies, then take another dose and drink a little Content and you'll be restored to your right senses."

Periwinkle: "Venus owns this herb and saith, That the leaves eaten by a man and wife together, cause love between them. The Periwinkle is a great binder, stays bleeding both at mouth and nose, if some of the leaves be chewed."

ENGLISH PUDDING

One pound raisins, 1 pound currants, 1 pound suet, 1 cup molasses, 1 cup milk, 2 nutmegs ground, allspice, cloves—teaspoonful, ½ teaspoon soda, 4 eggs. Boiled 4 or 5 hours, or steamed. Serve with hard sauce made of 1½ cups granulated sugar, ½ cup butter, beat until it is very white and to a cream. Add a little brandy. This Hard Sauce is also nice for batter puddings and dumplings.

GRATED APPLE PUDDING

One quart of grated sour apples, 5 eggs, ¼ pound butter, 1 pound sugar, juice and grated rind of 2 lemons. Bake an hour and a quarter. Eat cold.

BREAD PUDDING

One quart of milk; 2 cups of stale, fine, bread crumbs, soaked in the milk; 4 eggs, 2 tablespoons of melted butter; 1 cup sugar, nutmeg to taste; ¼ teaspoon soda, dissolved in vinegar. Apples cut up and placed at the bottom of the dish, is quite an addition. It can be baked or boiled.

INTERESTING FACTS REGARDING WINE GRAPES AS RECORDED IN A 400 YEAR OLD HERBAL

The sunne must give to the wine strength and vertue, and the night his sweetness and the moone shine his ripenes. And therefore are the wines of Canarie, of Candie, and other the like hot countries, both sweete and strong: for the sunne shineth vehemently in those countries, and the nights be longer than in this countrie. And for this consideration the wine of Rheine, and of other the septentrionall or north regions are weaker, and not so sweete and pleasant, bicause the nights in those countries be shorter, and the sunne hath not so much strength. And for the same cause also it groweth not in Norweigh, Swedland, Denmarke, Westphale, Prusse, and other cold countries: for the nights be there in sommer short and the power of the sunne is but small.

RAISIN WINE

Ingredients: To every gallon of spring water allow 8 pounds of good raisins, brandy of the finest quality. Stir the fruit and water in a large tub every day for a month; then press the raisins in a horsehair bag as dry as possible; put the liquor into a cask, and when it has done hissing, pour in a bottle of the best brandy; stop it close for twelve months; then rack it off, but without the dregs; filter them through a bag of flannel of three or four folds, add the clear to the quantity, and pour one or two quarts of brandy according to the size of the vessel. Stop it up, and at the end of three years you may either bottle it or drink it from the cask. Raisin wine would be extremely good if made rich of the fruit, and kept long, which improves the flavor greatly.

ELDERBERRY WINE

Mash 1 bushel of picked elderberries, and, having added 10 gallons of water, boil all together for a few minutes. Then strain. To every quart of juice add ¾ of a pound of sugar; and, while the liquid is still warm, put in ½ a pint of yeast. Let it ferment in a cask for ten days, and then bung up. In three months draw off the wine, and bottle.

RHUBARB WINE

Take the large juicy stalks of the rhubarb, or pie-plant, and press out the juice; to every gallon add 7 pounds of brown sugar dissolved in 1 gallon of water. Fill a cask with this proportion, and keep pouring in sweetened water as it works over, until clear; then bung up tight, and keep in a cool place.

GRAPE WINE

Ingredients: 20 pounds of fresh fruit, 1½ gallons water, 10 pounds granulated sugar. Put the grapes into a crock, pour over the water, which must be boiling; when conveniently cool, press well with the hands. Let it remain three days on the pomace covered over with a cloth. Then squeeze out all the juice and add the sugar. Leave for a week longer in the crock. Then remove the scum. Strain and bottle, leaving uncorked until the fermentation is over. Then strain and rebottle, corking tight. Place the bottles on their sides in a cool place.

GOOSEBERRY WINE

Ingredients: 6 pounds of green gooseberries to every gallon of water, 3 pounds of white sugar. The gooseberries must be green (*not* ripe) and must be perfectly sound. Top and tail them, place in a tub and bruise them. Be particular that every berry is broken, but do not crush the seeds; warm the water and pour on the fruit. Now press and squeeze it to a pulp; cover for a day and a night. Meantime prepare a coarse bag, and at the end of the stated time strain through it, extracting all the juice. Put into a tub, add sugar, stir until it is dissolved, and set in a warm place; keep it closely covered, allowing it to ferment for two days. At the end of that time draw into clean casks, tilt them a little on one side, and when the scum has settled, remove it and fill with the remaining juice. As soon as the fermentation has stopped, plug the casks upright, filling a third time, if needful, put the bungs in loosely and when the fermentation is over drive the bungs in tightly, and a small hole made to give vent. After six months draw off from the dregs into casks rinsed with brandy. Allow to stand a month, then examine, and if clear, bottle, if not, clear with one ounce of isinglass to eight gallons of wine.

DANDELION WINE

Soak 6 quarts Dandelion flowers in four quarts of water three days and three nights. Strain. Add 4 pounds sugar, 2 sliced lemons, 2 tablespoons yeast, then let stand 4 days and 4 nights. It is then ready to bottle. Take 1 to 2 tablespoonsful at a time. It is good for your stomach.

Submitted by K. A. B., North Lima, Ohio.

ROOT-BEER

"Gather a half bushel basket of spruce boughs, Sassafras roots, Sarsaparilla roots, sweet fern leaves, wintergreen leaves, black birch bark, black cherry bark, and dandelion and yellow dock roots. Boil in 6 gallons of water with a large handful of hops, and a quart of wheat bran. Strain through a sieve—turn in 3 quarts of molasses, and, if very strong, add a gallon or two of cold water. When cool, put in ½ pint of yeast, and when it begins to work, make a very slight vent for the escape of gas. In 3 days it will be ready for use. Excellent and healthful."—From an 1887 Cook Book.

How different this recipe is from most of the so-called "Root Beers" offered to-day.

ANGELICA LIQUOR

Pick the leaves of a couple of Angelica twigs, cut them in small pieces and put them in good alcohol mixed with sugar, dissolved in water; a few cloves and a little cinnamon. Let it stand and soak for 6 weeks, and then filterate it. Ingredients are: ½ pound Angelica, 1½ pounds alcohol, sugar to suit, and 2 quarts water.

ANISETTE

Ten ounces Anise seed, is to be put in a gallon of alcohol with the yellow rind of 2 or 3 lemons and a little cinnamon. This is set aside for a month. After that time strain the extract and dilute it with 3 quarts of water and 4 pounds sugar boiled down to a thick syrup, cooled and cleared. Work it like punch, then bottle.

BLACKBERRY CORDIAL

One quart blackberry juice, two pounds loaf sugar, one ounce cloves, one ounce cinnamon, one ounce allspice, one ounce nutmeg. Pulverize the spice, and tie in a clean cloth; boil all together for half an hour, and skim well. Then bottle while hot and seal.

ROOT BEER

Boil 2 ounces, each, of burdock, yellowdock, sarsaparilla, dandelion and spikenard roots well bruised, in 4 gallons of water for about twenty minutes; then strain, and add 10 drops, each, of the oils of wintergreen, sassafras and spruce. When the mixture is quite cool, put in 3 tablespoonfuls of yeast and 1 pound of sugar. Let it work about two hours; then bottle.

EPPS' BEER

Boil 1 pint of pressed hops, 2 quarts of bran and 2 ears of corn, roasted black, in 4 gallons of water, for half an hour. Strain, and add 1 pint of molasses; and, when cold, ½ pint of yeast. Let it remain in an open jar until it begins to ferment; then bottle, or put into a small cask.

Ginseng is used as a cordial; steeped in wine or spirits.

FRUIT PUNCH

Mix ½ pint of pineapple sirup with ½ pint raspberry or strawberry sirup, 1 gill of orange juice, 1 gill of lemon juice, and 1½ pints of water; taste, if not sweet enough, add a little sugar. Put this into a freezer, and when it begins to thicken add the beaten whites of 3 eggs; continue to freeze until firm; remove the paddle, let stand covered until five minutes before serving, then add ½ pint Rhine wine; mix quickly, and serve in glasses. The wine may be omitted if not liked.

GINGER ALE

Put 15 gallons well water over the fire, and when boiling immerse 1½ pounds sugar, ½ pound pounded ginger and less than 4 ounces cream of tartar, take it immediately from the fire and pour it into a wooden vessel adapted for fermentation. Squeeze out the juice of 6 lemons and strain it with ½ pint of rum, added into the liquid, which now must stand covered a while. When tepid add a pint of yeast and leave it 30 minutes, strain the ale through a linen cloth and bottle it; keep in a cool room.

GINGER BEER

White Sugar, 20 pounds
Honey, 1 pound
Water, 18 gallons
Lemon Juice, 8 fluid ounces
Bruised Ginger, 17 ounces

Boil the ginger in three gallons of water for half an hour, then add the lemon juice, sugar and honey with the remaining water, and strain; when cold add the white of an egg together with half an ounce of essence of lemon. After standing four days, bottle.

JUNIPER ADE

For 30 gallons ade take 2 gallons Barley malt and 2 gallons ripe and rinsed Juniper berries, which are to be pounded by a piece of birch in a big stone mortar or otherwise an iron kettle. Then put the berries in a tub, pour fresh well water on them and let them stand over night. Over another tub put wooden sticks and straw, well cleaned; pour the berries thereon and let the liquid run through 3 or 4 times until it looks clear. Meanwhile scald ½ pound of Hops and put it with some water over the fire to boil with steady stirring. Then add this to the Juniper liquid and stir so as to make it a little warm. Then stir into it some good beer yeast; now cover it with a clean cloth and on that a felt, and thus it must remain until it rises. Press out the substance in the straw by hot water and add to it the risen ade, making the keg full. It is to be preserved in a cellar or other cool place.

Milky juice of Fig trees is used to remove warts, ring and tetter worms.

BOTANICAL BREWS AND MIXTURES

The vast botanical kingdom offers unlimited variety of materials for brews and mixtures. Man has taken several plant products, and concocted them in such a manner that their taste has won favor with peoples over the entire globe.

The coffee bean had to be roasted before it became the world's greatest breakfast beverage.

Cocoa in its natural form is disagreeable and bitter. The early Spaniards took this Indian beverage, and "doctored" it up with vanilla and milk, to make a smooth drink, relished the world over.

A popular soda fountain beverage of today was originally concocted as a medicine! New brews and mixtures, that "catch the taste" of multitudes, still offers great commercial possibilities for its lucky discoverer.

The following recipes represent popular concoctions of various locales and times.

Wholesome summer beverage used for generations by Louisiana Creoles

4 bunches of Sassafras roots (about 2 oz. of dried root), 1½ pints of honey, 3½ pints molasses, 1 tablespoonful Cream of Tartar, ½ teaspoonful carbonate of soda. Boil Sassafras in enough water to make 2 quarts of tea. Strain. Set to boil again, and when it boils add 1½ pints of honey and 3½ pints of molasses. Add a tablespoonful cream of tartar. Stir well, and set to cool, then strain. Pour in clean bottles—cork tightly, and put in a cool place. In a day it will be ready for use. When serving, put a tablespoonful of it into a half glass of ice water, and stir in ½ teaspoonful of carbonate of soda. Drink while effervescing.

Old Fashioned Beer Recipes

Root Beer: Take one ounce each of Sassafras, Allspice, Yellow Dock, and Wintergreen; ½ ounce each of Wild Cherry Bark and Coriander; ¼ ounce of Hops, and 3 quarts molasses. Pour boiling water on these ingredients and let them stand for 24 hours; filter the liquor and add ½ pint of yeast, and it will be ready for use in 24 hours.

Pipsissewa Beer: ½ lb. Pipsissewa, 1 gal. water. Boil, strain and add: 1 lb. sugar, ¼ oz. powdered Ginger, yeast, q.s. Keep it in a moderately warm place, to excite a brisk fermentation; the next day decant the liquor and strain it through a cloth; allow it to work for another day or two, according to the weather; then skim it, again decant or strain, and put it into bottles, the corks of which should be tied down with wires. This preparation has been recommended by some in scrofulous affections of the joints, in doses of half a tumblerful.

Flavored Cider

The following was taken from John Worlidge's 265-year-old "Treatise of Cider": "Ginger may be added with good success, making the cider more brisk and lively than otherwise it would be."

"Cloves and Cinnamon added, not only gives it a fine Aromatick flavour, but tingeth it with a fine colour."

"Dried Rosemary may be added in the Vessel, and doth not make it very unpleasing."

"Wormwood imbib'd therein, produceth the effect that it doth in Wine."

Ginger Recipes

Ginger Beverage: 1 pt. of molasses, 2 oz. of Jamaica Ginger, 1 gal. warm water. Stir well together and add a cup of fresh yeast. Let stand 2 days—strain, bottle, and tie corks down.

Gingerette: 1 gal. water, 1 lb. sugar, ½ oz. Jamaica Ginger, ¼ oz. Cream of Tartar, 2 sliced lemons. Boil Ginger and lemons for 10 minutes in a part of the water; dissolve sugar and Cream of Tartar in cold water; mix all and add 1 gill yeast. Let it ferment through the night. Strain and bottle in the morning.

"A Little Wine for Thy Stomach's Sake"

Wine is an antiseptic which kills cholera microbes. Red wines kill typhoid fever microbes in two hours; dry wines, in twenty minutes. Colibacilli sometimes found in oysters are killed by white wine. In small quantities wine has a good effect on gastric secretions and on the functions of the liver. —From Golden Age.

Would you, my friend, the power of death defy?
Pray keep your inside wet, and your outside dry.

TAMARIND

Tamarind is a tropical tree of India bearing pods with a sweetish sour soft brown pulp. This pulp contains considerable proportion of tartaric acid and invert sugar, having mild laxative, astringent, febrifuge and refrigerant properties.

Tamarind pulp may be preserved in sugar or syrup, or cooked and strained to a sauce for making Tamarind-ade or a refreshing cold drink. Parkinson wrote in 1641, in regard to this beverage: "It doth exceedingly helpe to asswage the thirste, if an ounce thereof be dissolved in faire water, or taken of it selfe; for the people of the hot countries doe usually eate thereof in their long travells to quench their thirst, which they were never able to indure without it to refresh themselves in the great heate, both of the Summer, and of those drie places, where no water is to be had."

Tamarind whey was a popular recipe in many of our early cook books. It was made by boiling an ounce of Tamarind pulp with a pint of milk. The liquid was strained, then sweetened.

In the Orient a brine is made of Tamarind pulp for pickling fish, and an acid jelly made to serve with fish and cold meats. Rice cooked with Tamarind pulp is also eaten with fish or meats.

As a laxative, Tamarind pulp is generally used with Senna to modify the action of the latter.

Beverage Tea for Motherhood

Instead of tea or coffee, drink Alfalfa tea—it is a rich source for vitamins. Add Peppermint leaves to Alfalfa tea to improve taste. Never make herbal teas in aluminum utensils.

JUNIPER BERRIES

The first day begin with four berries, the second day take five berries, the third day, six, the fourth, seven, and so increase by one berry every day as agreeable until the twelfth, on which they will take fifteen berries; then continue for five days longer, taking each day one berry less. Many whose stomach filled with gasses have been relieved by this simple berry-cure.

Likes Honey with Yerba Mate

I want to tell you how much we enjoy the Yerba Mate sweetened with honey. Do try it, if you haven't already. The honey gives it a grand flavor.—Submitted by Mrs. C. A. Moore, Oakland, Calif.

A Few Useful Herbs

"An infusion of 6 drachms of Blessed Thistle leaves to a pint of cold water, forms an elegant bitter infusion, which is very efficacious in loss of appetite and dyspepsia.

"A weak infusion of Rosemary leaves furnishes a pleasant substitute for tea, and is particularly agreeable to some dyspeptic stomachs.

"Chamomile is a powerful tonic and stomachic, and inferior to no other, when properly administered. It is an excellent and popular remedy for a weakened state of stomach, attended by the ordinary symptoms of indigestion, such as heartburn, loss of appetite, flatulency, etc. In such affections, particularly if accompanied by a sluggish state of the intentinal canal, the cold infusion, made with half an ounce of the flowers to a pint of water, and combined with aromatics and alkalies, is grateful to the stomach; or, should hot water be employed, it must be allowed to stand on the flower ten minutes only—the time recommended in the London Pharmacopea; unless, indeed, we wish to excite or encourage vomiting, when a tepid strong infusion will do both."
—From "Medical Botany" by J. Stephenson, M.D., F.L.S. and J. M. Churchill, F.L.S.

HOW WORMWOOD WAS USED IN OLDEN TIMES

For a bad smell from the mouth, if it proceeds from the stomach, Wormwood is of excellent effect.

Whoever is suffering from torpidity and resultant melancholy, let him take the little box of Wormwood Powder instead of his snuff box, and put a pinch of its contents into his first spoonful of soup or sprinkle it like pepper on his food once or twice a day. Persons whose breath has been, as it were, laced up by the foul air and often still more foul juices—real dung-hills of the stomach—will breathe more freely again.

Travelers who are much troubled with simple indigestion should never forget to take with them as a faithful companion their little bottle of Wormwood tincture.

Wormwood tea, used as eye water, has often rendered the best services in eye complaints.

TIPS FROM AN OLD COOK BOOK

Allow a free admission of light into your house. Health of the inmates depends upon it.

Always lay your table neatly, company or not.

For ventilation, open your windows, top and bottom; inviting the fresh air one way, and the foul the other.

Be cordial when serving at the table, but not importunate.

Morning's milk yields more cream than evening's, at the same temperature.

See that nothing is thrown away that can be used in your own family, or some other.

If you would be happy, strive to make others so. Kind words make other people good-natured.

Pay respectful attention to elderly persons; serving them first at your table.

A night's intemperance, either in eating or drinking, has deprived many an individual of existence.

It is not what we eat, but what we digest, that makes us fat.

Not what we read, but what we remember, that makes us learned.

More have been ruined by servants than by masters.

A person will perform one fifth more work in a well ventilated room than in one badly ventilated.

Cater frugally for the body if you would feed the mind sumptuously. Modify all appetites, especially those acquired.

When particular what you will have from the butcher, purchase yourself.

Eat slowly and you will not over-eat.

Do first what presses most; and having determined what is to be done, lose no time in doing it.

Be hearty in your salutations.

Hope for the best, think for the worst, and bear whatever happens.

CLOVES FOR THE THROAT

For those who have to clear their throats so often during a talk there is a simple, inexpensive, harmless, effective remedy: Cloves—try it. A little box of Cloves costs but little, and lasts for weeks. Just before going on the radio, or just before beginning a public talk, put two or three cloves in the mouth and chew and swallow slowly. That is all.

I used to be troubled with the throat-clearing habit constantly, but Cloves have solved the problem. (The first time you try the Clove, it might 'bite" the throat a bit, but that is the healing process of the rasped and irritated throat lining, and after that there is no trouble, but a lot of throat comfort instead.) Reach for a Clove instead of a pill; they're kind to your throat.

Scratches on furniture: Rub the fresh broken kernel of walnut to scratch.

OLD FASHIONED BEERS

Spruce Beer: Take 1 ounce Hops, ½ ounce Ginger, and 1 gallon water, boil it well, and add 1 pint molasses, ½ ounce essence of Spruce. When cold, add a teacupful of yeast and put it in a clean, tight cask. Let it stand 24 hours, then bottle it.

Small Beer: Boil 1 ounce Hops, 1 ounce Ginger, and 2 quarts molasses in 2 gallons water, strain and keg it, and when blood warm, put in your yeast.

RECIPE FOR HANGOVER

This is a very old and favorite recipe of the Chinese: Make a decoction of Ginseng root—allow to stand until cool. Strain and add lemon juice to taste.

BLACKBERRY WINE

Measure your berries and bruise them; to every gallon add one quart of boiling water; let the mixture stand twenty-four hours, stirring occasionally; then strain into a cask; to each gallon add two pounds of sugar, stir till well dissolved; cork tight, and let stand till the following October, then draw off into bottles, putting two or three raisins into each bottle; cork tight, keep in a dry, cool place.

SIMPLE INSOMNIA

Cut out tea and coffee and take the following herbal mixture: A half ounce of Passion Flower to one ounce each of Scullcap, Mistletoe and Valerian. Pour on these herbs three pints of boiling water. When cold strain. Drink a wineglassful after meals and at bedtime. Sleeplessness may soon vanish and better

RECIPE FOR SPICE JAR

Half a pound of common salt, half a pound of bay salt, half an ounce each of nutmeg, cinnamon, cloves, allspice, benzoin, and borax; half an ounce of orris root pounded separately, and mixed afterwards, together with the salt; some lemon and orange peel dried and pounded, and half a drachm of musk.

HERB LORE

Want to call forth a whole army of demons? Lay coriander, parsley, hemlock, liquid of black poppy, fennel, sandalwood, and henbane in a heap and set a match to them. According to old beliefs this is a sure way of invoking evil spirits. Want to marry the first man you meet tomorrow, miss? Put a sprig of sandalwood under your pillow tonight. It's an old-time superstition, but what can you lose? A good love philtre, in case you're interested, is water distilled from the leaves and flowers of myrtle, according to the ancients, who were up on such things. If your swain is going off to the wars, a loaf of bread or a cup of wine seasoned with cumin and served to the one you love will prevent his being untrue to you.

INDEX

INDEX

Agar-Agar, 39, 240
Agrimony, 56
Alder, 26, 34, 59
Aletris, 85
Alkanet, 37, 39, 212
Allspice, 39, 217
Almonds, 35
Aloe, 25, 57, 134, 140
Ammonia, 180, 188
Angelica, 57, 60, 247
Anise, 33, 39, 54, 56, 77, 247
Angostura, 39
Annato, 40
Apples, 77, 135, 198, 241, 245
Arrowroot, 102, 217
Arsmart, 32
Ash, 30, 48
Asofoetida, 35, 40
Avens, 24

Baking Soda, 180
Balm, 21
Balm of Gilead, 84, 203
Balsam of Peru, 40
Balsam of Tolu, 40
Bananas, 30
Banyan Tree, 93
Baobab Tree, 92
Bathing, 211
Bay, 30, 217, 220
Bayberry, 58-59
Beauty Aids, Grandmother's, 195-197
Bees, 140-141, 143, 161
Bee Balm, 140
Beech Drops, 81
Beef Recipes, 227, 232, 233, 234, 235, 236, 238, 243
Beers, 178, 223, 247, 248, 250
Beliefs, Strange Old, 74, 105
Betel Nut, 40
Betony, 57
Beverages, 75, 102, 197, 221, 223, 235, 247, 248
Birch, 34
Bitters, 182
Black Alder, 26, 59
Blackberry, 85
Black Cohosh, 85
Black Poplar, 34
Bladderwrack, 81
Blessed Thistle, 249
Blue Cohosh, 85
Boneset, 85
Borage, 32, 37, 55, 140

Borax, 181
Botanic Age, 19-36
Botanicals, Spices, Gums From World Over, 38-52
Boteka, 83, 217
Bouncing Bet, 29, 155
Bread Recipes, 217, 223, 226, 236, 241, 242, ·244
Breath, Bad, 171, 203
Buchu, 40
Buckthorn, 26
Bugle Weed, 85
Burdock, 60, 129, 154
Butterfly Weed, 87
Butternut, 86

Cabbage, 26-27, 57, 136
Cakes, 216, 231, 238, 241, 242, 244
Calamus, 24-25, 40-41, 83, 86, 186
Canada Snake Root, 109, 115
Canary, 185, 190
Candy Recipes, 225, 231, 238, 239, 244
Canella, 41, 217
Capsicum, 27, 178, 217, 237, 240
Caraway, 32, 41, 56, 220
Cardamon, 41, 220
Carpeting Herbs, 178
Cascara, 109, 126
Cascarilla, 41
Cassia Fistula, 42
Catnip, 21, 142, 161, 186
Cattle, 129, 130, 132, 133, 135
Cedar, 59
Celandine, 29, 164
Chamomile, 24, 55, 77, 97, 101, 197, 201, 202, 249
Charms, Herbal, 65, 89, 122, 124, 224, 250
Cherries, 35, 245
Chervil, 58, 230
Chickweed, 32, 195
Chicory, 154
Chirata, 42
Chives, 139, 186, 216, 220
Chlorogalum, 126
Chlorophyll, 100
Cinnamon, 42, 190, 197, 217, 237
Clary Sage, 22, 152, 203
Cleavers, 28
Clove Pink, 152
Clover, 31, 182, 185
Cloves, 42, 63, 188, 217, 250
Cocculus Indicus, 36, 42, 144
Coltsfoot, 37, 64, 98
Columbine, 34

Comfrey, 82, 140
Cookies, 218, 223, 231, 239, 241, 244
Coriander, 42, 220
Corn Mush, 230
Costmary, 22, 56, 152, 154, 186
Crackers, 241
Cranesbill, 86
Creeping Jenny, 142
Cubebs, 42
Cucumber, 179, 195, 198
Cudbear, 42
Cumin, 43, 56–57, 220
Curry Powder, 240
Cypress, 30

Daisy, 60
Damiana, 83
Dandelion, 32, 147, 154, 168
Dill, 146, 217
Dittany, American, 156
Deer's Tongue, 43
Dog Grass, 34
Dragon's Blood, 35, 43
Duck, Preparing Wild, 147
Dulse, 43

Eggs, 131, 216, 237
Elder, 25, 61, 57, 130, 135, 195–196
Elecampane, 54, 60
Eryngium, 56
Essences, 225, 237
Eucalyptus, 145
Evergreen, 84, 171
Eyebright, 37, 77
Eyes, 74, 112

False Saffron, 26
Fennel, 32, 43–44, 54, 60, 155, 197, 217, 220
Fenugreek, 33, 44, 57
Ferns, 33, 60, 186
Feverbush, 86
Feverfew, 24, 152, 186
Fish, 143, 146, 220, 229, 234
Fishing, 120–122, 144, 145, 148
Flax, 44, 75, 129, 197, 203
Fringe Tree, 86
Fritters, 241
Fruit Tree, 129, 134, 145, 157, 172, 183
Fumitory, 27, 212

Galangal, 44
Galbanum, 60
Garden Burnet, 28, 216
Garlic, 58, 77, 98–99, 160, 212, 217
Gentian, 27
Ginger, 45, 89, 217, 221–223, 248
Ginseng, 90–91
Glasswort, 27, 77

Gobernadora, 84
Goldenrod, 37, 89
Goldenseal, 81
Goldfish, 168
Gold Thread, 86
Grains of Paradise, 45
Grapes, 35
Guarana, 45
Gum Arabic, 45–46, 75
Gunnera, 92

Hair, 126, 196, 199, 200–204
Hazelnut, 29
Henna, 46, 200–204
Health Maxims, 53–54, 76, 181, 187, 189
Herbal, Notes from Dodoen's, 55–60
Herbal, Gerard's 1597, 37
Herbs And Old Sayings, 158–160
Herbs, Scented, As Medicine, 210
Horses, 129, 130, 133, 179
Holly, 30
Hollyhock, 57
Honey, 160
Hops, 46–47, 60, 95, 182, 197
Horehound, 21, 60
Horsetail Grass, 34, 81, 212
Hound's Tongue, 28, 56, 156
Household Hints, 65, 190
Houseleek, 31, 60, 140
Hunting, 120, 143, 144
Hydrangea, 168
Hyssop, 54, 56, 140

Iceland Moss, 47, 83, 102
Incense, 208–209
Indian:
    Dye, 123
    Lore, 118–124
    Medicine, 109–115, 125, 126
    Soaps and Shampoos, 126
Indian Turnip, 148
Insect Control, 129, 132, 135, 156, 161, 166, 177, 179, 186, 188, 190
Irish Moss, 47, 75, 82, 103
Ivy, 57, 60, 61, 77, 164

Jelly Recipes, 102, 223, 230, 232, 235, 238, 239, 240, 242
Jewel Weed, 124
Job's Tears, 27
Joe Pye Weed, 84
Juniper, 47, 59, 142, 249

Kali, 27
Kidney Bean, 33

Lady's Slipper, 86
Lamb Recipes, 216, 227, 233, 234, 236, 237

Lamb's Quarters, 147, 154
Lavender, 142, 186, 210
Leaves, Skeletonizing, 166, 169, 170
Lemon, 198, 237, 242
Licorice, 48, 96–97
Life Everlasting, 86, 209
Liquors, 245, 247
Livestock, 129, 130, 133, 135, 156, 179
Logwood, 48, 201
Longevity, 53, 68–71, 76, 191
Lovage, 33, 57, 144
Lucerne, 83
Luminous Moss, 39

Mandrake, 83, 87
Mangrove, 92
Manna, 48
Marigold, 152, 190, 202
Marjoram, 20, 216
Marshmallow, 27, 48, 57–58, 178
Master-of-the-Woods, 28, 49, 57
Mastic, 35, 59, 60
Mate, 83, 106, 197
Meadowsweet, 29, 152
Medlar Fruit, 30
Melissa, 140, 182
Mints, 21, 56, 77, 186
Mistletoe, 167
Moon Lore, 138–139
Mother of Thyme, 20, 56
Motherwort, 60
Mouse-ear, 31
Mugwort, 24, 55, 186
Mulberry, 30
Mullein, 22, 60, 202
Mustards, 32, 218, 220, 235
Myrrh, 36, 49
Myrtle, 58, 164

Nature's Laboratory, 81–83
Nasturtium, 77, 147
Nitrogen, 168
Nutmeg, 49, 64

Oleander, 57
Olives, 59
Onion, 54, 58, 173, 211, 235, 237, 238
Orris, 26, 49, 190, 207

Pancake, Potato, 238
Papaya, 220
Paprika, 77, 185, 217
Parakeet, 185
Parsley, 33, 56, 77, 133, 146, 161, 186
Peach, 35
Pear, 31, 54
Pennyroyal, 21, 56, 87, 137, 142, 177
Peony, 58

Pepper Grass, 147
Peppermint, 131, 181, 197
Perfume, 203, 205–207, 245
Physic Root, 87
Pies, 223, 240
Pine, 35, 59, 211
Pioneers and their Medicine Men, 116–117
Pipsissewa, 87, 248
Plantain, 28, 132, 145, 154
Plants, Organic Substance of, 106
Plants, Rustic Names of, 104–105
Plants, Useful Around Farm, 140
Plant World, Wonders of, 92–94
Poke, 88, 133, 147
Pork Recipes, 179, 216, 220, 227, 230, 233, 234, 243
Poultices, 75, 125
Poultry, Care of, 132, 133, 136, 166
Poultry, Recipes, 227, 233, 235, 236
Preserving Flowers, 166, 167, 170, 174, 206
Preserving Food, 131, 136, 146, 171, 178, 179
Preserving Leaves, 148, 161, 166, 169, 170
Prickly Ash, 87
Psyllium, 49
Pudding Recipes, 226, 236, 239, 241, 245
Purslane, 154

Quassia, 50, 143, 156, 172, 186, 188
Quince Fruit, 30, 201

Rabbit, Roasted, 140
Race That Lived With Nature, 118–119
Ragweed, 88
Rampions, 29
Red Raspberry, 88
Repellents, Herbal, 65, 123, 129, 132, 141–142, 156, 161, 166, 179, 186, 190
Resurrection Plant, 94
Rhamnus, 59, 109
Rose, 156, 164, 170, 197, 206
Rosemary, 22, 56, 199, 202, 212
Rue, 24, 54, 56, 140, 142

Sachet, 207
Sage, 21–22, 54, 75, 77, 95, 152, 201, 202, 216, 235
Salad, 147, 236, 243
Salad Dressing, 235
Salt, 157, 180, 218
Sandalwood, 50, 187
Sandarac Gum, 50
Sargassum Weed, 93
Sassafras, 36, 50, 67, 88, 186, 197
Sauce Recipes, 218, 219, 232, 234, 235, 237, 240, 241, 243
Savin, 59
Savory, Summer, 20, 56, 60, 216
Savory, Winter, 140, 141

Seneca Snake Root, 88
Senna, 25, 51, 75
Sensitive Plant, 93
Serpentaria, 88
Sesame Seed, 26, 51
Sheep, 129, 130, 133, 156
Shepherd's Purse, 37
Simaruba, 52
Slippery Elm, 75, 97, 125, 132
Skin, 195, 196, 198, 203
Soap, 179
Solomon's Seal, 31, 37, 212
Sorrel, 60, 140, 147, 216
Soup Recipes, 102, 228, 229, 230, 231, 232, 234, 237, 243
Southernwood, 24, 55, 153, 155, 212
Sow Thistle, 32
Spot and Stain Removal, 145, 177, 180, 181, 183, 184
Spearmint, 77
Speedwell, 64
Spice, 63, 215, 217, 218
Spice Bush, 110, 147
Spikenard, 36, 88
Spurry, 28
Squaw Vine, 88
Squill or Sea Onion, 58, 82
Star Anise, 52
St. Jameswort, 60
St. John's Bread, 52, 217
St. Johnswort, 28, 55, 203
Stinging Nettle, 27, 76, 141, 202
Stone Root, 88
Strangler Fig, 93
Sugar, 239
Sulphur, 103, 145, 165
Sunflower, 56
Sweet Basil, 20, 140, 216
Sweet Fern, 88
Syrup Recipes, 223, 235, 239

Tamarind, 26, 178, 235, 240, 249
Tansy, 82, 129, 142, 153, 154, 186
Taragon, 216, 235
Teeth, 94, 196
Telegraph Plant, 94
Temperance, 68–71, 191
Thyme, 56, 141, 142, 178, 216
Tobacco, 31
Tomato, 57, 171, 190, 198
Tonquin, 52
Tragacanth Gum, 52
Trapping, 143, 144
Trefoil, 30
Turmeric, 52, 217
Turtlebloom, 89

Vanilla, 225
Vegetables, 235, 236, 237, 238, 240
Venus Flytrap, 94
Vinegars, 215, 216, 218, 219

Walnut, 34–35, 60, 201
Watercress, 60, 142, 212
Water Lily, 55, 89, 92, 142
Watermint, 37
Weather, 137, 138, 179
White Ash, 89
Wild Yam, 89
Willow, 59, 60
Wines, 197, 218, 223, 246, 250
Wintergreen, 89
Witch Hazel, 89
Wood Betony, 29
Woodruff, 28, 57, 212
Wormwood, 24, 55, 61, 141, 162, 166, 174, 186, 202, 249

Yarrow, 31, 55, 77, 164
Yellow Dock, 83, 141, 147, 155
Yew, 34
Yucca, 202